A Civil Society with no Hierarchy

A Civil Society with no Hierarchy

The Covenantal Societal Model

Edited by
Ilie Bădescu and Joseph Livni

LEXINGTON BOOKS
Lanham • Boulder • New York • London

Published by Lexington Books
An imprint of The Rowman & Littlefield Publishing Group, Inc.
4501 Forbes Boulevard, Suite 200, Lanham, Maryland 20706
www.rowman.com

86-90 Paul Street, London EC2A 4NE

British Library Cataloguing in Publication Information Available

Library of Congress Cataloging-in-Publication Data Available

Names: Bădescu, Ilie, editor. | Livni, Joseph, editor.
Title: A civil society with no hierarchy : the covenantal societal model / edited by Ilie Bădescu and Joseph Livni.
Description: Lanham : Lexington Books, [2023] | Includes bibliographical references and index. | Summary: "Acephalous societies live in the rainforest or on prairies as nomadic pastoralists. The covenantal societies are acephalous; however, they inhabit the sedentary civilized world. This collection of up-to-date research focuses on the sociology, politics, justice administration, relations with hierarchies, successes, and failures of these societies"—Provided by publisher.
Identifiers: LCCN 2023001934 (print) | LCCN 2023001935 (ebook) | ISBN 9781666903706 (cloth) | ISBN 9781666903713 (epub)
Subjects: LCSH: Civil society. | Political science—Anthropological aspects. | Covenants—Political aspects. | Social structure—Political aspects.
Classification: LCC JC337 .C5698 2023 (print) | LCC JC337 (ebook) | DDC 306.209—dc23/eng/20230210
LC record available at https://lccn.loc.gov/2023001934
LC ebook record available at https://lccn.loc.gov/2023001935

Contents

Introduction

In the beginning there was the covenant. No one claims that Daniel J. Elazar (1934–1999) coined the term *covenant.* We know that even the proto-Israelites were not the authors of the term. Long before the ethno-genesis of Israel, Hittite and Mesopotamian emperors prepared and ratified covenant treaties.[1] Israel was the first to sign a covenant with an immortal sovereign. This new type of covenant gave birth to a new society. Elazar coined the term *covenantal model* for this society and he dedicated his career to the study of this society.

Surprisingly, sociologists, historians, and legal scholars studied the same covenantal model independently. The French medievalist Barraqué called his societies pactist societies of Gascony, the French divinity scholar Paravy and others studied the Alpine Waldensian communities, and the Romanian sociologist Henri Stahl (1901–1991) researched communities like the one in the Vrancea region because they showed "a very interesting system of administration."[2] Elazar didn't know about them and they didn't know about Elazar.

This collection binds together updated sociological, political, and juridical knowledge about these separate societies. The message of this joint look at various aspects of these seemingly unconnected organizations is to show how similar they are in spite of their historical and geographical disconnection. These similarities are striking not only because of the geographical isolation, but also because they contrast with the surrounding administrations. It is worthwhile to illustrate these fundamental characteristics of the covenantal society.

OPPOSITION TO HIERARCHY

Before one discusses opposition to hierarchy one should discuss what we mean by *hierarchy*. The words of two wise scholars are helpful to clarify what we refer to as *hierarchy*.

1. Aristotle describes a form of *monarchy* in which the "king acts as the embodiment of the law."[3] For the purpose of this book, such a monarchy or ecclesiastical power structure is hierarchical.
2. Elazar[4] describes hierarchy where rulers sit at the apex of the pyramid and where the administration takes precedence over politics.

For the purpose of this book the term *hierarchy* conforms to these two descriptions.

Using anthropological terminology the covenantal societies are *acephalous*.[5] Chapter 1 by Joseph Livni describes how the archetype of the covenantal society grew from one of many acephalous nomadic pastoralist tribal associations.

Biblical archaeologists consistently report about a rankless society in Israel of the Judges[6] confirming the biblical text stating that in the period of the Judges there was no king in Israel.[7] In Early Christian congregations (*ecclesiae*) "the community did not conceive of authority in any individuals who functioned as leaders at times as leaders, but rather in the group as a whole."[8] In other words "the people were undoubtedly first in authority."[9] Edwin Hatch exemplifies several aspects of the anti-hierarchical culture of apostolic Christianity.[10] In the Romanian *obşte* "the entire community was omnipotent."[11] This observation justifies the term *comunal society* utilized by Romanian sociologists for the covenantal society.[12] English Puritans opposed arbitrary ascendancy.[13] The tradition of Jewish diaspora (see more in chapter 3 by Joseph Livni) conserved the conviction of Israel of the Judges that "sovereignty is God's.[14] In the Pyrenean zone of Gascony the *vesiau* or the vicinal community "it was the lord who had to earn the respect of the people,"[15] while the people "asserts a genuine right to violence."[16] Barraqué calls this vicinal system "political pactisme."[17] Several sources state that the Waldensians opposed hierarchy as well.[18] So did the Puritans[19] and the Pilgrims.[20]

According to the Waldensian creed "what God has not forbidden is permitted without the Pope."[21] Similarly Peter Mazzacano (chapter 7) observes that in the case of American Puritans opposed "the arbitrariness of rulers." The chapters of this book will show how political opposition to hierarchy sometime generated the need for political envoys facing external rulers like the *Patriarch* of Roman Palestine (chapter 2 by Zeev Safrai), the *shtadlan* of

Jewish Communities (chapter 3 by Joseph Livni), and "natural leaders [who] were to rule in the best interests of the community" in Puritan America (chapter 7 of Peter Mazzacano).

COVENANT

The term *covenantal* indicates that the main distinction from other acephalous society consists of a covenant that guides everything in the organization: government, justice, culture, family, and individual life. Various scholars separately describe this in various covenantal organizations: Early Christians,[22] Waldensians,[23] Gascon neighborhoods,[24] Romanian village communities,[25] Puritans,[26] and Presbyterians.[27]

Mădălina Măndiță, (chapter 5) researches the meaning of covenant starting with its prototype: the *berith* of ancient Israel. The chapter brings to surface a covenant as described by the Scriptures.

Various scholars from a diversity of fields noticed this particular mutation in an acephalous arrangement and consequently the term *covenant* shows up in various terms such as *covenant* ;[28] Hebrew *berith*; German *Bund*; English *covenant*,[29] pact/compact,[30] *system of commandments*,[31] *supreme customary justice*,[32] *Fors*, etc. Of all the terms I find that Stahl's term *supreme customary justice* is helpful being almost self-explanatory. Nevertheless, I will dissect the term. The term *justice* implies judge, administration of law, or as in our case "an outcome in which vice is punished and virtue rewarded."[33] By itself this idealized desire for fairness exists in any society.

The Jewish sages determined three components of human decency in a society regardless whether it is covenantal or not: *justice*, *truth* and *peace*.[34] Jo R. Formicola in chapter 9 mentions the preference of the "church to ally itself with those seeking the values of *truth, freedom, justice, love, and peace*." For the purpose of dissecting the meaning of covenant the focus should be on *justice.* Consequently, the term *justice* is not associated uniquely to the covenantal society. Nevertheless, Stahl talks about *customary justice.* Even this term is not yet *covenant* because "for custom to be regarded as law, more than simple usage must be and is required, even if the usage is general and has long flourished. The principal issue is that one cannot derive an *ought* from an *is*."[35] However, the term *supreme customary justice* does mean *covenant* because the adjective *supreme* not only converts the *is* (custom) to an *ought* (living law) but it also adds the meaning of *indisputable.* I find Stahl's expression powerful not only because it points at what *covenant* means, but also because it also associates it with its two precursors:

1. Custom—inherited from nomadic roots see Joseph Livni, chapter 1

2. Living law—present in practically any civilized society, see section *Covenant, Living Law, and Jurisprudence* below.

The term used in the Pyrenees is *Fors*. It is not in use in any living language. The term is clarified as follows:

> The Fors are a disparate collection of legal regulations in various states of evolution through customary practice, detailed decisions and judgments, decrees by the Viscount and the Court of Béarn and charters issued, all covering a long period, 11th–14th centuries.[36]

FEDERATIVE NETWORK

According to the conventional wisdom, acephalous societies are simple organizations with small populations. "It appears that an acephalous tribe is the largest social scale a human group can achieve without the benefit of centralized organization."[37] Israel of the Judges settled next to the Canaanites cities and one cannot rule out that it imitated the loose federative linkage among city-states without copying their internal oligarchic organization. "The existence of a tribal confederation in Canaan can be inferred in the 13th century B.C.E. based on archaeological evidence, namely the Merenptah stele."[38]

Such a tribal confederation overcomes the constraint of small population size of acephalous societies. It allows a common philosophy of maintaining the internal peace and protecting the external peace for a considerable population size while maintaining "the distribution of powers among multiple centers of the matrix, not the devolution of powers from a single center or down a pyramid."[39]

Most covenantal organizations are described keeping these federative circles (Part A in figure 0.1). For example the Early Christians ecclesiae were grouped into collectives of ecclesiae (e.g., Ignatius network) and a loose network (e.g., Asia Minor).[40] Presbyterians had an inner circle called *presbytery* (e.g., Pittsburgh) and an outer circle called *synod* (e.g., Pennsylvania).[41] Jewish communities follow the same pattern of Kehilah (*congregation*), Va'ad (*regional confederation*), and Medinah (*national confederation*).[42] The Waldensians are described as decentralized and multinuclear.[43] In the Pyrenees several vesiau were called *Cam Vésiau*[44] and the whole valley constituted a small *Republic*.[45] Romanian sociologists of the Romanian covenantal model describe the three-level networks in Romania: *village* (sat), *inter-village confederation* (ocol),[46] and *land* (ţara).

It is important to distinguish between covenantal federative network and departmentalization by territory of governmental civil service. The power

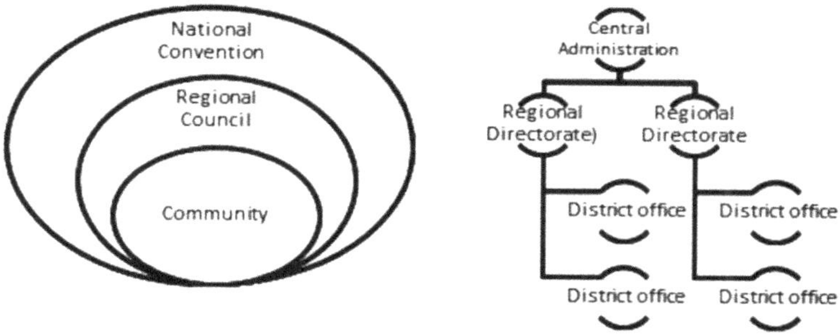

Figure 0.1 Covenantal Network Compared to Hierarchic Civil Service. *Source*: Prepared by the author.

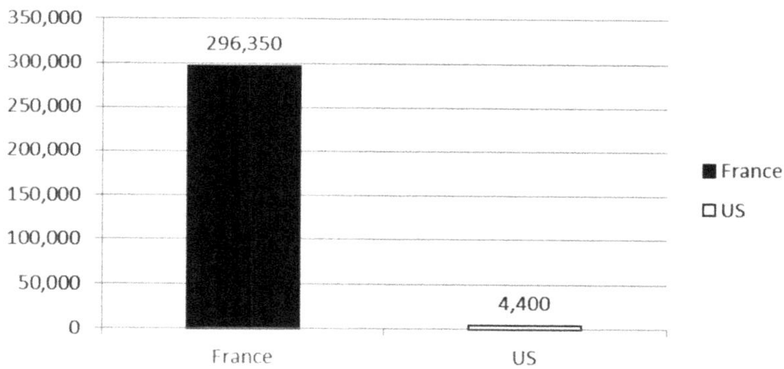

Figure 0.2 Centralized v. Decentralized Government. *Source*: Prepared by the author.

flow of covenantal federative network is bottom-up, that is, the community holds the decision authority by which it consents to harmonize regional issues within the regional council and national issues within the national convention.

Chapter 7 of Peter Mazzacano describes the Puritan covenantal network of Colonial New England. This organization (figure 0.1) served as model of the political organization of the United States. The community manages its police department, its education, its fire department, its zoning, its budget, among others. From Colonial times, the community had a say in all public affairs (Part A of figure 0.1). France is organized according to Part B in figure 0.1. In France, parents have no say in what their children are taught in public schools; the curriculum is determined by the Directorate in charge of pedagogic scheduling (DGP, Ministry of National Education, Paris).[47]

Figure 0.2 offers another comparison of the two approaches. The U.S. Department of Education retains 4,400 employees,[48] while the administrative staffs of the Ministry of National Education counts 296,350 employees.[49]

This number doesn't include the 866,500 teachers who are also employees of the Ministry.

The comparison of figure 0.2 has nothing to do with the quality of education in either of the systems. It has everything to do with the level of public involvement in the planning, administration, and human resource management including staffing. The Ministry of National Education of France manages almost everything regarding education in every region of France.[50]The U.S. Department of Education has very few functions.[51] The rest of the functions are carried out by personnel employed by states and districts; these employees are not counted in the U.S. figures of figure 0.2. The lower the level of government, the higher is the public involvement in its decision. This explains why American parents have a say in their children's education. This approach is inherited from the federative network system of the Puritan covenantal towns of colonial New England.

JUSTICE ADMINISTRATION

The covenantal society is distinct from other acephalous societies among others because it doesn't practice restorative justice consisting of cycles of offense and retaliation ending with a mediated settlement.[52] Instead, the covenantal society obeys a covenant distinguishing between right and wrong. This covenant may be written or oral. The oral covenant is distinct from ordinary customary law because it guides local justice administration.[53]

In most civil societies the virtue is to mind one's own business.

Reasonably, not everybody is righteous all the time. Therefore the covenantal society has to deal with detecting infractions, assigning guilt, and punishing transgressors.

In a society where there is no king there is no dedicated law enforcement either. In a society in which the "principal body of leadership of the group is the group itself,"[54] the group is in charge of detecting, judging, and correcting wrongdoings. This can take place only if the community has the "right to interfere in the particular life of every household."[55]

Maimonides interpreting Leviticus 19:17 affirms that sometimes one has no choice but to name and shame transgressors in public.[56] Henri Stahl discusses "the right of interference in the life of families."[57] Adela Şerban (chapter 6, section *The Social Control in Romanian Traditional Society*) describes the mode of operation in the Romanian *obşte* (figure 0.3). The similarity with the instruction of Maimonides is not a coincidence. The Waldensians survived among others because of "collective discipline."[58] Pilgrims and Puritans watched their neighbors while being watched.[59]

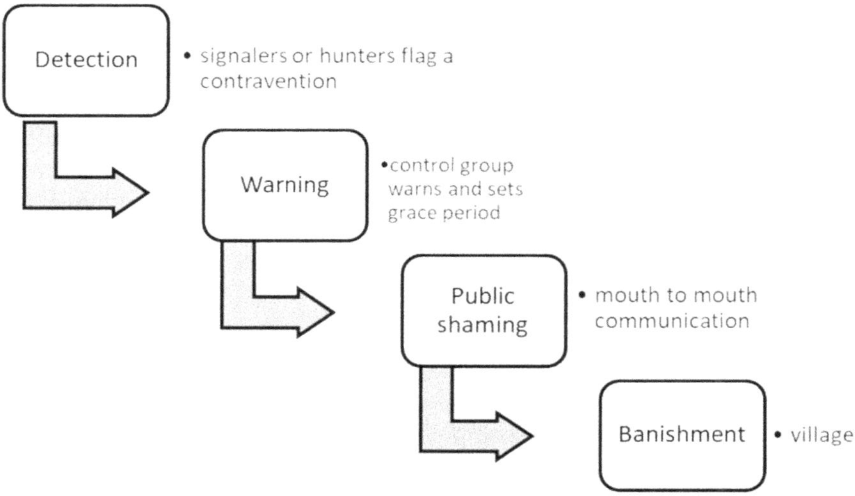

Figure 0.3 Justice Administration in the Romanian Traditional Village. *Source*: Prepared by the author based on description of Adela Şerban, chapter 6.

ASSEMBLY GOVERNMENT

The archaeological evidence confirms that pre-monarchic Israel was acephalous and rankless. That implies that the "day-to-day governance [was] in the hands of the people."[60] The covenantal society may imply a government in religious matters. The readers of the chapters will see that *religious matters* for this purpose include everything. For example in Roman Palestine "halakhic problems involved in paving the road to the maximum width, the confiscation of required land and so on; the archaeological findings provide the factual evidence for the existence of the network of roads" see Zeev Safrai, chapter 2. Several scholars confirm that Early Christian *ecclesiae* adopted the same principle of community assembly government.[61] Joseph Livni, chapter 3, surveys the self-government in the Jewish communities of the Diaspora. Léger,[62] Paravy,[63] and Antoine Monastier[64] describe the assembly governments of Waldensian communities; Bidot-Germa[65] and Gustave Bascle de Lagrèze[66] testify to the assembly government of the Gascon neighborhoods; Romanian village communities[67] and the Pilgrim's organization[68] are described in separate unrelated investigations.

Why did rulers allow the self-government of covenantal networks within their dominion? The main duty of every ruler is maintaining the peace, both internally and externally. If there is a system that can administer itself the ruler has a choice to take advantage of this capability or not. Rulers opted more often to allow than to prohibit a limited autonomy for the following reasons:

1. Military
   a. The ruler of the Romanian principality of Moldova Grigore Callimachi (1735–1769) testifies that the covenantal free villages served him as military safeguards.[69]
   b. In the Pyrenean areas the communities evolved to become *milites castri* (military forts).[70]
2. Financial reasons see Joseph Livni, chapter 3, regarding the autonomy of Jewish communities.
3. Economic and political reasons—The Crown of Aragon of the thirteenth–fourteenth century considered the Jewish minority as an ally for economic and political reasons.[71] Delegating justice administration is advantageous both economically and politically. Therefore, "[t]he fundamental principle of justice in Bigorre is that the count never judges."[72] Likewise the Romanian landlord "owned the houses on his estate, the tithe of the seeds, the pond, the forest, the mill and the pub, but never the right to judge and punish."[73]

ELDERS

The assembly legislated and judged, however decisions had to be carried out. Not everyone is willing and capable to deal with public matters. Those who could did and they became office holders. In biblical Israel these people were called *elders*, [Judges 21:16]. Biblical archaeologists note that even in monarchic Israel "local *elders* and local assemblies kept their prestige and authority."[74] The function subsisted in the Babylonian exile[75] and in Roman Palestine.[76] The Early Christians translated the word *elder* and their office holders were called *Presbiteroi* .[77] The Waldensian office holders were called Barbes.[78] The Calvinists, including Puritans and Pilgrims, returned to the elder (*ancien*) designation.[79] The Romanians called them *oameni buni şi bătrâni*.[80] In the Gascon neighborhoods, they were called *bonni homines*.[81]

One needs to make clear that these elders were not aristocracy in the true sense. The function was not inheritable.[82] The elders were either elected or recognized because they were competent and only as long as they were competent.[83] Adela Şerban (chapter 6) designates this pattern of leadership using the term *meritocracy* and rightly so. The elders were governed by the assembly (e.g., Early Christians,[84] Romanians,[85] Waldensians,[86] early New England settlements,[87] among others).

No doubt, a vibrant popular wisdom was always a component of the traditional continuity of all covenantal structures (section *Cultural Communitarianism and Historical Change* in chapter 4 by Ilie Bădescu). Nevertheless, some elders functioned as learned individuals and their skill was knowledge of the covenant and a cerebral approach toward its practical application; for example, the sages of Roman Palestine (chapter 2 by Zeev Safrai), the *bishops* of Apostolic Christianity,[88] the Jewish Diaspora Rabbis (chapter 3 by Joseph Livni), the *Barbas* of the Waldensian Community,[89] the *preaching presbyters* of English Puritans, and the *ministers* of American Puritans (chapter 7 by Peter Mazzacano). However, the example of the Salem Witch Trials (chapter 8 by Rachel Christ-Doane) points at a weakness due to exaggerated relying on popular perceptions. In the particular case of Salem not only notions of witches and devils penetrated the popular awareness, but also the learned ministry whose role was to shepherd the community away from such misconceptions reinforced it if not even originated the departure from reality.[90]

COVENANT AND CONSTITUTIONALISM

The combination of viable federative network, traditional justice administration, law enforcement by peer pressure, assembly government, and an ambiguous elder's empowerment shows that the study of the Scripture is not sufficient to set up a workable covenantal arrangement. For example we cited earlier Leviticus 19:17 prescribing a persistent vigilance of every individual over his/her neighbor's compliance with the commandments. It is very unlikely that any presumed founder of a covenantal system would notice this verse, or would understand that is absolutely essential to success, or would be able to instill in his flock that the new virtue is minding other people's business and setting up a system of detecting, judging, and removing contraventions (figure 0.3). This alone is sufficient to conclude that all viable covenantal organizations are direct descendants of the first prototype by inheriting obvious and written rules together with hidden and unwritten practices. In other words, one cannot find a viable covenantal society using the Scriptures as blueprint.[91] This raises the question: How did the first covenantal society come into existence? Chapter 1 makes the case that it appeared as a random mutation within a standard acephalous society of nomadic pastoralist by elevating their customary law to the perception of covenant; transgressions of commandments were detected and handled by prescribed procedures of attributing guilt and administering punishment. These practices are not found in nomadic societies. The Israelite nomads took up these measures during sedentarization adopting them from neighboring hierarchical states without giving up their opposition to hierarchy. The chapter substantiates that the success of such a hybrid acephalous system with laws, judicial procedures, and enforced correction has a low chance of survival. The particular case of Israelites prevailed because their customs included frequent general assemblies, and institutions that enhanced cohesion such as combatting extreme poverty and cultural cohesion.

The reader can judge by the similarities to the ideal type and by the similarities between each other that the real ancestral type could not be far from the ideal one described in chapter 5. The comparison between Măndiţă's prototype (chapter 5) and Mazzacano's description of the American Puritans' implementation of the covenant principle (chapter 7) is worthy of consideration. The chapter reiterates the view that "The rise of legalistic constitutionalism after the Revolutionary War in America was the logical outcome of Puritan thought." This observation can be traced back to Tocqueville: "the destiny of America embodied in the first Puritan who landed on those shores, just as the human race was represented by the first man."[92] Many other analyses of several disciplines came to the same conclusion[93]. Some scholars disagree.[94] This volume adds another dimension to the validity of Tocqueville's thesis.

COVENANTAL FAILURES

The covenantal organization is odd, nevertheless it works; this collection brings several successful examples that struggled and survived against all odds. However, the covenantal system is far from ideal. This volume treats the witch hunt of Salem as an example in which the covenantal intolerance went too far. The witch trials of Salem occurred within the covenantal system. Here, the absence of truth created an epidemic of hysteria and the consequential killing of twenty innocent people and of an additional 140 superfluous arrests. Chapter 8 of Rachel Christ-Doane of this volume is a suitable contribution discussing that event. The chapter illustrates how the justice administration of a covenantal system is not immune to irremediable injustice. The covenantal justice administration relies exclusively on the community. As discussed earlier (see *Justice Administration*) detection of transgression is nourished by the essential minding of other people's business or in the chapter's words "Ever vigilant in their duty to uphold their covenant with God, residents of New England naturally harbored suspicions and personal misgivings against their neighbors' potentially sinful behavior." This atmosphere generates an excessive peer pressure on the judicial process. Nevertheless, the chapter also indicates that "by early October protests against the proceedings could no longer be ignored." The same peer pressure mechanism that spread the support for injustice turned to brake and stop the process. Reasonably, other covenantal societies suffered similar outbreaks of severe malfunction. This example indicates that the system has an inherent auto-immune function enhancing its resilience.

COVENANT, LIVING LAW, AND JURISPRUDENCE

From the previous discussion of the term covenant one deduces a duality of messages:

1. The covenant is a customary law that is sanctioned by an intangible supreme sovereign.

   In every society there is an unwritten code of morality, decency, and mostly importantly expectation of peace and justice. Section *Covenant* related this to Ehrlich's notion of living law discussing similarities and differences between the two concepts: *living law* and *covenant*. Each society has a *living law*; only covenantal societies are ruled by a *covenant*.
2. *Living law* is a collection of norms of social associations such as communities, guilds, and professional fellowships. Beyond penal law, the living law covers morality, decency, tact, etiquette, and fashion.[95] Jewish sages treat community decency norms using the term "the way of the land"[96] (*derekh eretz* in Hebrew). A research exploring the meaning of the expression found among others: the way the inhabitants of the land should conduct themselves, manners, acceptable customs, good behavior, fundamental value, measure of proper behavior, good deed, and moral behavior.[97] I submit that this convincingly allows using the terms *living law* and *the way of the land* interchangeably. The sages distinguish between *covenant* and *the way of the land* "The *way of the land* preceded the Torah by twenty six generations."[98] As the *covenant,* the *living law* refers to a set of values nurtured by the people; however the *living law* has existed longer than the *covenant* and it is present in both covenantal and non-covenantal societies. As opposed to the *covenant* the *living law* is neither enforced nor enforceable.

That being said, *peace* and *justice*, two pillars of any living law did impact even the most powerful autocratic hierarchies. The proof is the extensive use of propaganda since antiquity when imperial monuments depicted "accounts of past acts and events, ritualized expressions of loyalty and consent."[99] Moreover in some exceptional cases popular expectations of *peace* or *justice* forced changing directions of government actions. Three examples where the absence of *justice* threatened internal peace come to mind. In all three examples, public resistance produced tangible shifts within the administrative culture of two of the most formidable successors of the Roman imperial hierarchy: the French Army and the Catholic Church. The three examples are:

1. The kidnapping of Edgardo Mortara – In Bologna of 1858 the officers of the Inquisition raided the Jewish home of Momolo and Marianna

Mortara and kidnapped their son Edgardo. Kertzer offers a dramatic account not only of the personal tragedy of the Mortara family, but also of the major role played by this papal confrontation with new perceptions of decency budding in Western Europe in those years:

Arturo Carlo Jemolo, the foremost historian of Church-state relations in Italy, cites Pope Pius IX's actions in the Mortara affair as among the most significant of his papacy, a papacy that was the most consequential in Church history.

Pius IX's principal biographers similarly make the connection between his handling of the Mortara affair in 1858 and his loss of his earthly kingdom in the following year.[100]

2. The trial of Emile Zola, a consequence of the Dreyfus affair, was fueled by two typically hierarchic organizations: the Army and the Church.[101] The absence of truth was the source of punishment of a decent person. The unjust condemnation of Dreyfus is principally attributed to antisemitism. In the case of Emile Zola, the decent Christian defender of Dreyfus's innocence, antisemitism played a minor role. Zola's unjust sentence resulted from a malfunction of the hierarchic system where the absence of truth played an instrumental role.
3. The cover up of the sex abuse of children in North America was steered by the Catholic Church, a typical hierarchic system. Chapter 9 of Jo R. Formicola discusses how divergence in dealing with immoral acts drove not only the perpetuation of indecency, but also its cover-up. The chapter discusses not only this malfunction of the hierarchic system but also sheds light on corrective actions prompting the Vatican to adopt the policy that recognized molestations as a grave sin and now as a crime.

NOTES

1. Moshe Weinfeld, "Covenant Making in Anatolia and Mesopotamia," *Journal of the Ancient Near Eastern Society* 22, no. 1 (1993).

2. Henri H. Stahl, *Nerej, un village d'une région archaïque: monographie sociologique*, vol. V. 1 (Bucarest: Institut de sciences sociales de Roumanie, 1939), 291.

3. Aristotle, Benjamin Jowett, and Henry William Carless Davis, *Politics*, Kindle edition ed. (Mineola, NY: Dover Publications, 2000), Kindle location 193.

4. Daniel J. Elazar, *Covenant & Constitutionalism: The Great Frontier and the Matrix of Federal Democracy* (New Brunswick, NJ: Transaction Publishers, 1997), 1–3.

5. Alan Barnard and Jonathan Spencer, *Encyclopedia of Social and Cultural Anthropology* (London, New York: Routledge, 1996), 594.

6. Avraham Faust, *Israel's Ethnogenesis: Settlement, Interaction, Expansion and Resistance* (London: Equinox Pub., 2006); Israel Finkelstein, Amihai Mazar, and

Brian. B. Schmidt, *The Quest for the Historical Israel: Debating Archaeology and the History of Early Israel, Sixth Biennial Colloquium of the International Institute for Secular Humanistic Judaism* (Atlanta: SBL Press, 2007); William .G. Dever, *What Did the Biblical Writers Know and When Did They Know It?: What Archeology Can Tell Us About the Reality of Ancient Israel*, Kindle ed. (Grand Rapids, Michigan: Eerdmans Publishing Company, 2002)..

7. Judges 21:25.

8. Paul Trebilco, *The Early Christians in Ephesus from Paul to Ignatius* (Grand Rapids, MI: Eerdmans Publishing Company, 2007), 489.

9. John Laurence Mosheim and Archibald Maclaine, *An Ecclesiastical History Antient and Modern from the Birth of Christ to the Beginning of the Eighteenth Century, in which the Rise, Progress, and Variations of Church Power are Considered in Their Connexion with the State of Learning and Philosophy and the Political History of Europe During that Period* (London: Strahan and Preston, 1811), 99.

10. Edwin Hatch, *The Organization of the Early Christian Churches* (London: Rivingtons, 1882), Lecture V.

11. our translation of Stahl, *Nerej, un village d'une région archaïque: monographie sociologique*, V. 1, 285.

12. Ilie Bădescu, "Communal Society and the "Dual System" Equality and Inequality In the Carpathian Valleys," *Revista română de sociologie anul* XXX, no. 3–4 (2019).

13. Daniel Neal and Joshua Toulmin, *The History of the Puritans, or Protestant Non-conformists* (Boston: Charles Ewer, 1817), Appendix IX.

14. Daniel J. Elazar, "Judaism and Democracy: The Reality," *Jerusalem Letter*, no. 48 (1986): 288.

15. Gustave Bascle de Lagrèze, *Histoire du droit dans les Pyrénées - comté de Bigorre* (Paris: Imprimerie Impériale, 1867), Chapter V.

16. Hélène Couderc-Barraud, *La violence, l'ordre et la paix: résoudre les conflits en Gascogne du XIe au début du XIIIe siècle* (Presses universitaires du Mirail, 2008), iii.

17. Jean Pierre Barraque, "Pactisme et pactismes," in *Mélanges en l'honneur du Professeur Christian Desplat. Espaces nationaux et identités régionales*, ed. Adrián Blázquez Garbajosa and Philippe Chareyre (Ortez: Gascogne, 2004).

18. Antoine Monastier, *Histoire de l'Eglise vaudoise depuis son origine et des Vaudois du Piémont jusqu'à nos jours: - Tome I*, vol. 1 (Geneva: Kessmann, 1847), 12; Gabriel Audisio, *The Waldensian Dissent: Persecution and Survival c. 1170-c. 1570*, trans. Claire Davison (Cambridge: Cambridge University Press, 1999), 16.

19. John Boxton Marsden, *The History of the Later Puritans . . .* , 2nd edition (London: Hamilton, Adams&Company; T. Hatchard, 1854), 61.

20. Enoch Lois Lowe, *Discourse Delivered at the Commemoration of the Landing of the Pilgrims of Maryland: Celebrated May 12, 1845, at Mt. St. Mary's, Near Emmitsburg, Md* (Gettysburg: H.C. Neinstedt, 1845), 13.

21. Monastier, *Histoire de l'Eglise vaudoise depuis son origine et des Vaudois du Piémont jusqu'à nos jours: - Tome I*, 1, Chapter 12.

22. Hatch, *The Organization of the Early Christian Churches*, 7.

23. Muston Alexis, *L'Israël des Alpes: première histoire complète des Vaudois du Piémont et de leurs colonies*, vol. I (Paris: Libr. de Marc Ducloux, 1851), 11; Jean Rodolphe Peyran and Thomas Sims, *An Historical Defence of the Waldenses Or Vaudois: Inhabitants of the Valleys of Piedmont* (London: C. & J. Rivington, 1826), 130, 31; Chap XXXI, Jean Léger, *Histoire generale des eglises evangeliques des Vallees de Piemont ou Vaudoises* (Leiden: Jean le Carpentier, 1669), 190–99; Audisio, *The Waldensian Dissent: Persecution and Survival c. 1170-c. 1570*, 27.

24. footnote 3 of Dominique Bidot-Germa, "The Specific Features of Medieval Notaries North and South of the Pyrenees: The Example of Béarn," *Imago temporis: medium Aevum* 5 (2011): 176.

25. Dimitrie Cantemir, *Descrierea Moldovei* (Grup Editorial Litera, 2016), 79; Henri H. Stahl and Paul H. Stahl, *Contribuții la studiul satelor devălmașe românești: Procesul de aservire feudală a satelor devălmașe*, vol. 3 (Cartea Românească, 1998), 138.

26. D. Neal and J. Toulmin, *The History of the Puritans or Protestant Non-conformists*. repr. from dr. Toulmin's ed (London: Thomas Tegg and son, 1837), 102.

27. Ibid., 362.

28. e.g. Daniel Judah Elazar, "Federalism and covenant" (1980); "The Almost-covenanted Polity" (paper presented at the Workshop in the covenant idea and the Jewish political tradition, Ramat Gan, Israel, 1982); Daniel J. Elazar, *Covenant & Commonwealth: From Christian Separation through the Protestant Reformation* (New Brunswick, NJ: Transaction Publishers, 1995); *The Covenant Tradition in Politics*, vol. 1 (Transaction Publishers, 1995); Daniel Elazar, *Covenant and Polity in Biblical Israel: Volume* 1, Biblical Foundations and Jewish Expressions: Covenant Tradition in Politics (Routledge, 1995); Elazar, *Covenant & Constitutionalism: The Great Frontier and the Matrix of Federal Democracy; Covenant and Polity in Biblical Israel* (New Brunswick, NJ: Transaction Publishers, 1998); D.J. Elazar et al., *The Covenant Connection: From Federal Theology to Modern Federalism* (Lexington Books, 2000); Filippo Sabetti, "Covenant Language in Canada" (paper presented at the Workshop on Covenant and Politics, Center for the Study of Federalism, Temple University, 1980); Steven Alan Samson, "Covenant Origins of the American Polity," *Faculty Publications and Presentations*. 5. Liberty University (1994); Shaun A. De Freitas, "Samuel Rutherford on Law and Covenant: The Impact of Theologico-Political Federalism on Constitutional Theory" (University of the Free State, 2003).

29. Max Weber, *Das Antike Judentum* (FV Éditions, 2017), Chapter Die Jahwebund und seine Organe.

30. e. g. Barraque, "Pactisme et pactismes"; Aero Mayflower Transit Co and William Bradford, *The Mayflower Compact* (The Company, 1955).

31. Émile Durkheim, *Moral Education* (Mineola, NY: Dover Publications, 2012), 31.

32. H.H. Stahl, "Nerej, un sat dintr-o regiune arhaică," Sociologie Românească, an IV (1942)., cited by ; Iancu Filipescu, "Din contribuțiile profesorului Henri H. Stahl la dezvoltarea sociologiei istoriei," [Contributions of Professor Henti Stahl to the development of history's sociology.] *Sociologie Romanească* IV, no. 3 (2006).

33. T. Britannica, "poetic justice," in *Encyclopedia Britannica*, ed. Editors of Encyclopaedia (2013).
34. Pirkey avot 1:18.
35. Alan Watson, "An approach to customary law," University of Illinois Law Review (1984).
36. Dominique Bidot-Germa, *Un notariat médiéval: droit, pouvoirs et société en Béarn* (Toulouse: Presses universitaires du Mirail-Toulouse, 2008).
37. Peter Turchin and Sergey Gavrilets, "Evolution of complex hierarchical societies," *Social Evolution & History* 8, no. 2 (2009).
38. Thomas E. Levy and Augustin F.C. Holl, "Migrations, ethnogenesis, and settlement dynamics: Israelites in iron age Canaan and Shuwa-Arabs in the Chad Basin," *Journal of Anthropological Archaeology* 21, no. 1 (2002).
39. Daniel J. Elazar, "Contrasting Unitary and Federal Systems," *International Political Science Review / Revue internationale de science politique* 18, no. 3 (1997).
40. Cavan W. Concannon, *Assembling Early Christianity: Trade, Networks, and the Letters of Dionysios of Corinth* (Cambridge: Cambridge University Press, 2017), 226.
41. Presbyterian Church in the U.S.A. Synod of Pennsylvania, Minutes of the . . . Annual Session of the Synod of Pennsylvania of the Presbyterian Church in the United States of America (1909), 11.
42. Daniel J. Elazar and Stewart Cohen, *The Jewish Polity: Jewish Political Organization from Biblical Times to the Present* (Bloomington, IN: Indiana University Press, 1985), 186, 87.
43. Audisio, *The Waldensian Dissent: Persecution and Survival c. 1170-c. 1570*, 159.
44. Gustave Bascle de Lagrèze, *La féodalité dans les Pyrénées, comté de Bigorre, mémoire lu à l'Académie des sciences morales et politiques* (Paris: A. Durand, 1864), 78.
45. Ibid., 73.
46. Henri .H. Stahl, Contribuţii la studiul satelor devālmaşe romineşti: Confederaţii de ocol, structuri teritoriale şi tehnici agricole (Bucharest: Editura Academiei Republicii Populare Romine, 1958), 178, 82, 96.
47. Article 20 of DECREE N°2020-1025, Government of France.
48. "Overview and Mission Statement," ed. Department of Education (Washington, DC: US Department of Education, 1992).
49. Bernard Javet, "L'éducation nationale en chiffres 2020," in *Les personnels et établissements, ed. Direction de l'évaluation de la prospective et de la performance (DEPP)* (Paris: Ministère de l`éducation nationale, de la junesse et des sports, 2020).
50. Among others (see DECREE N°2020-1025, Government of France):
    1. Education Projects and Development
    2. Communications
    3. Pre-K, K, Elementary, Middle and High Schools as well as Higher Education Institutions
    4. Curricula
    5. Regional Departments of Education

51. The functions are:

1. Establishing policies on federal financial aid for education, and distributing as well as monitoring those funds.
2. Collecting data on America's schools and disseminating research.
3. Focusing national attention on key educational issues.
4. Prohibiting discrimination and ensuring equal access to education.

Everything else is managed by the school districts, and by the state departments of education. "Overview and Mission Statement."

52. e. g. Jyotirmoy Pal Chaudhuri, "Conflicts in Africa and the Palavers," in *Searching for Non-Western Roots of Conflict Resolution: Discourses, Norms and Case Studies*, ed. Mr Shantanu Chakrabarti (KW Publishers Pvt Ltd, 2013); Walter Hawthorne, *The Interior Past of an Acephalous Society: Institutional Change Among the Balanta of Guinea-Bissau, c. 1400-c. 1950* (Stanford Stanford University, 1998), 16; David .J. Bederman, *International Law in Antiquity* (Cambridge, UK: Cambridge University Press, 2001), 48.

53. Gascony-Frédéric Le Play, *L'organisation de la famille selon le vrai modèle signalé par l'histoire de toutes les races et de tous les temps* (A. Mame et fils, 1895), 127; Couderc-Barraud, *La violence, l'ordre et la paix: résoudre les conflits en Gascogne du XIe au début du XIIIe siècle*, 41; Roman Palestine-Hatch, *The Organization of the Early Christian Churches*, 58; Romania-Cantemir, *Descrierea Moldovei*, 79; Stahl, *Nerej, un village d'une région archaïque: monographie sociologique*, V. 1, 102, 228, 34.

54. *Nerej, un village d'une région archaïque: monographie sociologique*, V. 1, 232–33.

55. Ilie Bădescu, *Ozana Cucu-Oancea, and Gheorghe Şişeşte, Dicţionar de sociologie rurală* (Editura Mica Valahie, 2005), 539.

56. Leviticus 19:17 Maimonides explains the verse teaching that "in heavenly i.e. religious matters [Covenant! my note] if he (the sinner) doesn't turn after a secret [rebuke], we may put him to shame in multitude [public] , make his sins public, reprove him in his presence, abuse and curse him until he turns for the better" Moses Maimonides and Hermann H. Bernard, *The Main Principles of the Creed and Ethics of the Jews, Exhibited in Selections from the Yad Hachazakah of Maimonides* (Cambridge: Deighton, 1832), 186.

57. H.H. Stahl, *Les anciennes communautés villageoises roumaines: asservissement et pénétration capitaliste* (Editions de l'Académie de la République socialiste de Roumanie, 1969).

58. Pierrette Paravy, *De la chrétienté romaine à la Réforme en Dauphiné. Évêques, fidèles et déviants (vers 1340-vers 1350)*, vol. 1, Collection de l'école française de rome (Rome: École française de Rome, 1993), 1026.

59. Nathanel Philbrick, *Mayflower: a Story of Courage, Community, and War*, Kindle Edition ed. (New York: Penguin Publishing Group, 2006), Kindle Loc. 265; Stacy Schiff, *The Witches: Suspicion, Betrayal and Histeria in 1692 Salem*, Kindle Edition ed. (New York Boston London: Little Brown, 2015), 48.

60. Elazar, "Judaism and Democracy: The Reality," 288.

61. Mosheim and Maclaine, *An Ecclesiastical History Antient and Modern from the Birth of Christ to the Beginning of the Eighteenth Century, in which the Rise, Progress,*

and Variations of Church Power are Considered in Their Connexion with the State of Learning and Philosophy and the Political History of Europe During that Period, 99; Elazar, *Covenant & Commonwealth: from Christian Separation through the Protestant Reformation*, 41, 42; Trebilco, *The Early Christians in Ephesus from Paul to Ignatius*, 489.

62. Chap XXXII, Léger, Histoire generale des eglises evangeliques des Vallees de Piemont ou Vaudoises, 199.

63. Paravy, *De la chrétienté romaine à la Réforme en Dauphiné. Évêques, fidèles et déviants (vers 1340-vers 1350)*, 1, 1026.

64. Monastier, *Histoire de l'Eglise vaudoise depuis son origine et des Vaudois du Piémont jusqu'à nos jours: - Tome I*, 1, Chapter 12.

65. Bidot-Germa, "The Specific Features of Medieval Notaries North and South of the Pyrenees: The Example of Béarn."

66. de Lagrèze, *Histoire du droit dans les Pyrénées - comté de Bigorre*.

67. Stahl and Stahl, *Contribuții la studiul satelor devălmașe românești: Procesul de aservire feudală a satelor devălmașe*, 3, 161; Stahl, *Nerej, un village d'une région archaïque: monographie sociologique*, V. 1, 232–33; Bădescu, Cucu-Oancea, and Şişeşte, *Dicționar de sociologie rurală*, 542.

68. Philbrick, *Mayflower: A Story of Courage, Community, and War*, Kindle Loc. 257.

69. Victor Tufescu, "Răspândirea satelor de răzeşi: contibuţiuni la studiul populării Moldovei," *Arhivele Basarabiei* 1 (1934).

70. Monique Bourin, "Historiographie des communautés de la France méridionale," in *La formation des communautés d'habitants au Moyen Âge. Perspectives historiographiques*, ed. Ludolf Kuchenbuch, Dieter Scheler, and Joseph Morsel (Xanten, Germany, 2003).

71. Claire Soussen Max, ""Iudei Nostri", pouvoir royal, communautés juives et société chrétienne dans les territoires de la Couronne d'Aragon au XIIIe et première moitié du XIVe siècle" (St Quentin en Yvelines, 2005); Shlomo Dov Goitein and Jacob Lassner, *A Mediterranean Society: An Abridgment in One Volume* (Berkley: University of California Press, 1999), 93.

72. my translation of Couderc-Barraud, La violence, l'ordre et la paix: résoudre les conflits en Gascogne du XIe au début du XIIIe siècle, 29.

73. my translation of Nicolae Iorga, "Scrisori de Boieri Scrisori de Domni," in *Din publicațiile casei școalelor*, ed. Casa şcoalelor (Vălenii de Munte, Romania: Editura casei şcoalelor; Datina Românească, 1925).

74. The evidence regarding elders consist of analysis of the archaeological findings Avraham Faust, "The Rural Community in Ancient Israel during Iron Age I I," *Bulletin of the American Schools of Oriental Research* (2000).

75. The evidence regarding elders consist of analysis of the archaeological findings ibid.

76. Ze'ev Safrai, *The Economy of Roman Palestine* (London-New York: Taylor & Francis, 2003), 25.

77. Hatch, *The Organization of the Early Christian Churches*, 39.

78. Audisio, *The Waldensian Dissent: Persecution and Survival c. 1170-c. 1570*, 125; William Stephen Gilly, *Waldensian Researches During a Second Visit to the Vaudois of Piemont* (London: Rivington, 1831), 140, 228, 35.

79. Isabella M. Watt et al., *Registres du Consistoire de Genève au temps de Calvin. Tome I, 1542–1544* (Geneva: Librairie Droz, 1996), viii.

80. Bădescu, Cucu-Oancea, and Şişeşte, *Dicţionar de sociologie rurală*, 532.

81. Couderc-Barraud, *La violence, l'ordre et la paix: résoudre les conflits en Gascogne du XIe au début du XIIIe siècle*, 96; Le Play, *L'organisation de la famille selon le vrai modèle signalé par l'histoire de toutes les races et de tous les temps*, 132; de Lagrèze, *Histoire du droit dans les Pyrénées - comté de Bigorre*, 100.

82. Mosheim and Maclaine, *An Ecclesiastical History Antient and Modern from the Birth of Christ to the Beginning of the Eighteenth Century, in which the Rise, Progress, and Variations of Church Power are Considered in Their Connexion with the State of Learning and Philosophy and the Political History of Europe During that Period*, 177; Chap XXXII, Léger, *Histoire generale des eglises evangeliques des Vallees de Piemont ou Vaudoises*, 199.

83. Mosheim and Maclaine, *An Ecclesiastical History Antient and Modern from the Birth of Christ to the Beginning of the Eighteenth Century, in which the Rise, Progress, and Variations of Church Power are Considered in Their Connexion with the State of Learning and Philosophy and the Political History of Europe During that Period*, 101; Charles A. Frazee, "The Origins of Clerical Celibacy in the Western Church," *Church History* 41, no. 2 (1972): 151; Le Play, *L'organisation de la famille selon le vrai modèle signalé par l'histoire de toutes les races et de tous les temps*, 127; Emilio Comba, *History of the Waldenses of Italy: From Their Origin to the Reformation, trans. Teofilo Comba* (London: Truslove & Shirley, 1889), 91, 190.

84. Mosheim and Maclaine, *An Ecclesiastical History Antient and Modern from the Birth of Christ to the Beginning of the Eighteenth Century, in which the Rise, Progress, and Variations of Church Power are Considered in Their Connexion with the State of Learning and Philosophy and the Political History of Europe During that Period*, 99; Frazee, "The Origins of Clerical Celibacy in the Western Church," 151; Hatch, *The Organization of the Early Christian Churches*, 119; Trebilco, *The Early Christians in Ephesus from Paul to Ignatius*, 415.

85. Stahl, *Nerej, un village d'une région archaïque: monographie sociologique*, V. 1, 290; Bădescu, Cucu-Oancea, and Şişeşte, *Dicţionar de sociologie rurală*, 542.

86. Alexis, *L'Israël des Alpes: première histoire complète des Vaudois du Piémont et de leurs colonies*, I, 11; Peyran and Sims, *An Historical Defence of the Waldenses or Vaudois: Inhabitants of the Valleys of Piedmont*, 130, 31; Chap XXXI, Léger, *Histoire generale des eglises evangeliques des Vallees de Piemont ou Vaudoises*, 190–99; Audisio, *The Waldensian Dissent: Persecution and Survival c. 1170-c. 1570*, 27.

87. Alexis de Tocqueville, *Democracy in America*, trans. Henry Reeve, Kindle Edition ed., vol. 1 (Project Gutenberg, 2006), 42.

88. Edwin Hatch, *The Organization of the Early Christian Churches: Eight Lectures Delivered Before the University of Oxford, in the Year, 1880, on the Foundation of the Late Rev. John Bampton, M. A* (Rivingtons, 1882), Lecture V.

89. Monastier, *Histoire de l'Eglise vaudoise depuis son origine et des Vaudois du Piémont jusqu'à nos jours: - Tome I*, 1, Chap. 12.

90. See Cotton Mather, *Memorable Providences Relating to Witchcraft and Possessions a Faithful Account of Many Wonderful and Surprising Things that Have Befallen Several Bewitched and Possessed Persons in New England* (Boston: R.P, 1689).

91. See also chapter "Inventing a Covenantal Society is Impossible" in Joseph Livni, *The Biblical Roots of American Constitutionalism - From 'I am the Lord' to 'We the People'* (Lanham, MD: Lexington Books, 2021).

92. Tocqueville, *Democracy in America*, 1, 233.

93. e. g. G.A. Moots, *Politics Reformed: The Anglo-American Legacy of Covenant Theology* (Columbia, MO: University of Missouri Press, 2010), 112; Ismael Kurun, *The Theological Origins of Liberalism* (Lanham, MD: Lexington Books, 2016); De Freitas, "Samuel Rutherford on Law and Covenant: The Impact of Theologico-Political Federalism on Constitutional Theory"; Elazar, *Covenant & Constitutionalism: The Great Frontier and the Matrix of Federal Democracy*; Donald S. Lutz, *The Origins of American Constitutionalism* (Baton Rouge, Louisiana: Louisiana State University Press, 1988); Steven Alan Samson, "Theological Sources of American Constitutionalism," Faculty Publications and Presentations, 54. Liberty University (1991); "Covenant Origins of the American Polity"; see also "parallels between the American system and the biblical system"; Sanford Levinson, *Constitutional Faith* (Princeton, NJ: Princeton University Press, 2011), 11; Livni, *The Biblical Roots of American Constitutionalism - From 'I am the Lord' to 'We the People'*.

94. e. g. Steven K. Green, *Inventing a Christian America: The Myth of the Religious Founding* (Oxford: Oxford University Press, 2017), 68.

95. Marc Hertogh, "From Men of Files" to "Men of the Senses": A Brief Characterisation of Eugen Ehrlich's "Sociology of Law," in *Living Law: Reconsidering Eugen Ehrlich*, ed. Marc Hertogh (Oxford and Portland, OR: Hart Publishing, 2009), 3.

96. A Romanian word for customary law is obiceiuul pamântului (the habit of the land) Cristinel Nicu C. Trandafir, "Valori europene în „obiceiul pământului" specific satelor devălmaşe româneşti (sec. XIV–XIX)," in Cultura română şi modele culturale europene cercetare, sincronizare, durabilitate (Bucharest: Romanian Academy, 2015).

97. Shmuel Safrai, "The Term Derekh Ereẕ," Tarbitz (1991).

98. Leviticus Raba (Margaliot) Jerusalem (1952), 179.

99. Bjorn.C. Ewald and Carlos .F. Noreña, *The Emperor and Rome: Space, Representation, and Ritual, ed. Bjorn.C. Ewald and Carlos .F. Noreña* (Cambridge, UK: Cambridge University Press, 2010), 33.

100. David I. Kertzer, *The Kidnapping of Edgardo Mortara* (New York: Vintage, 2008).

101. See details in Winthrop E. Dwight, "An Episode in the Affaire Dreyfus," *The Yale Law Journal* 8, no. 6 (1899).

REFERENCES

Aero Mayflower Transit Co, and William Bradford. *The Mayflower Compact*. Fenton, MO: The Company, 1955.

Alexis, Muston. *L'israël Des Alpes: Première Histoire Complète Des Vaudois Du Piémont Et De Leurs Colonies*, Vol. I. Paris: Libr. de Marc Ducloux, 1851.

Aristotle, Benjamin Jowett, and Henry William Carless Davis. *Politics*. Kindle edition. Mineola, NY: Dover Publications, 2000.

Audisio, Gabriel. *The Waldensian Dissent: Persecution and Survival C. 1170–C. 1570*. Translated by Claire Davison. Cambridge: Cambridge University Press, 1999.

Bădescu, Ilie. "Communal Society and the "Dual System" Equality and Inequality in the Carpathian Valleys." *Revista română de sociologie anul* XXX, nos. 3–4 (2019): 179–221.

Bădescu, Ilie, Ozana Cucu-Oancea, and Gheorghe Şişeşte. *Dicționar De Sociologie Rurală*. Editura Mica Valahie, 2005.

Barnard, Alan, and Jonathan Spencer. *Encyclopedia of Social and Cultural Anthropology*. London, New York: Routledge, 1996.

Barraque, Jean Pierre. "Pactisme Et Pactismes." In *Mélanges En L'honneur Du Professeur Christian Desplat. Espaces Nationaux Et Identités Régionales*, edited by Adrián Blázquez Garbajosa and Philippe Chareyre, 25–44. Ortez: Gascogne, 2004.

Bederman, David J. *International Law in Antiquity*. Cambridge, UK: Cambridge University Press, 2001.

Bidot-Germa, Dominique. "The Specific Features of Medieval Notaries North and South of the Pyrenees: The Example of Béarn." *Imago temporis: medium Aevum* 5 (2011): 175–91.

———. *Un Notariat Médiéval: Droit, Pouvoirs Et Société En Béarn*. Toulouse: Presses universitaires du Mirail-Toulouse, 2008.

Bourin, Monique. "Historiographie Des Communautés De La France Méridionale." In *La formation des communautés d'habitants au Moyen Âge. Perspectives historiographiques*, edited by Ludolf Kuchenbuch, Dieter Scheler, and Joseph Morsel. Xanten, Germany, 2003.

Britannica, T. "Poetic Justice." In *Encyclopedia Britannica*, edited by Editors of Encyclopaedia, 2013.

Cantemir, Dimitrie. *Descrierea Moldovei*. Grup Editorial Litera, 2016.

Chaudhuri, Jyotirmoy Pal "Conflicts in Africa and the Palavers." In *Searching for Non-Western Roots of Conflict Resolution: Discourses, Norms and Case Studies*, edited by Shantanu Chakrabarti. New Delhi: KW Publishers Pvt Ltd, 2013.

Comba, Emilio. *History of the Waldenses of Italy: From Their Origin to the Reformation*. Translated by Teofilo Comba. London: Truslove & Shirley, 1889.

Concannon, Cavan W. *Assembling Early Christianity: Trade, Networks, and the Letters of Dionysios of Corinth*. Cambridge: Cambridge University Press, 2017.

Couderc-Barraud, Hélène. *La Violence, L'ordre Et La Paix: Résoudre Les Conflits En Gascogne Du Xie Au Début Du Xiiie Siècle*. Toulouse: Presses universitaires du Mirail, 2008.

De Freitas, Shaun A. *Samuel Rutherford on Law and Covenant: The Impact of Theologico-Political Federalism on Constitutional Theory*. Thesis, University of the Free State, 2003.

de Lagrèze, Gustave Bascle. *Histoire Du Droit Dans Les Pyrénées - Comté De Bigorre*. Paris: Imprimerie Impériale, 1867.

———. *La Féodalité Dans Les Pyrénées, Comté De Bigorre*. Mémoire Lu À L'académie Des Sciences Morales Et Politiques. Paris: A. Durand, 1864.

Dever, William .G. *What Did the Biblical Writers Know and When Did They Know It?: What Archeology Can Tell Us About the Reality of Ancient Israel*. Kindle edition. Grand Rapids, MI: Eerdmans Publishing Company, 2002.

Durkheim, Émile. *Moral Education*. Mineola, NY: Dover Publications, 2012.

Dwight, Winthrop E. "An Episode in the Affaire Dreyfus." *The Yale Law Journal* 8, no. 6 (1899): 272–79.

Elazar, D. J., J. Kincaid, J. W. Baker, J. D. Bratt, H. Fisch, D. S. Lutz, W. S. Reid, and F. Sabetti. *The Covenant Connection: From Federal Theology to Modern Federalism*. Lanham, MD: Lexington Books, 2000.

Elazar, Daniel. *Covenant and Polity in Biblical Israel: Volume 1, Biblical Foundations and Jewish Expressions: Covenant Tradition in Politics*. New York: Routledge, 1995.

Elazar, Daniel J. "Contrasting Unitary and Federal Systems." *International Political Science Review/Revue internationale de science politique* 18, no. 3 (1997): 237–51.

———. *Covenant & Commonwealth: From Christian Separation Through the Protestant Reformation*. New Brunswick, NJ: Transaction Publishers, 1995.

———. *Covenant & Constitutionalism: The Great Frontier and the Matrix of Federal Democracy*. New Brunswick, NJ: Transaction Publishers, 1997.

———. *Covenant and Polity in Biblical Israel*. New Brunswick, NJ: Transaction Publishers, 1998.

———. "Judaism and Democracy: The Reality." *Jerusalem Letter*, no. 48 (1986): 1–5.———. *The Covenant Tradition in Politics*. Vol. 1. New Brunswick, NJ: Transaction Publishers, 1995.

Elazar, Daniel J., and Stewart Cohen. *The Jewish Polity: Jewish Political Organization From Biblical Times to the Present*. Bloomington, IN: Indiana University Press, 1985.

Elazar, Daniel Judah. "Federalism and Covenant." 1980.

———. "The Almost-Covenanted Polity." Paper Presented at the Workshop in the Covenant Idea and the Jewish Political Tradition, Ramat Gan, Israel, 1982.

Ewald, Bjorn C., and Carlos F. Noreña. *The Emperor and Rome: Space, Representation, and Ritual*. Edited by Bjorn C. Ewald and Carlos F. Noreña. Cambridge, UK: Cambridge University Press, 2010.

Faust, Avraham. *Israel's Ethnogenesis: Settlement, Interaction, Expansion and Resistance*. London: Equinox Pub., 2006.

———. "The Rural Community in Ancient Israel During Iron Age I I." *Bulletin of the American Schools of Oriental Research* (2000): 17–39.

Filipescu, Iancu. "Din Contribuţiile Profesorului Henri H. Stahl La Dezvoltarea Sociologiei Istoriei." [In Romanian]. *Sociologie Romanească* IV, no. 3 (2006): 27–33.

Finkelstein, Israel, Amihai Mazar, and Brian B. Schmidt. *The Quest for the Historical Israel: Debating Archaeology and the History of Early Israel*. Sixth Biennial Colloquium of the International Institute for Secular Humanistic Judaism. Atlanta: SBL Press, 2007.

Frazee, Charles A. "The Origins of Clerical Celibacy in the Western Church." *Church History* 41, no. 2 (1972): 149–67.

Gilly, William Stephen. *Waldensian Researches During a Second Visit to the Vaudois of Piemont*. London: Rivington, 1831.

Goitein, Shlomo Dov, and Jacob Lassner. *A Mediterranean Society: An Abridgment in One Volume*. Berkley, CA: University of California Press, 1999.

Green, Steven K. *Inventing a Christian America: The Myth of the Religious Founding*. Oxford: Oxford University Press, 2017.

Hatch, Edwin. *The Organization of the Early Christian Churches*. London: Rivingtons, 1882.

———. *The Organization of the Early Christian Churches: Eight Lectures Delivered Before the University of Oxford, in the Year, 1880, on the Foundation of the Late Rev. John Bampton, M. A.* Rivingtons, 1882.

Hawthorne, Walter. *The Interior Past of an Acephalous Society: Institutional Change Among the Balanta of Guinea-Bissau, C. 1400–C. 1950*. Stanford, CA: Stanford University, 1998.

Hertogh, Marc. "From 'Men of Files' to 'Men of the Senses': A Brief Characterisation of Eugen Ehrlich'S Sociology of Law." In *Living Law: Reconsidering Eugen Ehrlich*, edited by Marc Hertogh, 1–17. Oxford and Portland, OR: Hart Publishing, 2009.

Iorga, Nicolae. "Scrisori De Boieri Scrisori De Domni." In *Din publicațiile casei școalelor*, edited by Casa şcoalelor. Vălenii de Munte, Romania: Editura casei şcoalelor; Datina Românească, 1925.

Javet, Bernard. "L'éducation Nationale En Chiffres 2020." In *Les personnels et établissements*, edited by Direction de l'évaluation de la prospective et de la performance (DEPP). Paris: Ministère de l'éducation nationale, de la junesse et des sports, 2020.

Kertzer, David I. *The Kidnapping of Edgardo Mortara*. New York: Vintage, 2008.

Kurun, Ismael. *The Theological Origins of Liberalism*. Lanham, MD: Lexington Books, 2016.

Le Play, Frédéric. *L'organisation De La Famille Selon Le Vrai Modèle Signalé Par L'histoire De Toutes Les Races Et De Tous Les Temps*. A. Mame et fils, 1895.

Léger, Jean. *Histoire Generale Des Eglises Evangeliques Des Vallees De Piemont Ou Vaudoises*. Leiden: Jean le Carpentier, 1669.

Levinson, Sanford. *Constitutional Faith*. Princeton, NJ: Princeton University Press, 2011.

Levy, Thomas E., and Augustin F. C. Holl. "Migrations, Ethnogenesis, and Settlement Dynamics: Israelites in Iron Age Canaan and Shuwa-Arabs in the Chad Basin." *Journal of Anthropological Archaeology* 21, no. 1 (2002): 83–118.

Livni, Joseph. *The Biblical Roots of American Constitutionalism - From 'I Am the Lord' to 'We the People'*. Lanham, MD: Lexington Books, 2021.

Lowe, Enoch Lois. *Discourse Delivered at the Commemoration of the Landing of the Pilgrims of Maryland: Celebrated May 12, 1845, at Mt. St. Mary's, Near Emmitsburg, Md.* Gettysburg: H.C. Neinstedt, 1845.

Lutz, Donald S. *The Origins of American Constitutionalism*. Baton Rouge, Louisiana: Louisiana State University Press, 1988.

Maimonides, Moses, and Hermann H. Bernard. *The Main Principles of the Creed and Ethics of the Jews, Exhibited in Selections from the Yad Hachazakah of Maimonides*. Cambridge: Deighton, 1832.

Marsden, John Boxton. *The History of the Later Puritans*. Second edition. London: Hamilton, Adams & Company; T. Hatchard, 1854.

Monastier, Antoine. *Histoire De L'eglise Vaudoise Depuis Son Origine Et Des Vaudois Du Piémont Jusqu'à Nos Jours: - Tome I*. Vol. 1. Geneva: Kessmann, 1847.

Moots, G. A. *Politics Reformed: The Anglo-American Legacy of Covenant Theology*. Columbia, MO: University of Missouri Press, 2010.

Mosheim, John Laurence, and Archibald Maclaine. *An Ecclesiastical History Antient and Modern From the Birth of Christ to the Beginning of the Eighteenth Century, in Which the Rise, Progress, and Variations of Church Power Are Considered in Their Connexion With the State of Learning and Philosophy and the Political History of Europe During That Period*. London: Strahan and Preston, 1811.

Neal, D., and J. Toulmin. *The History of the Puritans or Protestant Non-Conformists*. Repr. from Dr. Toulmin's edition. London: Thomas Tegg and Son, 1837.

Neal, Daniel, and Joshua Toulmin. *The History of the Puritans, or Protestant Non-Conformists*. Boston: Charles Ewer, 1817.

"Overview and Mission Statement." Edited by Department of Education. Washington, DC: US Department of Education, 1992.

Paravy, Pierrette. *De La Chrétienté Romaine À La Réforme En Dauphiné. Évêques, Fidèles Et Déviants (Vers 1340–Vers 1350)* [in Français]. Collection De L'école Française De Rome. Vol. 1. Rome: École française de Rome, 1993.

Peyran, Jean Rodolphe, and Thomas Sims. *An Historical Defence of the Waldenses or Vaudois: Inhabitants of the Valleys of Piedmont*. London: C. & J. Rivington, 1826.

Philbrick, Nathanel. *Mayflower: A Story of Courage, Community, and War*. Kindle edition. New York: Penguin Publishing Group, 2006.

Presbyterian Church in the U.S.A. Synod of Pennsylvania. *Minutes of the . . . Annual Session of the Synod of Pennsylvania of the Presbyterian Church in the United States of America*. 1909.

Sabetti, Filippo. "Covenant Language in Canada." Paper Presented at the Workshop on Covenant and Politics, Center for the Study of Federalism, Temple University, 1980.

Safrai, Shmuel. "The Term Derekh Ereẕ." [In Hebrew]. *Tarbitz* (1991): 147–62.

Safrai, Ze'ev. *The Economy of Roman Palestine*. London, New York: Taylor & Francis, 2003.

Samson, Steven Alan. "Covenant Origins of the American Polity." *Faculty Publications and Presentations* 5. Liberty University, 1994.

———. "Theological Sources of American Constitutionalism." *Faculty Publications and Presentations* 54. Liberty University, 1991.

Schiff, Stacy. *The Witches: Suspicion, Betrayal and Histeria in 1692 Salem*. Kindle edition. New York, Boston, London: Little Brown, 2015.

Soussen Max, Claire. ""Iudei Nostri", Pouvoir Royal, Communautés Juives Et Société Chrétienne Dans Les Territoires De La Couronne D'aragon Au Xiiie Et Première Moitié Du Xive Siècle." St Quentin en Yvelines, 2005.

Stahl, H. H. *Les Anciennes Communautés Villageoises Roumaines: Asservissement Et Pénétration Capitaliste*. Editions de l'Académie de la République socialiste de Roumanie, 1969.

———. "Nerej, Un Sat Dintr-O Regiune Arhaică." *Sociologie Românească, an* IV (1942): 7–12.

Stahl, Henri H. *Contribuţii La Studiul Satelor Devālmaşe Romineşti: Confederaţii De Ocol, Structuri Teritoriale Şi Tehnici Agricole*. Bucharest: Editura Academiei Republicii Populare Romine, 1958.

———. *Nerej, Un Village D'une Région Archaïque: Monographie Sociologique* [in French]. Vol. V. 1, Bucarest: Institut de sciences sociales de Roumanie, 1939.

Stahl, Henri H., and Paul H. Stahl. *Contribuţii La Studiul Satelor Devălmaşe Româneşti: Procesul De Aservire Feudală a Satelor Devălmaşe*. Vol. 3. Cartea Românească, 1998.

Tocqueville, Alexis de. *Democracy in America*. Translated by Henry Reeve. Kindle edition. Vol. 1. Project Gutenberg, 2006.

Trandafir, Cristinel Nicu C. "Valori Europene În 'Obiceiul Pământului' Specific Satelor Devălmaşe Româneşti (Sec. Xiv–Xix)." In *Cultura română şi modele culturale europene cercetare, sincronizare, durabilitate*. Bucharest: Romanian Academy, 2015.

Trebilco, Paul. *The Early Christians in Ephesus From Paul to Ignatius*. Grand Rapids, MI: Eerdmans Publishing Company, 2007.

Tufescu, Victor. "Răspândirea Satelor De Răzeşi: Contibuţiuni La Studiul Populării Moldovei." *Arhivele Basarabiei* 1 (1934).

Turchin, Peter, and Sergey Gavrilets. "Evolution of Complex Hierarchical Societies." *Social Evolution & History* 8, no. 2 (2009): 167–98.

Watson, Alan. "An Approach to Customary Law." *University of Illinois Law Review* (1984): 561.

Watt, Isabella M., Homas A. Lambert, Robert M. Kingdon, Jeffrey R. Watt, Paule H. Dubuis, and Sandra Coram-Mekkey. *Registres Du Consistoire De Genève Au Temps De Calvin. Tome I, 1542–1544*. Geneva: Librairie Droz, 1996.

Weber, Max. *Das Antike Judentum*. FV Éditions, 2017.

Weinfeld, Moshe. "Covenant Making in Anatolia and Mesopotamia." *Journal of the Ancient Near Eastern Society* 22, no. 1 (1993): 2396.

Chapter 1

Nomadism and the Sociological Seed of Pre-Monarchic Israel

Joseph Livni

NOMADISM

Archaeology has shed light on the history of civilizations with powerful tools of analysis of material cultures of every inhabited corner of the planet. There are however societies like nomadic pastoralists "that do not leave behind detectable residues of their existence."[1]

Pastoralist nomads have been viewed by ancient civilization such as Sumer,[2] Greco-Roman culture,[3] China,[4] and Byzantium[5] as barbarians.

For some, *civilization* means the opposite of *barbarism*;[6] this may infer that pastoralist nomads have wandered around the civilization without contributing anything to it. Archaeology inadvertently concurs: "Archaeologists rarely consider that pastoralists were present in the sites they excavate or that they had an impact on the physical or sociological characteristics of the settlements."[7]

This chapter surveys investigations showing that the impact of these nomads has been significant in many aspects of our lifestyle: nutrition, health, political, sociological, law, military, among others.

The chapter will show examples of unveiling the secrets of nomadism by multidisciplinary investigation. Subsequently it will focus on innovations that we owe to nomadic pastoralists. The chapter dedicates a section arguing against the view that nomadic pastoralists are simple societies compared to the "complex" sedentary civilizations. We cannot talk about nomadism without touching the subject of sedentarization of nomads.

A whole section is dedicated to a most amazing socio-political organization, the civil society with no hierarchy that unintentionally stepped on the scene of history when a few tribes of pastoralist nomads settled down on the Central Hill of the Land of Israel.

INTERDISCIPLINARY APPROACH

Archaeology is a science. As physics, or biology, archaeology follows the three steps of the scientific method: observation, theory. and verification. The specialization and sub-specialization of scientific method to various branches of science is very fruitful. Only super-specialized scientist could show that "RNA signals through human TLR3, TLR7, and TLR8, but incorporation of modified nucleosides m5C, m6A, m5U, s2U, or pseudouridine ablates activity."[8] However, super-specialized science has its disadvantages. For example the equation of diffusion through space of an advantageous gene[9] was derived by Sir Ronald Fisher, one of the founders of modern statistics. The extension of the same equation to the spread of innovation in general and its application to the spread of farming in Europe in particular is an extraordinary achievement in . . . archaeology. Yet it was carried out by Cavalli-Sforza and Feldman[10] whose background was not at all archaeology. Interdisciplinary cross-fertilization is a new rage. Our experience shows that it is not an easy endeavor. It involves among others understanding jargons, tolerating analogies, and mutual trust in the integrity and rigor of hardly understandable derivations and determinations. This section treats interdisciplinary efforts that allowed overcoming weaknesses in treating nomadic presence with purely archaeological tools. Yes, there are such weaknesses. For example in biblical archaeology:

> In essence, this flaw, which cuts across all schools of biblical archaeology, is the prevailing, overly simplistic approach applied to the identification and interpretation of nomadic elements in biblical-era societies. These elements have typically been described as representing only one form of social organization which is simple and almost negligible in historical reconstructions.[11]

Some written chronicles of Priscus, Jordanes, Marcellinus Comes, and Paschal mention the Huns and their empire. However, no material archaeological evidence would testify to the historicity of a Hunic Empire. All we know is that Attila's capital was on the Hungarian plains.[12] In other words no palaces, temples, and architectural accomplishments testify to the greatness of Attila the Emperor of Huns. Could a bunch of pastoralist nomads run a vast empire and successfully battle the Roman, Byzantine, and Parthian Empires? Applying minimalist philosophy Attila was a little bandit from the prairies who managed to scare some chroniclers. Multidisciplinary investigations, however, revealed the secrets of the success of this typical steppe nomadic pastoralist confederation.

For example, multidisciplinary investigation produced the following breakthroughs in the study of nomadic pastoralism:

A. Proteomic analysis of dental calculus discovered in the nomadic pastoralists of the western Eurasian steppe a major transition to dairy product consumption at the beginning of the Bronze Age.[13] Reasonably, these pastoralists were meat consumers. The dairy products enhance one's dental health and allow longer periods of consuming meat which contribute to general health of the population. This affects among other demographic growth. All these factors contributed to the spread of Indo-European languages considering findings that these nomads indeed spread into Europe (see more about the sedentarization of Yamnaya nomads in section *Sedentarization*).
B. A study of a wide spectrum of specializations such as history, geo-genetics, environmental archaeology, ethno-archaeology, Nordic Studies and Linguistics, Bio and Health Informatics, Anthropology, and Genomics arrived at the process of "formation of a new material culture, the Corded Ware Culture, and of a new dialect, Proto-Germanic."[14] The third-millennium Corded Ware culture is further discussed in section *Sedentarization.*
C. A truly multidisciplinary investigation of Archaeology, Anthropology, Molecular Genetics, and Linguistics summarizes "shifts in ancestry across generations as particular human populations expanded or died out, as well as labeling migrants and their genes as they moved across geographic space."[15]
D. Ancient DNA analysis determined the contribution of Late Neolithic / Early Bronze Age pastoralist nomads from the Pontic-Caspian region to the spread of Indo-European languages into Europe. Ancient DNA analysis also calculates genetic distances[16] between various pairs of populations; however migration trends appear more noticeable when the DNA is harvested from ancient human remains rather than from current populations.[17]
E. Zoo-archaeological investigation of bit wear on horses' teeth revealed the difference of wear between horse used for riding and wagon pulling.[18] Accordingly one can time the use of horse as a transport animal to earlier than 4000 BCE and horseback-riding to the interval of 3400–2700 BCE (see also figure 1.1).
F. The reconstruction of a Scythian saddle and its test showed its advantages of riding a horse without stirrups.[19]
G. A socio-physics investigation proves that the first Israelite settlement at the beginning of Iron Age were of nomadic pastoralists that immigrated from the East.[20]
H. Analysis of Variance (*ANOVA*) post-processing of *zoo-archaeological* evidence and analogy to classical industrial *control engineering* concluded that pre-monarchic Israel stepped forward from customary *law* to enforced law.[21]

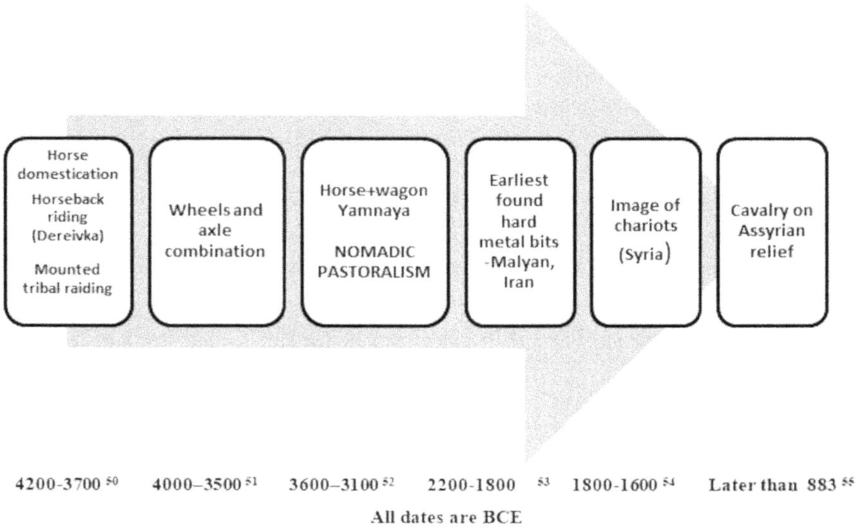

Figure 1.1 Innovations of Steppe Nomads; from Horse Domestication to Nomadic Pastoralism to Cavalry Warfare. *Source*: Prepared by the author.

INNOVATIONS

This section lists important innovations of pastoralist nomads that significantly changed the course of the history of civilizations regardless of including the nomadic herders into civilization.[22]

Before I list the innovations of these shepherds, cowboys, and raiders that knew little astronomy and presumably no physics I need to remind the reader that inventions are random modifications of products, tools and methods of production, transport, maintenance, among others.

> Humiliating to human pride as may be, we must recognize that the advance and even the preservation of civilization are dependent upon a maximum of opportunity for accidents to happen.[23]

Naturally, the most obvious nomadic pastoralist invention is . . . nomadic pastoralism. The earliest archaeological evidence of total separation between farming and herding took place at the beginning of the third millennium BCE in the *Yamna* territory North of the Black and Caspian seas (figure 1.2).[24] The earliest mention of Amorites in the Near East is in the second half of the same millennium.[25]

More "recent" inventions of nomadic pastoralists worthwhile mentioning are:

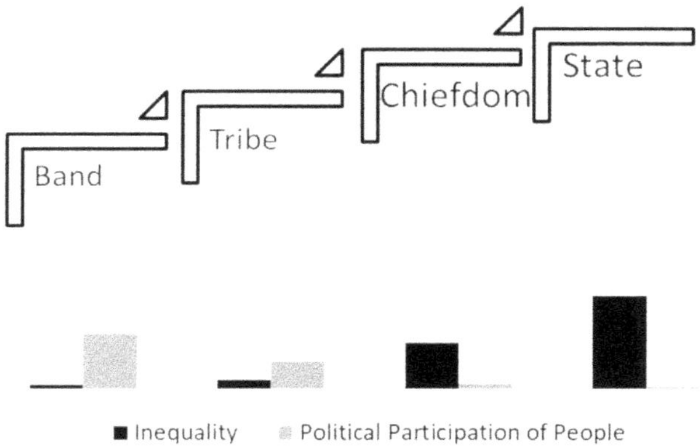

Figure 1.2 Observed Link between Complexity, Inequality, and Political Participation of the Popular Masses. Note:The chart indicates that as complexity grows the inequality increases and political participation decreases; this is likely true for Pharaonic Egypt and the Roman Empire. The generalization of this inference has never been substantiated. *Source: Prepared by the author*

A. The Scythian saddle[26] fifth–third century BCE
B. The composite, recurved Scythian bow[27] tenth century BCE
C. The asymmetric Hun bow fifth century[28] allowed to "employ the bow as mass weapon from horseback."[29]

The next section treats sociological prototypes created within nomadic pastoralist people.

SOCIAL MODELS

Scholars point at various factors determining the social models of pastoralist nomads. We shall show that the main constraining factors consist of culture[30] followed by vastness of territory and mobility and types of herds.[31] For example, one finds demographic, economic, cultural, and geographic (e.g., semi-desert, steppe, forest-steppe, intermountain valleys, high-mountain ranges) factors.[32]

Pastoralist nomads roam a vast territory and the distances between clans and tribes are not comparable to sedentary farming and trading societies evolved into city-states. The mobility of nomads adds another dimension of the sense of freedom because no one can profit from constraining pastoralists to any territory. These factors have a primary role in ruling out hierarchic models of such societies. Therefore, pastoralist nomads have social models that are on a variable scale between egalitarian federations and ranked empires consisting on a confederation linked with patron–client arrangements. The mobility of nomads is strongly related to their socio-political organization.[33] As a result of their mobility their ties to the clan or tribe are set by the equilibrium between centripetal forces that keep them within the tribe and the centrifugal forces enticing them to leave. The centripetal forces are the need to belong to a group in society in general and to the group they are familiar with in particular. The centrifugal forces consist in disagreement with arbitrary decisions that conflict with their sense of security. This creates a dynamics where transients of disequilibrium "enable association and dissociation without unpleasant rupture."[34] In other words, clans or even individuals can move out.

The tribe needs the tribesmen and the tribesmen need the tribe (centripetal forces). Conflicts can be reconciled either by a general acceptance of the authority of elders or where an egalitarian ethos[35] prevails one involves everybody in decision making:

A. To move or not to move. There are several reasons why the tribes move: greener grass elsewhere, maximizing the supply of resources, biological factors (e.g. tsetse flies), lack of pasture or water, economic and social relations with other groups, or states, and social relations between individuals within the nomadic tribe.[36]
B. Where to go? "The tribesmen never knew very much ahead of time what might be the best destinations."[37] Reasonably they weighed knowledge and reports about destination. "Go; view the land, especially Jericho."[38] The historicity of the collapse of Jericho has been contested by archaeologists;[39] however, the necessity to "view the land" is credible. Pastoralists herding different species prefer different destinations;[40] consequently even the animals had a say in the decisions about destinations.[41]

The culture before the society turned to nomadic pastoralism is the dominant factor controlling which of the two social models is adopted. Salzman convincingly shows how Plains Indians of North America conserved their previous views regarding political equality as they converted their lifestyle to horse-mounted hunting of bison.[42] Salzman observes that under identical environmental conditions tribes that previously had strong formal leadership, police, and so on remained ranked, while those who came from unranked organizations maintained an egalitarian organization.

The ranked pastoralist arrangement is the more frequent and probably the more sustainable model. Fundamental institutions like the oaths institution (see more in section *Covenant*), the patron client (ranked), and guest–host (egalitarian) relationships[43] led to "well tested political and social structures to integrate communities across geographic distances."[44]

The patron–client relationship is prevalent in pastoralist complex societies. The sedentary Egyptian Pharaonic model of empire was based on conquest followed by submission of the vanquished. The pastoralist patron–client institution also started with forceful penetration in foreign territories. However the pastoralist patron did not seek the total submission of the conquered population; the patron–client relationship maintained the client's function to manage his food production operation; however the patron took his share of the yield.[45]

The oscillatory dynamics of the pastoralist food production, random and incoherent variations of vegetation, water, tribe population, and herd size created fluctuations of abundance and scarcity.[46] This doesn't provide proof of historicity of the biblical story about Joseph and his brothers; however the need to look for food in Egypt seems very credible in light of this analysis. Similarly to the biblical account, the remedy of pastoralists consists of getting food during famine periods from sedentary societies. Their interrelations with sedentary societies "varied from direct exchange, trade, trade mediation and other related services, or mercenarism, to raids, looting, blackmailing, [and] occasional payments."[47]

It is noteworthy that trade relations contributed not only to the economy of both trade partners,[48] but also opened avenues of international trade like the silk road.[49] As explained above, the most frequent method was extracting revenues through the patron–client relationship.

Examples of such societies include the Yamnaya,[50] the Xiōngnú, the Yuèzhī, the Wusun,[51] the Huns of Attila,[52] and the Mongols of Genghis Khan.[53]

The egalitarian arrangement is less frequent. Egalitarian societies have no ruler because "the rank and file avoid being subordinated by vigilantly keeping alpha-type group members under their collective thumbs."[54] In these acephalous organizations there are initiators (elders); however they are under a constant watch of the community. Boehm coined the term *reverse dominance hierarchy* to distinguish it from the classical pyramidal hierarchy.[55]

Acephalous egalitarian organizations are not the result of democratic visionaries who lead by example and initiate egalitarian institutions; the essence of the *egalitarian ethos* is that it "disapproves of hierarchical behavior in general and of bossiness in leaders in particular."[56] This note is consistent with the previous observation that egalitarian pastoralist nomads transitioned from egalitarian hunter-gatherers when they turned to pastoralism. Hunter-gatherers who transitioned to pastoralism from a ranked organization will need a ranked pastoralist arrangement of the patron–client type. On the other hand an "egalitarian relation between followers and their leader is deliberately made to happen by collectively assertive followers."[57]

Scholars report examples of egalitarian pastoralist organizations such as:

F. Nuer, of South Sudan and Ethiopia; Sambutu of Kenya; Ruwallah Bedouin of northern Arabia and the Syrian Desert, including modern-day Jordan; Yomut Turkmen, and the Sarhad of Iranian Baluchistan;[58]
G. The Somali pastoralists;[59]
H. The Turkana of North-West Kenya;[60]
I. The Shuwa Arabs of Cameroon, Nigeria, and Western Chad;[61]
J. The Ilparakuyo and Maasai of Kenya and Tanzania.[62]

COMPLEXITY

The classical social typology of band-tribe-chiefdom-state[63] serves as a scale of social inequality of sociopolitical organizations.

There is no verifiable relationship between political complexity and inequality. One hurdle is that as long as the magnitudes of complexity, inequality, among others, are not defined the chart of figure 1.2 describes a qualitative link between unmeasurable magnitudes and its interpretation as a substantiated relationship is questionable.

Let me try to arrive at a more quantitative approach. Chiefdoms are the lowest step of the evolutionary staircase of figure 1.2 where one finds "pervasive inequality of persons and groups in the society."[64] The next step is the state: "The growing complexity of the society made it inevitable to develop mechanisms to ensure that rules and regulations were carried out—if necessary by force. In this way a reasonable degree of order in the overcrowded forts was reached and safety as well as a sufficient flow of food and goods was ensured."[65]

This explanation is helpful. Complexity is an expression of social problems: rules, regulations, enforcement of rules, safety, food flow, and goods availability. In most farming civilizations such problems were indeed overcome by hierarchy and centralization of power. For example table 1.1 lists some of the problems the Roman Empire faced in the fourth century.

In order to arrive at a quantifiable magnitude the column S*tate Variable* links each such problem with a measurable quantity. I proposed therefore to define *complexity* as the number of *state variables* faced by a social organization on the band-tribe-chiefdom-state scale.[66] This brings us to the question of *equilibrium* and *stability*[67] or in terms used by archaeologists[68] *sustainability* and *resilience*.[69] The investigation proved that indeed growing *complexity* brings the socio-political system closer to the point of collapse.[70]

At this point I am ready to claim that nomadic pastoralist social models of both kinds: ranked and egalitarian were more stable than the centralized hierarchic states even when they dealt with the same number of problems (i.e., even when they reached the same complexity). The reason for that is

Table 1.1 Quantifying Complexity of the Roman Empire in the Fourth Century by means of Problems and Assessable-Related State Variable

#	*Problem*	*State variable*
1	Defense from outsiders	Number of incursions
2	Justice (protection from insiders)	Number of free criminals, conspirators, traitors etc
3	Pagan senatorial aristocracy (a)	Number of pagan senators.
4	Public dole (b)	Number of poor
5	State of Roads (c)	Miles needing pavement
6	Fire protection (d)	Cost of insurance against fire losses
7	Ports efficiency (e)	expected time a boat is tied up at dock
8	Contract enforcement (f)	time and cost for resolving a commercial dispute
9	Duty evasion (g)	Number of smugglers
10	Safety of international commerce	Probability of loss due to piracy
11	Rebellions	Man-years tied-up to put down insurgencies
12	Epidemics	Number of death cases
13	Land abandonment (h)	Square meters of unused arable land
14	Rigged weighing scales (i)	Probability of acceptable exchange of goods
15	Political conspiracy	Probability of rulers' unnatural demise
16	Safety of internal commerce (j)	Probability of loss due to bandits
17	Theft	Number of thieves
18	Ruler's legitimacy	Number of skeptics
19	Control of provinces (k)	Number of usurper-governors
20	Tax	Tax cheaters
21	Military discipline and moral (l)	Number of deserters
22	Smuggling (m)	Number of smugglers

Source: Compiled by the author using data from:

a) The second half of the fourth century witnessed the beginning of a massive conversion to Christianity. Religious conflicts between Christians and Pagans as those among Christian divisions may be studied in light of differences in "political alignments rather than theological understanding" Joyce.E. Salisbury, *Rome's Christian Empress: Galla Placidia Rules at the Twilight of the Empire* (Baltimore: Johns Hopkins University Press, 2015), 24. In the Western Empire, Christianization was a result of a trickle-down effect from the aristocracy to the masses Peter Heather, *The fall of the Roman Empire: A New History* (Hampshire, UK: Pan Books, 2010), 127; Michele Renee Salzman, *The making of a Christian aristocracy: social and religious change in the western Roman empire*, Kindle Edition ed. (Cambridge, MA: Harvard University Press, 2002), Kindle loc. 114–19.

b) Alan Bowman, "Quantifying Egyptian Agriculture," in *Quantifying the Roman Economy. Methods and Problems, Oxford* (Oxford: Oxford University Press, 2009), 190.

c) Edward Gibbon, *The History of the Decline and Fall of the Roman Empire*, Kindle Edition ed. (Boston: Little, Brown, 1854), Kindle loc. 242.

d) Ibid., Kindle Loc. 5450.

e) Maria.T. Boatwright, *Hadrian and the Cities of the Roman Empire* (Princeton: Princeton University Press, 2000), 119.

f) Cameron Hawkins, "Contract, Coercion, and the Boundaries of the Roman Artisanal Firm," in *Work, Labour, and Professions in the Roman World* (Leiden: Brill, 2017), 41.

g) Stanley Bonner, *Education in Ancient Rome: From the Elder Cato to the Younger Pliny* (New York: Routledge, 2012), 317; Gibbon, *The History of the Decline and Fall of the Roman Empire*, Kindle loc. 4014.

h) Joseph A. Tainter, *The Collapse of Complex Societies* (Cambridge: Cambridge University Press, 1990), 145.

i) Ruth Kassinger, *Gold: From Greek Myth to Computer Chips* (Brookfield, CT: Twenty-First Century Books, 2003), 19.

j) Gibbon, *The History of the Decline and Fall of the Roman Empire*, Kindle loc. 7444.

k) Ibid., Kindle loc. 7616.

l) Gibbon, *The History of the Decline and Fall of the Roman Empire*, Kindle loc. 15708.

m) *The History of the Decline and Fall of the Roman Empire*, Kindle loc. 4929; William Smith, *Dictionary of Greek and Roman Antiquities* (London: C.C. Little and J. Brown, 1853), 945.

their descentralization.[71] Needless to say in an egalitarian confederation of egalitarian tribes the tribal autonomy was even less limited.

Some nomadic pastoralist organization have lasted until present presumably since the Neolithic; nevertheless many ceased to exist. Pastoralist organization exited history mainly through sedentarization; unlike collapse sedentarization is a gradual transient process going through a semi-nomadic step. The next section provides a brief summary of some sedentarization processes; section *Pre-monarchic Israel* details the particular case that gave birth to a new societal type: a sedentary society governed by a covenant, laws, and statutes, and yet without hierarchy.

SEDENTARIZATION

Today still there are nomadic pastoralist for example in Mongolia,[72] Tibet,[73] Egypt,[74] Siberia, Nigeria, Somalia, Kenya, and Algeria.[75] Nevertheless many pastoralist groups transitioned to sedentary lifestyle. Within these nomadic groups sedentary farming developed.[76] For example the Khazars,[77] the Hungarians,[78] the Pechenegs,[79] the Bulghars of Crimea,[80] and the Uighurs of East-Turkistan[81] were semi-nomadic people practicing pastoralism and farming in transition to sedentary lifestyle. How did the transition affect their social organization?

We shall distinguish three types of transitional political systems. The first two types described by Khazanov are due to sedentarization on land where there was a native population. The third type is a particular case when the nomads occupy a practically uninhabited territory.

The first type takes place when the dominant nomads and the sedentary population live separately. The two components are linked in patron–client relationship where nomads are the patrons and sedentary are the clients.[82] For example the Khazars had a patron–client relationship with more than twenty-five tribute-paying people.[83]

One early example of nomads settling down and imposing a change of culture is the sedentarization of Yamnaya pastoralists in Northern Europe (figure 1.3). Not only this immigration generated the new material culture called Corded Ware (2900 BCE–2350 BCE), but also it is associated with the spread of all the Indo-European languages spoken currently in Europe.[84] We know "that people of the largely-immigrant-descended Corded Ware and mostly local Globular Amphorae cultures remained genetically quite distinct for centuries."[85] There could be no textual evidence from ~3000 BCE proving that the *Yamnaya* migrants maintained a patron–client relationship with the local *Globular Amphorae* culture. Reasonably, the *Yamnaya* adopted their "inherited well tested political and social structures to

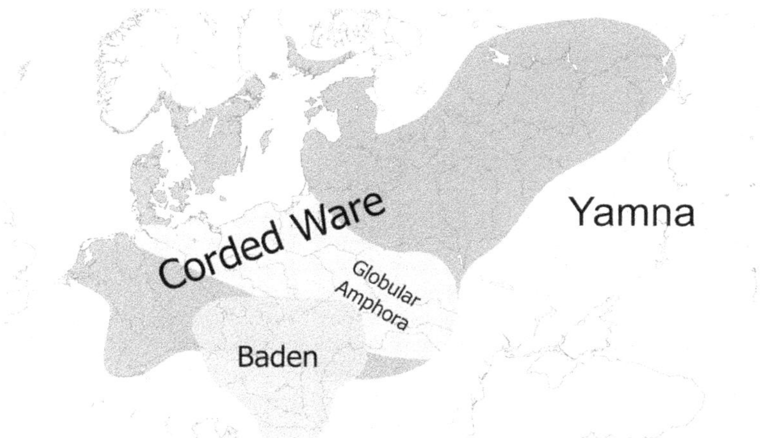

Figure 1.3 Corded Ware Culture (~3000–2900 BCE). *Source*: Public Domain, CC BY-SA 3.0 credit: Alexrk2.

integrate communities across geographic distances."[86] Moreover, the association with the spread of the Indo-European languages hints that in spite of the separation the population of both cultures the language of the Yamnaya was predominant.

A more recent event where an immigrant language displaced an indigenous language is the spread of Spanish in South America. If the strongly hierarchical Spanish conquistadores arrived at a patron–client relationship with the Inca elites, a fortiori the pastoralist Yamnaya also maintained the patron–client pattern which is characteristic to pastoralist conquerors.

The second type of transition to sedentary life takes place when the conqueror nomads replace the indigenous dynasties and subsequently a political integration of both components of the population; the elite of the previously nomadic component becomes the ruling class over the sedentary population.[87]

Two contradictory examples of sedentarization in practically uninhabited land will show that this category of sedentarization may vary along a large scale of possibilities:

For a long period after the Edomites settled in the Aravah desert they maintained their nomadic lifestyle: The Edomite "tribes of the entire Aravah and neighboring regions formed a strong coalition in order to exploit the ore bodies more efficiently, to facilitate trade and to better protect the sensitive enterprise."[88]

Only after the copper mining yields significantly diminished and "the main economy of Edom shifted to the Arabian trade"[89] they transitioned to a desert kingdom.[90]

The second example consists of the Israelite tribes that settled on the Central Hill of the Land of Israel. This example is detailed in the next section.

PRE-MONARCHIC ISRAEL

Sedentarization of Nomads or a Separation from Canaanite Culture

The biblical text teaches that the Israelites were slaves in Egypt; they escaped from bondage in Egypt and wandered in the wilderness of the desert for many years.

The biblical text mirrors the national memory of the Israelites transmitted orally until it was written down and subsequently copied and recopied. Scholars attempted to verify, corroborate, or refute the biblical narrative and not surprisingly arrived at contradictory results. The difficulty consists of the fact that the sources of information are scarce and unreliable, and the little information they carry is subject to interpretation.

Scholars disputed even the very appearance of Israelites in the Land of Canaan until 1896, when one discovered an Egyptian inscription specifying that a nation called Israel was annihilated[91] in Canaan by the Egyptian pharaoh. The inscription is known as the Merneptah Stele and its cross-examination of the biblical narrative by an independent Egyptian source put to rest the doubts in the minds of most scholars regarding the existence of an Israelite entity at the dawn of the Iron Age (twelfth century BCE).

We owe a great deal to biblical archaeologists for their work consisting of planning, determining the site locations, excavating evidence, stratifying sites into layers of consecutive periods, examining and cross-examining the findings with tools of other scientific disciplines, and finally evaluating the significance of their findings. No doubt they are scientists and we owe them a great deal for providing knowledge or information. However, it would be a mistake to accept every archaeological evaluation as proven fact. The proof to the contrary is provided by competing theories of various archaeologists regarding the significance of the same set of evidence.

The scientific method consists of three steps: observation, theory, and proof. In science proof of a theory is understood as ruling out any contradicting theory. There are archaeological theories that are proven in a similar fashion. However many theories formulated by archaeologists are controversial and the origin of the Israelites is one of them.

Some archaeologists hypothesize that the Israelites migrated from outside the Land of Canaan and others claim that they were Canaanites that split out of other Canaanites because they adopted a new variant of religion, ideology, cultural variation whatever one may want to call it.

I published an investigation that uses methodology of physics, namely the diffusion equation which rules out the theory cultural separation of Canaanite subgroups.[92] The mathematical model predicts that if Israel came into being though an ideological split from Canaan then the border would to be a line from West to East[93] (figure 1.4). However the detected borders are oriented in the North–South direction (figure 1.5). The conclusion is that the borders were not generated by an internal ideological split but by population immigration of Israelites from the East and of Philistines from the sea, or West.

That said the Israelites of the Central Hill (figure 1.4) were not any more nomads. They farmed grains, olives, and grapes.[94] The beginning of the Period of the Judges was a transition period from nomadic to sedentary lifestyle. The next sections deal with specific nomadic features that were brought from their nomadic lifestyle and conserved into a novel societal type.

The societal type of pre-monarchic Israel is called *covenantal society*. It reconciles the contradiction between the egalitarian ethos found in some

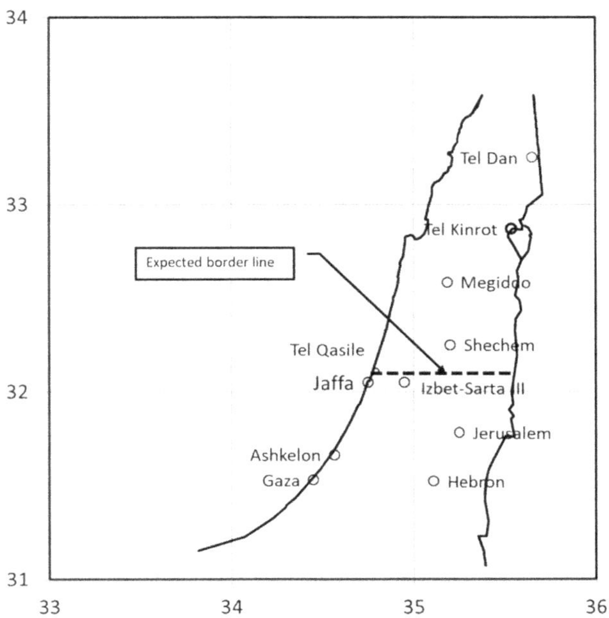

Figure 1.4 Expected Border Resulting by Split of a Different Ideology, Culture, or Faith. Note: The split may start anywhere e.g. Hebron, North of Megiddo or Jericho; it will propagate by cultural diffusion (random population exchange within a geographic neighborhoods); the idea propagates faster in the short East-West direction and when it stops the border is between South and North. *Source*: Prepared by the author.

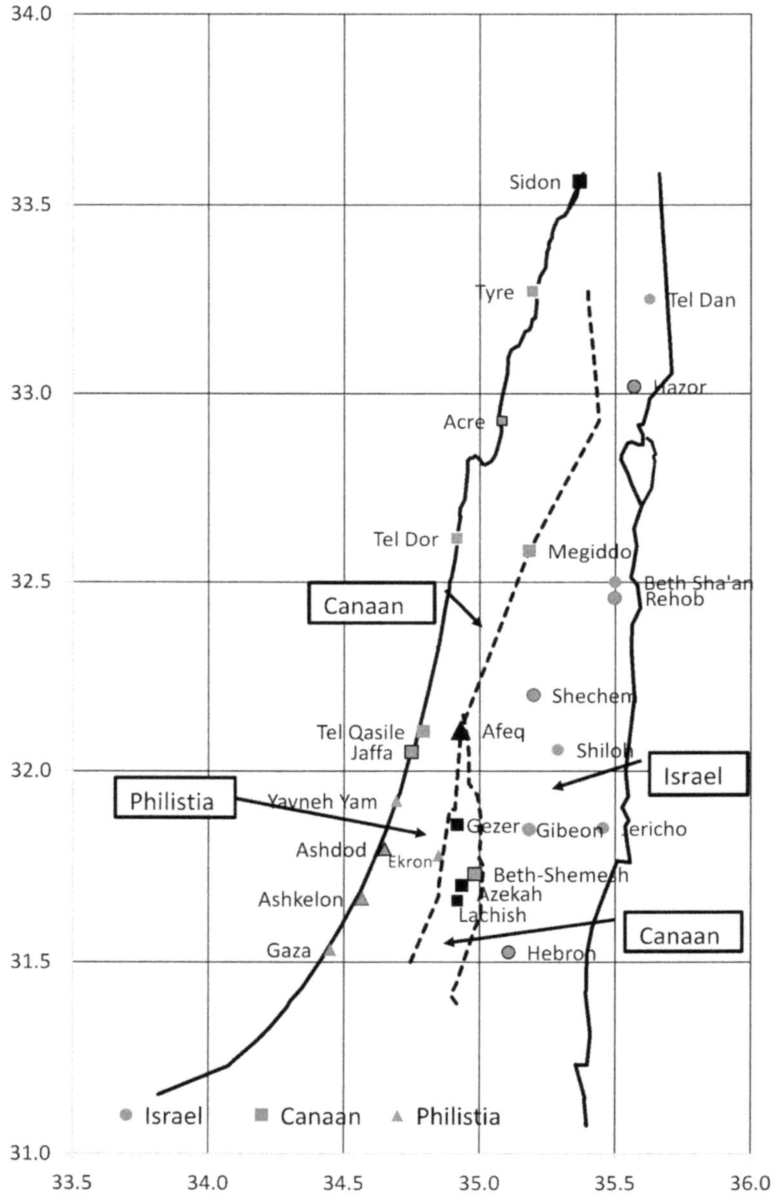

Figure 1.5 Actual Borders. Note: The borders South of 32nd parallel N are based on a published archaeological research (Avraham Faust and Hayah Katz, 2011). The border South of 32nd parallel N is assessed from several researches of the settlement pattern (see Figure 1-6). *Source*: Prepared by the author.

nomadic arrangements and sedentary lifestyle. The egalitarian ethos fueled the settlers' *opposition to hierarchy*. In general egalitarian existence is incompatible with a sedentary lifestyle. The Israelites developed from their nomadic habits institutions reconciling the contradiction: covenant, federative network, community-based justice administration, and assembly government with compulsory weekly participation. They are described in the following sections.

OPPOSITION TO HIERARCHY

"In those Days there was no King in Israel;
Every man did what was right in his own eyes."[95]

I shall not dwell on the multitude of interpretations of Judges 21:25. Readers of the clause translate it according to the cognitive map which is a result of their heritage,[96] education, peer models,[97] and social experience.[98] Consequently, most people who grew up in ranked societies will store in their cognitive map the corollary that a hierarchical structure is mandatory to maintain law and order.[99] From such a background even the archaeological data of pre-monarchic Israel "evince the pattern of socio-cultural polities" specific to complex chiefdoms.[100] Miller clarifies that he means hierarchies.[101] He concludes that the archaeological evidence indicates a non-egalitarian pre-monarchic Israel.[102] This point of view interprets Judges 21:25 that before the monarchy Israel was ruled by chiefs.

However, the consensus among archeologists is that pre-monarchic Israel was egalitarian in spite of the presence of rich and poor.[103] As explained earlier (see section *Social Models*), the egalitarian ethos should be understood as leveling authority and power, not wealth. Consequently, the egalitarian ethos doesn't imply economic equality. It doesn't restrict wealth; however it forbids displaying opulence. A lot of textual evidence testifies to an egalitarian ethos. "Even if all the textual evidence is no more than 'propaganda' its very existence proves that there was an audience for it."[104] In any society "[c]ollectively, followers control the behavior of leaders."[105] Therefore, the egalitarian ethos resists stratification and hierarchy.

As a consequence, the archaeological evidence interprets Judges 21:25 that pre-monarchic Israel was an acephalous society with no king, no chieftain, and no hierarchy. That should not be interpreted as anarchy.

The egalitarian ethos was brought by the nomadic pastoralist tribes. As both ranked and unranked societal modals of nomadic pastoralists pre-monarchic Israel developed institutions from the nomadic pastoralist heritage that allowed its functioning after sedentarization in spite of the opposition to hierarchy. The next section will show that the institution of *covenant* was inherited from the nomadic institution of *oath.* A federative network is also typical political arrangement of nomadic pastoralists providing military might necessary to balance the might of powerful sedentary hierarchies.

As mentioned earlier pre-monarchic Israel was egalitarian; consequently the pastoralist tribes that settled down on the Highlands of Israel were of the unranked type. A combination of sedentary life, covenant and egalitarian ethos create contradictory constraints; pre-monarchic Israel developed customs inherited from the nomadic past into institutions of law enforcement (see section *Justice Administration*) and of *reverse dominance hierarchy* (see more in section *Assembly Government*).

Covenant

Semitic-speaking Amorite nomads "those who have no cities, those who have no houses" wandered in the steppe long before the Israelites appeared on the scene of history.[106] Textual evidence shows that Shamshi-Addu the Ammorite ruler considers the allegiance of other nomads such as Yaminites, Simalites, and Rabeeans questionable because they didn't take yet an "oath of fealty."[107]

Naturally, the oath institution of nomadic pastoralists (see section *Social Models*) predated the writing; nevertheless later documented oaths hint about the form and content of such a loyalty oath. Most importantly one finds that in the Hittite (Indo-European) "treaty a great part of the covenantal stipulations was devoted to the commitment of the overlord to come to the aid of his vassal when necessary."[108] This is indeed a "patron–client" relationship in which the patron has also commitments.

Opposed to that is the *hierarchical* covenant of Egyptian Pharaoh[109] or of the Assyrian King.[110] The Egyptian and Assyrian oaths crystalized as *hierarchical* interethnic relationship. The Pastoralists embracing an *egalitarian* lifestyle also made treaties among tribes; some were put into practice by invoking the supernatural power (God) to punish those who break the oath.[111] This type of oath and ceremony "create the possibility and social space where both truth and forgiveness are validated and joined rather than a framework in which one must win over the other."[112]

We are ready to postulate that the similarly egalitarian pastoralist tribes that settled on the central hill of the Land of Canaan formed an alliance sanctioned by a Covenant in which the patron was the Lord.

The covenant of pre-monarchic Israel was not a Pharaonic kind of unilateral declaration of dominance because the Israelites descended from pastoralist *nomads.* The covenant was not an Indo-European steppe pastoralist patron–client oath either because it reflected the *egalitarian ethos* of their *nomadic* pastoralist ancestors.

The historicity of the covenant has been considered risky because there is no extra-biblical physical evidence of it. However, once one accepts that the proto-Israelites were descendants of nomadic pastoralists the denial of a covenant becomes problematic. We saw earlier that both patron–client and acephalous pastoralists adopted an institution of oath to establish the mutual commitments when forging alliances. The covenant played a role in harmonization of certain traditions which became uniformly followed all over the alliance. Traditional customs are inherently maintained by vertical cultural transmission[113] in a lineage-based extended family known in Israel as *beyt av*. The towns in pre-monarchic Israel (figure 1.6) were formed by a union of such families; the kinship in such unions was either genuine or fictive.[114]

A union of tribes will reasonably consist of a mosaic of clan traditions, tribal traditions, and a few traditions common to the whole union. The *complexity* of such a union grows when the common traditions are not only accepted but also enforced. That is consistent with the previous explanation of *social complexity* (section *Complexity*). Later section *Justice Administration* will discuss that in pre-monarchic Israel these common traditions switched from customs to enforced law. Although pre-monarchic Israel was a society that opposed hierarchy, it adopted institutions of legislation and law enforcement of the neighboring stratified cultures. Reasonably, the acephalous pre-monarchic Israel was more complex than the tribes of pastoralist nomads that founded it.

This section showed that Israel has had its covenant and a covenantal spirit since its very beginning. That said, the content of the first covenant is not necessarily the wording of its later written versions. Judging by the example of a currently existing nomadic pastoralist people where tribal treaties are sanctioned invoking God and spirits,[115] a preamble like "I am the Lord" is quite credible.

FEDERATIVE NETWORK

Unlike the covenant the historicity of the alliance is indisputable. Thus, the existence of a tribal confederation in Canaan can be inferred in the thirteenth century BCE based on archaeological evidence, namely the Merenptah Stele.[116]

Elazar distinguishes between two types of federative networks: confederation and federation.

A confederation is created when existing polities agree to a mutual interdependence for military, administrative, or trade purposes.[117] The patron–client relationship between nomadic pastoralist tribes is therefore

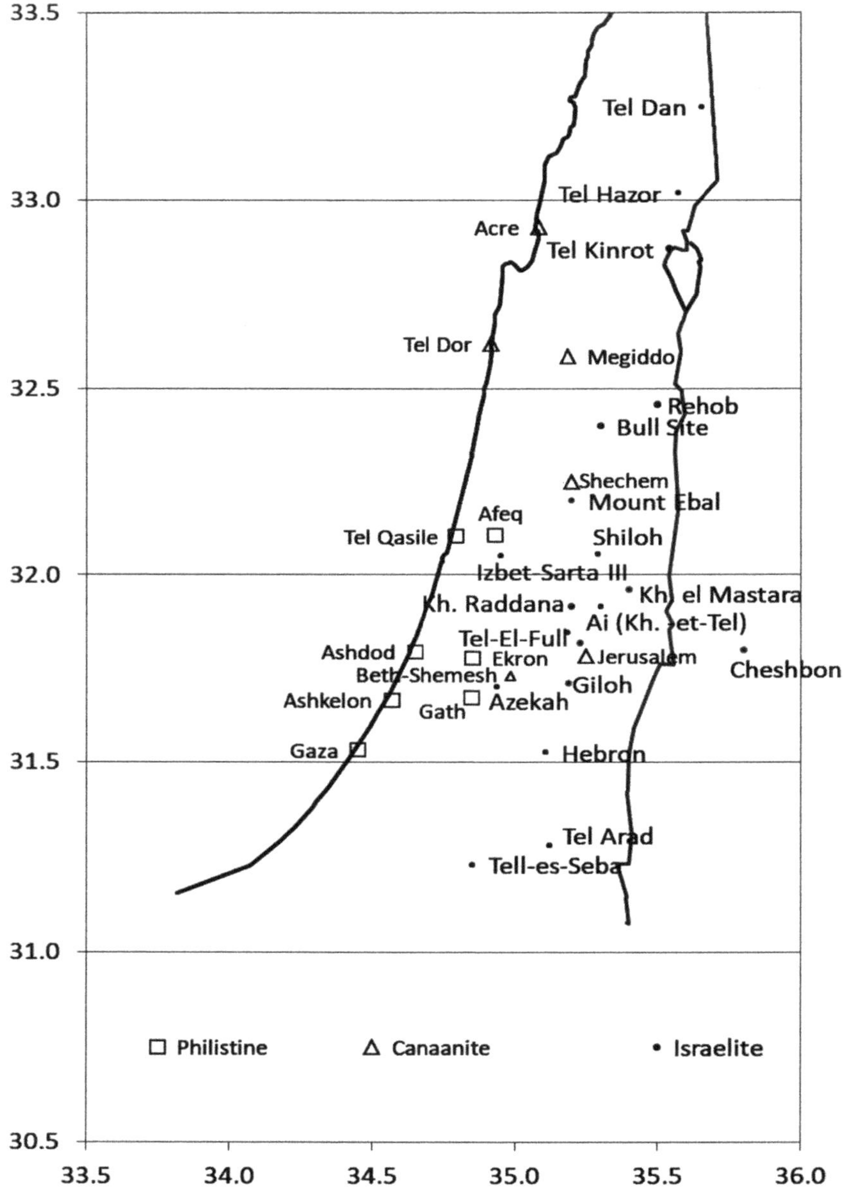

Figure 1.6 Archaeological Sites of Settlements of Pre-monarchic Israel. Note: The map shows only a few of the 130 sites discussed in the literature, for example, Israel Finkelstein, "[De] formation of the Israelite State: A Rejoinder on Methodology," Near Eastern Archaeology 68, no. 4 (2005). *Source*: Prepared by the author.

a confederation. The leagues of Greek and Canaanite city-states are also confederations. The advantages of a confederation over a unitary hierarchic state is that the constituent polities can balance military power or trade bargaining with powerful hierarchic empires while the local government of the constituent polities can more efficiently administer themselves. For example the military power of nomadic pastoralists was enhanced by the fact that every military-age man was counted in the military might of the confederation. Empires allowed only the army and the police to bear arms. The advantage of local administration of the confederate entities provided them more internal stability because each unit handled fewer problems and thus it was less complex as explained earlier in section *Complexity*. Nevertheless the total the survival of such confederations was guaranteed only by the common military or trade arrangement purpose. A confederation doesn't impose unity of political culture among its constituents (e.g., Sparta and Athens). As soon as the purpose of unification is relaxed the confederation is in danger to fall apart.

Pre-monarchic Israel formed a covenantal federation. It had a covenant which was based on a common tradition of government, laws, and law enforcement. The tribes also shared similar religions, morals, and concepts of justice.

The fundamental unit of the federation was the town. It started as small congregation of a few extended families, for example Izbet Sarta (see map of figure 1.6, Coordinates 32.1 N, 35 E). Izbet Sarta is one of the earliest sites discovered by archaeological excavations; its "oval layout" (figure 1.7) "indicates the pastoralist origin of the inhabitants"[118] because it is similar to nineteenth-century CE Bedouin encampment.

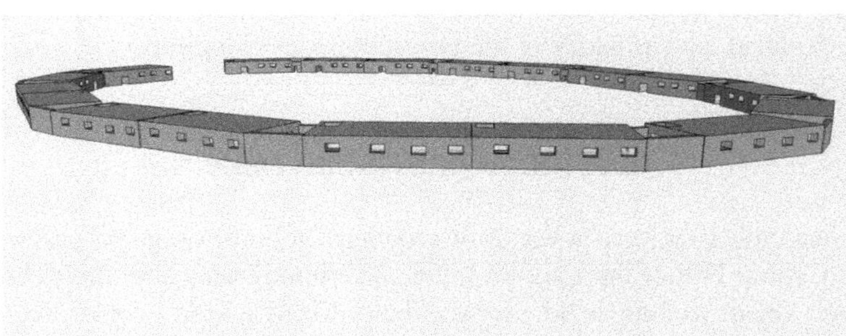

Figure 1.7 Izbet Sarta Iron Age I. *Source*: Creative visualization by author of a published diagram in Finkelstein and Silberman, The Bible Unearthed: 111.

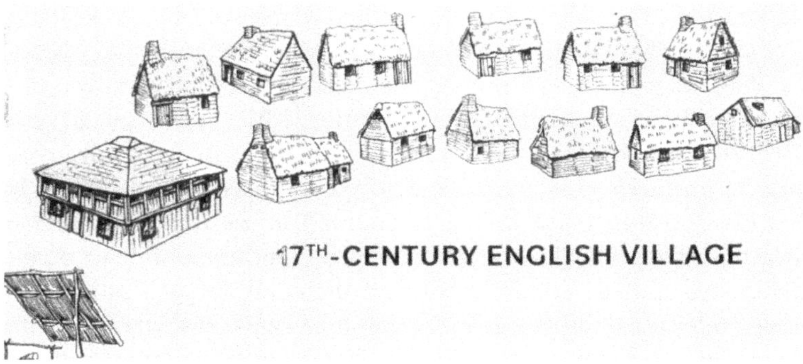

Figure 1.8 Replicated Layout of the Original Settlement of the Plymouth Colony of the Pilgrims. *Source*: Illustration reprinted courtesy of Plimoth Patuxet Museums, 137 Warren Avenue, Plymouth, MA.

For the reader of this book it is also noteworthy to point at the resemblance of this early beginning of a Promised Land with the similar beginning of the American covenantal tradition. Figure 1.8 illustrates the layout of the Pilgrims' settlement in Plymouth. The only remarkable difference is the meeting house that stands out. Sure in Izbet Sarta there were also meetings. One could hardly imagine how one could avoid meeting one's neighbors in such a small area. The only reason not to meet them is one's daily work in the nearby cultivated land and pasture.[119] However in Israel of the Judges there were compulsory[120] weekly meetings called "sacred convocation" (see more in section *Assembly Government*); it seems that the meetings in this earliest stage took place outdoors.

The resemblance in the layout cannot be attributed to direct cultural copying of settlement planning. The opposition to elitism is the principle that was transmitted from one covenantal society to the other. This feature combined with the similarity of circumstances, that is, a beginning in a new Promised Land, explains the similarity of the two settlement blueprints.

JUSTICE ADMINISTRATION

Pre-monarchic Israel was a result of sedentarization of nomadic pastoralists on the Central Hill of the Land of Israel. The immigrants kept their customs and their values as long as the new sedentary lifestyle didn't contradict them. One can reverse engineer this process from knowing habits of pastoralists, understanding their contradiction with sedentary existence, and considering archaeological evidence combined with anthropological considerations. Archaeologists provide the background:

> The political and economic context of the Levant during the second half of the 2nd millennium B.C. is characteristically that of shifting interaction between an imperial power (Egypt), Canaanite chiefdoms and city-states, and more or less autonomous agriculturalists and herders from the peripheries.[121]

Herders have conflicts and conflict resolution processes. We are told that "all the social contradictions between nomads have been settled in the context of traditional institutions of keeping the internal political stability."[122] This is true for Tibetan nomadic pastoralists[123] and for egalitarian pastoralists of Afar.[124]

According to Genesis 34, the pastoralist ancestors of proto-Israel practiced similar customs. "The mass murder of the clan of Hamor by Dina's brothers fits somewhere between hot-blooded revenge and cold-blooded deterrence."[125] The historicity of the reprisal against the rapists of Shechem may be in doubt; however the fact that the story circulated attests that similar events did take place.

On the other hand we know that pre-monarchic Israel did decree prohibition of crimes and those prohibitions were obeyed.[126] In other words criminal offenses were not dealt by reprisal/mediation as in the nomadic past, but by attribution of guilt and punishment as in the hierarchical sedentary Egypt or Canaan. Naturally, the content of the law itself was obviously not Egyptian or Canaanite; it was drawn from pastoralist customs imported by the immigrants.

An egalitarian pastoralist society has no police. Proto-Israel conserved the culture of questioning the authority of any mortal to detect transgression, to arrest, and to punish. Therefore in pre-monarchic Israel, detection of misbehavior, judgment, and subsequent correction were the responsibility of the whole community. This requires watching, judging, and punishing one's neighbor. The custom of minding other people's business is essential in such societies and it is a segment of cultural DNA that was inherited by all cultural descendants of pre-monarchic Israel—the first covenantal society.

Figure 1.9 schematically illustrates how wrongdoing is kept under control in general. As long as crime pays it is contagious. Therefore some susceptible individuals are corrupted and become criminals. Criminals are detected, arrested, and convicted. In the neighboring Egypt and Canaanite city-states dedicated policemen were responsible to arrest criminals, judges convicted them, and the service of corrections executed the sentences. As mentioned earlier, in pre-monarchic Israel everything was done by the community. The repentance mechanism consisted of an arsenal of community pressure borrowed from the nomadic past: rebuking, ridiculing, finger pointing, shunning, shaming, banning, and according to the biblical text even stoning to death.[127] Reasonably in some cases the transgressor became righteous. As condition changed mostly due to extreme poverty or to the influence of foreign idolatrous cultures some lapsed into the susceptible category.

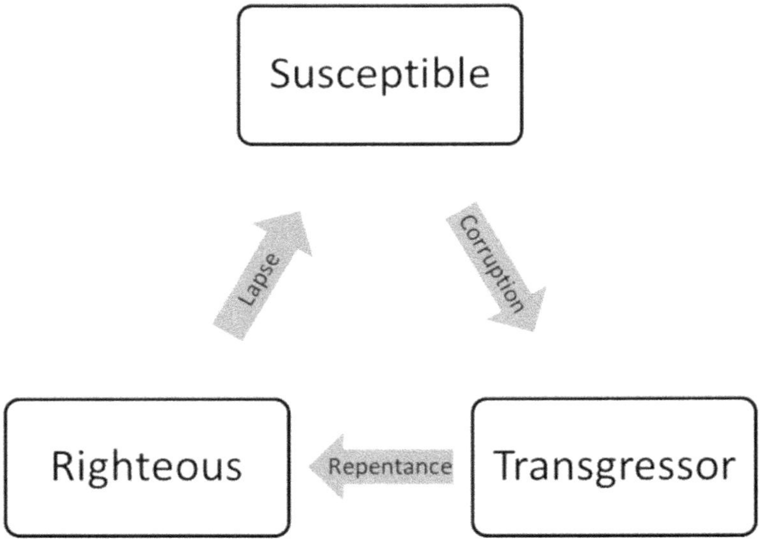

Figure 1.9 Control of Misbehavior. *Source*: Prepared by the author.

ASSEMBLY GOVERNMENT

In covenantal organizations the community is the highest authority in the political decision-making process.

The assembly government was not a revolutionary upset of a previous sociological reality as suggested by the "Peasant Revolt Model."[128] This particular theory is inconsistent with the archaeological evidence[129] and as mentioned earlier the borders between the hypothetical old (Canaanite) ideology and the new (Israelite) ideology are inconsistent with predictions of the laws of diffusion of innovations.[130] This chapter describes the appearance of an assembly government in the settlements of pre-monarchic Israel as an outcome of their nomadic past.

Section *Social Models* mentioned earlier that wandering was not without conflicts. Tribes espousing elitist creed solve these conflicts by debate within the council of elders. Eventually if such tribes put down roots they will tend to become oligarchies. The egalitarian ethos however imposes a bigger hurdle requiring arriving at a tribal consensus. The principal difficulty consists of two elements:

(1) Ensuring full participation of the whole local community in the decision-making process.
(2) The town assemblies need to be held frequently.[131]

Cultivating crops requires continuous work; consequently full participation is rarely achieved. There are reports of "Near Eastern democracy" in sedentary societies.[132] Faust's primary source is the article of Jacobsen about two Mesopotamian cities. Examining this source, we find that the assemblies were at a variable intervals and full participation was not achieved.[133] This type of "democracy" is oligarchical as Jacobsen himself admits.[134]

In Israel the weekly frequency of assemblies and full participation at them is achieved by prohibiting work on Sabbath and decreeing the day of Sabbath a "sacred convocation."[135] The prohibition of work on that day assures full participation.[136] Partial participation leads to oligarchy as the Mesopotamian "democracy" exemplifies.

One could hypothesize that the decree was issued later than pre-monarchic times. A previous research examined this hypothesis and showed that the unranked society of pre-monarchic Israel would have fallen apart in a matter of few months had they not observed weekly convocations.[137]

It is important to note that this principle was not invented either by the settlers or by their nomadic ancestors. Reasonably it came into existence as a random habit. Many nomadic and sedentary people celebrate periodic events together. Such celebrations help crystallizing shared ethnic habits and institutions. New Moons and Full Moons are examples of quite frequent assemblies. Unfortunately, the interval between New Moon and Full Moon is too long to allow an effective assembly government.[138] The random mutation that saved the pre-monarchic Israelite covenantal society from extinction was an unusual habit of assemblies with a frequency of seven days. The seven-day interval was unusual because the week is not related to a natural period. The week was not invented; it is a random cultural mutation that in evolutionary terms explains the survival of the covenantal society.

Since the archaeological evidence shows that the unranked society prevailed for a long time, one should conclude that in the pastoralist past of the tribes there was a Sabbath-like tradition, with periodic assemblies, as explained in a previous research.[139]

Reasonably, the nomadic pastoralist past of the tribes, their egalitarian ethos, and a tradition of periodical meetings explain how the assembly government of pre-monarchic Israel came into existence.

TRANSITION TO MONARCHY

The previous sections discussed the evolution from egalitarian nomadic pastoralist tribes to a decentralized alliance of egalitarian network of quasi-sedentary communities administrated by strong local assembly governments. The term pre-monarchic Israel however divulges that the next phase was monarchy. The biblical narrative teaches that the alliance transitioned into a United Monarchy. This gave rise to two questions that merit a summary discussion before closing the chapter.

1. Did a United Monarchy Exist?

The previous discussion leads to an affirmative answer. A negative answer stems from lack of evidence of a powerful centralized kingdom. Archaeologists who looked for traces of typical ancient empires such as Egypt, Babylon, and the Roman Empire found nothing of the sort:

> we still have no archaeological evidence—despite the biblical descriptions of its grandeur—that Jerusalem was anything more than a modest highland village in the time of David, Solomon and Rehoboam.[140]

The historicity of such a United Monarchy is questioned also because "David and Solomon's homeland of Judah was conspicuously underdeveloped—and there is no evidence whatever of the wealth of a great empire."[141] Additionally, the population of Judah estimated from the total inhabited area was about 5,000 people, a population too little for state formation.[142]

The *Jerusalem Journal of Archaeology* dedicated a whole volume[143] of contributions of prominent archaeologists answering yes to the question. This section provides additional support to their affirmative answer from the point of view of the nomadic pastoralist ancestry of the pre-monarchic Israeli culture.

This analysis is also helpful in examining the question of the historicity of the United Monarchy. The biblical story also hints at military reasons for the monarchy; the people asked for "a king to lead us and to go out before us and fight our battles."[144] We don't know when was this verse edited and introduced into the Bible. The archaeological evidence of an external threat and of a significant reaction in the form of mass abandonment of villages[145] indicates that the narrative of the text circulated orally from the actual time when the opposition to monarchy declined.

The nomadic pastoralist origin of the Israelites provides a clue to reconciling the controversy. Ignoring the knowledge about more powerful pastoralist nomadic empires such as the Huns of Attila and the Mongols of Genghis Khan (section *Social Models*) would lead the analysis of the physical archaeological evidence they left to the conclusion that they were little bandits on the prairie.

I already disputed the figure of 5,000 inhabitants of Judah and found it impossible based on population growth examination; the investigation indicates that the error is also attributable to continued existence of pastoralism in Judah.[146]

As far as the *grandeur* of Jerusalem is concerned the interpretation of the biblical description grew from an "expectation of material expressions of political power, including the centralization of that power."[147] Pre-monarchic Israel inherited many cultural traits from its pastoralist nomad ancestors. Therefore it is reasonable that the biblical claims of domination over territories outside the highland area are "a result not of conquest but of various forms of alliances and different modes of patron-client relations, by which various local rulers (temporarily?) submitted to the emerging polity."[148] This type of decentralized patron–client relationship is typical to large nomadic pastoralist alliances (see section *Social Models*). Moreover, the archaeological evidence of Iron Age II in areas outside the Iron Age I territory indicates an extension of Israelite habits outside pre-monarchic Israel's boundaries.[149]

Therefore, given the alliance of Israelite tribes existed already in the time of Merenptah, given that they were descendants of nomadic pastoralists, and given there is evidence of a sudden external threat, the strengthening of the unity makes more sense than the hypothesis of divergence; in other words the theory denying the historicity of the United Monarchy is less convincing than its opposing hypothesis.

2. Did the monarchy end the egalitarian covenantal spirit of Israel?

The answer of this chapter is negative. No doubt once "all the people shouted, and said, God save the king,"[150] the opposition to hierarchy was seriously challenged. Nevertheless, at least in the new rural areas the evidence left "no real signs of socioeconomic stratification."[151] The semi-autonomy of the villages and the position of elders were also conserved.[152] The standing of the Covenant was not challenged. On this question the Bible editors left no doubt. The divine authority of its commandments is alive in the Bible not because of the monarchy but in spite of it. In other words the sacrosanctity of the commandments is a result of the spirit of the people and not of royal or priestly ideology.

Would it be the same outcome if the ancestors of the Israelites were Canaanite farmers and not nomadic pastoralists?

CONCLUSION

It is feasible that other pastoralists also attempted to maintain a similar egalitarian oath of alliance after turning to farming. A previous research shows that such an attempt succeeds if the covenant is accompanied with other attributes such as frequent assemblies requiring compulsory participation, a tradition of watching others' compliance with the covenant, of accepting being similarly watched, of resisting other cultures, and of practicing poverty relief.[153] The covenantal society was born because the tribes arrived at a covenant similar to the oath of the Turkana. However, the society survived after turning to sedentary life because the tribes also brought with them the complementary traditions listed earlier.

NOTES

1. Anne Porter, *Mobile Pastoralism and the Formation of Near Eastern Civilizations: Weaving Together Society* (Cambridge: Cambridge University Press, 2012), 10.

2. Minna Lönnqvist, "How to control nomads," *A Case Study Associated with Jebel Bishri in Central Syria. West Semitic Nomads in Relation to the Urban World: RAI* 53, no. 2 (2010): 134.

3. "In Greco-Roman culture, Scythians are either hailed as the noblest, or most backward of barbarians"; Troy Martin, "The scythian perspective in Col 3: 11," *Novum Testamentum* 37, no. Fasc. 3 (1995).

4. Sergey A. Vasjutin, "Typology of pre-states and statehood systems of nomads," in *Nomadic Pathways in Social Evolution*, ed. D. M. Bondarenko, A. V. Korotayev, and N. N. Kradin (Moscow: Center for Civilizational and Regional Studies of the Russian Academy of Sciences, 2003), 56; Christine Hofmann, "A study of central eurasian innovations in warring states china and their impact on war and domination" (University of Vienna, 2012), 45.

5. Konstantin M. Klein, "Marauders, daredevils, and noble savages: Perceptions of Arab nomads in late antique hagiography," *Der Islam* 92, no. 1 (2015).

6. Fernand Braudel, *A History of Civilizations* (New York: Penguin Books, 1993), 4.

7. Porter, *Mobile Pastoralism and the Formation of Near Eastern Civilizations: Weaving Together Society.*

8. This observation was an essential step to develop thePfizer and Moderna vaccines against the COVID-19 virus Katalin Karikó et al., "Suppression of RNA recognition by Toll-likereceptors: the impact of nucleoside modification and the evolutionary origin ofRNA," *Immunity* 23, no. 2 (2005).

9. [1] Ronald A. Fisher, "The Wave of Advance of Advantageous Genes," *Annals of Eugenics* 7 (1937).

10. Luigi Luca Cavalli-Sforza and Marcus W Feldman, *Cultural Transmission and Evolution* (Princeton, NJ: PrincetonUniversity Press, 1981), 42–44.

11. Erez Ben-Yosef, "The architectural bias in current biblical archaeology," *Vetus Testamentum* 69, no. 3 (2019).

12. Patrick Howarth, *Attila, King of the Huns: Man and Myth* (New York: Barnes & Noble Books, 1995), 157.

13. Shevan Wilkin et al., "Dairying enabled early bronze age yamnaya steppe expansions," *Nature* (2021).

14. Kristian Kristiansen et al., "Re-theorising mobility and the formation of culture and language among the corded ware culture in Europe," *Antiquity* 91, no. 356 (2017).

15. David Anthony and Dorcas Brown, "Molecular archaeology and Indo-European linguistics: Impressions from new data," in *Usque Ad Radices: Indo-European*

Studies in Honour of Birgit Anette Olsen, ed. Bjarne Simmelkjær Sandgaard Hansen, et al. (Copenhagen: Museum Tusculanum Press, 2017).

16. Genetic distance expresses the difference in mutations between two sets of genetic material extracted from the same segment of two individuals. There are various methods of calculating genetic distance; in my view the *principal component analysis* (PCA) method is the most educating. This methodology expresses the mutation set of each individual as a weighted combination of a large number of mutation sets (principal components); the method shows that a combination of two or three principal components is a 'good enough approximation' provided one selects the proper two three principal components. The term *good enough approximation* is associated with an error and one can evaluate its magnitude. The method will plot the weighting coefficient of each individual on a two or three-dimensional plot. In a two dimensional plot one axis is the weighting coefficient of principal component 1 and the second axis will represent the coefficient of principal component 2. Two individuals that show the same mutations will thus be located at the same position. Two individual with slight differences will be located close to each other. If one analyses *ancient DNA* then one can see distances as a function of history, see for example 2a of Wolfgang Haak et al., "Massive migration from the steppe was a source for Indo-European languages in Europe," *Nature* 522, no. 7555 (2015)..

17. For example DNA samples from ancient burial sites in Germany indicate massive migration of Yamnaya people the from Volga-Don-Black Sea-Caspian Sea region, ibid. Analysis of the DNA of current Germans and of current inhabitants of that Russian region would probably not reveal the same migration.

18. Dorcas Brown and David Anthony, "Bit wear, horseback riding and the Botai site in Kazakstan," *Journal of Archaeological Science* 25, no. 4 (1998).

19. Elena V. Stepanova, "Reconstruction of a scythian saddle from Pazyryk Barrow № 3," *The Silk Road* 14 (2016).

20. Joseph Livni, "Testing competing archaeological theories of Israel's origins using computation techniques," *Archeologia e Calcolatori* 28, no. 1 (2017).

21. *The Biblical Roots of American Constitutionalism - From 'I am the Lord' to 'We the People'* (Lanham, MD: Lexington Books, 2021), 35–46.

22. Braudel lists several meanings of *civilization* among others that "it is all that humanity has achieved" Braudel, *A History of Civilizations*, 5. This meaning rules out excluding pastoralist nomads from *civilization.*

23. Fridrich A. Hayek, *The Constitution of Liberty* (University of Chicago Press, 1978), 29.

24. Michael D. Frachetti, *Pastoralist Landscapes and Social Interaction in Bronze Age Eurasia* (Berkeley, Los Angeles, London: University of California Press, 2009), 20.

25. Aaron A. Burke, *The Amorites and the Bronze Age Near East: The Making of a Regional Identity* (Cambridge: Cambridge University Press, 2020), 18.

26. Stepanova, "Reconstruction of a scythian saddle from Pazyryk Barrow № 3."

27. Renate Rolle, *The World of the Scythians* (Berkeley and Los Angeles: University of California Press, 1989), 65; Mike Loades, *The Composite Bow* (New York: Bloomsbury Publishing, 2016), 10.

28. "The asymmetrical bow excels in really high poundages (the amount of power needed to draw back the string), which gives greater range and power, is faster to fire, and performs far better with a thumb ring." Samual Rumschlag, "One bow (or stirrup) is not equal to another: A comparative look at Hun and Mongol military technologies," *The Silk Road* 16 (2018); Ian Hughes, *Aetius: Attila's nemesis*, Kindle Edition ed. (Barnsley, UK: Pen and Sword, 2012), Kindle loc 1826.

29. *Aetius: Attila's nemesis*, Kindle Loc. 1716.

30. Philip Carl Salzman, "Pastoralists," in *Oxford Research Encyclopedia of Anthropology* (2020), 34, 39; Peter Rigby, "Pastoralism, egalitarianism, and the state: The Eastern African case," *critique of anthropology* 7, no. 3 (1988): 21.

31. Mark J. Dwyer and Kirill V. Istomin, "Theories of nomadic movement: A new theoretical approach for understanding the movement decisions of Nenets and Komi reindeer herders," *Human ecology* 36, no. 4 (2008).

32. Ibid.; Matthew Baker, Erwin Bulte, and Jacob Weisdorf, "The origins of governments: From anarchy to hierarchy," *Journal of Institutional Economics* 6, no. 2 (2010); Vasjutin, "Typology of pre-states and statehood systems of nomads."

33. Porter, *Mobile Pastoralism and the Formation of Near Eastern Civilizations: Weaving Together Society*, 3.

34. Ibid., 12.

35. ". . . a strong adherence to notions of egalitarianism. These ideological concepts are embedded in the age set and kinship structures, and are materialized in all forms of speech and discourse, whether in the everyday praxis of pastoralism or in the rituals that mark crucial periods in the lives of boys and girls, and men and women."

36. Dwyer and Istomin, "Theories of nomadic movement: A new theoretical approach for understanding the movement decisions of Nenets and Komi reindeer herders"; Hanne Kirstine Adriansen and Thomas Theis Nielsen, "Going where the grass is greener: On the study of pastoral mobility in Ferlo, Senegal," *Human Ecology* 30, no. 2 (2002).

37. Salzman, "Pastoralists."

38. Hebrew Bible Joshua 2

39. Israel Finkelstein and N.A. Silberman, *The Bible Unearthed: Archaeology's New Vision of Ancient Israel and the Origin of Sacred Texts* (Simon & Shuster, 2002), 82.

40. "sheep are grazers, while goats and camels are browsers" Salzman, "Pastoralists."

41. Dwyer and Istomin, "Theories of nomadic movement: A new theoretical approach for understanding the movement decisions of Nenets and Komi reindeer herders."

42. Horse-mounted hunting of large herbivores is not yet pastoralism; nevertheless the transition to nomadic pastoralism is also associated with the beginning of horse-back riding David W. Anthony, "Two IE phylogenies, three PIE migrations, and four kinds of steppe pastoralism," *Journal of Language Relationship* 9, no. 1 (2013): 16.

43. Ibid.

44. Ibid., 18.

45. Anthony explains this relationship by analogy to current days franchise relationship, see " ibid., 13.

46. Anatoly M. Khazanov, "Nomads of the Eurasian steppes in historical retrospective," in *Nomadic Pathways in Social Evolution*, ed. Dmitri M. Bondarenko, Andrey V. Korotayev, and Nikolay N. Kradin (Moscow: Center for Civilizational and Regional Studies of the Russian Academy of Sciences, 2003), 28.

47. Ibid., 31. see also "Until modern times the role of the Central Eurasians was often reduced to the one of the villain, the intruder, the raider, encroaching on and feeding upon the material and intellectual wealth of the great agricultural empires on the periphery" Hofmann, "A study of Central Eurasian innovations in warring states China and their impact on war and domination," 6.

48. for example the "lucrative" trade between Indo-European Tokharian speaking Yuezhi and Chinese farmers "A study of Central Eurasian innovations in warring states China and their impact on war and domination," 21, 22.

49. Ibid., 7.

50. Haak et al., "Massive migration from the steppe was a source for Indo-European languages in Europe"; Anthony, "Two IE phylogenies, three PIE migrations, and four kinds of steppe pastoralism"; Wilkin et al., "Dairying enabled early bronze age Yamnaya steppe expansions"; Alin Frînculeasa, Bianca Preda, and Volker Heyd, "Pit-graves, Yamnaya and Kurgans along the Lower Danube: Disentangling IVth and IIIrd millennium BC burial customs, equipment and chronology," *Praehistorische Zeitschrift* 90, no. 1–2 (2015).

51. Hofmann, "A study of Central Eurasian innovations in warring states China and their impact on war and domination."

52. e. g. Howarth, *Attila, King of the Huns: Man and Myth*; N. Fields and S. Noon, *Attila the Hun* (Bloomsbury Publishing, 2015).

53. e. g.Vasjutin, "Typology of pre-states and statehood systems of nomads," 54.

54. Cristopher Boehm, *Hierarchy in the Forest* (Cambridge, MA: Harvard University Press, 2001), 11.

55. Christopher Boehm et al., "Egalitarian behavior and reverse dominance hierarchy [and comments and reply]," *Current anthropology* 34, no. 3 (1993).

56. Ibid.

57. Ibid., 233.

58. Philip.Carl Salzman, *Pastoralists: Equality, Hierarchy, And The State* (Milton Park, UK: Taylor & Francis, 2018), Chap. 3.

59. Ioan .M. Lewis, *Blood and Bone: The Call of Kinship in Somali Society* (Lawrenceville, NJ: Red Sea Press, 1994), 233.

60. Sarah Mathew and Robert Boyd, "Punishment sustains large-scale cooperation in prestate warfare," *Proceedings of the National Academy of Sciences* 108, no. 28 (2011): 11375.

61. Thomas E. Levy and Augustin F.C. Holl, "Migrations, ethnogenesis, and settlement dynamics: Israelites in iron age Canaan and Shuwa-Arabs in the Chad Basin," *Journal of Anthropological Archaeology* 21, no. 1 (2002).

62. Rigby, "Pastoralism, egalitarianism, and the state: The Eastern African case."

63. Robert L. Carneiro, "Process vs. Stages: A false dichotomy in tracing the rise of the state," *Alternatives of Social Evolution* (2000): 87. Citing from Elman Rogers Service, *Primitive Social Organization: An Evolutionary Perspective* (New York: Random House, 1962).

64. Christopher S. Peebles and Susan M. Kus, "Some archaeological correlates of ranked societies," *American Antiquity* 42, no. 3 (1977). Quoting from Elman Rogers Service, *Primitive Social Organization. An Evolutionary Perspective* (New York: Random House, 1971), 145.

65. Henri J.M. Claessen, "Was the state inevitable?," *The Early State, Its Alternatives and Analogues* (2004): 76.

66. Joseph Livni, "Investigation of collapse of complex socio-political systems using classical stability theory," *Physica A: Statistical Mechanics and Its Applications* 524 (2019).

67. The connection of hierarchy, complexity and stability is mentioned by Dmitri M. Bondarenko, Andrey V. Korotayev, and Nikolay N. Kradin, "Introduction: Social evolution, alternatives, and nomadism," in *Nomadic Pathways in Social Evolution*, ed. Nikolay N. Kradin, Dmitri M. Bondarenko, and Thomas J. Barfield (Moscow: Center for Civilizational and Regional Studies of the Russian Academy of Sciences, 2003), 6.

68. See for example in Joseph A. Tainter, "Social complexity and sustainability," *Ecological Complexity* 3, no. 2 (2006).

69. "Sustainability is the capacity to continue a desired condition or process, social or ecological"; Joseph A. Tainter, "Social complexity and sustainability," *Ecological Complexity* 3, no. 2 (2006). – Physicists call this *equilibrium.* "Resiliency is the ability of a system to adjust its configuration and function under disturbance"; ibid. Physicist call this *stability.*

70. The more interrelated problems a state tries to solve the closer it brings to collapse, Livni, "Investigation of collapse of complex socio-political systems using classical stability theory."

71. Nikolay N. Kradin, "Nomadic empires: Origins, rise, decline," in *Nomadic Pathways in Social Evolution*, ed. Nikolay N. Kradin, Dmitri M. Bondarenko, and Thomas J. Barfield (Moscow: Center for Civilizational and Regional Studies of the Russian Academy of Sciences,, 2003).

72. Maria E. Fernandez-Gimenez, "The role of Mongolian nomadic pastoralists' ecological knowledge in rangeland management," *Ecological Applications* 10, no. 5 (2000).

73. Daniel J. Miller, "Tough times for Tibetan nomads in western China: Snowstorms, settling down, fences and the demise of traditional nomadic pastoralism," *Nomadic Peoples* (2000).

74. John Briggs et al., "Indigenous and scientific knowledge: The choice and management of cultivation sites by Bedouin in Upper Egypt," *Soil Use and Management* 14, no. 4 (1998).

75. Saverio Krätli, "Education provision to nomadic pastoralists: A literature review" (2001).

76. Khazanov, "Nomads of the Eurasian steppes in historical retrospective," 39.

77. Thomas S. Noonan, "Some observations on the economy of the Khazar Khaganate," in *The World of the Khazars*, ed. Peter Golden, Hagai Ben-Shamai, and Andras Rona-Tas (Leiden boston: Brill, 2007), 209.

78. Ibid., 217.

79. Ibid., 218.

80. Ibid., 216, 17, 21.

81. Khazanov, "Nomads of the Eurasian steppes in historical retrospective," 40.

82. Khazanov describes then as "vassal-tribute and other undeveloped and not always completely institutionalized forms of collective dependence ibid., 39.

83. Noonan, "Some observations on the economy of the Khazar Khaganate," 208; Khazanov, "Nomads of the Eurasian steppes in historical retrospective," 39.

84. David W. Anthony, "Migration, ancient DNA, and bronze age pastoralists from the Eurasian steppes.," in *Migration Nomads from the East IEMA*, ed. Megan Daniels (Buffalo, NY: SUNY Press, 2021).

85. Ibid.

86. Anthony, "Two IE phylogenies, three PIE migrations, and four kinds of steppe pastoralism," 17.

87. For example the Kushans Empire; the Khitan and Jürchen states in China, the Qarakhanid state in Central Asia, the Saljuk state in the Middle East, the Yüan in China and the Hülegüid state in Iran, and the Shaybani state in Central Asia Khazanov, "Nomads of the Eurasian steppes in historical retrospective," 40.

88. Ben-Yosef, "The architectural bias in current biblical archaeology," 372.

89. Ibid., 373.

90. "A strong coalition of tribes led by kings"; ibid.

91. The inscription's words are "Israel is laid waste and its seed is not" Kenton L. Sparks, *Ethnicity and Identity in Ancient Israel: Prolegomena to the Study of Ethnic Sentiments and Their Expression in the Hebrew Bible* (Winona Lake, IN: Pennsylvania State University Press, 1998).

92. Livni, "Testing competing archaeological theories of Israel's origins using computation techniques."

93. Similar historical cultural borders along the shorter dimension of a country were: the Roman Empire split between East and West, The US North-South cultural conflict of the 19th century, Norway and Italy show distinct cultural traits between North and South.

94. It is interesting to note that even today the habits of Jewish people reflect these three farming branches; on eve of the Sabbath Jews recite three blessings: on the candles (olives), on the wine (grapes), and on the bread (grains).

95. Judges 21:25.

96. In early childhood we adopt a neutral markers (traits that do not affect our ability to function in the society) according to a weighted average of that trait among the socializers we contacted during childhood (parents, relatives, close neighbors etc.) Robert Boyd and Peter J. Richerson, "The evolution of ethnic markers," *Cultural Anthropology* 2, no. 1 (1987): 72.

97. Adolescents "are predisposed to imitate individuals who have similar [neutral] marker traits"; ibid.

98. During their mature phase, "individuals modify both their adaptive and marker traits by imitating the successful individuals among their local young adult peers".

99. For example : "The transition from amorphy to anarchy and on to hierarchy, triggered by the accumulation of wealth ('lootable assets'), implies an evolutionary trajectory

characterized by (i) the absence of thieving and raiding, followed by (ii) the rise of thieving and raiding and decentralized defense levels, which in turns might give way to (iii) the emergence of hierarchic structure to provide efficient levels of law and order, see Baker, Bulte, and Weisdorf, "The origins of governments: From anarchy to hierarchy."

100. In the literature Complex chiefdoms are ranked see for example Peter Turchin and Sergey Gavrilets, "Evolution of complex hierarchical societies," *Social Evolution & History* 8, no. 2 (2009).

101. Robert .D. Miller, *Chieftains of the Highland Clans: A History of Israel in the 12th and 11th Centuries BC* (Eugene, OR: Wipf & Stock Publishers, 2012), 81.

102. Miller observes that there were distinctions between rich and poor. Robert D. Miller II, *Chieftains of the Highland Clans: A History of Israel in the 12th and 11th Centuries BC* (Eugene, OR: Wipf and Stock Publishers, 2012), 98.

As explained earlier *egalitarian* does not exclude the presence of rich and poor.

103. e. g. Avraham Faust, *Israel's Ethnogenesis: Settlement, Interaction, Expansion and Resistance* (London: Equinox Pub., 2006); Israel Finkelstein, Amihai Mazar, and Brian. B. Schmidt, *The Quest for the Historical Israel: Debating Archaeology and the History of Early Israel*, Sixth Biennial Colloquium of the International Institute for Secular Humanistic Judaism (Atlanta: SBL Press, 2007); William G. Dever, *What Did the Biblical Writers Know and When Did They Know It?: What Archeology Can Tell Us About the Reality of Ancient Israel*, Kindle ed. (Grand Rapids, MI: Eerdmans Publishing Company, 2002)..

104. Faust, *Israel's Ethnogenesis: Settlement, Interaction, Expansion and Resistance*, 105.

105. Peter J. Richerson and Robert Boyd, "Complex societies," *Human Nature* 10, no. 3 (1999).

106. Karen Radner and Eleanor Robson, *The Oxford Handbook of Cuneiform Culture* (OUP Oxford, 2011), 676.

107. Porter, *Mobile Pastoralism and the Formation of Near Eastern Civilizations: Weaving Together Society*, 36.

108. Moshe Weinfeld, "Covenant making in Anatolia and Mesopotamia," *Journal of the Ancient Near Eastern Society* 22, no. 1 (1993).

109. Ibid.

110. Ibid.

111. J.K. Chelang'a and M. Chesire, "Analysis of conflict resolution strategies among Pastoralist Communities of Kenya," *Journal of African Interdisciplinary Studies* 4, no. 4 (2020); Josiah Osamba, "Peace building and transformation from below: Indigenous approaches to conflict resolution and reconciliation among the pastoral societies in the borderlands of eastern Africa," *African Journal on Conflict Resolution* 2, no. 1 (2001).

112. Chelang'a and Chesire, "Analysis of conflict resolution strategies among Pastoralist Communities of Kenya."

113. Cultural transmission from parents to offspring is called vertical transmission Luigi Luca Cavalli-Sforza and Marcus W. Feldman, *Cultural Transmission and Evolution* (Princeton, NJ: Princeton University Press, 1981), 77–129.

114. Philip J. King and Lawrence E. Stager, *Life in Biblical Israel* (Louisville, KY: Westminster John Knox Press, 2001).

115. Osamba, “Peace building and transformation from below: Indigenous approaches to conflict resolution and reconciliation among the pastoral societies in the borderlands of eastern Africa.”

116. Levy and Holl, “Migrations, ethnogenesis, and settlement dynamics: Israelites in iron age Canaan and Shuwa-Arabs in the Chad Basin,” 91.

117. Daniel J. Elazar, *Exploring Federalism* (Tuscaloosa and London: University of Alabama Press, 1987), 104, 05.

118. Finkelstein and Silberman, *The Bible Unearthed: Archaeology's New Vision of Ancient Israel and the Origin of Sacred Texts*, 111.

119. Ibid., 110.

120. A visit at the small site of Izbet Sarta makes it obvious that a covenant prohibiting work on Sabbath (Exodus 20:10) renders the participation at the meeting compulsory.

121. Levy and Holl, “Migrations, ethnogenesis, and settlement dynamics: Israelites in iron age Canaan and Shuwa-Arabs in the Chad Basin,” 97.

122. Bondarenko, Korotayev, and Kradin, “Introduction: Social evolution, alternatives, and nomadism,” 10.

123. Robert B. Ekvall, “Peace and war among the Tibetan nomads 1,” *American Anthropologist* 66, no. 5 (1964): 1124.

124. Chelang’a and Chesire, “Analysis of conflict resolution strategies among Pastoralist Communities of Kenya.”

125. Alan M. Dershowitz, *The Genesis of Justice* (New York: Warner Books, 2000), 147.

126. Livni, *The Biblical Roots of American Constitutionalism - From ‘I am the Lord’ to ‘We the People’*, 35–46.

127. Exodus 31:15, Leviticus 20:13, Leviticus 24:16, Deuteronomy 21:18–21.

128. George E. Mendenhall, “The hebrew conquest of Palestine,” *The Biblical Archaeologist* 25, no. 3 (1962); Norman Gottwald, *Tribes of Yahweh: A Sociology of the Religion of Liberated Israel, 1250-1050 BCE* (Sheffield: Bloomsbury Publishing, 1999).

129. Levy and Holl, “Migrations, ethnogenesis, and settlement dynamics: Israelites in iron age Canaan and Shuwa-Arabs in the Chad Basin,” 104; Finkelstein and Silberman, *The Bible Unearthed: Archaeology’s New Vision of Ancient Israel and the Origin of Sacred Texts*; Faust, *Israel's Ethnogenesis: Settlement, Interaction, Expansion and Resistance*, 96–98.

130. Livni, “Testing competing archaeological theories of Israel’s origins using computation techniques.”

131. A rankless society needs a frequency of less than 14 days in order to maintain law and order; if such a frequency was not achieved then the law enforcement was carried out by a police which contradicts the hypothesis of rankless society, see Joseph Livni and Lewi Stone, “The stabilizing role of the Sabbath in pre-monarchic Israel: A mathematical model,” *Journal of Biological Physics* 41 (2015).

132. Faust, *Israel's Ethnogenesis: Settlement, Interaction, Expansion and Resistance*, 98.

133. the text indicates that the assemblies were ad-hoc: "after an assembly was established" Thorkild Jacobsen, "Primitive democracy in ancient Mesopotamia," *Journal of Near Eastern Studies* 2, no. 3 (1943): 166; see also "Even the men may not have put in an appearance in numbers which we should consider an adequate representation of the citizenry"; ibid., 163.

134. Ibid., 159.

135. Leviticus 23:3.

136. Full participation requires not only that the adult men in the community stop working; the command specifies that "neither you, nor your son or daughter, nor your manservant or maidservant or livestock, nor the foreigner within your gates" are allowed to work, Exodus 20:10.

137. Joseph Livni, "The cultural evolution of an institution: The Sabbath," *Cliodynamics* 8 (2017).

138. Livni and Stone, "The stabilizing role of the Sabbath in pre-monarchic Israel: A mathematical model."

139. Livni, "The cultural evolution of an institution: The Sabbath."

140. Finkelstein and Silberman, *The Bible Unearthed: Archaeology's New Vision of Ancient Israel and the Origin of Sacred Texts*, 158.

141. Ibid., 140.

142. Ibid., 143.

143. Avraham Faust, Yosef Garfinkel, and Madeleine Mumcuoglu, "The study of the 10th century BCE in the early 21st century CE: An overview," *Jerusalem Journal of Archaeology* 1 (2021).

144. 1 Samuel 10:21.

145. Avraham Faust, "Chronological and spatial changes in the rural settlement sector of ancient Israel during the iron age: An overview," *Revue Biblique (1946-)* (2015): 254.

146. Joseph Livni, "Investigation of population growth of ancient Israel," *Edited by Manfried Dietrich and Ingo Kottsieper. Ugarit-Forschungen* 46 (2015).

147. Ibid.

148. Avraham Faust, "The "united monarchy" on the ground: The disruptive character of the iron age I–II transition and the nature of political transformations," *Jerusalem Journal of Archaeology* 1 (2021): 50.

149. [T]he (re)building of new cities without temples is clearly not a coincidence; rather, it shows the large scope of the expanding polity and probably indicates direct control; ibid.

150. 1 Samuel 10:21.

151. Faust, "Chronological and spatial changes in the rural settlement sector of ancient Israel during the iron age: An overview," 260.

152. A strong local administration is evidenced by "well-organized industrial areas, boundary walls around the perimeter of the settlements, terrace systems, communal facilities for storage, and more"; ibid.

153. Livni and Stone, "The stabilizing role of the Sabbath in pre-monarchic Israel: A mathematical model."

REFERENCES

Adriansen, Hanne Kirstine, and Thomas Theis Nielsen. "Going Where the Grass Is Greener: On the Study of Pastoral Mobility in Ferlo, Senegal." *Human Ecology* 30, no. 2 (2002): 215–26.

Anthony, David, and Dorcas Brown. "Molecular Archaeology and Indo-European Linguistics: Impressions From New Data." In *Usque Ad Radices: Indo-European Studies in Honour of Birgit Anette Olsen*,

edited by Bjarne Simmelkjær Sandgaard Hansen, Adam Hyllested, Anders Richardt Jørgensen, Guus Kroonen, Jenny Helena Larsson, Benedicte Nielsen Whitehead, Thomas Olander, and Tobias Mosbæk Søborg. Copenhagen: Museum Tusculanum Press, 2017.

Anthony, David W. "Horses, Ancient Near East and Pharaonic Egypt." In *The Encyclopedia of Ancient History*, edited by Roger S. Bagnall, Kai Brodersen, Craige B. Champion, Andrew Erskine, and Sabine R. Huebner. Chichester, UK: Blackwell Publishing, 2013.

———. "Migration, Ancient DNA, and Bronze Age Pastoralists From the Eurasian Steppes." In *Migration Nomads From the East IEMA*, edited by Megan Daniels. Buffalo, NY: SUNY Press, 2021.

———. "Two Ie Phylogenies, Three Pie Migrations, and Four Kinds of Steppe Pastoralism." *Journal of Language Relationship* 9, no. 1 (2013): 1–22.

Anthony, David W., and Dorcas R. Brown. "The Secondary Products Revolution, Horse-Riding, and Mounted Warfare." *Journal of World Prehistory* 24, no. 2 (2011): 131–60.

Audisio, Gabriel. *The Waldensian Dissent: Persecution and Survival C. 1170–C. 1570*. Cambridge: Cambridge University Press, 1999.

Baker, Matthew, Erwin Bulte, and Jacob Weisdorf. "The Origins of Governments: From Anarchy to Hierarchy." *Journal of Institutional Economics* 6, no. 2 (2010): 215–42.

Ben-Yosef, Erez. "The Architectural Bias in Current Biblical Archaeology." *Vetus Testamentum* 69, no. 3 (2019): 361–87.

Boatwright, Maria.T. *Hadrian and the Cities of the Roman Empire*. Princeton, NJ: Princeton University Press, 2000.

Boehm, Christopher, Christoph Antweiler, I. Eibl-Eibesfeldt, Susan Kent, Bruce M. Knauft, Steven Mithen, Peter J. Richerson, and David Sloan Wilson. "Emergency Decisions, Cultural-Selection Mechanics, and Group Selection [And Comments and Reply]." *Current Anthropology* 37, no. 5 (1996): 763–93.

Boehm, Christopher, Harold B. Barclay, Robert Knox Dentan, Marie-Claude Dupre, Jonathan D. Hill, Susan Kent, Bruce M. Knauft, Keith F. Otterbein, and Steve Rayner. "Egalitarian Behavior and Reverse Dominance Hierarchy [And Comments and Reply]." *Current anthropology* 34, no. 3 (1993): 227–54.

Boehm, Cristopher. *Hierarchy in the Forest*. Cambridge, MA: Harvard University Press, 2001.

Bondarenko, Dmitri M., Andrey V. Korotayev, and Nikolay N. Kradin. "Introduction: Social Evolution, Alternatives, and Nomadism." In *Nomadic Pathways in Social*

Evolution, edited by Nikolay N. Kradin, Dmitri M. Bondarenko, and Thomas J. Barfield, 1–24. Moscow: Center for Civilizational and Regional Studies of the Russian Academy of Sciences, 2003.

Bonner, Stanley. *Education in Ancient Rome: From the Elder Cato to the Younger Pliny*. New York: Routledge, 2012.

Bowman, Alan. "Quantifying Egyptian Agriculture." In *Quantifying the Roman Economy. Methods and Problems, Oxford*, 177–204. Oxford: Oxford University Press, 2009.

Boyd, Robert, and Peter J. Richerson. "The Evolution of Ethnic Markers." *Cultural Anthropology* 2, no. 1 (1987): 65–79.

Braudel, Fernand. *A History of Civilizations*. New York: Penguin Books, 1993.

Briggs, John, Iian D. Pulford, Maharshi Badri, and Alan S. Shaheen. "Indigenous and Scientific Knowledge: The Choice and Management of Cultivation Sites by Bedouin in Upper Egypt." *Soil Use and Management* 14, no. 4 (1998): 240–45.

Brown, Dorcas, and David Anthony. "Bit Wear, Horseback Riding and the Botai Site in Kazakstan." *Journal of Archaeological Science* 25, no. 4 (1998): 331–47.

Burke, Aaron A. *The Amorites and the Bronze Age Near East: The Making of a Regional Identity*. Cambridge: Cambridge University Press, 2020.

Carneiro, Robert L. "Process Vs. Stages: A False Dichotomy in Tracing the Rise of the State." *Alternatives of Social Evolution* (2000): 83–94.

Cavalli-Sforza, Luigi Luca, and Marcus W. Feldman. *Cultural Transmission and Evolution*. Princeton, NJ: Princeton University Press, 1981.

Chelang'a, J. K., and M. Chesire. "Analysis of Conflict Resolution Strategies Among Pastoralist Communities of Kenya." *Journal of African Interdisciplinary Studies* 4, no. 4 (2020): 4–21.

Claessen, Henri J. M. "Was the State Inevitable?" *The Early State, Its Alternatives and Analogues* (2004): 72–87.

Dershowitz, Alan M. *The Genesis of Justice*. New York: Warner Books, 2000.

Dever, William .G. *What Did the Biblical Writers Know and When Did They Know It?: What Archeology Can Tell Us About the Reality of Ancient Israel*. Kindle edition. Grand Rapids, MI: Eerdmans Publishing Company, 2002.

Dwyer, Mark J., and Kirill V. Istomin. "Theories of Nomadic Movement: A New Theoretical Approach for Understanding the Movement Decisions of Nenets and Komi Reindeer Herders." *Human Ecology* 36, no. 4 (2008): 521.

Ekvall, Robert B. "Peace and War Among the Tibetan Nomads 1." *American Anthropologist* 66, no. 5 (1964): 1119–48.

Elazar, Daniel J. *Exploring Federalism*. Tuscaloosa and London: University of Alabama Press, 1987.

Faust, Avraham. "Chronological and Spatial Changes in the Rural Settlement Sector of Ancient Israel During the Iron Age: An Overview." *Revue Biblique (1946-)* (2015): 247–67.

———. *Israel's Ethnogenesis: Settlement, Interaction, Expansion and Resistance*. London: Equinox Pub., 2006.

———. "The "United Monarchy" on the Ground: The Disruptive Character of the Iron Age I–II Transition and the Nature of Political Transformations." *Jerusalem Journal of Archaeology* 1 (2021): 15–66.

Faust, Avraham, and Hayah Katz. "Philistines, Israelites and Canaanites in the Southern Trough Valley During the Iron Age I.". *Ägypten und Levante/Egypt and the Levant* 21 (2011): 231–47.

Faust, Avraham, Yosef Garfinkel, and Madeleine Mumcuoglu. "The Study of the 10th Century Bce in the Early 21st Century Ce: An Overview." *Jerusalem Journal of Archaeology* 1 (2021).

Fernandez-Gimenez, Maria E. "The Role of Mongolian Nomadic Pastoralists' Ecological Knowledge in Rangeland Management." *Ecological Applications* 10, no. 5 (2000): 1318–26.

Fields, N., and S. Noon. *Attila the Hun*. Utgivere: Bloomsbury Publishing, 2015.

Finkelstein, Israel. "[De] Formation of the Israelite State: A Rejoinder on Methodology." *Near Eastern Archaeology* 68, no. 4 (2005): 202–8.

Finkelstein, Israel, Amihai Mazar, and Brian. B. Schmidt. *The Quest for the Historical Israel: Debating Archaeology and the History of Early Israel*. Sixth Biennial Colloquium of the International Institute for Secular Humanistic Judaism. Atlanta: SBL Press, 2007.

Finkelstein, Israel, and N. A. Silberman. *The Bible Unearthed: Archaeology's New Vision of Ancient Israel and the Origin of Sacred Texts*. New York: Simon & Shuster, 2002.

Fisher, Ronald A. "The Wave of Advance of Advantageous Genes." *Annals of Eugenics* 7 (1937): 355–69.

Frachetti, Michael D. *Pastoralist Landscapes and Social Interaction in Bronze Age Eurasia*. Berkeley, Los Angeles, London: University of California Press, 2009.

Frînculeasa, Alin, Bianca Preda, and Volker Heyd. "Pit-Graves, Yamnaya and Kurgans Along the Lower Danube: Disentangling Ivth and Iiird Millennium Bc Burial Customs, Equipment and Chronology." *Praehistorische Zeitschrift* 90, nos. 1–2 (2015): 45–113.

Gibbon, Edward. *The History of the Decline and Fall of the Roman Empire*. Kindle edition. Boston: Little, Brown, 1854a.

———. *The History of the Decline and Fall of the Roman Empire*. Boston: Little, Brown, 1854b.

Gottwald, Norman. *Tribes of Yahweh: A Sociology of the Religion of Liberated Israel, 1250-1050 BCE*. Sheffield: Bloomsbury Publishing, 1999.

Haak, Wolfgang, Iosif Lazaridis, Nick Patterson, Nadin Rohland, Swapan Mallick, Bastien Llamas, Guido Brandt, S. Nordenfelt, E. Harney, K. Stewardson, and Q. Fu. "Massive Migration from the Steppe Was a Source for Indo-European Languages in Europe." *Nature* 522, no. 7555 (2015): 207–11.

Hawkins, Cameron. "Contract, Coercion, and the Boundaries of the Roman Artisanal Firm." In *Work, Labour, and Professions in the Roman World*, 36–61. Leiden: Brill, 2017.

Hayek, Fridrich A. *The Constitution of Liberty*. Chicago, IL: University of Chicago Press, 1978.

Heather, Peter. *The Fall of the Roman Empire: A New History*. Hampshire, UK: Pan Books, 2010.

Hofmann, Christine. "A Study of Central Eurasian Innovations in Warring States China and Their Impact on War and Domination." University of Vienna, 2012.

Howarth, Patrick. *Attila, King of the Huns: Man and Myth*. New York: Barnes & Noble Books, 1995.

Hughes, Ian. *Aetius: Attila's Nemesis*. Kindle edition. Barnsley, UK: Pen and Sword, 2012.

Jacobsen, Thorkild. "Primitive Democracy in Ancient Mesopotamia." *Journal of Near Eastern Studies* 2, no. 3 (1943): 159–72.

Karikó, Katalin, Michael Buckstein, Houping Ni, and Drew Weissman. "Suppression of Rna Recognition by Toll-Like Receptors: The Impact of Nucleoside Modification and the Evolutionary Origin of RNA." *Immunity* 23, no. 2 (2005): 165–75.

Kassinger, Ruth. *Gold: From Greek Myth to Computer Chips*. Brookfield, CT: Twenty-First Century Books, 2003.

Keimer, Kyle H. "Evaluating the "United Monarchy" of Israel: Unity and Identity in Text and Archaeology." In *State Formation Processes in the 10th Century BCE Levant*, 2021.

Khazanov, Anatoly M. "Nomads of the Eurasian Steppes in Historical Retrospective." In *Nomadic Pathways in Social Evolution*, edited by Dmitri M. Bondarenko, Andrey V. Korotayev, and Nikolay N. Kradin, 25–49. Moscow: Center for Civilizational and Regional Studies of the Russian Academy of Sciences, 2003.

King, Philip J., and Lawrence E. Stager. *Life in Biblical Israel*. Louisville, KY: Westminster John Knox Press, 2001.

Klein, Konstantin M. "Marauders, Daredevils, and Noble Savages: Perceptions of Arab Nomads in Late Antique Hagiography." *Der Islam* 92, no. 1 (2015): 13–41.

Kradin, Nikolay N. "Nomadic Empires: Origins, Rise, Decline." In *Nomadic Pathways in Social Evolution*, edited by Nikolay N. Kradin, Dmitri M. Bondarenko, and Thomas J. Barfield, 73–87. Moscow: Center for Civilizational and Regional Studies of the Russian Academy of Sciences, 2003.

Krätli, Saverio. "Education Provision to Nomadic Pastoralists: A Literature Review." (2001).

Kristiansen, Kristian, Morten E. Allentoft, Karin M. Frei, Rune Iversen, Niels N. Johannsen, Guus Kroonen, Łukasz Pospieszny, T. D. Price, S. Rasmussen, K. G. Sjögren, and M. Sikora. "Re-Theorising Mobility and the Formation of Culture and Language Among the Corded Ware Culture in Europe." *Antiquity* 91, no. 356 (2017): 334–47.

Levy, Thomas E., and Augustin F. C. Holl. "Migrations, Ethnogenesis, and Settlement Dynamics: Israelites in Iron Age Canaan and Shuwa-Arabs in the Chad Basin." *Journal of Anthropological Archaeology* 21, no. 1 (2002): 83–118.

Lewis, Ioan M. *Blood and Bone: The Call of Kinship in Somali Society*. Lawrenceville, NJ: Red Sea Press, 1994.

Livni, Joseph. "Investigation of Collapse of Complex Socio-Political Systems Using Classical Stability Theory." *Physica A: Statistical Mechanics and Its Applications* 524 (2019): 553–62.

———. "Investigation of Population Growth of Ancient Israel." Edited by Manfried Dietrich and Ingo Kottsieper. *Ugarit-Forschungen* 46 (2015): 214–34.

———. "Testing Competing Archaeological Theories of Israel's Origins Using Computation Techniques." *Archeologia e Calcolatori* 28, no. 1 (2017): 109–28.

———. *The Biblical Roots of American Constitutionalism - From 'I Am the Lord' to 'We the People'*. Lanham, MD: Lexington Books, 2021.

———. "The Cultural Evolution of an Institution: The Sabbath." *Cliodynamics* 8 (2017): 59–74.

Livni, Joseph, and Lewi Stone. "The Stabilizing Role of the Sabbath in Pre-Monarchic Israel: A Mathematical Model." *Journal of Biological Physics* 41 (2015): 203–21.

Loades, Mike. *The Composite Bow*. New York: Bloomsbury Publishing, 2016.

Lönnqvist, Minna. "How to Control Nomads." *A Case Study Associated With Jebel Bishri in Central Syria. West Semitic Nomads in Relation to the Urban World: RAI* 53, no. 2 (2010): 69.

Martin, Troy. "The Scythian Perspective in Col 3: 11." *Novum Testamentum* 37, no. Fasc. 3 (1995): 249–61.

Mathew, Sarah, and Robert Boyd. "Punishment Sustains Large-Scale Cooperation in Prestate Warfare." *Proceedings of the National Academy of Sciences* 108, no. 28 (2011): 11375–80.

Mazar, Amihai. "Archaeology and the Biblical Narrative: The Case of the United Monarchy." In *One God - One Cult - One Nation. Archaeological and Biblical Perspectives*, edited by R. G. Kratz, H.Spieckermann, B. Corzilius, and T. Pilger. Berlin, New York: de Gruyter, 2010.

Mendenhall, George E. "The Hebrew Conquest of Palestine." *The Biblical Archaeologist* 25, no. 3 (1962): 66–87.

Miller, Daniel J. "Tough Times for Tibetan Nomads in Western China: Snowstorms, Settling Down, Fences and the Demise of Traditional Nomadic Pastoralism." *Nomadic Peoples* (2000): 83–109.

Miller, Robert D., II. *Chieftains of the Highland Clans: A History of Israel in the 12th and 11th Centuries BC*. Eugene, OR: Wipf and Stock Publishers, 2012.

Noonan, Thomas S. "Some Observations on the Economy of the Khazar Khaganate." In *The World of the Khazars*, edited by Peter Golden, Hagai Ben-Shamai, and Andras Rona-Tas, 207–44. Leiden, Boston: Brill, 2007.

Osamba, Josiah. "Peace Building and Transformation from Below: Indigenous Approaches to Conflict Resolution and Reconciliation Among the Pastoral Societies in the Borderlands of Eastern Africa." *African Journal on Conflict Resolution* 2, no. 1 (2001): 22–28.

Paravy, Pierrette. *De La Chrétienté Romaine À La Réforme En Dauphiné. Évêques, Fidèles Et Déviants (Vers 1340–Vers 1350)* [in Français]. Collection De L'école Française De Rome. Vol. 1. Rome: École française de Rome, 1993.

Peebles, Christopher S., and Susan M. Kus. "Some Archaeological Correlates of Ranked Societies." *American Antiquity* 42, no. 3 (1977): 421–48.

Porter, Anne. *Mobile Pastoralism and the Formation of Near Eastern Civilizations: Weaving Together Society*. Cambridge: Cambridge University Press, 2012.

Potts, Daniel T. *Nomadism in Iran: From Antiquity to the Modern Era*. Oxford: Oxford University Press, 2014.

Pouzet, Philippe. "Les Origines Lyonnaises De La Secte Des Vaudois." *Revue d'histoire de l'Église de France* 22, no. 94 (1936): 5–37.
Radner, Karen, and Eleanor Robson. *The Oxford Handbook of Cuneiform Culture*. Oxford: Oxford University Press, 2011.
Richerson, Peter J., and Robert Boyd. "Complex Societies." *Human Nature* 10, no. 3 (1999): 253–89.
Rigby, Peter. "Pastoralism, Egalitarianism, and the State: The Eastern African Case." *Critique of Anthropology* 7, no. 3 (1988): 17–32.
Rolle, Renate. *The World of the Scythians*. Berkeley and Los Angeles: University of California Press, 1989.
Rumschlag, Samual. "One Bow (or Stirrup) Is Not Equal to Another: A Comparative Look at Hun and Mongol Military Technologies." *The Silk Road* 16 (2018): 78–90.
Salisbury, Joyce E. *Rome's Christian Empress: Galla Placidia Rules at the Twilight of the Empire*. Baltimore: Johns Hopkins University Press, 2015.
Salzman, Michele Renee. *The Making of a Christian Aristocracy: Social and Religious Change in the Western Roman Empire*. Kindle edition. Cambridge, MA: Harvard University Press, 2002.
Salzman, Philip Carl. "Pastoralists." In *Oxford Research Encyclopedia of Anthropology*, 2020.
———. *Pastoralists: Equality, Hierarchy, and the State*. Milton Park, UK: Taylor & Francis, 2018.
Service, Elman Rogers. *Primitive Social Organization: An Evolutionary Perspective*. New York: Random House, 1962.
———. *Primitive Social Organization: An Evolutionary Perspective*. New York: Random House, 1971.
Smith, William. *Dictionary of Greek and Roman Antiquities*. London: C.C. Little and J. Brown, 1853.
Spalding, Karen. "Social Climbers: Changing Patterns of Mobility Among the Indians of Colonial Peru." *Hispanic American Historical Review* 50, no. 4 (1970): 645–64.
Sparks, Kenton L. *Ethnicity and Identity in Ancient Israel: Prolegomena to the Study of Ethnic Sentiments and Their Expression in the Hebrew Bible*. Winona Lake, IN: Pennsylvania State University Press, 1998.
Stepanova, Elena V. "Reconstruction of a Scythian Saddle from Pazyryk Barrow № 3." *The Silk Road* 14 (2016): 1–18.
Tainter, Joseph A. "Social Complexity and Sustainability." *Ecological Complexity* 3, no. 2 (2006): 91–103.
———. *The Collapse of Complex Societies*. Cambridge: Cambridge University Press, 1990.
Turchin, Peter, and Sergey Gavrilets. "Evolution of Complex Hierarchical Societies." *Social Evolution & History* 8, no. 2 (2009): 167–98.
Vasjutin, Sergey A. "Typology of Pre-States and Statehood Systems of Nomads." In *Nomadic Pathways in Social Evolution*, edited by D. M. Bondarenko, A. V. Korotayev, and N. N. Kradin, 50–62. Moscow: Center for Civilizational and Regional Studies of the Russian Academy of Sciences, 2003.

Weinfeld, Moshe. "Covenant Making in Anatolia and Mesopotamia." *Journal of the Ancient Near Eastern Society* 22, no. 1 (1993): 2396.

Wilkin, Shevan, Alicia Ventresca Miller, Ricardo Fernandes, Robert Spengler, William T.-T. Taylor, Dorcas R. Brown, David Reich, D. J. Kennett, B. J. Culleton, L. Kunz, and C. Fortes. "Dairying Enabled Early Bronze Age Yamnaya Steppe Expansions." *Nature* 598 (2021): 1–5.

Chapter 2

Power Structure within Autonomy in Roman Palestine

Zeev Safrai

HISTORICAL BACKGROUND

From the end of the second century BCE until 63 BCE there was an independent Jewish kingdom, "Hasmonean Judea." "Judea" started out in the small district of and developed into a mini empire throughout the territory of the "Land of Israel" as the Hasmoneans perceived it.

This independence began even before the collapse of the Seleucid Empire that governed Judea earlier and preceded the national awakening in the adjacent areas. Jewish independence was naturally accompanied by a national awakening that was reinforced by the biblical heritage and the religious Jewish laws.

In 63 BCE the kingdom was captured and annexed to the Roman Empire. From then until the year 10 CE Judea was a vassal kingdom, which split into a series of subkingdoms. The vassal kingdom maneuvered, with some difficulty, between the Jewish national interest and loyalty to the global Roman Empire.

From 6 CE the vassal Kingdom was gradually transferred to direct Roman rule. The elimination of the vassal kingdoms in the East was a general process. But in each province it had a different effect. In the Hasmonean Land of Israel Roman rule was met with a combination of strong hostility, religious and national strengthening, and an anti-Roman trend. Until 70 CE there was a system of national institutions, headed by the high priest, who was chosen by the Romans in rotation (out of a number of families considered "of prestigious lineage").

Between 66 and 70 CE a national rebellion erupted in the province of Judea, which was characterized by the elimination of the existing national institutions (the murder of the high priest) and an internal revolution that was led by a series of independent commanders, who emerged from the grass roots, rather than from the existing leadership class (the priestly leadership).

Of course, these commanders eliminated one another in internal battles. However, there was some kind of national system that was concentrated on the Temple, a new high priest was chosen, coins were minted, and a kind of national court was established, in the structure of the Sanhedrin, a concept that will be clarified later.[1] The national framework functioned in part, simultaneously to intense internal battles.[2]

The rebellion was suppressed by the Romans, and the Temple was destroyed. After the Destruction the job of high priest was eliminated. This short period of the Great Revolt is particularly interesting because it brings to the surface the national desires, and the national utopian ideal, which the empire made sure to destroy and dismantle.

In the years 132–135 another revolt erupted, this time with a single leader who was acceptable to everyone, who specifically described himself as "Shimon ben Kosba, the Patriarch and Economic Leader of Israel"("Nasi" and "Parnas").[3] It is not clear who appointed this Patriarch; apparently, he himself. In addition, in the first year of the revolt another leader appears on the coins of the revolt "state," "Elazar the Priest," whose status is unclear, and who disappeared later in the revolt.

The Roman government considered the Jewish religion a "recognized religion," with the exception of the short periods when anti-religious decrees were legislated (130–139).

SOURCES

For the beginning of the period, Josephus and the New Testament Gospels are the main sources, and for the later period the Talmudic Jewish sources, most of which were edited from the early third century on. Josephus focuses mainly on the political history of the Jewish people. The Gospels were written for religious reasons, and most of the relevant information appears in narrative and religious texts. The rabbinic sources, however, are a collection of discussions and rulings on a great variety of laws; they also include homilies, which for the most part do not reflect historical truths. Historical nuggets may be found scattered throughout the literature.

There has been a longstanding debate about the nature of the rabbinic sources and their historical reliability. The intensity of the debate and its strongly minimalist stance has unfortunately inhibited the study of the period.

The sages and editors of the Talmudic writings have been "accused" by the minimalists of being "recruited" for religious purposes because of their utopian views, focusing only on intellectual elite, the result being a heavily edited and redacted product. In this chapter, the use of sages' literature will be made in an intermediate way. Sages' literature must be trusted, but it is of course biased. This chapter discusses the topic where sages have a desire to present themselves as an establishment. Yet I am aware of this bias and believe that the great richness of this testimony makes it possible to discern when the description is biased and "diverted," and what its real roots are.

The System of Government in The Roman Empire

The system of the Jewish autonomy was of course adapted to the structure of the Roman provincial government. In order to assess it, we must begin with a short survey of the Roman provincial structure. This chapter will deal only with the eastern part of the empire, which eventually became (at 314 CE) the Byzantine Empire. The empire was aware (perhaps not consciously) of the difference between the eastern provinces and the west of the empire.

The difference between the provinces lay in the degree of Hellenization on the one hand, and the sense of nationalism on the other. In the whole empire the main distinction was between the city and the rural areas. The city was Roman-Hellenist in nature, and was formally considered independent, although in effect it was of course subject to the Roman procurator. In the whole empire the polis had an elected leadership that managed its affairs, the tax collection, and the many municipal services. The municipal elite class was also a class characterized by friction and bridging with the autochthonous masses, which were less Hellenistic. The Roman city was global. Although there were local differences, the overall structure, language, and architecture were global in nature.

The village was for the main part autochthonous. It was less Hellenized and it was to a great degree independent. There is no evidence of a mixed village (Jews and Christians). There are few findings that presumably attest to two religious groups in a single village, and this is not the place to expand on that.

In both Syria and Egypt, the village had communal systems, which differed from one another in their job titles and the variety of positions. In the Syrian village there was a *demo* (an assembly) and a Boule (council), and in Egypt there were no such institutions. The local community in both provinces collected the local taxes (in other words, the tax was imposed on the village as a group, and the independent leadership divided it among the taxpayers, based on a periodical census).

The method of distribution was presumably dictated by the empire, but the local leadership was allowed to decide that X would pay 1/12 of his assets, and Y would pay 1/20. The leadership built temples, bathhouses, and rural roads, and provided a few services (such as policing, courts, and a little more).

Apparently throughout the Roman Empire (including the Western empire) the village had the option of internal organization, which was exploited to a different degree in each locale. There is a great deal of research on this subject and there has yet to be a comprehensive study about the entire Roman or Byzantine rural area.[4]

The Jewish village was highly organized. On the one hand, no temples were built in it, and bathhouses were rare. But they did build a synagogue and roads between villages and between the village and its fields. There was a kind of local militia, a school, and a type of compulsory education law (for boys only). There was also a well-developed charity system. These two latter services were an innovation of Jewish society.

The Autonomous Government Power structure of Jewish Society

The Jewish self-government consisted of three combined layers[5]

A. The national level
B. The local level, which is divided between the city and the village
C. The sages

The first two were formal institutions and the third was informal.

In Alexandria, as in first-century BCE Cyrenaica, there was a *politeuma*, in other words an internal Jewish community which was an equal partner of the general community.[6] In effect there is competition between the communities, which is fueled by mutual hostility, and clearly the leadership of the polis had a built-in advantage and seniority over the Jewish *politeuma*.

This general description is based on inscriptions (from Cyrenaica) and additional evidence, such as a sentence in the Letter of Aristeas, the writings of Philo, and more. Such a *politeuma* is also described in Antiochia in the fourth century, and there were scholars who discounted the evidence and maintained that such a structure lacks administrative logic and is impossible, and that the *politeuma* was nothing more than an empty name. But recently a series of papyri from such a *politeuma* from the Ptolemaic era were discovered in the city of Hierakonpolis in Egypt[7] and there is no doubt that occasionally the term is used in a literary form to describe ordinary or second-class citizenship.[8]

However, it is also clear that that this is how the Jewish community in Diaspora cities was managed.[9] All these sources are from the first century BCE and the first century CE and perhaps the early second century CE. That does not mean that this structure stopped operating later on, and it is implied in the words of Chrysostomos (fourth-century Syria).

Politeuma is not a term just for a Jewish community, there was such a *politeuma* of Idumeans in Memphis, Egypt, a community of Cilicians and of other foreign nations. Sometimes it was a voluntary association of a brotherhood of foreigners in a city, or of worshippers of a specific god.[10] It was therefore the way the Ptolemaic administration made it easier to absorb immigrants in the cities under the jurisdiction of its kingdom, and the Romans adopted the structure in other provinces as well. We can assume that in the Palatine province the situation was similar.

During the reign of the independent kingdom, the Jews administered the cities, and perhaps in a number of cities with a non-Jewish majority (Caesarea) their rule was controversial. Later on, or at least after the Destruction of the Temple, the inhabitants of the non-Jewish cities composed the leadership and the Jews made do with a *politeuma* at best. There were several cities with a solid Jewish majority (Tiberias, Sepphoris, or Lydda), but the leadership of the city was also non-Jewish in nature, and the Jews were forced to make do with a *politeuma*.

What was the scope of the *politeuma*'s activity? Clearly it was the organization that built the synagogues and handled the network of community services that we will describe below, and it is also clear that it established a judiciary. In Hierakonpolis the *politeuma* had the right to an independent judiciary that was restricted only by the Roman procurator (in other words, a right equal to that of the polis itself).

Did the *politeuma* enjoy autonomy in the economic sphere as well? Did it set prices and issue weights? There is some evidence that this was the case, judging by the number of weights from all over the province (Caesarea, Ashdod, and Antiochia in Syria) with Jewish symbols.[11] This situation is explained by a number of Jewish sources, which have not as yet been properly discussed in the research, and which indicate that the Jewish community handled the payment of municipal taxes.[12]

In that case, the Jews used and took advantage of an old Hellenistic communal structure and preserved it (with the consent of the Roman authorities, and despite the opposition of the polis institutions). The Jewish community expanded this structure by deciding on internal practices and communal obedience. Of course! In the event of a legal conflict between a Jew who was a citizen of the *politeuma* and a non-Jewish citizen of the polis, the case was probably brought to the leadership of the polis (which usually served as a court).

Moreover, any Jew could decide that he would avoid his obligation to his own people and turn to the polis leadership. There was probably constant competition for positions of power between the two institutions as well. But Jewish obedience and solidarity preserved the communal structure.

THE RURAL COMMUNITY

Even before the description we should add a methodological comment. The Jewish sources were created in small study groups that were active in the cities, the towns, and the villages. The texts in our hands were edited in the large Study Halls in the villages, which gradually became concentrated in the cities (Sepphoris and Tiberias). It is usually difficult to determine whether a specific saying reflects the rural town or Jewish life in the polis. But as a rule, and most probably, the Jewish sources in general reflect the situation in the rural town.

According to Jewish sources and the archaeological findings that have been preserved, the Jewish community was highly established.[13] It was much more developed than those of its neighbors in the East (Syria, Egypt, Arabia, Asia Minor) and far more than those in the West (Spain, Gaul, and Britain) in which there were fewer rural towns than in the East.

The rural Jewish community in Judea built schools and paid the teachers' salaries. All the local boys studied in these schools (boys only). The community established charitable institutions that provided food for the poor as well as financial support, helped to pay for weddings, were involved in redeeming captives, and supported the weak and the sick. The community built roads to the agricultural areas and to adjacent communities. The sages discuss the *halakhic* problems involved in paving the road to the maximum width, the confiscation of required land and so on, and the archaeological findings provide the factual evidence for the existence of the network of roads. Usually the village did not have a wall, with the exception of border communities.

As opposed to the polis, the communities did not supply food to the town markets, and usually there was no need for that. However, the Agoronomos (in charge of the market and the trade) who operated in the Jewish town was involved in supervising weights and on rare occasions also supervised prices. A special Roman law confirms the right of the Jewish authorities to set their own prices.[14]

In the village there were cisterns and public pools, a *mikveh*,[15] a public bathhouse (rarely) and of course a synagogue and additional public services. In large communities there was even street lighting, which was rare even in the polis; it was probably found only on main streets.

The medieval Jewish community financed itself by providing religious services such as ritual slaughter, burials, or weddings. On the other hand, during the period of the Mishna and the Talmud these needs were not defined as "religious services," the community was not involved in providing them, and they were considered ordinary commercial services, which were provided on a commercial and individual basis. The community did not define itself on this religious basis at all and was a clearly municipal body.

Anyone could be elected to a public position, and as opposed to the polis there were no special requirements in terms of pedigree or wealth. Of course, in effect, the wealthy had a natural advantage, but it was not translated into a formal restriction. Candidates had to be of a minimum age (20 or 25), but again this was not a legal restriction but rather an existing practice. In Jewish-Roman Palestine women were not allowed to fill public positions.

The rural community was inspired by the polis, but it was designed in a different social and ideological format. Some of the services were a partial imitation of what the villagers were familiar with in the polis. For example, the person responsible for economic activity was called an *agoronomos* and the scope of his activity was based on that of the polis. However, the basic principles of the community differed. Educational and charitable services were unknown in the non-Jewish polis, and these services were inspired by Jewish-religious ideology under the leadership of the sages.

As far as the government was concerned, in the polis tax collection was the principal job of the autonomous leadership. The Jewish community also handled tax collection for the Roman authorities, despite the problematic relations between the government and the Jewish settlement.[16]

In general, we can state that the Jewish community was more populist in nature. The leaders were not necessarily wealthy, and as opposed to the polis, these leaders were not required to pay for their appointment. The funding of the community was based on taxation and on popular contributions; it was not imposed on the wealthy and was not dependent on their good will.

Supplementary evidence of that can be found in dozens of synagogue-inscriptions of dedication and thanks for paying tribute by relatively small contributions of one-third of a dinar, or the donation of a lintel or a column. All that is opposed to both: the polis and the Syrian villages, where donations of entire public buildings are mentioned. The system of services was also designed mainly for the benefit of the general public and the poor of the community in particular. The structure of the Jewish community therefore reflected Jewish social ideology inspired by Hellenistic-Roman administrative structures.

There were few public buildings in the village. There was a synagogue in almost every Jewish community from the third century on (see below). Additional buildings were rare, but we know of marketplace structures, a public fountain, and a number of other exceptional examples. Here too there is a big difference between the Jewish community and the Syrian village, which had more public buildings and fewer communal services.

Of course, these services did not operate in every community, and the description here is an optimal list of the services that operated in all the communities (as described in rabbinical sources). We can assume that in every village different local entities were active, leading to the expansion or the reduction of the system of services. In other words, we have evidence of all the services, and every one of them operated in some of the communities, but only in the large and developed community did all or most of these services exist.

The Jewish community was headed by an institution that was a kind of people's assembly. It was not called "demos," the Greek term, but had a Hebrew name. It had a town head who was called "resh omarim"[17] and referred to by the Greek term *archon* or simply "head." There was an organization of town leaders *tovei Haï`r* (usually seven, but apparently the number was not permanent). This council also served as a local court. Parallel to this court there was a kind of notary, *shahad*, who is mentioned not only in the Mishna[18] but in inscriptions as well.[19]

In large villages there may also have been a city council called a Boule, which may have existed only in villages that were capitals of a *toparchy*. From among the council members a court of law was assembled that had enforcement powers, including the right to incarcerate people.[20] The local appointed officials are called *parnasim*. That may be a distortion of a Greek term, but it was accepted as a Hebrew term for all intents and purposes. For example, there was a Boule in Beitar. In Syria there was a Boule only in important villages, which were sometimes called mater Metrakomia (mother village). The community paid for its activities, mainly from a tax imposed on the local residents and from public fundraising campaigns—*pesika* mentioned in several inscriptions. As opposed to the community in the Syrian village and in the polis, the Jewish community had no economic enterprises, land, or similar sources of income.

The community made its decisions in a democratic process, but appointments were apparently made by the Patriarch, who had to consult with the village residents but had the last word. That was the case both in the Land of Israel and in the Diaspora.

In that case, under the two-tiered imperial administration (the imperial government, and below it, the government in the regional polis) another administrative layer developed on both the national level (Council of Sages, Sanhedrin?) and on the local level (the community). All this in spite of the fact that the rural villages in Roman Palestine were, on average, smaller than those in Syria and Egypt (up to 100 dunams = 10 hectares at most).

In the past I thought that the Jewish community flourished thanks to the (limited) religious autonomy granted to those who practiced the Jewish religion. In other words it was an autonomy that turned into recognition of Judaism as a dispersed nation. But now I believe the opposite. Although the Patriarchy began as an expression of that religious autonomy, the village community exploited the imperial permission for rural organization and a limited community. The Jews took maximum advantage of this vacuum while adapting the behavior of the government to the cultural and social nature of the Jewish rural town.

One item that appears often in the Egyptian papyri is a request by citizens who are trying to exploit the tiered system of government. They complain to the procurator or to the government of the *toparchy* (or the polis) about an injustice caused to them by the local authorities, or about unsuitable service. In Roman Palestine no parallel papyri were preserved (due to the different climatic conditions). But in general, it seems that the Jewish institutions knew how to enforce their authority and even they fined anyone who turned to the foreign ruler.[21]

However, we hear about an application to "the courts of the non-Jews" not as an appeals court but a priori, in other words: two Jews who preferred to be judged in the non-Jewish institutions.[22] This probably refers to a polis, because in the village there were no such institutions. We also hear of a one-time case in which someone punished by the local Jewish government (in the polis of Tiberias) complained to the non-Jewish authorities, apparently to the government of the procuratorship.[23] In that case the Jewish activists in the capital city intervened and tried to reduce the blame (with a bribe of course) and were unsuccessful. We don't know how the affair ended, but this an example of the clash between the tiers of government, a clash in which the supreme authority has a built-in advantage over the lower levels of government.

THE FOURTH TIER: THE SAGES

Below these three tiers of government with a formal administration (empire, polis, Jewish autonomous community), there was another tier, the "sages." The sage is a unique figure in the Roman world. In vain scholars tried to compare him to the Roman philosopher, the temple priests in Rome or Egypt, or the Christian or perhaps pre-Christian holy men (like Apollonius of Tiana who was a single person and not a social class).[24]

The sages are a social elite group, some of them from the wealthy class and some from a lower economic class. Each sage convened a small group of students (*havura*—study group) who studied with him for several years. After an undefined and non-uniform number of years some turned themselves into sages who headed a study group, some stopped studying, some switched to another *havura* (study group), and some discontinued their intensive study and became ordinary community members with a certain amount of knowledge.

The leading sages held assemblies at various opportunities, mainly in the home of the Patriarch but also in buildings of the polis or the village, and there they held discussions and debated, and occasionally also made various religious decisions. In the court of the Patriarch there was such a group of leading sages who composed a skeleton of national leadership.[25]

The usual model is a sage who studies with his group, sometimes under a tree, or in the Study Hall adjacent to the synagogue. Upon his death the group disbands, the older members of the *havura* embark on a private path as ordinary householders, and the best ones study with their rabbi for many years (or with a number of rabbis), return to their village and start an independent study group there.

The content of the studies was decided by the sage himself. However the Mishna became the prevalent accepted textbook that was studied from the time of its redacting (220 CE). The text was memorized orally. The sages' studies, like their judging, were spontaneous and not institutionalized. The number of sages is unknown. In the rabbinic texts there are about 600 names of sages who were active over seven or eight generations (100–400). Of course, there were other sages who are unknown to us, but there were no more than several hundred in each generation. Not every village had a sage, and a sage was not a formal appointment, except the *semicha* as a sage that we will mention below.

The sage encountered the public on a daily basis, because he was a part of village society. There was an additional public encounter during the *drasha* (Torah sermon) on Shabbat, a kind of popular university, in which the sage discussed interpretations of the weekly Torah portion read that week, and guided the community tactfully and pleasantly with heartwarming words. The sages developed a magnificent culture including a judicial system, which competed with the Roman system and was not "culturally" inferior to it. They developed a system of popular sermons, myths, and a national culture. Sages are almost the only group in the empire that handed down a written culture to us in languages other than Greek or Latin (i.e., Hebrew and Aramaic) starting in the early Roman period.[26]

The rabbinical literature often describes the sage as an esteemed figure, but, generally speaking, there are no miracles attributed to him and the sage is not a professional healer of the sick or a rainmaker. At most he initiates (or approves) a public fast and decides who leads the public prayers. In the first and second centuries there were also outright holy men, who are called "Hasidim," who were not known for their teaching of Torah but only for healing the sick, bringing rain, and other holy acts.[27]

This type of holy man is familiar from Syrian and Egyptian society, mainly in the Christian period but apparently earlier as well. Jesus, for example, is far more similar to a typical *Hasid*, although he is also presented as unique sage, who is involved mainly in social and ethical issues and less in *halakha*.[28] There were scholars who did not distinguish between sages and *Hasidim* and therefore mistakenly attributed to sages,[29] activity as holy men.[30]

We can assume that when it comes to the sage's image the rabbinical literature is somewhat polemical and not objective. In fact, the sage was a respected figure but not necessarily the most esteemed figure in Jewish society. Here and there we also hear criticism of the sages and their decisions. Such critical comments are attributed to Jesus and his successors, with a minority of them also found by implication in the rabbinic literature itself.

Sages were engaged in all the *halakhic* issues, the laws of Shabbat, the laws of tithing, the laws of impurity (which were very popular until the second century), and legal issues (how to sell and how to buy, when the business owner is permitted to change his mind and when his promise irrevocable, how to marry, inheritance arrangements, writing contracts, and many other matters).

The sages believed that this knowledge is important, and that the public has a responsibility to learn it—it's open to everyone—and a scholar has to be familiar with all these subjects and know how to teach them. In the study group these subjects were studied systematically (with a system chosen by the teacher) and the public came with questions that the sage answered either during the study session or privately. The main role of the sages was to study and teach Torah and *halakha* and to be a perfect model of a Torah scholar. They have no formal authority or appointment from the public but at most an "internal" appointment whose significance is not sufficiently clear.

The sages developed a unique system of *halakha* whereby there were many details involved in the observance of each commandment. If according to the Torah there was an obligation to give a *teruma* (a heave offering) to the priest, the *halakha* determined the blessing to be recited by the donor, who was allowed to raise a heave offering, at what stage of the fruit a *teruma* could be given, and when it became obligatory, whether it is permitted to eat agricultural crops before the *teruma*, how to preserve the ritual purity of the offering, and endless similar details.

In general, the sages rejected the legitimacy of the Roman government and were hostile to it. On the other hand, they recognized the existence of a "civil" leadership system (Jewish of course), demanded the right to primary legislation (determining the *halakha*) and occasionally even intervened in "secondary legislation," but left the daily administration to the community leaders.[31]

The community and its institutions for their part worked to uphold the rabbis' value system and were therefore involved in values espoused by the sages, including education and charity. We can even say that the community "laws" were influenced to a great extent by the values of the sages, but the sages did not run the community. The synagogue was at the disposal of the sages every day, and occasionally classrooms or an actual study hall was built, financed by the community of course.

Sages determined (or demanded the right to determine) the limits of communal activity (what the majority is permitted to force on the minority). They demanded the construction of synagogues, decided on the nature of prayers but didn't actually lead them (as opposed to Christian priests). They decided on marriage and divorce arrangements but were not actively involved in them, and so on.

They of course also decided on halakhot on public issues, but these halakhot are for the most part matters of principle. For example, sages preach to the public to engage in many acts of charity, and even determine the norm regarding the amount of bread to be distributed to the poor or the amount of money to be donated to help a bride (the wedding needs for an impoverished bride), but they are not those in charge of charitable contributions.

It should be emphasized that frequently the *halakha* is no more than a legal version of the public custom, dating from some time in the distant past. But the sages are the ones who express it in words and reinforce it.

One *halakha* will illustrate the delicate position of the sages. Second Temple sages (from the end of the Second Temple period to the beginning of the first century CE) discuss whether it is permitted to make the *pesika* (promise to donate) on Shabbat, in other words, to promise a donation during the public collection in the synagogues. The fear is based on *halakha*, because such a promise is considered a monetary commitment, and doing business on Shabbat is forbidden.

In terms of *halakha* this is clearly forbidden. But practically speaking, the prayers on Shabbat are the most suitable time for a public appeal. Everyday needs therefore took precedence over *halakha*. In such a case, the *halakhic* debate apparently post-dates the practical custom. Some of the sages try to prevent the existing custom, while some permit it. But in this case, we can assume that the public determined the *halakha*, and the sages only approved an existing practice. However, in the ethos of the sages they are the ones who decide, and without their permission the community would not have done anything that contradicts the *halakha*.

At the same time there is evidence that the sages were beginning to assume public positions. They release people from vows, and they demand the authority to arrange divorces. In a multigenerational process that is taking place to this day, we see a trend of assuming as many public roles as possible. In the Roman period, the period of the Mishna and the Talmud, the process just began.

A more overt conflict, which the sages try to downplay, concerned judicial authority. Of course, the sages believed that only they were authorized to judge, because only they are familiar with the details of the halakhot, including those regarding legal procedures. Jewish law is very strict about legal procedures, and in any case is restricted to professional experts.

In practice, the sages' rabbinic court was voluntary. Anyone who so desired came to it, anyone who didn't want a sage's ruling, but still wanted a national-Jewish legal procedure, turned to the community court. Anyone who wanted enforcement turned to the community court, since the sage did not have the power of enforcement, but only personal prestige and charisma.[32]

The sages often describe the decisions of the sages' courts and almost ignore the municipal courts. They recognize the authority of the municipal courts, but have contempt for their prestige; they question their authority and always suspect them of a lack of knowledge and an absence of expertise. A description of "their" judicial system (that of the sages) is in effect a system of "marketing" and public relations, and perhaps sometimes even a covert attack against the municipal courts.

However, the sages could not object outright to the municipal courts. Such an overt attack would have (rightly) been seen as a confrontation with the institutions of the community whose existence the sages supported. All those who participated in the covert internal attack had a common "enemy," the Roman government, which united the internal rivals. The sages often preach in favor of internal "peace," since that was the only source of power against the non-Jewish government and against non-Jewish society and religion. These conflicts with the Roman authorities were vital for the survival of Jewish society and marginalized internal tensions, although it didn't cause their disappearance.

The sages didn't demand to become part of the municipal leadership. Occasionally there was a sage who did so as an individual, but the general ethos of the sages was a demand to avoid getting mired in communal needs, and to leave free time for study and for leadership "from a distance" from the study hall.

THE RELATIONSHIP BETWEEN THE PATRIARCH AND THE SAGES

The status of the sages on the national level was more complicated. According to the rabbinical literature, the Patriarch was the head of the sages. He was also the head of the Sanhedrin, and at least de jure he conducted its sessions. The council of sages was a limited group of sages who were active in the Patriarch's court, and constituted an active source of decision-making authority. Needless to say, the council was conducted by the Patriarch. A somewhat similar situation is presumably familiar from other arrangements, and it appears in three major varieties:

A. The ruler makes use of the existing elite and harnesses them for his needs, so that the elite become the backbone of his administration. The Emperor of China, for example, used the intellectual class—the students of Confucius—and gave them a central role in the government of the Chinese Empire.[33] The king joins the existing elite class and heads it. On the one hand he adds its prestige to the sages, and relies on its familiar and accepted legitimacy. On the other hand, he preserves the power of the elite and limits it from up close. For example, in many societies the king was also the high priest or the head judge. The Roman emperor was also the chairman of the Senate, and often the high priest. The King of England is the head of the Church of England.
B. From time to time the king is the symbolic head of the elite society, but in effect is not its ruler. In a similar process we can see that the King of England has, in the course of the past 700 years, been transformed from the acting leader of the Parliament to a symbol of government only. Sometimes the king is only "the first among equals."
C. The ruler fights the elite class and succeeds in crushing it (or fails to do so). That was the case of Herod, for example.

However, the relationship between the Patriarch and the sages (the Sanhedrin) was different for several reasons: During the entire Tannaitic period,[34] the Patriarch himself was a "professional" sage, and is even among the leading sages. He was an active, genuine, and full partner to the values and aspirations of this class. A king who wanted to serve as the high priest in any pagan temple required power that would enable him to seize this position, but beyond that he had no need of any exceptional professional training. But a Patriarch who wanted to be a sage required comprehensive training as well as ability (including a good memory). Rabban Gamliel in the Yavne generation, R. Shimon b. Gamliel, and R. Judah the Patriarch were not only ordinary sages, but they were among the chief speakers in the study hall. Their status as Patriarchs and sons of Patriarchs may have eased their promotion in the internal power structure of the study hall. As a participant in the study hall the patriarch was exposed to other opinions and took part in the halakhic debate as all other sages.

We have no specific information about the studies of the son of the Patriarch who preceded R. Judah the Patriarch, since his two predecessors grew up in period of rebellion and chaos. On the other hand, R. Judah the Patriarch grew up in a period of peace, and information was preserved as to how he studied in the study hall as a regular student. Once he complained to his father that he wasn't respected like the son of another sage, R. Eliezer the son of Shimon b. Yochai[35] and in another source reports how he was not allowed to join the study group of one of the sages.[36] Other evidence presents him as a member of the study group who studies and argues with his friends and his rabbis.

Some of the Patriarchs from the Amoraitic period[37] were also sages, although less important. R. Yehuda Nesiah (third century CE) was a sage, who is described by the sages as a "great man." A number of sayings were attributed to him in the *halakha* and the Aggadah. Rabban Gamliel b. Rabbi is also called "a great man."

On the other hand, we have no evidence about later Patriarchs who are active in the study hall. Apparently, the gap between the elite class of sages and the Patriarchs increased during those periods, although until the middle of the third century the Patriarchs on an individual level were members of the class of sages. Therefore, the tension between the Patriarch and the sages, whom we will discuss, is largely an internal struggle within the study hall, surrounding issues of an internal nature.

One of the areas of friction is the appointment of the sages themselves. The rabbinical literature often mentions the internal appointment of "Rabbi." In the research it is not clear to what exactly he was appointed, and whether he had real powers or whether it was an honorary title only.[38] In any case, in social terms it was part of the sage's promotion track. The appointment was made on the occasion of *semicha* (ordination). *Semicha* is a ceremony that symbolizes the transfer of divine grace and power by means of the chain of transmission from Mount Sinai. The ceremony of *semicha* inspired the model of the Christian ceremony of ordination.

Ordination was the source of legitimacy for the individual sage and for the group of sages. It also had implications for other areas of the sages' activity and their ability to teach and to make *halakhic* decisions, as well as for their status in the internal power structure and in society in general. A clear tradition explains the changes that took place in this sphere. At first (the Yavne generation, 100–135), every sage had autonomy to appoint his students. Later this was done in cooperation with the Patriarch. During a third stage (in the generation of Rabbi, 180–220), this source of power became the exclusive authority of the Patriarch, and finally came a process of joint appointments.[39]

Apparently, this is not only a historical fact (which is described schematically), but what is more important is the sages' acceptance of this situation. That doesn't enable us to claim that all the internal appointments were made by the Patriarch, but only that such a situation existed, and as mentioned, it is accepted by the sages with understanding. In fact, the Patriarch is violating the sages' internal autonomy and is controlling their prestigious professional advancement.

The study of Torah was the sages' principal preoccupation, and they and their students enjoyed total freedom. We have never found a Patriarch who intervened in the study arrangements, and determined, as Patriarch, what they will discuss, in which fields, and on which subject. But we should recall that the first Patriarchs, in the generations of Tannaim, were outstanding sages, and in practice headed the rabbinic court.

One of the jobs of the head of this court was to decide on the issues to be discussed in the institution, and the areas of study in the study hall of the council of sages. But we have never found that the Patriarch prevented any of the sages from studying Torah as he wished.

The editing of the Mishna acted as a restriction of sorts of the freedom of study, or perhaps was responsible for its institutionalization. However, the Mishna was not the work of the Patriarch, but was composed by the sages themselves, and R. Judah the Patriarch acted as the head of the sages and not as Patriarch. Moreover, often the opinion of Rabbi, as it appears in parallel sources, is not even included in the Mishna, which indicates that it was not a personal document.

The rabbinical literature contains overt and covert criticism of the Patriarch, and usually there is no indication that the Patriarch intervened in the contents of study and prevented criticism of himself. Only marginally is there mention of certain criticism of academic freedom in cases of disrespect for the Patriarch. The Patriarch responded angrily and even violently, the sages defended their right to deal with spiritual content as they wished, and the leading sages mediated and restored internal peace.[40]

In another case Rabban Gamliel ordered to shelve the translation of the Book of Job, and scholars have already debated the nature of the fault he found in the translation.[41] This story is evidence of the Patriarch's power and his ability to undermine the autonomy of other scholars. But it is doubtful whether the Patriarch really confronted the sage here or whether, on the contrary, this is evidence of the sages' supervision—under the sponsorship of the Patriarch—of the public, represented by an ordinary person.[42]

Usually, the freedom of debate was preserved. Even on the subject of sanctifying the new month Rabbi Dosa ben Hyrcanus was permitted to differ with the Patriarch. But the Patriarch was furious when another sage tried to cast doubt on the ruling itself. In the Yavne generation there was a continuing attempt on the part of the sages, under the leadership (and initiative) of Rabban Gamliel as the head of the rabbinic court (who apparently did not bear the title Patriarch, as mentioned above) to decide in the event of an internal controversy.[43] The decision process encountered the opposition of those sages who disagreed with the decision and caused a traumatic rift in the study hall.

At the end of the process, in the following generation, it was decided to try to refrain from *halakhic* decisions. And in any case, a sage who remains in the minority and preserves his autonomy and adheres to his opinion is not punished. That means that every sage enjoyed internal autonomy. However, this autonomy was found only among the sages or at most included a veteran student even if he hadn't been "appointed."[44] But the students and the general public did not have the right to adhere to their opinion when it contradicted the sage. The sources also stress that the individual sage does not have the right to impose his authority; the right belongs only to the sages as a group.

The absence of any formal organization in the way the sage teachers or judges is diametrically opposed to the description of the arrangements of the Sanhedrin, which have a detailed ceremonial order. That is one of the reasons why some scholars doubt whether the institution of the Sanhedrin actually existed.

In social terms the Patriarch is a kind of "king" or "ruler" who operates outside the elite class, and occasionally even clashes with it. But the image of the position of Patriarch in the Talmudic literature is undoubtedly as a part of the society of sages. Myth has it that the early sages were Patriarchs.[45] It is hard to know who benefited from this myth. Is the office of Patriarch a product of the prestige of the sages and of Hillel the Elder, or do the sages adopt the Patriarchs into their society, appropriate them, and co-opt them in the sense of "they are ours?"[46] There is a specific debate about that in the midrashim, which thereby reflect, with great sensitivity, the cooperation and the built-in conflict.[47]

The fact that the Patriarchs were also, or mainly, sages presents an additional research problem. Many activities of the Patriarchs were likely to be related either to their role as Patriarch, or alternatively, to their place as sages in the study hall. For example, the redaction of the Mishna in the time of Rabbi Judah the Patriarch could be interpreted as an act of the sages to institutionalize study perhaps to determine the *halakha*, but it can also be interpreted as an attempt by the Patriarch to limit the sages' autonomy and "academic" freedom, and to decide on a study "agenda."

Distinguishing between the activities of the Patriarch required by his position and his activity as a sage is difficult and sometimes impossible. Moreover, the distinction was in essence unclear already at the time when the events themselves took place.

The Patriarch's leadership team included several of the leading sages. The Patriarchs did not have a team of "ministers" or senior officials, and these roles were carried out by the sages. For example, on trips to Rome sages join the Patriarch, and other sages fill national roles such as responsibility for charity on the national level.

Sages also traveled to the southern towns in order to encourage the opening of schools.[48] Needless to say, opening a school was first and foremost an interest of the sages. Are they sent by the Patriarch or are they acting on their own initiative with his blessing? We have already mentioned the Council of Sages in whose context the leading sages worked with the Patriarch, and together constituted a leadership group that dealt with various public and *halakhic* issues. The activity of the leadership group reflected close cooperation between the Patriarch and the sages, the Patriarch's involvement in the study hall, and the involvement of the sages in the work of the Patriarch. The sages' involvement in the House of the Patriarch is therefore evident from many of our sources.

Apparently, the Patriarch also had followers who were not a part of the group of sages but were closely connected to it. For example, in the late second and third centuries the status of the office of Patriarch increased and the "system" at his disposal grew. Rabbi would enforce his directives by means of his ministers and policemen.[49] Another Patriarch had a senior slave named Gramana who acted on his behalf.

We can assume that all of these assistants were no more than low-ranking. Rabbi Judah the Patriarch began a process of adding wealthy men to the "Sanhedrin" (or the Council of Sages). We don't know how successful he was. In any case, the sages naturally fought this trend openly. In an inscription from Shikmona there is mention of Menachem, a senior official (lamprotates) who was also "Komitos and presbitethe." Although Menachem is not called Rabbi, the title "presbitethe," elder in Hebrew, enables us to say that he was from the circles of the sages.[50]

In another inscription from Hamat Gader an anonymous official boast that he is a protégé (tropths) of the Patriarchs. And he may have filled a senior role in the community and the court of the Patriarch without any connection to the sages.[51] It is possible that the rabbinical literature ignores officials who were not sages. The relationship between the sages and the Patriarch is discussed at length in the literature.[52] Alon noted the tension and the battles between the Patriarch and the sages, and Mantel[53] remarks on the strong cooperation between the Patriarch and the sages, two sides of the same coin.

We can sum up by saying that the rabbis criticize the aristocratic practices in the House of the Patriarch, mainly those of the house of R. Judah the Patriarch, and there is also personal criticism of the practices of specific Patriarchs in the *halakha*, mainly in connection with third-century Patriarchs. Apparently, the wording of the remarks and the reprimands is not particularly harsh; it does not exceed the usual practice among the sages themselves, and apparently the Patriarch was seen as a sage among the sages.

Even on the level below the Patriarch there is evidence of a certain tension and competition among the "zekenim" (the accepted term for the sages) and the heads (the term for local leadership and the city archon in particular). As is usual in the rabbinic midrash, the tension is described as a historic competition, as in the midrash that asks whom Moses and Joshua ben Nun preferred, the elders or the heads[54] or similar midrashim claiming that the real "head" is the elder.[55] These midrashim reflect the sages' utopian ideal rather than their actual status.

As mentioned, the sages' utopia is a historical given, since not only facts shape a reality, but occasionally a utopian ideal can also be influential. In addition, the utopia reveals the aspirations whose fulfillment is prevented by real life. The sages describe the monarchy as the ideal system of government,[56] in spite of the fact that in the Bible there are many chapters that imply criticism of the monarchy.

However, in the utopian kingdom the king is a weak figure, and the sages are the leaders. Lorberbaum described the Jewish king as a "disempowered king."[57] As opposed to the practice in the ancient world, the "Jewish" king is subordinate to the law, and the law is the *halakha* determined by the sages. In reality the king cannot be prosecuted,[58] although a king is also permitted to pass his own laws (in some areas) that bypass or contradict the laws of the rabbinical court.

Primarily, he is allowed to confiscate money even without legal authority (in other words, without approval of "the *halakha*" viz., the sages). The king is required to consult with the Sanhedrin, the sages' autonomous institution, and although he heads the Sanhedrin, the center of power is in the hands of the utopian Sanhedrin rather than the king.

DISCUSSION

The sages were a social elite, and the Patriarch was a type of ruler or king. Their mutual relations should be examined as a balance of power between a king and an elite class that is close to the king and works for him. The sages needed the Patriarch, just as the Patriarch needed the sages, and both sides recognized this "symbiotic" need. The sages were interested in the existence of the Patriarchy for several reasons.

a. The public needed a Jewish leader to represent them before the Roman government. Perhaps the sages were not in need of a permanent leader in the study hall, but the public was undoubtedly in need of a leader, and for the sages, leadership in the study hall was the "price" for the need for a national leader. As Rabbi Mana said: "I heard from Rabbi Yudan, and from all the rabbis, why does the Beit Din treat the (House of the Patriarch) with respect? To prevent disputes in Israel."[59]
b. We can assume that the sages preferred to appoint the Patriarch themselves, perhaps even to appoint him for short periods, in order to guarantee their power and their independence, but these things were not under their control. And it is doubtful whether the public would have accepted that; it certainly was not acceptable to the Roman authorities. Handing down the office of Patriarch from father to son made it difficult

for the sages to control the Patriarch, but also prevented the Romans from doing the same.

c. The Sages exploited the Patriarch's authority and power to promote their own preferred interests. At the same time, the Patriarch was also very interested in cooperation with the sages, for several reasons:
    1. The Patriarch himself was a member of the class of sages and probably shared their views.
    2. The Patriarch as ruler used the sages as an important component of the governmental system at his disposal.
    3. The Patriarch's power was supported by the Roman authorities, but his authority was based mainly on the voluntary cooperation of the Jewish public in Palestine and the Diaspora. The sages granted the office of Patriarch religious-public legitimacy, which under the conditions of the period was essential. The Jewish public was prepared to willingly accept the burden of the Patriarchy despite its mistakes and weaknesses, because that was the way to ensure the existence of the Jewish collective. The Patriarch embodied the image of the nation as a consolidated unit despite its political, geographical, economic, and to some extent cultural dispersal.

Observing the commandments and the study of Torah constituted the real content of the Jewish sense of solidarity. The myth of the Jewish people was in effect the ethos demanded by the sages and practiced by them. The Patriarchy was a national leadership that identified in public with the observance of the commandments and cooperated with the sages—the clear community leaders. The need for symbiosis prevented the outbreak of the tensions between the Patriarch and the sages, and the public demanded that they preserve the national collective.

The sages therefore developed their status as a level of government below the voluntary, national, and local level. On the national level we should recall the existence of the Sanhedrin, a national court that of course was clearly identified with the sages. It is doubtful whether such a court was active during the entire period, but it was always the subject of a utopian dream.

The existence of the sages and their natural desire to influence inevitably clashes with the local leadership. But at the same time the community leadership and the sages have a strong symbiotic relationship in which each side needs the other. That is how we can understand the many sermons of the sages in praise of "peace" and "compromise"—these are the ways and means of preserving the internal Jewish power structure without military might and without official authority (not the community leadership and certainly not the sage).

The Jewish autonomy and its structure and power is, by definition, a "covenant society" in the terms of Daniel Elazar.[60] It is a covenant because everyone could elect to participate or to quit, even without formal act of conversion.

The society of the Study Hall is certainly a covenant society. Membership requires active choice and genuine long-term intellectual effort. The internal hierarchy was naturally even less formal, and yet there was strong internal discipline. As we have described here, there were extreme incidents of violating discipline, and the society of the Study Hall was forced, in a short process lasting a single generation, to give up uniformity and to allow and contain disputes, while preserving the utopian idea that one day the Sanhedrin would be established and would eliminate such disputes.

Daniel Elazar emphasized that in a covenant society there is no hierarchy and no coercion, which is the essence of the covenant. In my opinion, based on his explanation, two additional components should be stressed.

a. In the covenant society of the Jewish community in general and in the Study Hall in particular, there were intimate rural societies, in which there was strong social pressure. Social pressure can sometimes serve as a substitute for a network of institutions responsible for punishment and enforcement. In modern times, in communities with large populations (which constitute the natural venue for modern research), social pressure has lost some of its power and validity. But in an intimate rural community social pressure is a highly influential, cruel, and very powerful social instrument.
b. Although the Jewish society had no nationwide mechanism of enforcement and punishment, for deviants there was divine punishment, which for those living at the time was considered no less concrete that the enforcement power of the earthly government. Tradition attributes to R. Yohanan b. Zakkai the spiritual bequest and the blessing: "May it be His will that the fear of Heaven shall be upon you like the fear of flesh and blood." (B. Berachot 28b). And within the Study Hall there is a repetition of this awareness that fear of the rabbi is like fear of God (M. Avot 4:12).

In a religious society, divine sanctions are more powerful than those of the earthly government. Added to this fact is the belief that the monopoly on divine sanction is reserved for the religious leadership, in other words, the sages.[61] This reinforced the alliance between the communal leadership and the sages. The alliance enabled the local leadership to exploit the concept of future punishment, and enabled the local sage to support communal activity and grant it religious legitimacy. The communal leadership, on the other hand, accepted the authority of sages in principle and in terms of legislation. The charity system (hesed) and the education system reflect and execute the aspirations of the sages and implement them in everyday life.

Daniel Elazar also stresses the power of mutual hesed. The system of hesed was the response to economic pressure and to the risk involved in a livelihood based on agriculture.[62] The Jewish community enhanced the system of hesed to levels that until then were not customary in the rest of the world.

The secret of the success of the internal power structure is obedience and the sense of being a persecuted collective. The Jewish ethos is one of an isolated nation under attack by everyone. Anyone who wanted the continuation of Jewish survival chose the path that strengthened the internal power structure.

Although the Patriarchy was eliminated in the middle of the fifth century, the sense of identity as a national collective was reflected in the Sanhedrin as a body that united the Jews of the province. At the same time there were many who gave up the struggle and abandoned the Jewish framework. Without getting into precise explanations, the system of the Jewish collective in the Land of Israel lasted, against all odds, for a long period of about 700 years during which the system was under attack.

At first it was an unorganized attack by Hellenism and global Romanization. Afterward it became an initiated and organized attack by Christianity, sponsored by the imperial governments. Under these conditions we have to ask not what finally caused the collapse of the internal power structure, but how they managed to maintain it for such a long period of time. The Jewish internal power structure is a "success story." It is the organizational tool that enabled the survival of the Jewish ethnic group and its local and national solidarity. Several basic conditions were responsible for this success.

A. The national solidarity and the sense of persecution of the Jewish community. The sense of persecution may have been exaggerated. In historical terms, it is doubtful whether it was more serious than that suffered by the Christian community during the Roman period, or that of the Manicheans, the Copts, or other religious groups in the Roman and Byzantine East. But it is not the facts that are important, but the ancient community's perception of the situation.
B. The sense of hostility and distance from the rest of the world in general, and Hellenistic culture in particular, and especially the Roman Empire. This feeling of hostility (which was usually mutual) was fed by the *halakha*: the perception of others as impure, the ban against marriage with them, the ban against eating their produce, and so on.
C. An imperial administrative framework that could have been a "juridical house" for the Jewish community. And in fact, the national institutions

(the Patriarchy and the Sanhedrin) were the first to suffer, since they had no accepted Roman parallel. The Jewish community expanded the existing frameworks through successful political lobbying and national solidarity. This solidarity was reflected in the fact that the few members of the Jewish community that were part of the imperial administration served as lobbyists for their fellow Jews.

D. The indifference of the Roman government to "religious" questions, and its lack of interest in what was happening in a village far from the Hellenist-Roman culture. In fact, in the Christian empire, this lack of interest turned into hostility and competition between the Christian establishment and the Jews. The national institution of the Patriarchy was undermined by that. The blow to the Sanhedrin is more doubtful, it is possible that it was just then that the Sanhedrin began to flourish. Rural autonomy was not harmed by the Christian assault. We don't know.

NOTES

1. Flavius Josephus, *The Jewish War* (Middlesex, UK: Harmondsworth, 1955), D 334-36.

2. Josephus and the Jewish sources stress the internal battles. In the research literature it is common to accept these sources literally, and to emphasize the civil war that ostensibly caused the destruction of the Temple and the conquest of the land. There is no question that there was great internal tension. However, a perusal of the processes of the war also indicates success in bridging between the sides and achieving combined activity, parallel to the internal wars. This subject is awaiting research, and the summary proposed here is to a certain degree the somewhat unusual personal opinion of the writer of the article, see for example Goodman 2011, Mladen Popović, *The Jewish Revolt Against Rome: Interdisciplinary Perspectives* (Leiden: Brill, 2011).

3. Ḥanan Eshel and Boaz Zissu, *The Bar Kokhba Revolt: The Archaeological Evidence* (Jerusalem: Yad Izhak Ben-Zvi, 2019).

4. The community in Syria is known from inscriptions William Kelly Prentice, "Officials charged with the conduct of public works in Roman and Byzantine Syria" (paper presented at the Transactions and Proceedings of the American Philological Association, 1912); Henry Innes MacAdam, "Studies in the History of the Roman Province of Arabia" (The University of Manchester, 1979); Chaker Ghadban, "Monuments de Hammara (Béqa'-Sud, Liban): Nova et vetera," *Ktèma* 10, no. 1 (1985); Maurice Sartre, "Communautés villageoises et structures sociales d'après l'épigraphie de la Syrie du Sud," *L'epigrafia del villaggio, Faenza* 127 (1993); Julien Aliquot, "Sanctuaries and Villages on Mt Hermon during the Roman Period," in *The Variety of Local Religious Life in the Near East*, ed. Kaizer Tad (Leiden: Brill, 2008); J.P. Rey-Coquais, "Villages du Liban et de la Syrie moyenne (de Dams au Coude de

l'Oronte)," in *L'epigrafia del villaggio*, ed. Alda Calbi, Amgela Donati, and Gabriela Poma (Faenza, 1993); George McLean Harper, "Village Administration in the Roman Province of Syria: A Dissertation Presented to the Faculty of Princeton University in Candidacy for the Degree of Doctor of Philosophy" (Princeton University Deptartment of Classics, 1928); Norman H. Baynes and Elsabeth S. A. Dawes, *Three Byzantine Saints: Contemporary Biographies of St. Daniel the Stylite, St. Theodore of Sykeon and St. John the Almsgiver* (London: St Vladimirs Seminary 1948), chap. 72, 111, 43.; Theodoros of Sykeon, chap 72, 111, 143, J. J. Jarri, "Inscriptions Arabes, Syriaques et Grecques du Massif du Belus du Nord," *Annales Islamologicques* 9, no. 281 (1970): 187–214; 215–219. Harper mentioned a series of office holders, starting from the kwmarchos, the village head, and up to elected officials such as epimelhtes, pistos et al. These office holders appear in two contexts, one as honorary title on tombstones and the other during the construction of public buildings, usually temples. Harper was unable to find a defined position, and duty for each elected official. This element is the basis for Grainger's criticism of Harper. In his opinion, the titles that are mentioned are for the most part honorary titles only John D Grainger, "'Village Government'in Roman Syria and Arabia," *Levant* 27, no. 1 (1995).. Grainger (like the other scholars) ignored the literary information about rural organization – like Theodor from Sykeon Baynes and Dawes, "Three Byzantine Saints: Contemporary Biographies of St. Daniel the Stylite, St. Theodore of Sykeon and St. John the Almsgiver." chapters 72, 111, who mentioned the head of the elders as a secular position. In Chapter 124, he mentions the village head (kwmarchos), in another chapter (143), for example, he tells about a rural community that constructed a bridge, a rural school (ch. 6, 26) and a public meal (ch. 143). The research also ignored the archaeological information about temples, bathhouses, public fountains and roads that are found in the rural area, and this is not the place to enumerate them. For example, an inscription on a public spring (πεγή Jarri 1970, inscriptions no. 181 in the village of Nebo [Northern Syria] reflects communal activity of the local community. See also Dar 1993: 156, 246, and mainly the map on p. 3, on which ancient roads between the small villages on the Hermon are sketched. Office holders don't appear in inscriptions from after the fourth century, but the historical and archaeological evidence continues up to the end of the Arab conquest (640 A.D.). The role of the community leadership in Syria and Arabia regarding tax collection does not appear, but it is clear from the general structure of the empire.

The community in Egypt is known mainly from papyri (the archaeological information has barely been examined, see Alan K. Bowman, *The Town Councils of Roman Egypt*, vol. 11 (Toronto: Hakkert, 1971); A.H. Macnaghten, "Local Administration in Egypt under Roman Rule, Fourth to Sixth Centuries AD: The Element of Corruption" (University of St Andrews, 1993); Adam Łukaszewicz, *Les édifices publics dans les villes de l'Égypte romaine: problèmes administratifs et financiers* (Warsaw: Wydawnictwo Uniwersytetu Warszawskiego, 2018); Ann Ellis Hanson, "Village Officials at Philadelphia: A Model of Romanization in the Julio-Claudian Period," *Egitto e etoria antiea dall'eLlenismo all'eta amba. Bilancio di 1m confronto* (1989); Constantin Zuckerman, "Du village à l'Empire: autour du Registre fiscal d'Aphroditô (525/526)," in *Centre de Recherche d'Histoire et Civilisation de*

Byzance. Monographies 16 (Paris: Peeters, 2005); Giovanni R Ruffini, *Life in an Egyptian Village in Late Antiquity: Aphrodito Before and After the Islamic Conquest* (Cambridge University Press, 2018); Micaela Langellotti, *Village Life in Roman Egypt: Tebtunis in the First Century AD* (Oxford: Oxford University Press, 2020), 43–53. Karolien Geens, *Panopolis, a Nome Capital in Egypt in the Roman and Byzantine Period (ca. AD 200-600)* (Dissertation, Leuven University, Leuven, 2014), 145–155.

In addition to the office holders, who are "elected" every year, there was a "village scribe" (κωμογραμματεί kwmogramatai) who was the appointed "professional." He was not an elected Arthur MFW Verhoogt and Sven Peter Vleeming, *The Two Faces of Graeco-Roman Egypt*, vol. 30 (Leiden: Brill, 1998).The tax collection system in Egypt underwent two important reforms, which we will not discuss further. There were rural communities in Egypt who enjoyed autopragia, in other words, the right to collect taxes independently Zuckerman, "Du village à l'Empire: autour du Registre fiscal d'Aphroditô (525/526)"; Ruffini, *Life in an Egyptian Village in Late Antiquity: Aphrodito Before and After the Islamic Conquest*; Langellotti, *Village Life in Roman Egypt: Tebtunis in the First Century AD*, 43–53.

5. Shmuel Safrai and Menachem Stern, "Jewish Self-government," in *The Jewish People in the First Century, Volume 1* (Brill, 1974).

6. Alan Appelbaum, *The Dynasty of the Jewish Patriarchs* (Tübingen: Mohr Siebeck, 2013).

7. Sylvie Honigman, "The Jewish Politeuma at Heracleopolis," *Scripta Classica Israelica* 21 (2002); James M.S. Cowey and Klaus Maresch, *Urkunden des Politeuma der Juden von Herakleopolis (144/3–133/2 v. Chr.)(P. Polit. Iud.)* (Wiesbaden: Springer-Verlag, 2013); Aryeh KASHER, "No longer a Historiographic Legend: New Papyri from a Forgotten Jewish Politeuma in Ptolemaic Egypt," *Tarbiz* 72, no. 1–2 (2003).

8. Epistle to the Philippians 3:20.

9. Patrick Sänger, "The Politeuma in the Hellenistic World (Third to First Century BC): A Form of Organisation to Integrate Minorities," in *Migration und Integration—wissenschaftliche Perspektiven aus Österreich, Vienna*, ed. Julia Reinprecht Dahlvik, Christoph Wiebke, and Sievers (Göttingen V&R Unipress, 2013); Walter Ruppel, "Politeuma. Bedeutungsgeschichte eines staatsrechtlichen Terminus," *Philologus* 82 (1927); Aryeh Kasher, "The Rights of the Jews of Antioch on the Orontes" (paper presented at the Proceedings of the American Academy for Jewish research, 1982); Gert Lüderitz, "What is the Politeuma?," in *Studies in Early Jewish Epigraphy*, ed. Pieter W. van der Horst and Jan Willem van Henten (Brill, 1994).

10. Sylvie Honigman, "'Politeumata' and Ethnicity in Ptolemaic and Roman Egypt," *Ancient Society* 33 (2003).

11. Ze'ev Safrai, "The Jewish Community in the Talmudic Period," *Jerusalem: The Zalman Shazar Center for Jewish History* (1995): 124–127.

12. (Babylonian Talmud Bava Batra 13a; 7b; Y Pe'ah 1:1 16a).

13. Moshe Weinberg, "Die Organisation der jüdischen Ortsgemeinden in der talmudischen Zeit (Schluss)," *Monatsschrift für Geschichte und Wissenschaft des Judentums*, no. H. 15 (1897); Ze'ev Safrai, "Boundaries and Administration in

Eretz-Israel in the Mishnah and Talmud Period," *Tel Aviv* (1980); Safrai and Stern, "Jewish self-government."

14. Roman Law, Imperatori Theodosiani Codex, Liber Decimus Sextus (CTH 16:8.10).

15. Ritual bath.

16. Jerusalem Talmud (Ketubot 1:10 34a).

17. Levi Yizhaq Rahmani, "A Bilingual Ossuary-Inscription from Khirbet Zif," *Israel Exploration Journal* (1972).

18. (Sanhedrin 3:1).

19. Safrai, "The Jewish Community in the Talmudic Period."

20. (Babylonian Talmud Sanhedrin 66b, Jerusalem Talmud. Kidushin 4:12 17a).

21. (Tosafta Baba Metzia 11.25).

22. (For example, Mishna Gittin 9:8).

23. Jerusalem Talmud Megillah 3.2 74a.

24. The use of the term "social class" is based on the fact that they know one another, help one another, often marry one another. They have a special mode of dress and try to wear elegant clothing despite the fact that they are commoners. They have a shared daily schedule, a unique language (Hebrew|) and mainly shared ethos, shared institutions, a weak internal power structure and additional components.

25. Safrai and Stern, "Jewish self-government"; Ben-Zion Rosenfeld, *Torah Centers and Rabbinic Activity in Palestine, 70-400 CE: History and Geographic Distribution* (Leiden: Brill, 2010).

26. In Egypt and Syria there was an autochthonous culture.

27. Ze'ev Safrai, "The Village in Judea," in *The Village in Judea*, ed. Shimon Dar and Ze'ev Safrai (Tel Aviv: Eretz, 1977).

28. The set of rules of the day-to-day life of a Jew; literally: *the path to walk.*

29. R. Shimon ben Yochai (180-220) is an exceptional sage who is known as a miracles worker as was R. Yehshua b. Levi, who was a sage and a Hasid.

30. William Scott Green and Wolfgang Haase, "Palestinian Holy Men: Charismatic Leadership and Rabbinic Tradition," *Religion (Judentum: Allgemeines; palästinisches Judentum [Forts.])* (1979); Baruch M Bokser, "Wonder-working and the rabbinic tradition: The case of Ḥanina Ben Dosa," *Journal for the Study of Judaism in the Persian, Hellenistic, and Roman Period* 16, no. 1 (1985).

31. Ze'ev Safrai and Chana Safrai, "The Process of the Sages` Takeover of Public Positions," in *Te`uda 25, Israel and the Diaspora in the Time of the Second Temple and the Mishnah" Aryeh Kasher Memorial Volume* (Tel Aviv: Tel Aviv University, 2008); Safrai, "The Jewish Community in the Talmudic Period."

32. "Higher than high," in *Judaism: A Dialogue Between Cultures*, ed. Yossie Turner, et al. (Jerusalem: Magness Press, 2000).

33. Ping-ti Ho, *The Ladder of Success in Imperial China* (New York: Columbia University Press, 1967).

34. Approximately (10-220 C.E.).

35. Jerusalem Talmud Shabat 1:5 12 c.

36. Babylonian Talmud Yevamot 84a.

37. From about 200 to 500 CE.

38. The tradition speaks of two appointments a year, so that the number of those receive the title could not have been more that 60-70 people in one generation.

39. Jerusalem Talmud Sanhedrin 1:1 19a.

40. Jerusalem Talmud Sanhedrin 1:4 19d.

41. Tosafot Shabat. 13(14):2.

42. (Babylonian Talmud Shabat 115a).

43. Gideon Leibson,. "Determing Factors in Herem and Nidui (Ban and Excommunication) During the Tannaitic and Amoraic Periods," *Annual of the Institute for Research in Jewish Law* 2 (1975): 292–345 (Heb.); Gideon Leibson "The Ban and Those Under it: Tannaitic and Amoraic Perspectives" *Shenaton ha-Mishpat ha-Ivri: Annual of the Institute for Research in Jewish Law* 6–7 (1979): 177–202 (Heb.).

44. Mishna Horayot 1:1).

45. (Mishna Hagigah 2:2).

46. For example, determining the calendar was an exclusive mandate of the Patriarch, who formed a court (from among the sages) under his leadership to decide on the issue. As far as the sages are concerned, these decisions are the decisions of sages, and the authority to determine the calendar is theirs (see Y. Rosh. 3:3 48c; Safrai 1994: 247–258).

47. Albeck, *Midrash bereshit rabbah.*

48. (Jerusalem Talmud Hagigah 1:1 76C).

49. Babylonian Talmud Berakhot 16c: 44a; Jerusalem Talmud Sanhedrin 1:4, 14d.

50. Shmuel Klein, Sepher Ha-Yshuv, Dvir Tel Aviv 1939 (He.):156.

51. Leah Rot-Gerson *The Greek Inscriptions from Synagogue in Eretz Israel. Yad Ben-Zvi, Jerusalem* 1997 (Heb.): 172–173.

52. Catherine, Hezser. *The Social Structure of the Rabbinic Movement in Roman Palestine*. Tübingen: Mohr Siebeck, 1997: 405–450; Alon, *Jews, Judaism and the Classical World: Studies in Jewish History in the Times of the Second Temple and Talmud*; Safrai 2010.

53. Mantel, *Studies in the History of the Sanhedrin.*

54. Jerusalem Talmud Horayot 3:5 48b.

55. Jerusalem Talmud Nedarim 1:8, 42b.

56. Goodblatt, *The Monarchic Principle: Studies in Jewish Self-Government in Antiquity.*

57. Yair Lorberbaum, *Disempowered King: Monarchy in Classical Jewish Literature*, vol. 9 (London: Bloomsbury Publishing, 2011).

58. That is the case in the Tannaitic literature. In Amoraitic literature we also find the opinion that even the ideal king can be prosecuted, while those same kings who are not absolutely perfect are likely to oppose the authority of a Beit Din and therefore, they cannot be prosecuted. In other words, there ןs a fear that prosecuting them will end in the failure of the judicial system.

59. Jerusalem Talmud Pesahim 1, 33a.

60. Daniel J. Elazar, *Covenant and Polity in Biblical Israel* (New Brunswick, NJ: Transaction Publishers, 1998).

61. Torah study was not the only religious activity. In the Jewish town there were also additional groups, such as mystics, holy men, biblical scholars who researched

the language and the exact version of the Bible, et al. See, Zeev Safrai, "Jewish Culture Outside of the Study Hall," *JAAJ* 8 (2020): 123–197.

But all these groups in the end accepted the authority of the sages and saw them as the religious leadership that determined the religious norms.

The general public, which naturally was not much preoccupied with Torah study, considered the sages their religious model. See for example Adiel Schremer, "The Religious Orientation of Non-Rabbis in Second-Century Palestine," in *Follow the Wise: Studies in Jewish History and Culture in Honor of Lee I. Levine*, ed. Zeev Weiss, et al. (Winona Lake, IN: Eisenbraun, 2010), 319–341. This final claim is a change in the dispute in the research, and I have expressed my opinion in detail in the abovementioned article.

62. Traditional agriculture in the Land of Israel is dependent on rain, and the amount of rain is unpredictable. In addition, agriculture was a livelihood that involved additional risks.

REFERENCES

Albeck, Chanoch. *Midrash Bereshit Rabbah*. Jerusalem: Wahrmann Books, 1965.

Aliquot, Julien. "Sanctuaries and Villages on Mt Hermon During the Roman Period." In *The Variety of Local Religious Life in the Near East*, edited by Kaizer Tad, 73–96. Leiden: Brill, 2008.

Alon, Gedalyah. *Jews, Judaism and the Classical World: Studies in Jewish History in the Times of the Second Temple and Talmud*. Jerusalem: Magnus Press, Hebrew University, 1977.

Appelbaum, Alan. *The Dynasty of the Jewish Patriarchs*. Tübingen: Mohr Siebeck, 2013.

Baynes, Norman H., and Elsabeth S. A. Dawes. *Three Byzantine Saints: Contemporary Biographies of St. Daniel the Stylite, St. Theodore of Sykeon and St. John the Almsgiver*. London: St Vladimirs Seminary, 1948.

Bokser, Baruch M. "Wonder-Working and the Rabbinic Tradition: The Case of Ḥanina Ben Dosa." *Journal for the Study of Judaism in the Persian, Hellenistic, and Roman Period* 16, no. 1 (1985): 42–92.

Bowman, Alan K. *The Town Councils of Roman Egypt*. Vol. 11, Toronto: Hakkert, 1971.

Cowey, James M. S., and Klaus Maresch. *Urkunden Des Politeuma Der Juden Von Herakleopolis (144/3–133/2 V. Chr.)(P. Polit. Iud.)*. Wiesbaden: Springer-Verlag, 2013.

Efron, Joshua. "The Sanhedrin as an Ideal and as Reality in the Period of the Second Temple." In *Studies of the Hasmonean Period*, edited by Joshua Efron, 250–92. Tel Aviv, 1967.

———. "The Sanhedrin as an Ideal and as Reality in the Period of the Second Temple." *Imanu'el* 2 (1973): 44–49.

Elazar, Daniel J. *Covenant and Polity in Biblical Israel*. New Brunswick, NJ: Transaction Publishers, 1998.

Eshel, Ḥanan, and Boaz Zissu. *The Bar Kokhba Revolt: The Archaeological Evidence*. Jerusalem: Yad Izhak Ben-Zvi, 2019.

Ghadban, Chaker. "Monuments De Hammara (Béqa'-Sud, Liban): Nova Et Vetera." *Ktèma* 10, no. 1 (1985): 287–309.

Goodblatt, David. *The Monarchic Principle: Studies in Jewish Self-Government in Antiquity*. Mohr, 1994.

———. "The Origins of Roman Recognition of the Palestinian Patriarchate." *Studies in the History of the Jewish People and the Land of Israel* 4 (1978): 89–102.

Goodman, Martin. "The Roman State and the Jewish Patriarch in the Third Century." In *The Galilee in Late Antiquity*, edited by Israel L. Levin. New York and Jerusalem: Harvard University Press, 1992.

Grabbe, Lester. "Sanhedrin, Sanhedriyyot, or Mere Invention?" *Journal for the Study of Judaism* 39, no. 1 (2008): 1–19.

Grainger, John D. "'Village Government'in Roman Syria and Arabia." *Levant* 27, no. 1 (1995): 179–95.

Green, William Scott, and Wolfgang Haase. "Palestinian Holy Men: Charismatic Leadership and Rabbinic Tradition." *Religion (Judentum: Allgemeines; palästinisches Judentum [Forts.])* (1979): 619–47.

Habas, Ephrat. "Rabban Gamaliel of Yavneh and His Sons: The Patriarchate Before and After the Bar Kokhva Revolt." *The Journal of Jewish Studies* 50, no. 1 (1999): 21–37.

Hanson, Ann Ellis. "Village Officials at Philadelphia: A Model of Romanization in the Julio-Claudian Period." *Egitto e etoria antiea dall'eLlenismo all'eta amba. Bilancio di 1m confronto* (1989): 432.

Harper, George McLean. "Village Administration in the Roman Province of Syria: A Dissertation Presented to the Faculty of Princeton University in Candidacy for the Degree of Doctor of Philosophy." Princeton University Department of Classics, 1928.

Ho, Ping-ti. *The Ladder of Success in Imperial China*. New York: Columbia University Press, 1967.

Honigman, Sylvie. "'Politeumata' and Ethnicity in Ptolemaic and Roman Egypt." *Ancient Society* 33 (2003): 61–102.

———. "The Jewish Politeuma at Heracleopolis." *Scripta Classica Israelica* 21 (2002): 251–66.

Jacobs, Martin. *Die Institution Des Jüdischen Patriarchen: Eine Quellen-Und Traditionskritische Studie Zur Geschichte Der Juden in Der Spätantike*. Vol. 52. Tübingen: Mohr Siebeck, 1995.

Josephus, Flavius. *The Jewish War*. Middlesex, UK: Harmondsworth, 1955.

Kasher, Aryeh. "No Longer a Historiographic Legend: New Papyri From a Forgotten Jewish Politeuma in Ptolemaic Egypt." *Tarbiz* 72, nos. 1–2 (2003): 5–36.

———. "The Rights of the Jews of Antioch on the Orontes." Paper Presented at the Proceedings of the American Academy for Jewish Research, 1982.

Langellotti, Micaela. *Village Life in Roman Egypt: Tebtunis in the First Century Ad*. Oxford: Oxford University Press, 2020.

Leṿin, Israel L. "The Status of the Patriarch in the Third and Fourth Centuries: Sources and Methodology." *The Journal of Jewish Studies* 47, no. 1 (1996): 1–32.

Levine, Lee I. "The Emergence of the Patriarchate in the Third Century." In *Envisioning Judaism: Studies in Honor of Peter Schäfer on the Occasion of His Seventieth Birthday*, edited by Raanan S. R. S. Boustan and Peter Schäfer, 235–63. Tubingen: Mohr-Siebeck, 2013.

Linder, Amnon *The Jews in Roman Imperial Legislation.* Edited by Israel The National Academy of Science. Detroit: Wayne State University Press, 1987.

Lorberbaum, Yair. *Disempowered King: Monarchy in Classical Jewish Literature.* Vol. 9. London: Bloomsbury Publishing, 2011.

Lüderitz, Gert. "What Is the Politeuma?" In *Studies in Early Jewish Epigraphy*, edited by Pieter W. van der Horst and Jan Willem van Henten, 183–224. Leiden: Brill, 1994.

Łukaszewicz, Adam. *Les Édifices Publics Dans Les Villes De L'égypte Romaine: Problèmes Administratifs Et Financiers.* Warsaw: Wydawnictwo Uniwersytetu Warszawskiego, 2018.

MacAdam, Henry Innes. "Studies in the History of the Roman Province of Arabia." The University of Manchester, 1979.

Macnaghten, A. H. "Local Administration in Egypt under Roman Rule, Fourth to Sixth Centuries Ad: The Element of Corruption." University of St Andrews, 1993.

Mantel, Hugo. *Studies in the History of the Sanhedrin.* Leiden: Brill, 2020.

Popović, Mladen. *The Jewish Revolt Against Rome: Interdisciplinary Perspectives.* Leiden: Brill, 2011.

Prentice, William Kelly. "Officials Charged With the Conduct of Public Works in Roman and Byzantine Syria." Paper Presented at the Transactions and Proceedings of the American Philological Association, 1912.

Rahmani, Levi Yizhaq. "A Bilingual Ossuary-Inscription From Khirbet Zif." *Israel Exploration Journal* (1972): 113–16.

Rey-Coquais, J. P. "Villages Du Liban Et De La Syrie Moyenne (De Dams Au Coude De L'oronte)." In *L'epigrafia Del Villaggio*, edited by Alda Calbi, Amgela Donati, and Gabriela Poma, 137–49. Faenza, 1993.

Rosenfeld, Ben-Zion. *Torah Centers and Rabbinic Activity in Palestine, 70–400 CE: History and Geographic Distribution.* Leiden: Brill, 2010.

Ruffini, Giovanni R. *Life in an Egyptian Village in Late Antiquity: Aphrodito Before and After the Islamic Conquest.* Cambridge: Cambridge University Press, 2018.

Ruppel, Walter. "Politeuma. Bedeutungsgeschichte Eines Staatsrechtlichen Terminus." *Philologus* 82 (1927): 268.

Safrai, Shmuel, and Menachem Stern. "Jewish Self-Government." In *The Jewish People in the First Century*, Vol. 1, 377–419. Leiden: Brill, 1974.

Safrai, Zeev. "Boundaries and Administration in Eretz-Israel in the Mishnah and Talmud Period." *Tel Aviv* (1980): 71.

———. "Higher Than High." In *Judaism: A Dialogue Between Cultures*, edited by Yossie Turner, Avi Sagi, Dudi Schwartz, and Yedidia Stern, 219–34. Jerusalem: Magness Press, 2000.

———. "The Jewish Community in the Talmudic Period." [In Hebrew]. *Jerusalem: The Zalman Shazar Center for Jewish History* (1995).

———. "The Village in Judea." In *The Village in Judea*, edited by Shimon Dar and Zeev Safrai. Tel Aviv: Eretz, 1977.

Safrai, Zeev, and Chana Safrai. "The Process of the Sages Takeover of Public Positions." In *Te`Uda 25, Israel and the Diaspora in the Time of the Second Temple and the Mishnah" Aryeh Kasher Memorial Volume*. Tel Aviv: Tel Aviv University, 2008.

Sänger, Patrick. "The Politeuma in the Hellenistic World (Third to First Century BC): A Form of Organisation to Integrate Minorities." In *Migration Und Integration—Wissenschaftliche Perspektiven Aus Österreich, Vienna*, edited by Julia Reinprecht Dahlvik, Christoph Wiebke, and Sievers, 51–68. Göttingen V&R Unipress, 2013.

Sartre, Maurice. "Communautés Villageoises Et Structures Sociales D'après L'épigraphie De La Syrie Du Sud." *L'epigrafia del villaggio, Faenza* 127 (1993).

Schremer, Adiel. "The Religious Orientation of Non-Rabbis in Second-Century Palestine." In *Follow the Wise: Studies in Jewish History and Culture in Honor of Lee I. Levine*, edited by Weiss Zeev, Irshai Oded, Magness Jodi, and Seth Schwartz, 319. Winona Lake, IN: Eisenbraun, 2010.

Stern, Sacha. "Rabbi and the Origins of the Patriarchate." *Journal of Jewish Studies* 54, no. 2 (2003): 193–215.

Verhoogt, Arthur M. F. W., and Sven Peter Vleeming. *The Two Faces of Graeco-Roman Egypt*. Vol. 30. Leiden: Brill, 1998.

Weinberg, Moshe. "Die Organisation Der Jüdischen Ortsgemeinden in Der Talmudischen Zeit (Schluss)." *Monatsschrift für Geschichte und Wissenschaft des Judentums*, no. H. 15 (1897): 673–91.

Zuckerman, Constantin. "Du Village À L'empire: Autour Du Registre Fiscal D'aphroditô (525/526)." In *Centre de Recherche d'Histoire et Civilisation de Byzance. Monographies 16*. Paris: Peeters, 2005.

Chapter 3

Jewish Communities of the Diaspora

Joseph Livni

An earlier study listed four essential categories explaining the Judaic spiritual system:[1]

1. Monotheism
2. Covenant
3. Prophetism
4. Messianism

By definition, the Covenant is the common fundamental feature of all covenantal societies. In the particular case of Jewish covenantal communities, the Covenant consists of fundamental laws decreed by the Torah and the Talmud; they covered all aspects of social life and "contributed to shaping the Jewish identity, representing sources of power, an example of survival in Exile and Diaspora."[2] This aspect is relevant to the topic of this volume; it is found repeatedly in all other covenantal organizations and therefore is the topic of this chapter.

The chapter focuses on the Diaspora from its very beginning (sixth century BCE) until the Enlightenment. This modern intellectual movement modernized Jewish sociology, identity, and culture triggering changes known as *emancipation*. Among others, the emancipation brought to surface the tension between *individual equality* and the traditional community autonomy.[3]

The Jewish community life changed after the emancipation. The process is outside scope for the purpose of this chapter; however it is well documented both as far as Sephardic and Ashkenazi Western communities are concerned.[4]

OPPOSITION TO HIERARCHY

Opposition to hierarchy should not be understood as resistance to host monarchs and their hierarchy. Before the Enlightenment the Jewish Diaspora lived within a hierarchic world. Jews accepted the ruler of the host country according to the Jewish statute affirming that the law of the kingdom is the law (*dina de malchuta dina*).[5] The opposition to hierarchy was exercised within the Jewish Autonomous Administration (see section *Assembly Government*).

The Jewish Diaspora did feature sometimes and in some places a prominent personality that could be erroneously seen as top of a hierarchy. For example we find functions such as *constable*, *head of the community* (rosh hakahal[6]), *Presbyter*,[7] *Hachambasha*,[8] *Jewish bishop*,[9] *Magister Judaeorum*, and so on.[10] These functions existed because of the hierarchic spirit of the host empires (Byzantine, Ottoman, Czarist Russia, etc.).[11] The imperial administrations needed a designated leader to represent communities and the office was created accordingly. For example the official head of congregation in Alexandria (tenth–thirteenth centuries) was recognized by the governor and by the chief of police. Nevertheless, as typically was the case, his authority was limited: "He had to have the approval, confidence, and cooperation of the people; otherwise he faced dissent and even dismissal."[12]

For example in Candia (Venetian Crete) job description of the "constable" reminds of chairing a session rather than top of hierarchy.[13]

COVENANT

As described earlier the Jewish Diaspora has opposed political hierarchy. Nevertheless, it has functioned within a constitutional authority in which one finds a hierarchy of covenantal statutes (figure 3.1). The Mishnah describes how the Covenant, the fundamental source of authority, constituted the first link of a hierarchical chain of constitutional decrees each deriving its authority from its predecessor: "Moses received the Torah from Sinai and transferred it to Joshua; Joshua to the Elders; the Elders to the Prophets; and the Prophets transferred it to the members of the Great Assembly."[14]

The Mishnah itself foresees further links to this chain by authorizing directives decreed to "make a fence around the Torah."[15] According to Maimonides this directive has been interpreted as an authority to sanction later edicts (*gezeiroth*), statutes (*takkanoth*,[16] *chazakot*,[17] *haskamot*,[18]*responsa*[19]). The authority was given on condition that the decrees move people away from transgression.[20]

The nature of takkanot ha-kahal inevitably implies that many of the statutes are collective works, whose validity is conditioned by the consensus

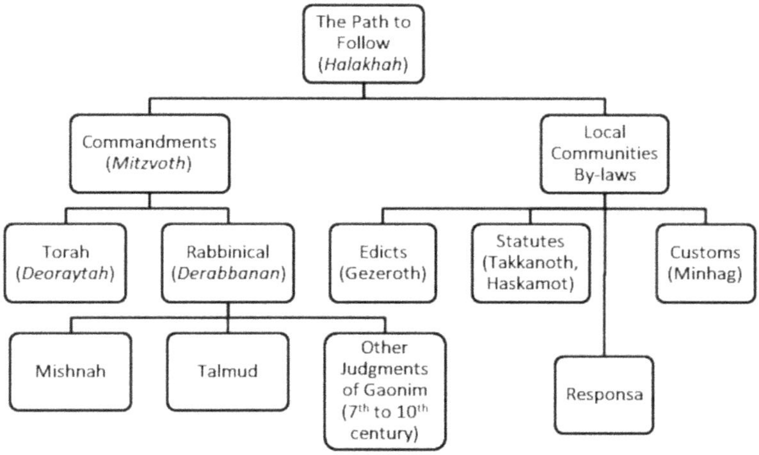

Figure 3.1 Hierarchy of Jewish Covenantal Legal System (Halakhah). *Source*: Prepared by the author.

of a larger body of communal representatives, for example, in takkanot of Kandia[21] and of Fez.[22] Even if in practice the council acted without consulting the community at large, the very pretention that they express "the words of the congregation" proves that the congregation at large was the source of authority.

These regulations did not supersede Halakha or any anteriorly edicts of Covenant. They regulated specific community tasks; for example one finds *takkanot* which regulate the appointment and conduct of synagogue cantors, particularities of marital law,[23] the appointment of the "bridegrooms of the Torah,"[24] and the economic life.[25] Life in diaspora created friction with the host population. Some decrees provided instructions of behavior in order "to give no reason to non-Jews for complaints or disregard for Jewish prayer practices."[26] We also find rules of ethics for justices "to recuse themselves in cases of conflicts of interest."[27]

FEDERATIVE NETWORK

In larger cities several communities coexisted. Frequently one found coexisting communities because of divergence in sects. For example in medieval Alexandria and Fustat (eleventh century) there were three congregations: Jerusalemite, Babylonian, and Karaite.[28] In fifteenth-century Rome, there were Italian, German, French, Castilian, Aragonese, and Catalan congregations.[29] In Fez, Morocco "the King of Fez and the native Fez Jews welcome the Castilian emigres and permitted them to establish in Fez a separate Jewish community, with its own laws and institutions."[30] In fifteenth-century Istanbul, there were also congregations organized according to the country or province of origin such as Ashkenaz, Hungary, Calbria, Castilia, Aragon, and Portugal.[31] In Salonica (fifteenth to seventeenth centuries) there were three congregations: Sephardic, Ashkenazi, and Romaniotes.[32] In the seventeenth century, Amsterdam had two congregations: Sephardi and Ashkenazi. These two congregations were found in several cities of Europe, for example, Bucharest (fifteenth after sixteenth century),[33] Alba Iulia (1591 and later),[34] Budapest (starting in 1461),[35] and Belgrade (thirteenth–fourteenth-century Ashkenazi, fifteenth-century Sephardi).[36] The congregations managed their affairs autonomously, "as each were a city onto itself."[37]

The various local and regional communities were linked in regional networks, The sphere of jurisdiction of these councils was called *galil* (e.g., Moravia and Western Hungary).[38]

A network of several *galil* councils was sometimes called *medina*. The *medina council* mostly dealt with negotiating with the host ruler. For example:

a) The *medina* of Moravia "encompassed three districts."[39]
b) In the three principalities of Romania there was an "extended network for obtaining and transmitting information necessary for the expanding Ottoman Empire."[40]
c) Similarly in Thessaloniki there was a federation, known as *kolel de la sivdad* (collective of the city), in order to represent their interests to the Ottoman state.[41]
d) In Lithuania a Council of Lithuania[42] managed inter-community affairs.
e) In Poland there was a Council of Four Lands (Greater Poland, Little Poland, Galicia incl. Podolia and Volhynia).[43]

JUSTICE ADMINISTRATION

One of the specific features of covenantal society is their capability to autonomously administer justice.[44] This attribute explains the autonomy conferred to the communities by non-Jewish rulers. Needless to say this capability was essential to the resilience of the communities. At the same time, it was advantageous to the host governments. Since one essential task of every government is justice,[45] it was easier to govern a population if one could delegate a great part of this burden to the communities. "Seventy percent of rulings made in pre-Emancipation communities dealt with commercial, civil, and even criminal cases."[46]

Almost every community established its judicial court (*beyt-din*).[47] However sometimes Jews requested non-Jewish tribunals because "law is one thing and life is another."[48]

The general rule in Jewish Communities was that "turning to a Gentile court on the same level as informing to the authorities (*'malshinut,' 'mesirah'*) and threatened the transgressor with excommunication and ostracism."[49] Several community leaders (e.g., Rashi of Troyes and Moses Isserless of Krakow) forbade adjudication before non-Jewish courts. We learn that this *haskama* was overridden in certain communities (e.g., Istanbul) under the *halakha* declaring that the law of the kingdom is the law *dina de-malchuta dina.* In Salonika, turning to non-Jewish courts "was less widespread, perhaps due to the firmness and solidarity of the Jewish community in that city." In 1770 in Altona, Hamburg, a dispute between Rabbi Jacob Emden and Rabbi Jonathan Eybeshutz was adjudicated by the king of Denmark because "no Jewish power could resolve the issue."[50] In Frankfurt am Main of the early seventeenth century the community lost confidence in its board of office holders, locally known as the *Havura of the Ten.* The office holders strayed into oligarchic direction; the foreseeable "communal unrest"[51] called for adjudication. However, the nature of the conflict worked against the cohesion forces within the community and the mediation ended up in Imperial and later municipal tribunals.[52] Another relevant situation came up when the community decided to dismiss its Rabbi. As in the previous case such a situation can only occur in a reversed dominance hierarchy. The Rabbi had no chance to win in the Jewish court (*beyt-din*) precisely because in the Jewish tradition the community hires and fires the Rabbi. Not surprisingly in the Rabbi's judgment the rabbinical tradition regarding *mesirah* and *malshinut* lost validity and the Rabbi Hersz Lejbowitz of Miedzyboz (1776) turned to Polish administrators for protection.[53]

High-intensity peer pressure was the only means of enforcing decisions of council. For example in the Ashkenazi shtetl[54] of Eastern Europe:

> A force which was operative in the shtetl but which has disappeared from Jewish life today is the pressure from public opinion[55]
>
> . . .
>
> The kehila[56] knew very well that it could not enforce its decisions, but it acted as though it could.[57]

As a consequence unpopular decisions had no chance of survival. Nevertheless, warranted decisions were imposed because the community exerted peer pressure and consequential punitive actions. For lesser offenses the community imposed fines,[58] and accepted public repentance through apologies.[59] One cannot neglect the power of community to honor the righteous or treat with disrespect the wicked. The Sabbath reading of the Torah generated a traditional opportunity to honor or disregard individuals.[60] Every call to read the Torah *(aliyah)* is an honor. The third and sixth calls to read the Torah (third and sixth *aliyoth*) are considered more prestigious than any other *aliyah*.[61] When other considerations are not present (donors, Bar-Mitzva, or bridegroom before wedding) the *aliyoth* and their sequence are naturally according to an unpublished scale of honors within the community. The wicked is called up rarely if at all.

This ritual and other traditions like "spreading the word" generated a scale of honor within the community. The power of this reputation scale went beyond rituals. It had an impact on the capability to do business, get loans, or success in matchmaking.

> The [matchmaker] shadchan considers the prospective bride and groom's character, interests, modesty, adherence to halakha, scholarship, family reputation, and any other relevant factor to create a good match.[62]

The Jewish town's reputation scale was analogous to a modern-day service of credit rating and/or of security clearance.

The pressure didn't spare office holders. They were subject to losing their status.[63]

Criminal offenses that jeopardize or harm the entire community were punishable with the most severe consequences like long time banishment or excommunication.

> [Excommunication was] a punishment for criminal offenses whose main thrust was to ostracize a person from Jewish society, isolating him and preventing him from having any religious, social, or communal relationship with his fellow Jews. In a small, closed religious society, such as Jewish society in the Middle Ages, this was a severe punishment, and it would not be an exaggeration to say it was even more severe than imprisonment, common today.[64]

Communities had to overcome defiance from within. Criticism against the community was somewhat tolerated, however unconcealed and remorseless rupture with the community could lead to excommunication, as was the case of Baruch Spinoza in Amsterdam in 1656.[65] Similarly, blatant offense against the edict of Rabbi Gershom (Mainz, c. 960–1040) prohibiting polygamy was punishable by excommunication;[66] hence the edict is prevalently called the *Ban of Rabbi Gershom*. Needless to say communities had to deal with external dangers; the threat of excommunication served as protection from repercussions from outside due to offenses against the Crown, such as dealing with fake coins.[67]

ASSEMBLY GOVERNMENT

The existence of Jewish self-government outside the Land of Israel has a long history. We know very little about the first Babylonian exile (587–539 BCE) and the source is mostly biblical: "Alongside priests and prophets, elders took up leadership positions and perhaps were able to build up limited self-government."[68]

The Persian rule followed the Babylonian exile period. Counterintuitively, the Jewish self-government gained momentum both in Persian Babylon and in the Land of Israel.[69] There is extra-biblical evidence of Jewish self-rule in Persian Yehud:

> This is not to suggest that Judah was not an autonomous entity with a series of governors already in the beginning of the Achaemenid[70] Period[71] and perhaps even earlier.[72] But signs of autonomy such as the minting of Yehud coins and standardized Aramaic stamp-seal impressions on local storage-jar handles, whether connected to the Judahite administrative authority or more likely simply to be explained as potter's marks,[73] probably did not appear before the fourth century.[74]

The following Hellenistic and Roman conquerors maintained the autonomy of the Jews in Judea.[75]The chapter of Zeev Safrai of this volume entitled "Power structure within Autonomy in Roman Palestine" treats precisely this period.

The next important Jewish existence outside the Land of Israel is in Ptolemaic Egypt of the second century BCE both in Heracleopolis and in Alexandria. The testimony is extra-biblical and it consists of a library of papyri. The Jewish communities shaped "a pattern providing the Jews with complete internal autonomy;"[76] these communities were called *politeuma.*

The pattern has been conserved for later Diaspora.

> As early as during the period of Frederick I Barbarossa (1152–1190), the Jews in the area of the Holy Roman Empire, meaning most of the Slovenian lands as well, were directly subordinate to the ruler and as such were designated as "servants of the Royal Chamber" (*servi camerae regis*).[77] Jewish servitude "(*Kammerknechtsschaft*)," though, despite the use of the term *servus* didn't imply classical servitude or vassalage, but rather only a direct subordination to the ruler, as Jews in fact represented a separate social class/estate.[78]

Similarly communal assemblies administered Jewish Communities all along the pre-emancipation period, for example, the semi-autonomous representative bodies of Prague (1254),[79] Candia (Venetian Crete—sixteenth century),[80] Venice (sixteenth century),[81] Istanbul (sixteenth century),[82] and Vilna.[83]

There were several reasons for princes to delegate government responsibilities to the communities. One finds, for example, the following grounds:

1. *Income to the rulers*—For example in England "for most of the thirteenth century the Jews were a regular source of royal revenue."[84] Later in the Polish-Lithuanian state:

   > Three parallel historical processes contributed to the formation of Jewish autonomy in the Polish-Lithuanian Commnwealth. . . . The first process was a by-product of the fiscal reforms that the commomwealth underwent, starting in the early sixteenth century. The purpose of the reform was to provide a steady income for the growing number of military units that were engaged in a seemingly endless series of wars.[85]

2. *Simplifying tax collection and/or keeping internal peace*—In Roman Palestine "Jewish autonomy generally extended beyond such matters as preserving civil order locally and collecting taxes."[86] The government of the host kingdoms preferred not to individually assess Jews. It was simpler to assess a whole community and let the community deal with assessing and collecting the tax. For example in Poland "[T]he Concil of Four Lands was created around 1580–1581 mainly for the purpose of collecting the Jewish poll tax (*poglowne żydowskie*)."[87] In the Ottoman Empire which held important Iberian Sephardic communities (e.g., Istanbul, Safed, Palestine, and Saloniki, Greece) and some Ashkenazi and Italian communities (Istanbul), "the communities were obliged to ensure the orderly payment of the taxes and other dues levied by the central and local authorities."[88]
3. *Funding rulers for financing occasional needs*—In Bohemia of the thirteenth century we learn:

   > Following the model of Hungarian King Bela IV's Jewish laws of 1251, King Premysl Otakar II issued his Royal Charter for the Jews in 1254. The charter contained the usual business legalisms: The Jews were protected as money lenders and as servants of the king, and were required to pay high taxes as well as supply occasional loans to the royal treasury.[89]

In Vilna (1797) the kahal was accused that it "undercounted the number of Jews so as to decrease the Jewish tax bill; underreported the amount of tax monies collected from the Jews; appropriated."[90]

The community government instituted houses of worship, schools, and guidelines of behavior among Jews; and with non-Jews (see section *Institutions*), it was in charge of family life and events and records (weddings, divorce, bar-mitzvah, burials, and mourning). The community government disputed and settled internal conflicts; it detected, adjudicated, and punished transgressions including criminal cases as well (see "Justice Administration"). The detection of social deviation was achieved by mutual watching of each individual. Chapter "The Covenant as Ideal Type" of Mădălina Mândiță refers to Weber pointing out that the individuals were "jointly responsible for one another."[91]

OFFICE HOLDERS

Assembly government means that in all public affairs the community directs, supervises, detects non-conformities, and guides corrective actions. That said, the community consists of people who make a living and very few actively participate in the actual execution of tasks such as hiring or firing rabbis, education, synagogue building and maintenance, collecting and administering taxes and finances,[92] library, burials, and running institutions supervising dietary rules.[93] These tasks were carried out by office holders starting from biblical times when they were called *elders*.

The non-hierarchic character of this arrangement consisted of the fact "that no office was held for life, much less could it be passed from father to son. This was true for elected leaders, as it was for paid functionaries."[94]

The elders carried out administrative tasks as instructed and agreed by the community:[95]

> It will be the constable's duty to] choose seven renowned men among the community's eminent men, and let them swear on the Torah scroll to be prepared and duly appointed to administer and uphold all that the community instructs and charges them [to do] in all the matters concerning our community.[96]

The term elder is ambiguous not only in Jewish or covenantal context but also in other tradition-based societies such as Aboriginal People of Canada: "we have misused the role of elder through our ignorance and failure to see that not all elders are teachers, not all elders are spiritual leaders and not all old people are elders."[97]

The term *elder* therefore designates experience, wisdom, and most importantly traditional continuity. They were sometimes elected by the congregation[98] and sometimes nominated;[99] therefore I would not describe the Jewish communities of the Diaspora using the term democracy. Another study of First Nations of Canada offers a well-defined explanation how eldership was acquired in the Jewish Diaspora as well:

> Elders are not born, they are not appointed, they emerge as the sum total of the experiences of life, they are a state of being. The category of "Elder" as described by individuals in this section is special because there are few older

> people available who are willing to take on the responsibilities of an Elder, the responsibility to teach correctly about tradition and the good life, and who have the necessary knowledge.[100]

In other words one becomes an elder if one follows tradition, one has experience, one participates at assembly debates, and one carries out daily tasks. Eldership comes to an end when the elder loses the confidence of the community in these capabilities.

The title of elders varied in time and location; very rarely the designation was more clarifying than the term elder. In Venetian Crete they were still called *elders* or *seven renowned men*.[101] Many Spanish and Portuguese called the council of elders "ma'amad."[102] The term *parnasim* is shared by both Sephardi and Ashkenazi Jews.[103] In the Romanian Principality of Moldavia we found the Slavic term *staroste* which means *elder*.[104] In the Ottoman Empire we find the Hebrew term *memunim* (appointed).[105] Not surprisingly, in Jewish communities of Roman Egypt the term was *presbyteroi*,[106] which is also the designation of the same function in Early Christian communities (see also chapter 3 of this book). Another term in Roman Egyptian Jewish communities was *archontes*.[107] The Hebrew term in Roman Palestine *tovei hair* means the good men of the town.[108] In Frankfurt am Main the council was called *Havura* or *the Ten*.[109]

INSTITUTIONS

Synagogue

Needless to say the term synagogue has Hellenistic roots. It is found in the Septuagint, the oldest known translation of the Torah (Pentateuch).[110] However, the Torah never mentions dedicated houses of prayers. Consequently, the term synagogue meant assembly,[111] congregation or the whole federation of Israel (see section *Federative Network*). For example in Exodus 12:47 the Hebrew text undoubtedly talks about the whole nation of Israel and the Septuagint translates it to the term *synagogue*. The term designated originally a Judean institution "dealing with their political, liturgical, social, educational, judicial, and spiritual challenges."[112] The institution had many alternative designations[113] among others ecclesia which originally also meant the people's assembly, for example, in democratic Athens.[114] The term *proseuche* is a more appropriate term used in the beginning of the Diaspora meaning *the house of worship*.[115] The term synagogue has been used by non-Jews and currently it is widely used by American Jews to designate *house of prayer*. However, the early Diaspora Jews rarely used the term. Instead they used other terms.[116]

Communities were in charge to build,[117] acquire,[118] and maintain[119] their house of prayer. The house of worship also served as meeting house, as school,[120] and as corrective institution. "It was there that warnings were issued, decrees of excommunications pronounced, and oaths taken, and it was exclusion from the synagogue that constituted the punishment for the disobedient."[121]

The term "meeting house" hints that the house of worship was originally a community center where assemblies were held.[122] It is not surprising that prohibition of secular talk "remained somewhat vague."[123] The fact that there are special sections of the liturgy where such talk is prohibited proves this point.[124] I mention this issue in order to clarify that in covenantal societies public administration, religion, and tradition are bound together. The question whether the synagogue was a house of worship also serving for public administration, or was it a community center also serving for prayers can be endlessly debated. Not surprisingly, American puritans also called their house of prayer meeting house.

The meeting house was in the midst of the Jewish quarter. Some Jewish quarters were called *Ghetto*, see figure 3.2; a *ghetto* was a neighborhood where Jewish inhabitants were restricted to live and consequently segregated from non-Jews.

However, even when they were not obliged, Jews chose to live walking distance from the prayer house because Jewish law forbids driving or riding on the Sabbath day. Consequently, they resided in predominantly Jewish neighborhoods called *Juderia* in Spain, see figure 3.3, or *Mellah* in

Figure 3.2 Rome, Ghetto, Arco delle Azimelle by Ettore Roesler Franz. Public domain.

Figure 3.3 Juderia, Girona, Spain—Street in an ancient Jewish Quarter. *Source*: Photo taken by the author.

Morocco, see figure 3.4. In central Europe there are streets called Jewish Street, for example, Judengasse in Salzburg and Židovská ulica in Ljubljana and Bratislava.

In Eastern Europe many Jews lived in small towns called *shtetl* where the population was mainly Jewish,[125] see figure 3.5.

Rabbi

The term *rabbi* has three meanings belonging to three separate institutions:

1. Rabbi—as scholar
2. Rabbi—as community minister
3. Rabbi—as Chief Rabbi

Rabbi—the scholar—The covenantal society is regulated by Scripture (see section *Covenant*). Everyday life creates friction, challenges, and difficulties that need answers according to the ordinances of the Scripture. Chapter 2 "Power structure within Autonomy in Roman Palestine" of Safrai explains how in Roman Palestine dedicated institutions of sages provided answers to practical questions. With a great amount of lenience one could offer an

Figure 3.4 Mellah, Casablanca, Morocco. Public domain.

Figure 3.5 Lubaczynska Street, shtetl of Lachva, Belarus. Public domain.

analogy to current-day research institutes or even to services of customer support. This tradition was maintained all along the Diaspora.

Rabbi—the community minister—This institution also traces its roots to Roman Palestine. As described by Safrai in chapter 2 "Power structure within Autonomy in Roman Palestine" sages started a tradition of discussing the weekly portion of the Torah at the meeting house (synagogue) of the community. In the Diaspora the community Rabbi continued this tradition. Rabbis were hired,[126] and possibly fired,[127] by community councils, thus subordinate to community government and became involved in many practical aspects of the Jewish life. The rabbi sometimes was called *Marbitz Torah*,[128] *doctor scholae*, *senior scholae*, or *episcopus Iudaeorum*.[129]

His job description included:

1. Mediation of property-related disputes between Jews and non-Jews[130]
2. Declaring an anathema[131]
3. Managing the school[132]
4. Make decisions regarding the *halakha*[133]
5. Judging disputes[134]
6. Officiate weddings[135]
7. Issuing divorce certificates[136]
8. Guiding Jewish Institutions (see section *Other Community Institutions*)

Chief Rabbi—As explained in chapter 2 "Power structure within Autonomy in Roman Palestine" of this volume the term *Rabbi* with no references to a particular name designates one historic figure namely Rabbi Judah the Patriarch, who functioned as the head of the Jewish population of Roman Palestine (c. 190–220).

The Romans were a hierarchic society and they extended their hierarchic methods of administration across all the provinces including Palestine. They delegated the power of representation of the communities to one dominant principal. The Patriarch therefore linked two worlds: the hierarchy of the Roman rulers and the covenantal Jewish network of communities that he represented. By being the sole representative of the Jewish communities he possessed power, privileges, and prestige; on the other hand the patriarch was a member of the council of sages, he was appointed by this council and "it is not clear to what exactly he was appointed, and whether he had real powers or whether it was an honorary title only."[137]

In later times hierarchic rulers of the host state also dealt with similar functions of sole representatives of the Jewish Communities. For example the Ottoman Sultans designated a position of Hachambasha in territories such as Baghdad,[138] Syria,[139]Yemen,[140] Kurdistan,[141] Moldavia,[142] and Bosnia.[143] In later years this function has been called Chief Rabbi. It is important to distinguish the title from hierarchic Church titles such as Pope, Cardinal, or Archbishop. The Chief Rabbi represented the Jewish communities in the non-Jewish world. Within the Jewish world his rabbinical prestige was according to his expertise in Halakha and tradition:

> Various Jewish communities, however, have seen practical advantages of having a chief rabbi even though, technically speaking, the religious authority of all rabbis is equal. The need, moreover, for some kind of national Jewish authority has often been recognized by both Jews and governments to protect Jewish interests and facilitate relations between non-Jewish governments and large Jewish populations. Sometimes Jews resented appointments by secular authorities when the choice seemed to have been made with a desire to manipulate the Jewish community.[144]

The function of representing a community, a regional or provincial council was not always carried out by Rabbis. Some communities had a function called *shtadlan* (intercessor); people with special negotiating skills (which are not necessarily acquired by rabbinical studies) carried out this function.[145]

Other Community Institutions

Charity—An investigation of Livni and Stone teaches that charity is not only a nice-to-have tradition in a covenantal structure but it is essential to its survival.[146] The work is mathematical; however the explanation of this discovery consists of the fact that even righteous individuals may become susceptible to transgression under conditions of absolute misery. The hierarchical society can isolate such individuals in prisons; however the covenantal community cannot. Therefore the institution of *gmilut hasadim* (loving kindness) had to exist in all communities not only in the ones evidence by records.[147]

Ritual slaughter—Dietary rules are a unique attribute to the Jewish covenantal societies described in this volume. That said, there are other religions prohibiting certain foods, for example, Islam and Hinduism. Jews not only prohibit certain foods, but also have ordinances specifying the rules of qualification of a ritual slaughterer (*shohet*) and how to verify the fitness of an animal for food and how to slaughter the animal. The communities of the Diaspora were in charge of maintaining ritual slaughter houses and employ certified slaughterers (*shohatim*).[148]

Burial service—In most places the institute in charge of burial services was called *Chevra Kadisha.* It is not surprising that one finds many records mentioning this institute. In Prague where the earliest record of Jewish existence dates to 960, the *Chevra Kadisha* was "modernized" in about 1564.[149] Before sharing taxation (1622), Jewish burial services were already shared by the three congregations of Amsterdam.[150] The existence of a burial society in Salonica is attested by records.[151]

The earliest known Jewish community of Romania was established in Alba Iulia in 1625;[152] its *Chevra Kadisha* was established in 1645.[153] In Oradea, Romania, the records attest to 68 members of the *Chevra Kadisha* established in 1781.[154] Finally, a detailed coverage of the structure, activity, and traditions of the *Chevra Kadisha* of Miskolc, Hungary is offered by Lupovitch.[155]

Ritual bath (mikveh) is an ancient institution and as consequence it was omnipresent: in Crete,[156] in Romania,[157] in Habani communities of Yemen,[158] in Afghanistan,[159] and in Georgia.[160] Women were not ruled out as managers of the ritual bath.[161] The oldest known mikveh of Europe is found in Syracuse, Sicily, Italy; Jews arrived to Sicily before Christianity, see figure 3.6.

Education—The term *am-haaaretz* means *the people of the land,* it is found in the Bible and it is a designation of a social status, "but whether the term denotes a defined institution with specific functions, or a political, economic, and social stratum is subject of divergent opinions among biblical scholars."[162] However, in the later Talmudic literature the term turned to designate an *ignoramus*.[163] This label entered the colloquial jargon of the Jewish street. Needless to say, it was a demeaning title and within the communities parents made an effort to guide their offspring away from it. As a matter of fact, with the apparition of the Pharisees (200 BCE) the trend in Palestine was "ensuring that all male Jewish children and adults could read the Torah (in Hebrew) in front of the Jewish community in the synagogue."[164] The tradition to call up the Bar-mitzvah child (on his thirteenth birthday) to read the Torah in the synagogue served among others as public confirmation that the parents carried out their implied duty to educate their child.

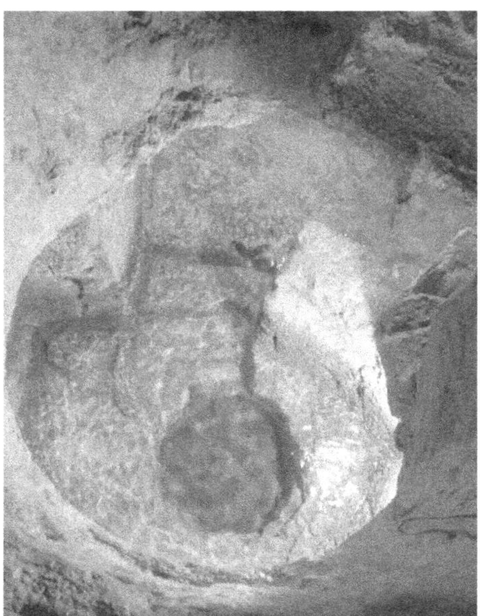

Figure 3.6 Mikveh of Syracuse, Italy. Public Domain, Credit Di CunctatorSr - CC BY-SA 4.0.

Therefore the institution of education was omnipresent leaving testimonial records in Sephardic, Ashkenazi, Italian, and other communities.[165] Some communities held a library.[166]

Tuition started early; children were introduced to the Hebrew alphabet as early as three.[167] There were no formal classes; children changed study groups according to their proficiency. Nevertheless, based on ancient accounts,[168] Goelman reconstructs a blueprint of Jewish education: at age five one studies the Bible, at age ten the Mishnah, and at age fifteen the Gemarrah:

> Where comprehension of the Bible appeared to depend largely on understanding the story line of the narrative, comprehension of the Mishnah demands that the child be able, in ibn Mahiri's words,[169] "to understand these texts on his own, independently, whenever he might need to."[170]

Assistance to the sick—The institution was called in most communities *Bikur Holim* and it was established in almost all the communities.[171] Its mission consisted of taking the sick to a doctor or to a hospital, visiting the sick, praying for the sick at the Sabbath service (*mi-she-beyrach for the sick*), and helping the family of the sick.

Taxation–Individuals paid taxes to the community and the community paid taxes to the host country.[172] The tax was imposed according to the capability of each household. The taxes were used for the expenses of the community and for taxes of the host Ruler.

RESILIENCE OF JEWISH COMMUNITIES

Is the Jewish Diaspora a success story? Some scholars investigate the reasons for its success:

> annual, weekly and daily rituals meant to inscribe the pollution–purification narrative contributed to the adaptive success of the Israelite cultural assemblage over the course of two millennia.[173]

This chapter also hints at success: two millennia of Jewish self-government, of opposing hierarchic elites, of a national network across the Old world, of managing justice, education, meeting house, poverty, and sickness assistance.

I propose to quantify the success of these communities by measuring their chance of survival. For this purpose demography comes to the rescue. In the year 100 CE there were about 3.8–4 million Jews in the world.[174] In 1825, at the beginning of the emancipation, there were 3.3 million Jews in the world.[175] The periods of eleventh to fourteenth century and the sixteenth to eighteenth century were periods of record growth rates of the pre-industrial world.[176] The population of England grew from 3.1 million to 7 million between the years 1501 and 1800[177] which amounts to a growth rate of 0.28 percent/year. Since this expresses a high growth rate for a pre-industrial population, one can conservatively consider one-third of this rate or .093 percent/year as a reasonable growth rate. Accordingly, in 1825 there should have been a Jewish population size of $3.8 \times e^{00093}$ = 19.4 million Jews. As a consequence I estimate the survival chance of a Jewish community, Pr_s to the ratio of what the population size actually was, that is, 3.3 million to what it should have been, that is, 19.4 million. Thus the probability of survival is $Pr_s = \frac{3.3}{19.4} = 16.9\%$.

The main reason for this low rate of community survival consists of conversion to Christianity or to Islam. That indicates that many communities did not possess one or more of the essential attributes such as opposition to elitism, adequate assembly government, justice administration, network cohesion, rabbinical guidance, education, and relief for poor and sick. The study of the actual reasons for conversions is out of scope. Nevertheless, two reasons are within the scope of this chapter because they are related to the covenantal fabric of the communities:

1. Education—The education reform within the Jewish communities that started already in Palestine of 200 BCE. A study concluded "that some Jewish farmers convert[ed]to other religions in response to the costly educational reform in Judaism."[178]
2. Extreme Peer Pressure—We saw that peer pressure was an essential ingredient for the survival of the communities. However, on an individual basis there will be individuals who fold under the pressure created by the never-ending vigilance of others.

On the other hand the 17 percent of communities that survived deserve a second look. The first extra-biblical mention of Israel is "the late thirteenth century BCE stela of Merneptah."[179] The monument makes known that "Israel is laid waste and his seed is not." Considering this report and that Israel's unusual socio-political system has existed in adverse circumstances for three millennia, there is a good reason to conclude that after all, the covenantal system is resilient.

CONCLUSION

The Jewish Diaspora continued the assembly government system of covenanted communities inherited from Second Temple times. It lived as almost identical autonomous entities within a great variety of host populations. It was knitted into a strong federative network across lands and continents. It possessed an anti-elitist philosophy, a vigorous justice administration, office holders, and very similar institutions (rabbi, court of justice, synagogue, education, loving kindness etc.). *For all purposes the Jewish Diaspora has been a nation.*

NOTES

1. Mădălina Măndiţă, *Compared Noology of Jewish and Romanian People* (Aachen: Shaker Verlag, 2017).
2. Ibid., 121.
3. Benjamin Nathans, *Beyond the Pale: The Jewish Encounter with Late Imperial Russia* (Berkley/LosAngeles/London: University of California Press, 2002), 77; Dale Van Kley, "The Abbé Grégoire and the Quest for a Catholic Republic," in *The Abbé Grégoire and His World*, ed. Jeremy D. Popkin and Richard H. Popkin (Dordrecht/Boston/London: Kluwer Academic Publishers, 2000).
4. e. g. Francesca Bregoli, *Mediterranean Enlightenment: Livornese Jews, Tuscan Culture, and Eighteenth-Century Reform* (Stanford: Stanford University Press, 2014), 3; Steven M. Lowenstein, American Council of Learned Societies, and Oxford University Press, *The Berlin Jewish Community: Enlightenment, Family, and Crisis, 1770-1830* (Oxford: Oxford University Press, 1994), 77, 98, 195; Joshua Schreier, "Napoleon's Long Shadow: Morality, Civilization, and Jews in France and Algeria, 1808-1870," *French Historical Studies* 30, no. 1 (2007).
5. e.g. Kenneth Stow, *Alienated Minority: The Jews of Medieval Latin Europe* (Cambridge, MA/London: Harvard University Press, 2009), 159.
6. Heszel Klépfisz, *Inexhaustible Wellspring: Reaping the Rewards of Shtetl Life* (Jerusalem, NY: Devorah Publishing, 2003), 202; Yaron Ben-Naeh, *Jews in the Realm of the Sultans: Ottoman Jewish Society in the Seventeenth Century* (Tubingen: Mohr Siebeck, 2008).
7. 12th century England Stow, *Alienated Minority: The Jews of Medieval Latin Europe*.
8. Ladislau Gyemant, "The Romanian Jewry: Historical Destiny, Tolerance, Integration, Marginalisation," *Journal for the Study of Religions and Ideologies* 1, no. 3 (2010); Elias Schwarzfeld, "The Jews of Moldavia at the Beginning of the Eighteenth Century," *The Jewish Quarterly Review* 16, no. 1 (1903); Alexandru Roitman, "Alegerile rabinice din oraşul Bălţi în anul 1877, după documente inedite," *Revista de Etnologie şi Culturologie* 26, no. 2 (2019).
9. 15th century Poland Hanna Zaremska, "The Rabbinate of Poznań in the Second Half of the Fifteenth Century," *Acta Poloniae Historica* 119 (2019): 163; 11th century Holy Roman Empire Stow, *Alienated Minority: The Jews of Medieval Latin Europe*, 160.
10. Carolingian title *Alienated Minority: The Jews of Medieval Latin Europe*, 160.
11. See for exemple note 1 of Roitman, "Alegerile rabinice din oraşul Bălţi în anul 1877, după documente inedite."

12. Shlomo Dov Goitein and Jacob Lassner, *A Mediterranean Society: An Abridgment in One Volume* (Berkley: University of California Press., 1999), 99. Similar limited authority the Jews "grudgingly tolerated" individuals nominated by thee external hierarchies, however they enjoyed "no monopoly over internal rule," Stow, *Alienated Minority: The Jews of Medieval Latin Europe*.

13. Martin Borysek, "Takkanot Kandiyah–A Collection of Legislative Statutes as a Source for the Assessment of Laymen's Legal Authority in a Jewish Community in Venetian Crete" (University of Cambridge, 2016), 140.

14. Mishna Avot 1:1.

15. Idem.

16. e. g. Borysek, "Takkanot Kandiyah–A Collection of Legislative Statutes as a Source for the Assessment of Laymen's Legal Authority in a Jewish Community in Venetian Crete"; Zaremska, "The Rabbinate of Poznań in the Second Half of the Fifteenth Century," 170; Ben-Naeh, *Jews in the Realm of the Sultans: Ottoman Jewish Society in the Seventeenth Century*; Debra Glasberg, "The Castilian Jews of Fez: An Early Modern Transformation from Spanish to North African Jews," *The Bernard Revel Graduate· School of Jewish Studies* (2010); Joseph Dana, "Between Influence and Authority: The Rabbinate of the Seventeenth Century Portuguese Jewish Community of Amsterdam" (Central European University, 2010).

17. Renzo Toaff, "Statuti e leggi della «Nazione ebrea» di Livorno. II: La legislazione dal 1655 al 1677.(Cont. ne)," *La Rassegna Mensile di Israel* 38, no. 5 (1972).

18. e. g. Ben-Naeh, *Jews in the Realm of the Sultans: Ottoman Jewish Society in the Seventeenth Century*, 171; Toaff, "Statuti e leggi della «Nazione ebrea» di Livorno. II: La legislazione dal 1655 al 1677.(Cont. ne)."

19. Rabbinical correspondence –Communities asked prestigious scholars for decisions on disputes between different local council members halakhic problems for which they could find no guidelines; see for example Zaremska, "The Rabbinate of Poznań in the Second Half of the Fifteenth Century."

20. Amy Karen Downey and Leo Percer, *Maimonides's Yahweh: Rabbinic Judaism's Attempt to Answer the Incarnational Question* (Eugene, OR: Wipf & Stock Publishers, 2019), 66. Maimonides did not institute the provision authorizing local councils to decree ordinances. He only explains why this authority survived in a constantly authority challenging covenantal society. In this commentary on the Mishnah Maimonides refers to the Sages' commandment to make a fence around the Torah and it further makes the case that this guideline's authority stems from the Torah "Watch over my watch" [Leviticus 18:30, authors' translation], In a covenantal society the source of authority of a rule is not the position of the ruler in the social hierarchy, but the location of the legal reference in the legal system hierarchy (e. g. REF _Ref98600220 \h * MERGEFORMAT Figure 1).

21. Borysek, "Takkanot Kandiyah–A collection of legislative statutes as a source for the assessment of laymen's legal authority in a Jewish community in Venetian Crete."

22. Glasberg, "The Castilian Jews of Fez: An Early Modern Transformation from Spanish to North African Jews."

23. Ibid.

24. Borysek, "Takkanot Kandiyah–A Collection of Legislative Statutes as a Source for the Assessment of Laymen's Legal Authority in a Jewish Community in Venetian Crete," 88.

25. Ibid.

26. Chazakah no 77 Toaff, "Statuti e leggi della «Nazione ebrea» di Livorno. II: La legislazione dal 1655 al 1677.(Cont. ne)," 38–39.

27. Chazakah no 87 ibid., 46.

28. Elinoar Bareket, *Fustat on the Nile: The Jewish Elite in Medieval Egypt* (Brill, 2021).

29. Anna Esposito, "The Sephardic Communities in Rome in the Early Sixteenth Century," *Imago Temporis - Medium Aevum* 1 (2007).

30. Glasberg, "The Castilian Jews of Fez: An Early Modern Transformation from Spanish to North African Jews."

31. Joseph Hacker, "The Sephardim in the Ottoman Empire in the Sixteenth Century," *The Sephardi Legacy* 2 (1992).

32. Devin E Naar, "The "Mother of Israel" or the "Sephardi Metropolis"? Sephardim, Ashkenazim, and Romaniotes in Salonica," *Jewish Social Studies* 22, no. 1 (2016).

33. e.g. Bucharest: Alina Popescu, "Architectural Survey of the Bucharest Synagogues," *Studia Hebraica*, no. 9–10 (2009); Alba Iulia, Romania: Daniel Dumitran, "Jewish Cemeteries of Romania: Alba Iulia Case Study," *Annales Universitatis Apulensis Series Historica* 19, no. 2 (2015); Belgrade: Jasmina Huber, "Competing Musical Traditions in the Holy Land in the 20th Century and How They Found Their Way into the Synagogue of Belgrade," *PaRDeS: Zeitschrift der Vereinigung für Jüdische Studien eV* 20 (2014).

34. Dumitran, "Jewish Cemeteries of Romania: Alba Iulia Case Study"; Marius Cazan, "Alba Iulia," ed. Institutul Național Pentru Studierea Holocaustului din România "Elie Wiesel" (Bucharest: Institutul Național Pentru Studierea Holocaustului din România "Elie Wiesel", 2000).

35. Vivian Mann, "Synagogues, Medieval and Modern," in *The Encyclopaedia of Judaism* 2nd Edition (Leiden/Boston: Brill, 2005).

36. Huber, "Competing Musical Traditions in the Holy Land in the 20th Century and How They Found Their Way into the Synagogue of Belgrade."

37. Naar, "The "Mother of Israel" or the "Sephardi Metropolis"? Sephardim, Ashkenazim, and Romaniotes in Salonica."

38. Jacob Katz, *Tradition and Crisis: Jewish Society at the End of the Middle Ages*, trans. Bernard Dov Cooperman (Syracuse, NY: Syracuse University Press, 2000), 103.

39. Ibid., 104.

40. Gyemant, "The Romanian Jewry: Historical Destiny, Tolerance, Integration, Marginalisation"; or for exemple the powerful Council of Four Lands: Greater Poland, Little Poland, Galicia (with Podolia) and VolhyniMoshe Rosman, "The Role of Non-Jewish Authorities in Resolving Conflicts within Jewish Communities in the Early Modern Period," *Jewish Political Studies Review* (2000); Klemen Jelinčič

Boeta, "Medieval Jewish Community of Maribor," *Unity and Dialogue* 75, no. 2 (2020).

41. Naar, "The "Mother of Israel" or the "Sephardi Metropolis"? Sephardim, Ashkenazim, and Romaniotes in Salonica."

42. Solomon Zeitilin, "The Council of Four Lands," *The Jewish Quarterly Review* 39, no. 2 (1948).

43. Ibid.; Rosman, "The Role of Non-Jewish Authorities in Resolving Conflicts within Jewish Communities in the Early Modern Period."

44. Andrea Yaakov Lattes, "Aspetti politici ed istituzionali delle comunita ebraiche in Italia nel Cinque-Seicento," *Zakhor II* (1998): 10; Gyemant, "The Romanian Jewry: Historical Destiny, Tolerance, Integration, Marginalisation"; Hacker, "The Sephardim in the Ottoman Empire in the Sixteenth Century"; Cazan, "Alba Iulia"; Data Base, "The Jewish Community of Alba Iulia," (Tel Aviv: The Museum of the Jewish People, 1996); Renata Segre, "Sephardic Settlements in Sixteenth-Century Italy: A Historical and Geographical Survey," *Mediterranean Historical Review* 6, no. 2 (1991); Slovenia, 1244 Boeta, "Medieval Jewish Community of Maribor"; Mann, "Synagogues, Medieval and Modern."

45. Philip A. Klein, *Beyond Dissent: Essays in Institutional Economics* (Armonk, NY: M.E. Sharpe, 1994), 22. Charles Howard McIlwain, *Constitutionalism: Ancient and Modern* (Clark, NJ: Lawbook Exchange, 2005), 84, see also reference to Pirkey Avot (Chapters of the Fathers) in the Introduction and to the Pontifical Council For Justice and Peace, *Compendium of the Social Doctrine of the Church* (Washington, DC: United States Conference of Catholic Bishops, 2004) in Chapter 9 "of Jo Renee Formicola.

46. Mark Avrum Ehrlich, *Encyclopedia of the Jewish Diaspora: Origins, Experiences, and Culture* (Santa Barbara, CA: ABC-CLIO, 2009), 419.

47. Ben-Naeh, *Jews in the Realm of the Sultans: Ottoman Jewish Society in the Seventeenth Century*, 159; Boeta, "Medieval Jewish Community of Maribor"; A Hebrew document dating from 1591 mentions a beit din (Jewish court) in Alba Iula, Transylvania Researchers of ANU, "The Jewish Community of Alba Iulia" (Tel Aviv: The Museum of the Jewish People, 1996); Stow, *Alienated Minority: The Jews of Medieval Latin Europe*; Eli Valley, *The Great Jewish Cities of Central and Eastern Europe: A Travel Guide and Resource Book to Prague, Warsaw, Crakow, and Budapest* (Lanham/Toronto/Oxford: Rowman & Littlefield, 2005), 297, 316, 28, 465.

48. Rosman, "The Role of Non-Jewish Authorities in Resolving Conflicts within Jewish Communities in the Early Modern Period."

49. Ben-Naeh, *Jews in the Realm of the Sultans: Ottoman Jewish Society in the Seventeenth Century.*

50. Rosman, "The Role of Non-Jewish Authorities in Resolving Conflicts within Jewish Communities in the Early Modern Period," 56.

51. Ibid., 57.

52. Ibid.

53. Ibid., 59.

54. A small Jewish town in eastern Europe in the past "entry - shtetl," in *Oxford Advanced Learner's Dictionary* (Oxford: Oxford University Press, 2022).

55. Klépfisz, *Inexhaustible Wellspring: Reaping the Rewards of Shtetl Life*, 42.

56. Community, congregation.

57. Klépfisz, *Inexhaustible Wellspring: Reaping the Rewards of Shtetl Life*, 170–171.

58. Ibid., 118.

59. Howard N. Lupovitch, *Jews at the Crossroads: Tradition and Accommodation During the Golden Age of the Hungarian Nobility, 1729-1878* (Budapest: Central European University Press, 2007), 92; Rosman, "The Role of Non-Jewish Authorities in Resolving Conflicts within Jewish Communities in the Early Modern Period," 56.

60. Katz, *Tradition and Crisis: Jewish Society at the End of the Middle Ages*, 153–154.

61. Ronald L. Eisenberg, *850 Intriguing Questions about Judaism: True, False, or In Between* (Lanham, MD: Rowman & Littlefield Publishers, 2015), 199.

62. Jeffrey Wildstein, *Judaism: An Introduction to Jewish Beliefs and History* (Indianapolis, IN: DK Publishing, 2015)., Chapter Breaking The Glass – Jewish Weddings.

63. Lupovitch, *Jews at the Crossroads: Tradition and Accommodation During the Golden Age of the Hungarian Nobility, 1729-1878*, 92.

64. Elimelech Westreich and Avishalom Westreich, "Jewish Law: Marriage," in *Routledge Handbook of Religious Laws*, ed. Rossella Ferrari Bottoni, Silvio (London: Routledge, 2019).

65. Gilles Deleuze, *Spinoza: Practical Philosophy* (San Francisco: City Lights Books, 1988), 5–14; Dana, "Between Influence and Authority: The Rabbinate of the Seventeenth Century Portuguese Jewish Community of Amsterdam," 38.

66. Westreich and Westreich, "Jewish Law: Marriage."

67. Ben-Naeh, *Jews in the Realm of the Sultans: Ottoman Jewish Society in the Seventeenth Century*; e.g. excommunication (cherem) is punishment for acquiring a house taken by force by a non-Jew from another Jew Toaff, "Statuti e leggi della «Nazione ebrea» di Livorno. II: La legislazione dal 1655 al 1677.(Cont. ne)," 33, 44.

68. Elelwani Farisani, "A Sociological Analysis of Israelites in Babylonian Exile," *Old Testament Essays* 17, no. 3 (2004). Citing (Jr 29:1; Ezk 7:1; 14:1; 20:1) and Rainer Albertz, *A History of Israelite Religion in the Old Testament Period, Volume II: From the Exile to the Maccabees* (Louisville, KY: Presbyterian Publishing Corporation, 1994), 373.

69. Yaacov Shavit and Barbara Harshav, "Cyrus King of Persia and the return to Zion: A Case of Neglected Memory," *History and Memory* 2, no. 1 (1990).

70. the First Persian Empire, founded by king Cyrus in 550 BCE.

71. The source cites Hugh G.M. Williamson, "Judah and the Jews," in *Studies in Persian Period History and Historiography*, ed. M. Brosius and A. Kuhrt (Leiden Brill, 1998).

72. The source cites Nadav Na'aman, "Royal Vassals or Governors? On the Status of Sheshbazzar and Zerubbabel in the Persian Empire," *Henoch* 22, no. 1 (2000).

73. The source cites Donald T Ariel and Yair Shoham, "Locally Stamped Handles and Associated Body Fragments of the Persian and Hellenistic Periods," *Excavations at the City of David* 1985 (1978): 137–169.

74. Alexander Fantalkin and Oren Tal, "Redating Lachish Level I: Identifying Achaemenid Imperial Policy at the Southern Frontier of the Fifth Satrapy," in *Judah and the Judeans in the Persian Period*, ed. Oded Oeming Lipschitz, Manfred (Winona Lake, IN: Eisenbrauns, 2006), 180.

75. Shmuel Safrai and Menachem Stern, "Jewish Self-government," in *The Jewish People in the First Century, Volume 1* (Brill, 1974).

76. Sylvie Honigman, "The Jewish Politeuma at Heracleopolis," *Scripta Classica Israelica* 21 (2002).

77. Valley, *The Great Jewish Cities of Central and Eastern Europe: A Travel Guide and Resource Book to Prague, Warsaw, Crakow, and Budapest*, 6; Stow, *Alienated Minority: The Jews of Medieval Latin Europe*, 275.

78. Boeta, "Medieval Jewish Community of Maribor."

79. Valley, *The Great Jewish Cities of Central and Eastern Europe: A Travel Guide and Resource Book to Prague, Warsaw, Crakow, and Budapest*, 7.

80. Borysek, "Takkanot Kandiyah–A Collection of Legislative Statutes as a Source for the Assessment of Laymen's Legal Authority in a Jewish Community in Venetian Crete," 140; Gyemant, "The Romanian Jewry: Historical Destiny, Tolerance, Integration, Marginalisation"; Hacker, "The Sephardim in the Ottoman Empire in the Sixteenth Century."

81. Segre, "Sephardic Settlements in Sixteenth-Century Italy: A Historical and Geographical Survey," 122.

82. Hacker, "The Sephardim in the Ottoman Empire in the Sixteenth Century."

83. Chaya Kessler, *Vilna Remembered and Vilna Imagined: The Struggle of the Vilna Jewish Community to Recreate Its Past* (Youngstown State University, 2005).

84. Robin R. Mundill, *The King's Jews: Money, Massacre and Exodus in Medieval England* (London/New York: Bloomsbury Publishing, 2010), 12.

85. Judith Kalik, *Scepter of Judah: The Jewish Autonomy in the Eighteenth-Century Crown Poland* (Leiden/Boston: Brill, 2009)., chapter 1

86. Safrai and Stern, "Jewish Self-government"; Esposito, "The Sephardic Communities in Rome in the Early Sixteenth Century"; Ben-Naeh, *Jews in the Realm of the Sultans: Ottoman Jewish Society in the Seventeenth Century*; Schwarzfeld, "The Jews of Moldavia at the Beginning of the Eighteenth Century"; ibid.

87. Mundill, *The King's Jews: Money, Massacre and Exodus in Medieval England*, 3.

88. Hacker, "The Sephardim in the Ottoman Empire in the Sixteenth Century."

89. Valley, *The Great Jewish Cities of Central and Eastern Europe: A Travel Guide and Resource Book to Prague, Warsaw, Crakow, and Budapest.*

90. Rosman, "The Role of Non-Jewish Authorities in Resolving Conflicts within Jewish Communities in the Early Modern Period."

91. Max Weber, *Ancient Judaism* (New York & London: Free Press, 2010), 258.

92. Esposito, "The Sephardic Communities in Rome in the Early Sixteenth Century"; Ben-Naeh, *Jews in the Realm of the Sultans: Ottoman Jewish Society in the Seventeenth Century.*

93. *Jews in the Realm of the Sultans: Ottoman Jewish Society in the Seventeenth Century.*

94. Katz, *Tradition and Crisis: Jewish Society at the End of the Middle Ages*, 90.

95. The community supervised the office holders including in public finances for example in Egypt of the Geniza period (10th-13th centuries) see Goitein and Lassner, *A Mediterranean Society: An Abridgment in One Volume*, 100.

96. Borysek, "Takkanot Kandiyah–A Collection of Legislative Statutes as a Source for the Assessment of Laymen's Legal Authority in a Jewish Community in Venetian Crete," 139.

97. Beatrice Medicine, "My Elders Tell Me," in *Indian Education in Canada, Volume 2*, ed. Jean Barman, Yvonne M. Hébert, and Don McCaskill (Vancouver, BC, Canada: UBC Press, 1987).

98. Ben-Naeh, *Jews in the Realm of the Sultans: Ottoman Jewish Society in the Seventeenth Century*, 197; Gyemant, "The Romanian Jewry: Historical Destiny, Tolerance, Integration, Marginalisation"; Boeta, "Medieval Jewish Community of Maribor."

99. Borysek, "Takkanot Kandiyah–A Collection of Legislative Statutes as a Source for the Assessment of Laymen's Legal Authority in a Jewish Community in Venetian Crete," 139.

100. Suzanne M Stiegelbauer, "What Is an Elder? What Do Elders Do?: First Nation Elders as Teachers in Culture-based Urban Organizations," *The Canadian Journal of Native Studies* 14 (1996): 50.

101. Borysek, "Takkanot Kandiyah–A Collection of Legislative Statutes as a Source for the Assessment of Laymen's Legal Authority in a Jewish Community in Venetian Crete," 139.

102. Hacker, "The Sephardim in the Ottoman Empire in the Sixteenth Century"; Gotthard Deutsch and Max Schloessinger, "MAHAMAD (more correctly MA'AMAD," in *Jewish Enciclopedia* ed. Isidore Singer, Isaac K. Funk, and Frank H. Vizetelly (New York: Funk & Wagnalls, 1906); Dana, "Between Influence and Authority: The Rabbinate of the Seventeenth Century Portuguese Jewish Community of Amsterdam," 29.

103. Hacker, "The Sephardim in the Ottoman Empire in the Sixteenth Century"; Boeta, "Medieval Jewish Community of Maribor"; Katz, *Tradition and Crisis: Jewish Society at the End of the Middle Ages*, 69, 105.

104. Schwarzfeld, "The Jews of Moldavia at the Beginning of the Eighteenth Century."

105. Ben-Naeh, *Jews in the Realm of the Sultans: Ottoman Jewish Society in the Seventeenth Century*, 197.

106. Honigman, "The Jewish Politeuma at Heracleopolis: ."

107. Ibid.

108. Ben-Naeh, *Jews in the Realm of the Sultans: Ottoman Jewish Society in the Seventeenth Century*, 197. Exactly this denomination is found in Catalan sources *boni homines villae* Monique Bourin, "Historiographie des communautés de la France méridionale," in *La formation des communautés d'habitants au Moyen Âge. Perspectives historiographiques*, ed. Ludolf Kuchenbuch, Dieter Scheler, and Joseph Morsel (Xanten, Germany2003).This Hebrew denomination of the office holders circulated in Roman Palestine see Safrai (Chapter 2 of this collection). In Gascony and Romania

we find similar designations i.e. *boni homines* (De La Greze, Chapter 8) and *oameni buni* (Bădescu, chapter 5).

109. In Frankfurt (1612-1628) Rosman, "The role of non-Jewish authorities in resolving conflicts within Jewish communities in the early modern period."

110. Sukho Billy Jang, "The Origin of the Synagogue" (University of the Holy Land, 2018).

111. Jutta Leonhardt, *Jewish Worship in Philo of Alexandria* (Tübingen: Mohr Siebeck, 2001), 81.

112. Jang, "The Origin of The Synagogue."

113. didaskelaion, hieron, topos, sabateion, beyt-hamidrash, oikos Ralph J. Korner, *The Origin and Meaning of Ekklēsia in the Early Jesus Movement* (Leiden: Brill, 2017). Other designations were beyt-hakneset (meeting house a designation also found in the American Puritan tradition), shul (school, ascola), e.g Altneuschul of Prague scuola e.g. Cinque Scuole in Rome, temple e.g. Templul Coral in Bucharest.

114. Peter .J. Rhodes, *Athenian Democracy* (Edinburgh Edinburgh University Press, 2019), 91.

115. Leonhardt, *Jewish Worship in Philo of Alexandria*, 81; Jang, "The Origin of The Synagogue."

116. The earliest term is Bet-Knesset - assembly house, or meeting house Dan Urman, "The House of Assembly and the House of Study," in *Ancient Synagogues: Historical Analysis and Archaeological Discovery*, ed. Dan Urman and Paul Virgil McCracken Flesher (Leiden: Brill, 1998), 243; Ashkenazi Jews: Shul, Shtieble Herbert M. Danzger, *Returning to Tradition: The Contemporary Revival of Orthodox Judaism* (New Haven/London: Yale University Press, 1989), 353; Sephardic Salonika: kahal Tamar Alexander-Frizer, *The Heart Is a Mirror: The Sephardic Folktale* (Detroit: Wayne State University Press, 2008), 99; Rome: Tempio, scuola Esposito, "The Sephardic Communities in Rome in the Early Sixteenth Century." The term Temple is found in many European locations among other Vienna, Amsterdam, Bucharest, Paris, Nürnberg, Hamburg, and Krakow Carol H. Krinsky, *Synagogues of Europe: Architecture, History, Meaning* (Mineola, NY: Dover Publications, 1996).

117. Gyemant, "The Romanian Jewry: Historical Destiny, Tolerance, Integration, Marginalisation"; Cazan, "Alba Iulia"; 13th century, Boeta, "Medieval Jewish Community of Maribor"; Segre, "Sephardic Settlements in Sixteenth-Century Italy: A Historical and Geographical Survey"; Table VIIILupovitch, *Jews at the Crossroads: Tradition and Accommodation During the Golden Age of the Hungarian Nobility, 1729-1878*, 168.

118. Esposito, "The Sephardic Communities in Rome in the Early Sixteenth Century."

119. Ibid.; Lupovitch, *Jews at the Crossroads: Tradition and Accommodation During the Golden Age of the Hungarian Nobility, 1729-1878.*

120. Urman, "The House of Assembly and the House of Study," 237.

121. Katz, *Tradition and Crisis: Jewish Society at the End of the Middle Ages*, 152.

122. Urman, "The House of Assembly and the House of Study," 237.

123. Katz, *Tradition and Crisis: Jewish Society at the End of the Middle Ages.*

124. e. g. The prayer called *Amidah*, and the Blessing of the Kohanim.

125. "According to the1897 census in the gubernii of the Pale of Jewish Settlement and Poland, there existed 462 small towns with an absolute Jewish majority, and 116 had a Jewish population of over eighty percent." Ben-Cion Pinchuk, "The shtetl," *Cahiers du monde russe* 41, no. 41/4 (2000).

126. Zaremska, "The Rabbinate of Poznań in the Second Half of the Fifteenth Century," 165; Roitman, "Alegerile rabinice din oraşul Bălţi în anul 1877, după documente inedite"; Dana, "Between Influence and Authority: The Rabbinate of the Seventeenth Century Portuguese Jewish Community of Amsterdam."

127. Zaremska, "The Rabbinate of Poznań in the Second Half of the Fifteenth Century," 166; or see for example the community of Miedzyboz sought to dismiss rabbi Hersz Lejbowicz in 1744 Rosman, "The Role of Non-Jewish Authorities in Resolving Conflicts within Jewish Communities in the Early Modern Period."

128. Hacker, "The Sephardim in the Ottoman Empire in the Sixteenth Century."

129. Zaremska, "The Rabbinate of Poznań in the Second Half of the Fifteenth Century," 164.

130. Ibid.

131. Ibid.

132. Ibid., 167.

133. Ibid.

134. Ibid.

135. Ibid.; Roitman, "Alegerile rabinice din oraşul Bălţi în anul 1877, după documente inedite."

136. Zaremska, "The Rabbinate of Poznań in the Second Half of the Fifteenth Century," 164.

137. See chapter "Power Structure within Autonomy in Roman Palestine" of this volume.

138. V. Shamash et al., *Memories of Eden: A Journey Through Jewish Baghdad* (Evanston, IL: Northwestern University Press, 2016), 116.

139. Yaron Harel, *Intrigue and Revolution: Chief Rabbis in Aleppo, Baghdad, and Damascus, 1774-1914* (Liverpool: Liverpool University Press, 2015), 112.

140. Ari Ariel, *Jewish-Muslim Relations and Migration from Yemen to Palestine in the Late Nineteenth and Twentieth Centuries* (Leyden: Brill, 2013), 30.

141. Kem Blady, *Jewish Communities in Exotic Places* (Northvale, NJ/Jerusalem: Jason Aronson, Incorporated, 2000), 167.

142. Gyemant, "The Romanian Jewry: Historical Destiny, Tolerance, Integration, Marginalisation," 304 ; Schwarzfeld, "The Jews of Moldavia at the Beginning of the Eighteenth Century"; Ben-Naeh, *Jews in the Realm of the Sultans: Ottoman Jewish Society in the Seventeenth Century*; Schwarzfeld, "The Jews of Moldavia at the Beginning of the Eighteenth Century."

143. Moric Levi, "Ruždi-pasha and the Jews of Sarajevo," *Duh Bosne* 6, no. 3 (2011).

144. T. Britannica, "chief rabbinate.," in *Encyclopedia Britannica*, ed. Editors of Encyclopaedia (2013).

145. Katz, *Tradition and Crisis: Jewish Society at the End of the Middle Ages*, 72–73.

146. Joseph Livni and Lewi Stone, "The Stabilizing Role of the Sabbath in Premonarchic Israel: A Mathematical Model," *Journal of Biological Physics* 41 (2015).

147. Esposito, "The Sephardic Communities in Rome in the Early Sixteenth Century," 33; Cazan, "Alba Iulia"; Claudiu Constantin Mitu, "Istoria Evreilor Din România" (Lucian Blaga University Sibiu Romania, 2020); Toaff, "Statuti e leggi della «Nazione ebrea» di Livorno. II: La legislazione dal 1655 al 1677.(Cont. ne)," 38; Table VIIILupovitch, *Jews at the Crossroads: Tradition and Accommodation During the Golden Age of the Hungarian Nobility, 1729-1878*, 168; see poor relief Ben-Naeh, *Jews in the Realm of the Sultans: Ottoman Jewish Society in the Seventeenth Century*; Shamash et al., *Memories of Eden: A Journey Through Jewish Baghdad*, 116; Dana, "Between Influence and Authority: The Rabbinate of the Seventeenth Century Portuguese Jewish Community of Amsterdam," 27; see Assistance for the poor and the sick Hacker, "The Sephardim in the Ottoman Empire in the Sixteenth Century," 120; in Buchara Blady, *Jewish Communities in Exotic Places*, 188; among Krinchak Jews of Crimeaibid, 120; in Daghestan ibid., 166.

148. Zaremska, "The Rabbinate of Poznań in the Second Half of the Fifteenth Century," 164; Esposito, "The Sephardic Communities in Rome in the Early Sixteenth Century"; Shamash et al., *Memories of Eden: A Journey Through Jewish Baghdad*, 95; in Yemen Blady, *Jewish Communities in Exotic Places*, 14; in Kurdistan ibid., 167; in Meshed, Persia ibid., 78; in Isfahan, Georgia ibid., 63.

149. Valley, *The Great Jewish Cities of Central and Eastern Europe: A Travel Guide and Resource Book to Prague, Warsaw, Crakow, and Budapest.*

150. Dana, "Between Influence and Authority: The Rabbinate of the Seventeenth Century Portuguese Jewish Community of Amsterdam."

151. Naar, "The "Mother of Israel" or the "Sephardi Metropolis"? Sephardim, Ashkenazim, and Romaniotes in Salonica."

152. Cazan, "Alba Iulia."

153. Ibid.

154. Mitu, "Istoria Evreilor Din România," 16.

155. Lupovitch, *Jews at the Crossroads: Tradition and Accommodation During the Golden Age of the Hungarian Nobility, 1729-1878.*

156. Borysek, "Takkanot Kandiyah–A Collection of Legislative Statutes as a Source for the Assessment of Laymen's Legal Authority in a Jewish Community in Venetian Crete," 88; Mitu, "Istoria Evreilor Din România."

157. Borysek, "Takkanot Kandiyah–A Collection of Legislative Statutes as a Source for the Assessment of Laymen's Legal Authority in a Jewish Community in Venetian Crete," 88; Mitu, "Istoria Evreilor Din România."

158. Blady, *Jewish Communities in Exotic Places*, 36.

159. Ibid., 202.

160. Ibid., 146.

161. Boeta, "Medieval Jewish Community of Maribor."

162. A'haron Oppenheimer, *Am Ha-aretz* (Leiden: E. J. Brill, 1977), 10.

163. Ibid., 69.

164. Zvi Eckstein and Maristella Botticini, "From Farmers to Merchants, Conversions and Diaspora: Human Capital and Jewish History," *Journal of the European Economic Association* 5(5) (2007).

165. Ben-Naeh, *Jews in the Realm of the Sultans: Ottoman Jewish Society in the Seventeenth Century*, 38; Gyemant, "The Romanian Jewry: Historical Destiny, Tolerance, Integration, Marginalisation"; Boeta, "Medieval Jewish Community of Maribor"; Kessler, "Vilna Remembered and Vilna Imagined: The Struggle of the Vilna Jewish Community to Recreate Its Past"; in Oradea, Carei and Sighetuul Marmaţiei, Romania Mitu, "Istoria Evreilor Din România"; Toaff, "Statuti e leggi della «Nazione ebrea» di Livorno. II: La legislazione dal 1655 al 1677.(Cont. ne)"; Valley, *The Great Jewish Cities of Central and Eastern Europe: A Travel Guide and Resource Book to Prague, Warsaw, Crakow, and Budapest*, 32–33; Lupovitch, *Jews at the Crossroads: Tradition and Accommodation During the Golden Age of the Hungarian Nobility, 1729-1878*; Hacker, "The Sephardim in the Ottoman Empire in the Sixteenth Century," 120; in Kurdistan the Hebrew school was called knishta Blady, *Jewish Communities in Exotic Places*, 103; in Tripolitania the name of the school was kutab. Ibid., 323; in Yemen the teacher was called mori, ibid., 14; in Afghanistan ibid., 201.

166. Boeta, "Medieval Jewish Community of Maribor."

167. Hillel Goelman, "Toward a Historical and Spiritual Understanding of Child Development: The Medieval Commentaries of Rabbi Moshe Yehuda ibn Mahiri," *Ethos* 29, no. 4 (2001).

168. Moshe Yehudah Ibn Mahiri, "Ben Hamesh l'Mikra" (Venice1598).

169. Ibid.

170. Goelman, "Toward a Historical and Spiritual Understanding of Child Development: The Medieval Commentaries of Rabbi Moshe Yehuda ibn Mahiri."

171. e.g in the Ottoman Empire Hacker, "The Sephardim in the Ottoman Empire in the Sixteenth Century"; in Romania Mitu, "Istoria Evreilor Din România"; in Rome Esposito, "The Sephardic Communities in Rome in the Early Sixteenth Century"; in the oldest Jewish Community of Romania Cazan, "Alba Iulia."

172. Hacker, "The Sephardim in the Ottoman Empire in the Sixteenth Century"; Schwarzfeld, "The Jews of Moldavia at the Beginning of the Eighteenth Century"; ibid.

173. Seth Abrutyn, "Pollution-Purification Rituals, Cultural Memory and the Evolution of religion: How Collective Trauma Shaped Ancient Israel," *AJCS* 3, no. 1 (2015).

174. Eckstein and Botticini, "From Farmers to Merchants, Conversions and Diaspora: Human Capital and Jewish History."

175. Sergio DellaPergola and J. Evan, "Some Fundamentals of Jewish Demographic History," *Papers in Jewish Demography* (1997).

176. Stephen P. Bensch, *Barcelona and Its Rulers, 1096-1291* (Cambridge: Cambridge University Press, 1995), 87; Yehogachin S. Brenner, *A Short History Of Economic Progress: A Course in Economic History* (London: Frank Cass & Co, 1969), 53; Peter Turchin, *Historical Dynamics: Why States Rise and Fall* (Princeton, NJ: Princeton University Press, 2003), 179; Carlo. M. Cipolla, *Before the Industrial Revolution: European Society and Economy* (London: Routledge, 1993), 130; Fekri A. Hassan, "Population Dynamics, (672 - 710), in r(ed..), Routledge, 1999," in *Companion Encyclopedia of Archaeology* (London: Routledge, 1999), 673.

177. see curve of Figure 10.1 of Roger S. Scholefield and Alain Bideau, *The Decline of Mortality in Europe* (Oxford: Oxford University Press, 1991), 403

178. Eckstein and Botticini, "From Farmers to Merchants, Conversions and Diaspora: Human Capital and Jewish History."

179. Ann E. Killebrew, *Biblical Peoples and Ethnicity: An Archaeological Study of Egyptians, Canaanites, Philistines, and Early Israel, 1300–1100 B.C.E* (Atlanta, GA: Society pf Biblical Lit., 2005).

REFERENCES

Abrutyn, Seth. "Pollution-Purification Rituals, Cultural Memory and the Evolution of Religion: How Collective Trauma Shaped Ancient Israel." *AJCS* 3, no. 1 (February 2015): 123–55.

Albertz, Rainer. *A History of Israelite Religion in the Old Testament Period, Volume II: From the Exile to the Maccabees*. Louisville, KY: Presbyterian Publishing Corporation, 1994.

Alexander-Frizer, Tamar. *The Heart is a Mirror: The Sephardic Folktale*. Detroit: Wayne State University Press, 2008.

Ariel, Ari. *Jewish-Muslim Relations and Migration From Yemen to Palestine in the Late Nineteenth and Twentieth Centuries*. Leiden: Brill, 2013.

Ariel, Donald T., and Yair Shoham. "Locally Stamped Handles and Associated Body Fragments of the Persian and Hellenistic Periods." *Excavations at the City of David* 1985 (1978): 137–69.

Bareket, Elinoar. *Fustat on the Nile: The Jewish Elite in Medieval Egypt*. Leiden: Brill, 2021.

Ben-Naeh, Yaron. *Jews in the Realm of the Sultans: Ottoman Jewish Society in the Seventeenth Century*. Tubingen: Mohr Siebeck, 2008.

Bensch, Stephen P. *Barcelona and Its Rulers, 1096–1291*. Cambridge: Cambridge University Press, 1995.

Blady, Kem. *Jewish Communities in Exotic Places*. Northvale, NJ, Jerusalem: Jason Aronson, Incorporated, 2000.

Boeta, Klemen Jelinčič. "Medieval Jewish Community of Maribor." *Unity and Dialogue* 75, no. 2 (2020): 167–79.

Borysek, Martin. *Takkanot Kandiyah – A Collection of Legislative Statutes as a Source for the Assessment of Laymen's Legal Authority in a Jewish Community in Venetian Crete*. Cambridge: University of Cambridge, 2016.

Bourin, Monique. "Historiographie Des Communautés De La France Méridionale." In *La formation des communautés d'habitants au Moyen Âge. Perspectives historiographiques*, edited by Ludolf Kuchenbuch, Dieter Scheler, and Joseph Morsel. Xanten, Germany, 2003.

Bregoli, Francesca. *Mediterranean Enlightenment: Livornese Jews, Tuscan Culture, and Eighteenth-Century Reform*. Stanford, CA: Stanford University Press, 2014.

Brenner, Yehogachin S. *A Short History of Economic Progress: A Course in Economic History*. London: Frank Cass & Co, 1969.

Britannica, T. "Chief Rabbinate." In *Encyclopedia Britannica*, edited by Editors of Encyclopaedia, 2013.

Cazan, Marius. "Alba Iulia." Edited by Institutul Naţional Pentru Studierea Holocaustului din România "Elie Wiesel". Bucharest: Institutul Naţional Pentru Studierea Holocaustului din România "Elie Wiesel", 2000.
Cipolla, Carlo M. *Before the Industrial Revolution: European Society and Economy*. London: Routledge, 1993.
Dana, Joseph. *Between Influence and Authority: The Rabbinate of the Seventeenth Century Portuguese Jewish Community of Amsterdam*. Central European University, 2010.
Danzger, Herbert M. *Returning to Tradition: The Contemporary Revival of Orthodox Judaism*. New Haven & London: Yale University Press, 1989.
Data Base. *The Jewish Community of Alba Iulia*. Tel Aviv: The Museum of the Jewish People, 1996.
Deleuze, Gilles. *Spinoza: Practical Philosophy*. San Francisco: City Lights Books, 1988.
DellaPergola, Sergio, and J. Evan. "Some Fundamentals of Jewish Demographic History." *Papers in Jewish Demography* (1997): 11–33.
Deutsch, Gotthard, and Max Schloessinger. "Mahamad (More Correctly Ma'amad." In *Jewish Enciclopedia*, edited by Isidore Singer, Isaac K. Funk, and Frank H. Vizetelly. New York: Funk & Wagnalls, 1906.
Downey, Amy Karen, and Leo Percer. *Maimonides's Yahweh: Rabbinic Judaism's Attempt to Answer the Incarnational Question*. Eugene, OR: Wipf & Stock Publishers, 2019.
Dumitran, Daniel. "Jewish Cemeteries of Romania: Alba Iulia Case Study." *Annales Universitatis Apulensis Series Historica* 19, no. 2 (2015): 235–58.
Eckstein, Zvi, and Maristella Botticini. "From Farmers to Merchants, Conversions and Diaspora: Human Capital and Jewish History." *Journal of the European Economic Association* 5, no. 5 (2007): 885–926.
Ehrlich, Mark Avrum. *Encyclopedia of the Jewish Diaspora: Origins, Experiences, and Culture*. Santa Barbara, CA: ABC-CLIO, 2009.
Eisenberg, Ronald L. *850 Intriguing Questions About Judaism: True, False, or in Between*. Lanham, MD: Rowman & Littlefield Publishers, 2015.
Esposito, Anna. "The Sephardic Communities in Rome in the Early Sixteenth Century." *Imago Temporis - Medium Aevum* 1 (2007): 177–85.
Fantalkin, Alexander, and Oren Tal. "Redating Lachish Level I: Identifying Achaemenid Imperial Policy at the Southern Frontier of the Fifth Satrapy." In *Judah and the Judeans in the Persian Period*, edited by Oded Oeming Lipschitz, Manfred, 167–97. Winona Lake, IN: Eisenbrauns, 2006.
Farisani, Elelwani. "A Sociological Analysis of Israelites in Babylonian Exile." *Old Testament Essays* 17, no. 3 (2004): 380–88.
Glasberg, Debra. "The Castilian Jews of Fez: An Early Modern Transformation From Spanish to North African Jews." *The Bernard Revel Graduate· School of Jewish Studies* (2010).
Goelman, Hillel. "Toward a Historical and Spiritual Understanding of Child Development: The Medieval Commentaries of Rabbi Moshe Yehuda Ibn Mahiri." *Ethos* 29, no. 4 (2001): 491–512.

Goitein, Shlomo Dov, and Jacob Lassner. *A Mediterranean Society: An Abridgment in One Volume*. Berkeley, CA: University of California Press, 1999.
Gyemant, Ladislau. "The Romanian Jewry: Historical Destiny, Tolerance, Integration, Marginalisation." *Journal for the Study of Religions and Ideologies* 1, no. 3 (2010): 85–98.
Hacker, Joseph. "The Sephardim in the Ottoman Empire in the Sixteenth Century." *The Sephardi Legacy* 2 (1992): 2.
Harel, Yaron. *Intrigue and Revolution: Chief Rabbis in Aleppo, Baghdad, and Damascus, 1774–1914*. Liverpool: Liverpool University Press, 2015.
Hassan, Fekri A. "Population Dynamics (672–710), in R (Ed.), Routledge, 1999." In *Companion Encyclopedia of Archaeology*. London: Routledge, 1999.
Honigman, Sylvie. "The Jewish Politeuma at Heracleopolis." *Scripta Classica Israelica* 21 (2002): 251–66.
Huber, Jasmina. "Competing Musical Traditions in the Holy Land in the 20th Century and How They Found Their Way into the Synagogue of Belgrade." *PaRDeS: Zeitschrift der Vereinigung für Jüdische Studien eV* 20 (2014): 87–98.
Ibn Mahiri, Moshe Yehudah. "Ben Hamesh L'mikra." Venice, 1598.
Jang, Sukho Billy. *The Origin of the Synagogue*. University of the Holy Land, 2018.
Kalik, Judith. *Scepter of Judah: The Jewish Autonomy in the Eighteenth-Century Crown Poland*. Leiden, Boston: Brill, 2009.
Katz, Jacob. *Tradition and Crisis: Jewish Society at the End of the Middle Ages*. Translated by Bernard Dov Cooperman. Syracuse, NY: Syracuse University Press, 2000.
Kessler, Chaya. *Vilna Remembered and Vilna Imagined: The Struggle of the Vilna Jewish Community to Recreate Its Past*. Youngstown State University, 2005.
Killebrew, Ann E. *Biblical Peoples and Ethnicity: An Archaeological Study of Egyptians, Canaanites, Philistines, and Early Israel, 1300–1100 B.C.E.* Atlanta, GA: Society pf Biblical Lit., 2005.
Klein, Philip A. *Beyond Dissent: Essays in Institutional Economics*. Armonk, NY: M.E. Sharpe, 1994.
Klépfisz, Heszel. *Inexhaustible Wellspring: Reaping the Rewards of Shtetl Life*. Jerusalem, New York: Devorah Publishing, 2003.
Korner, Ralph J. *The Origin and Meaning of Ekklēsia in the Early Jesus Movement*. Leiden: Brill, 2017.
Krinsky, Carol H. *Synagogues of Europe: Architecture, History, Meaning*. Mineola, NY: Dover Publications, 1996.
Lattes, Andrea Yaakov. "Aspetti Politici Ed Istituzionali Delle Comunita Ebraiche in Italia Nel Cinque-Seicento." *Zakhor* II (1998): 21–37.
Leonhardt, Jutta. *Jewish Worship in Philo of Alexandria*. Tübingen: Mohr Siebeck, 2001.
Levi, Moric. "Ruždi-Pasha and the Jews of Sarajevo." *Duh Bosne* 6, no. 3 (2011).
Livni, Joseph, and Lewi Stone. "The Stabilizing Role of the Sabbath in Pre-Monarchic Israel: A Mathematical Model." *Journal of Biological Physics* 41 (2015): 203–21.
Lowenstein, Steven M., American Council of Learned Societies, and Oxford University Press. *The Berlin Jewish Community: Enlightenment, Family, and Crisis, 1770–1830*. Oxford: Oxford University Press, 1994.

Lupovitch, Howard N. *Jews at the Crossroads: Tradition and Accommodation During the Golden Age of the Hungarian Nobility, 1729–1878*. Budapest: Central European University Press, 2007.

Măndiţă, Mădălina. *Compared Noology of Jewish and Romanian People*. Aachen: Shaker Verlag, 2017.

Mann, Vivian "Synagogues, Medieval and Modern." In *The Encyclopaedia of Judaism*,

2nd ed. Leiden, Boston: Brill, 2005.

McIlwain, Charles Howard. *Constitutionalism: Ancient and Modern*. Clark, NJ: Lawbook Exchange, 2005.

Medicine, Beatrice. "My Elders Tell Me." In *Indian Education in Canada, Volume 2*, edited by Jean Barman, Yvonne M. Hébert, and Don McCaskill. Vancouver, BC, Canada: UBC Press, 1987.

Mitu, Claudiu Constantin. *Istoria Evreilor Din România*. Lucian Blaga University Sibiu Romania, 2020.

Mundill, Robin R. *The King's Jews: Money, Massacre and Exodus in Medieval England*. London, New York: Bloomsbury Publishing, 2010.

Na'aman, Nadav. "Royal Vassals or Governors? On the Status of Sheshbazzar and Zerubbabel in the Persian Empire." *Henoch* 22, no. 1 (2000): 35–44.

Naar, Devin E. "The "Mother of Israel" or the "Sephardi Metropolis"? Sephardim, Ashkenazim, and Romaniotes in Salonica." *Jewish Social Studies* 22, no. 1 (2016): 81–129.

Nathans, Benjamin. *Beyond the Pale: The Jewish Encounter With Late Imperial Russia*. Berkley/LosAngeles/London: University of California Press, 2002.

Oppenheimer, A'haron. *Am Ha-Aretz*. Leiden: E. J. Brill, 1977.

Oxford Advanced Learner's Dictionary. Oxford: Oxford University Press, 2022.

Pinchuk, Ben-Cion. "The Shtetl." *Cahiers du monde russe* 41, no. 41/4 (2000): 495–504.

Popescu, Alina. "Architectural Survey of the Bucharest Synagogues." *Studia Hebraica*, nos. 9–10 (2009): 123–34.

Researchers of ANU. *The Jewish Community of Alba Iulia*. Tel Aviv: The Museum of the Jewish People, 1996.

Rhodes, Peter J. *Athenian Democracy*. Edinburgh: Edinburgh University Press, 2019.

Roitman, Alexandru. "Alegerile Rabinice Din Oraşul Bălţi În Anul 1877, După Documente Inedite." *Revista de Etnologie şi Culturologie* 26, no. 2 (2019): 119–26.

Rosman, Moshe. "The Role of Non-Jewish Authorities in Resolving Conflicts Within Jewish Communities in the Early Modern Period." *Jewish Political Studies Review* (2000): 53–65.

Safrai, Shmuel, and Menachem Stern. "Jewish Self-Government." In *The Jewish People in the First Century, Volume 1*, 377–419. Leiden: Brill, 1974.

Scholefield, Roger S., and Alain Bideau. *The Decline of Mortality in Europe*. Oxford: Oxford University Press, 1991.

Schreier, Joshua. "Napoleon's Long Shadow: Morality, Civilization, and Jews in France and Algeria, 1808–1870." *French Historical Studies* 30, no. 1 (2007): 77–103.

Schwarzfeld, Elias. "The Jews of Moldavia at the Beginning of the Eighteenth Century." *The Jewish Quarterly Review* 16, no. 1 (1903): 113–34.
Segre, Renata. "Sephardic Settlements in Sixteenth-Century Italy: A Historical and Geographical Survey." *Mediterranean Historical Review* 6, no. 2 (1991): 112–37.
Shamash, V., T. Rocca, M. Rocca, and S. Moreh. *Memories of Eden: A Journey Through Jewish Baghdad*. Evanston, IL: Northwestern University Press, 2016.
Shavit, Yaacov, and Barbara Harshav. "Cyrus King of Persia and the Return to Zion: A Case of Neglected Memory." *History and Memory* 2, no. 1 (1990): 51–83.
Stiegelbauer, Suzanne M. "What Is an Elder? What Do Elders Do?: First Nation Elders as Teachers in Culture-Based Urban Organizations." *The Canadian Journal of Native Studies* 14 (1996): 37–66.
Stow, Kenneth. *Alienated Minority: The Jews of Medieval Latin Europe*. Cambridge, MA, London: Harvard University Press, 2009.
Toaff, Renzo. "Statuti E Leggi Della «Nazione Ebrea» Di Livorno. Ii: La Legislazione Dal 1655 Al 1677.(Cont. Ne)." *La Rassegna Mensile di Israel* 38, no. 5 (1972): 33–48.
Turchin, Peter. *Historical Dynamics: Why States Rise and Fall*. Princeton, NJ: Princeton University Press, 2003.
Urman, Dan. "The House of Assembly and the House of Study." In *Ancient Synagogues: Historical Analysis and Archaeological Discovery*, edited by Dan Urman and Paul Virgil McCracken Flesher, 232–55. Leiden: Brill, 1998.
Valley, Eli. *The Great Jewish Cities of Central and Eastern Europe: A Travel Guide and Resource Book to Prague, Warsaw, Crakow, and Budapest*. Lanham, Toronto, Oxford: Rowman & Littlefield, 2005.
Van Kley, Dale. "The Abbé Grégoire and the Quest for a Catholic Republic." In *The Abbé Grégoire and His World*, edited by Jeremy D. Popkin and Richard H. Popkin. Dordrecht/Boston/London: Kluwer Academic Publishers, 2000.
Weber, Max. *Ancient Judaism*. New York & London: Free Press, 2010.
Westreich, Elimelech, and Avishalom Westreich. "Jewish Law: Marriage." In *Routledge Handbook of Religious Laws*, edited by Rossella Ferrari Bottoni, Silvio, 221–38. London: Routledge, 2019.
Wildstein, Jeffrey. *Judaism: An Introduction to Jewish Beliefs and History*. Indianapolis, IN: DK Publishing, 2015.
Williamson, Hugh G. M. "Judah and the Jews." In *Studies in Persian Period History and Historiography*, edited by M. Brosius and A. Kuhrt, 145–63. Leiden: Brill, 1998.
Zaremska, Hanna. "The Rabbinate of Poznań in the Second Half of the Fifteenth Century." *Acta Poloniae Historica* 119 (2019): 157–74.
Zeitilin, Solomon. "The Council of Four Lands." *The Jewish Quarterly Review* 39, no. 2 (1948): 211–14.

Chapter 4

Communal Society and the Societal "Dual System"

Equality and Inequality in Carpathian Valleys

Ilie Bădescu

In the memory of H. H. Stahl

SOCIOLOGY REVISITED: THE COVENANTAL SOCIETY PARADIGM

Covenantal or Contractual Society?

One of the greatest challenges for sociology is to explain the survival of egalitarian social communities within the hierarchical, inequality-based societal formations.[1] Such communities have survived in several geographical areas. This type of societal formation persisted in the area stretching around the Carpathian Mountains since immemorial time until nowadays. It has run unchanged for thousands of years next and often under the layers of superimposed systems of dominations with their own taxing apparatus and military bodies. Our purpose in the present study is to investigate how the continuity for such long periods of the egalitarian, non-hierarchical, and rankless social formations is possible within the ascent of hierarchical, inequality-based formations. First of all, we have to understand the principal difference between the two types of societies. Finding out the answer to this problem results from the definition of the ownership system.

Using Livni's designation, we may speak of a communal structure and organization when both land partitioning of property, between family households and justice system, belong to the community which runs them out of any kind of external hierarchy and intrusion. We say, in such situations, that the community takes precedence over the political and military system, however complex it would be. Based on its communal organization, the community takes control of even economy.[2]

As a rule, sociology takes its cue to undertake such analysis, from the relation between the "frontstage" (surface) phenomena and deep structures of society. H. H. Stahl advanced a new method, that he named *social archaeology*, to investigate such deep structures. Sociologists like Spencer (at the end of a prestigious sociological series) believed that such a profound unit-study of sociology is the *social contract.* Spencer's response assumes a model of societal organization where economy takes precedence over the community. This is but a particular situation and it denotes, apparently, a defining model for a late historical era and for a small area, that of Western Europe. In other geographic areas and for long historical periods, the organizational model was one in which "community seems to take precedence over economy."[3] There are more other essential traits needed to circumscribe the ideal type of communal culture and society.

This type of culture and society must be concomitantly general and intuitive in order to be on the same time intelligible to common people and at handy for the purpose of giving the salutary answer to the more general (universal)/ challenge: *how to live honestly, rightly, that is, justly.*

In a way, we may assume, as J. Livni underlines, that "*justice and seeing straight have remained associated since land have been owned, the connection is not only found* in Indo-European cultures; the Hebrew Bible also uses the term *straight* for *just* (Judges, 21:25)."[4] In the Proto-Romanian communalist society and culture, the partitioning land between villages and, within them, between family households, was based, as H. H. Stahl disclosed, on this pattern of the "straight line." The issue of the land appropriation is part of the same deep root, and it lays the foundation of the "natural" societal order itself.

The *Book of Genesis* tells us that God Himself made man to be the master of land and, following the consequences of the lapsing moment, not only that God has not taken back from man the creational gifts but He, additionally, bestowed upon man a superadded ability, that of being able to work the land and to harvest its fruits in a way that is pleased to God, that is, by living and sharing everything justly, that is, *straight.*

That biblical narration reveals us that human destiny is deeply "hidden in God" and that the whole story of human being is founded on *the covenant between God and man* (starting with the first one between God and Adam whom God created upon His own image and likeness), a covenant that man has broken by not observing God's *protecting commandment* of not eating from the forbidden tree (as a matter of fact, from *the mortal fruit*).

The main purpose of the covenantal (communitarian) culture is, in all times and places, the preservation of the foundational semasiology enabling us to discern intuitively the profile of a *good orderliness* in society and to deposit it in the vernacular languages by those families of words through which a kind of pre-reflexive semantic paradigm is propagated in large populations. Within our latent mind, we do not mistake as to what is the ideal type of societal justice, that is, a latent societal type helping us, pre-reflexively, to recognize the state of a given society as being a just/right or an unjust one. This inner "social mind" (Mead) has universally and irretrievable been testified in Bible. Thanks to it we are self-reinforced within a primeval "looking glass self," as Cooley named it, and which makes us spontaneously able to comprehend the fundamentals of a "straight society," and to make difference between *social justice* and *societal injustice*.

In the Covenantal order, between me, as an individual, and the higher order, there is nothing to interfere, nothing to watch, but God. The societal order based on the ranks and the king, as a ruler with supreme power in this world, is an alternative to the covenantal order, because the king alleges for him the role of a mediator, who interferes between me and the incorruptible divine order, claiming for him the role of the representative of a higher order. The history of mankind mirrors the struggle between two types of social order: a rankless, non-hierarchical one, based on the common observance of divine orderliness, and a hierarchical, non-egalitarian one, based on the implicit obedience to the power of the ruler and his elite.[5] Is there beneath of such a struggle a deeper order in which the model of a "good society" is mirrored?

"COMMUNAL VILLAGES" AND "DUAL SYSTEM"

From Communal Culture to the "Dual System": Fundamentals of H. H. Stahl's Sociology of Communal Societies

The communal structure and organization may last unchanged for thousands of years, underlines H. H. Stahl, next and often under the layers of superimposed nomads, under the burden of domination systems with their own taxing apparatus and military bodies. These burdensome states of occupation did not manage to destroy the old communal structure, so that the indigenous population existed by its own communal organization, which consisted of the communal villages progressing toward the larger network of the Confederation communal villages to culminate in their first form of state organization called *Voivodates*. Stahl defines the communal social formation by the "family households association," based on a "shared territory," in which the "community as such has rights prior to and above the rights of the comprising households"; these rights were controlled by a "governing body" called *obstie* (collective assembly).[6]

Concomitant with the emergence of a hierarchical order in society, the buds of inequality appear themselves. What is odd at the process of the progressive escalation of inequality is that, despite the terrible force backing it historically, its vigor within certain types of communities and cultural areas appears to be rather low, being marked by constant failures to enlarge over there. *The terrible domination systems, empires, and different types of imperialism grow outside, above, become burdensome, oppressive but cannot penetrate communities, cannot dismantle their sub-structures.* Thus, a dualistic system is born, which we will examine in this study. Such failures can be recorded within those types of societies called, with H. H. Stahl's general term, *communal societies.* This term "relates to a particular *rankless* societal model governed by a rule (covenant) rather than by a ruler."[7] The roots of this type of society descend directly into the Bible so that they can be certified in the people of Bible, namely in ancient Israel. Moreover, the scientist will discover this type of society also within some other areas as in the ancient communal society from the Carpathian region of Romania. H. H. Stahl and N. Iorga researched the ancient communal institution of "the good and old men" (*oamenii buni si batrani*), meaning those who were called to make justice based on the orally transmitted ancient wisdom and collective rule. Stahl used to explain this type of societal organization as one stemming from "that order based on the diffuse tradition." This is a representative type of a rankless society governed by rule rather than by a ruler. The hierarchy of ranks could not be born in such a community. It is appropriate to name it "communal society" or by Elazar's term *covenantal society.* We shall notice that, as Stahl demonstrated, the communal type of society resisted long time along and in parallel with the hierarchical type of social organization (based on the authority of the ruler and ruling elite). The history of inequality bypassed such a communal/ covenantal order. Inequality emerged outside the local communal society as a network of relationships between two separate societies, so that we may observe the non-hierarchical society evolving unbroken until the twentieth century in rural Romania. The study of inequality has a long tradition[8] but the study of the "non-hierarchical societies" has a short tradition rooted typologically like Elazar's research of the covenantal society or in the field-works like that of H. H. Stahl's on the communal society (ancient equalitarian village communities), in Romania and, historically, in Iorga's works on the ancient institutions of " the good and old men" (*boni viri anziani* or *boni homines*) collectively assumed to be those most honest and righteous men within a free, non-hierarchical community. In Romanian "batran" (the oldest in a family or within a community) means not only the eldest one (from the Latin *veteranus*), but also "forefather" (*moş*, a traco-illyric etymology), a sort of "patriarch," a genealogical predecessor. A village is divided genealogically on more "forefathers" (mosi) with their lands (moşii), a sort of genealogical estates. H. H. Stahl draws attention on the two totally different ways of feudalism penetration in rural local communities: the Western type of feudalism based on the internal hierachization of local community (the first form of feudalism) and the Romanian type, where the class of lords could exploit the peasants organized nevertheless in free, non-hierarchical village communities, that is, based on a system of internal non-hierarchical organization. The two components of such a society evolve totally in parallel the only link between them being a tribute-based one in the form of fiscal dues in produce and labor. This type of social organization could be denoted as a *dual societal system*. Peculiarity of such a dual system consists in their contrastive evolution: while the first system, let us call it the *communal system*, moves non-transformatively, almost linearly, and non-reflexively, the other one, let's call it *the hierarchical type*, is un-equalitarian, reflexive, having a mirroring elite.[9] The hierarchical type and the non-hierarchical one coexist next to each other. As Stahl showed, "the lords can exploit village communities without owning them, by the simple imposition of a tribute, according to a state fiscal system."[10] The only way of feudalization by Western type occurred, paradoxically, during the period of penetration of capitalism in the Romanian rural society beginning with the nineteenth century. The two systems of *societal organization*, a hierarchical, un-equalitarian one and a non-hierarchical, rankless one, coexisted and periodically have come into collision with each other. This historical path characterized by the *dual system* concluded into a second serfdom within the full capitalist age, but even then, the free communal society continued to exist until nowadays. We need to explain the survival of communal society throughout the long historical cycles of inequality. Our hypothesis combines two theories: Stahl's theory of a dual societal system and Elazar's theory of the covenantal society. Our own hypothesis assumes the theory of autochthony of the people whose proprietary connection with their land originates in a primordial time, *in illo tempore*. That kind of man's connection with his land was collectively remembered as the "holy bond," legitimating the hereditary rights to strip of land based on the divine covenant.

Such an orderliness which asks everybody to live and share everything justly, that is, straight, is obviously the very root of communal culture and society. This type of societal organization, certified by the field-research, is precisely the main and irrefutable argument of the autochthony of a people who had lived in that way from the immemorial times until nowadays. Peasantry is indeed the main document of the historical continuity of that people on its land called *patria communis*—homeland, motherland, or fatherland. The peasantry people reveal, therefore, as being prior to any type of empire or ethnic newcomers despite of their success to build the oppressive, superimposed forms of statehood, based on a transient domination, a purely *temporariness.*

FREE VILLAGE AND COMMUNAL SOCIETY

Rural areas preserved the sociological model of community culture, which remained unchanged until the establishment of statehood.[11] From that event moment, until the twentieth century, H. H. Stahl noted: "Since free villages *(răzeşi* and *moşneni)* still existed between the two world wars they could be subjected to field research, undertaken as monographs between 1925 and 1946 by the School of Sociology directed by my teacher, Professor Dimitrie Gusti."[12] Free villages (*razesi* and *mosneni*) were subjected, therefore, to field research for a while of twenty years. The challenging aspect of those free villages' organizational pattern is its networking structure so that it could extend over large areas in the form of villages confederation. The information and goods circulated within such a confederation on such a network basis. The prototype of this archaic pattern was the small and extended genealogical structure. Large "family lineage" pattern often encompassed the whole village and sometimes an entire surrounding village region. The genealogical pattern was probably used as an organizational model in the process of communal organization of the village. All the male inhabitants of the villages grouped on the valleys, for instance, addressed each other with the appellative "brother," even though there was no consanguineous relationship between them.

In such a form of communal existence we encounter two traits:

1) the inhabitants claim "that they formed a single large family lineage descended from a single ancestral hero believed to have been the founder of the village;
2) they settled their patrimonial rights in the whole of the village territory according to a family genealogy, either memorized or written."[13]

The "myth" of the ancestral hero as a founder of the village emerged later when "the original community begins to decay and divides its property into unequal, hereditary parts, and then into private property."[14]

Therefore, the genealogical pattern is not the founding structure of village, but its function is nevertheless working within a village as a "measure of hereditary rights to strip of land."[15] Moreover, there are villages where the genealogical type followed a non-genealogical one, so that the founding structure of the village is not confused, at its beginning, with the genealogical structure. Therefore, we need to understand the transition from one to another to make clear the features of a primary communalist culture and society. Theoretically, communal villages could be defined by at least these traits: (a) as a group of households, that are holders of a territory, (b) maintain relations among them over a vast territory; (c) share a package of the rules acknowledged by all and encompassed in what we may call the oral Law enforced by diffuse tradition and by strict observance of representatives of the general assemblies. In those villages fallen under "the domination of a feudal lord, *the lord takes over, by force, the old rights of general assemblies* which, thus, lose their powers, even though the village remains 'communal.'"[16]

Despite the expropriation of the village of its old rights, the communal structure remains unchanged until the threshold of capitalism penetration in the Eastern European societies. Only the market economy will provoke changes that undermine the communal organization of the villages. Let us see first the internal organization of such a communal village and then we shall approach the way of transition from one type to another to make clear the network structure that explains *the transitional process.*

Anyway, the two types of societal order, one based on the enveloping hierarchical system (with a state apparatus destined to military functions and to tribute taxation) and the other one based on the general assemblies of community and, eventually, on the authority of "the good and old men," continued to coexist until twentieth century, argues H. H. Stahl. Beneath such a co-evolutionary structure persist hidden conflicts and periodical clashes coming out between those two societal systems. H. H. Stahl's sociology approached this dual system in all its joints during the long period of Romanian social history and throughout the Carpathian-Danubian territory. Moreover, as we shall see bellow, in Transylvania, the dual societal system takes on an ethnocratic color. The superimposed element is ethnically foreign to the population of villages whose rights were encroached on by the regime of foreign domination.

COMMUNALISM VERSUS STATEHOOD: HOW TO RECONCILE THEM?

The concepts of "humanity" and "civilization," used to define the world system, were exclusively Eurocentric, argues C. Schmitt: "civilization" meant European civilization. Non-European space was considered to be uncivilized or half-civilized, leaderless, even empty. The belief in "European civilization" was essential to the whole structure of *Volkerrecht*, and was part and parcel of European consciousness."[17] The challenging issue is that, as a matter of fact, social history testifies two evolutionary ways for the European society: one based on the passage from communal society to hierarchical order; the other one consisting in the dualist system, that is, the persistence of a rankless communal society concomitant with the emergence of the hierarchical state order. In Romanian area there was neither a feudal order like the Western feudal system nor even a slave state order, but a communal type of social organization parallel with a state hierarchical order. The only relationship between the two societal systems was a tribute-like one. All interpersonal issues within communal society (free villages) were solved based on the communal non-hierarchical, oral "institution" ("oral Law") of what usually was called *the good and old men*, as an old judicial act testifies it.

> Behold, coming Ion, our servant, with his woman and with their children, in front of us and our Moldavian boyars, of high and low ranks, presented in front of us a zapis (a testimonial file), as testimony from the good and old men (*oameni buni si bătrâni*), namely: Ionaşcu from the Fair of Suceava (Targul Sucevei) and Ion Vulpe of Nelineşti and Isaia from there too, and Vasile sin Captain also from there, witnessing that, in front of those good and old men, Gligore from Lipaiesti, the brother of Constantin, the son of the Patroaia, sold, willingly, untold of no one, nor oppressed, and gave his share (a jerbie: a strip) from the village of Lipaiesti with the place of land and village and with all his income to. . . .[18]

The *good and old men*, as the representatives within community, judging based on the oral Law, known and shared by all members of community, served as a pattern even for the organization of the early form of state, called voivode-state, in its first stage of historical evolution. N. Iorga argues: "Voivode-Rulers had no court, and they were rounding, necessarily, in those first decades (of the century), only by advisers (*sfetnici*), dressed in Romanian (traditional) clothes, similar to elders called to peasant judgments."[19]

Such communities, noted H. H. Stahl in his works, have existed as the oldest type of social organization forms and continued to exist and preserve their autonomy until nowadays. Moreover, the communal villages, argued Stahl, were organized in confederations of free villages to serve afterward as the basis for early forms of state called Romanian Principalities. On the other hand, beyond and distinct of them, there emerged from outside of these free communal confederations a reorganized type of hierarchical state after a pattern partly rooted in local traditions, partly from influences of those types of voluminous conquering states brought in the area by invading peoples finally settled next or around the natives (autochthonous communal society). As Iorga argues: "in the Romanian Country, the first boyars were necessarily foreigners, but in short time, those Greco-Slavs beneficiaries remained very few and they can barely be recognized among the others."[20] In a certain sense, they have come to be assimilated thus forming the local elite. Despite such a statist impulse, there was a totally different communal order preserved, beyond and linked to that hierarchical organization of society. This non-hierarchical social order relies on the genealogy that goes up to its spiritual origin confirmed and strengthened in the form of a covenant which asks the people to respect the spiritual teachings sheltered by it and springing out of it. When the signs of a tendency to a type of hierarchical order starts emerging (in which a "race" claims for itself a leading role, a dominant position), the different genealogical stocks start to collide with each other. But, even in the midst of such a contest an older type of community survived where people look at those who respect the covenant as to "brothers and sisters." This order is communally shared and respected, and taken for granted, so that, in such a society the genealogical contest and clashes are lacking or vanish. The observance of communal rule is the access gate into such a group. The European civilization evolved in that way, that is, by the progressive sharing of the same Judeo-Christian covenantal teachings by all European peoples (nations). This covenantal evolution was carried out parallel to a progressive development of the hierarchical order (statehood order centered on the ruler and on the leading elite). The only difference, argued H. H. Stahl, is that in some societies, the Romanian one being included, the communal order, parallel with the statehood, survived as a distinct social order, that is, rankless, leaderless, and internally non-hierarchical, up to the twentieth century.

A rank-based social order could not emerge within a communal society by its inner evolution but by external admixture due either to an external source, an occupation, that is, a war and/or a domination effect, and therefore to an act of external imposition, or to the reaction against such an external intrusion.

> The boyar was the owner only in the margins (within the boundaries) of the Lord's reward for his comrades in the battle, his faithful in the expelling, for his lenders on the hard days. What could the Lord have given? Of course, that only what he had: first of all, his voivodship's rights to the free peasant land, i.e. the tithe, from which then, in time and by coercion, could be taken out greater rights, and then from the possession of his inheritance, on the confiscated patrimonies from cunning or traitors, and on the wilderness without owner. The colonization, more and more stretched, as well as the ever-increasing confiscation in the fights for the seat of the aspirants, established finally, from the 15th century on, the bond between the beneficiaries and the great owner, and these processes made so to emerge a Romanian aristocracy: when the aristocracy lacked the power of the rank, it had the houses of the estate, with the tithe of the harvest, with the dominion of the pond, the forest, the mill and of the tavern, but never the right of judgment and punishment.[21]

Therefore, and I stress on the last statement in the citation from Iorga's book, the ruler (*voivode*) and its elite could get a lot of rights in society and over the communal society *but never the right of judgment and punishment*. This was *the right of the community itself* and it was granted by the oral Law. As I have already mentioned, this type of societal organization relies, Stahl demonstrated, on that sort of order based on the *diffuse tradition*. With a supplementary observation: the order has its root in the spiritual authority founded on the authority of divine covenant not on the authority of a given tradition. Otherwise, it will be hard to explain its power of subsistence and of withstanding the test of time. The relation between the two types of social structures could take over either the form of coexistence or the form of conflict. This conflict was between the two social patterns: one based on equality and the other on inequality or hierarchy. The inequality exerted pressure over equality, the communalism reacting against this intrusion of the principle of inequality. This fight could take the form of a Reconquista or of a boycott form, that is, a rejection by unassuming and thus by total abandonment of the system itself. The problem of such a dual society was to solve this conflict, to harmonize the parts, to transfigure the confines into confluences, that is, to reconcile the statehood (and hierarchical organization) with communalism (an equalitarian pattern).

Based on the covenantal society theory we may comprehend specific phenomena as the struggle for the right over a territory called country and the inter-ethnical disputes on the territorial areas, as in Transylvania where the communal order was primordial compared to any historical regulation (written Law), this one ensuing from an ulterior hierarchical organization of society, imposed by occupation and/or by conquest. That is the source of the distinction between the autochthony, that is, the covenantal rights over a country land, and the historically evolved rights resulting from a historical secular act and embracing the form of the written Law. The autochthony is founded on the covenantal oral Law and embraces the form of an imprescriptible communal right known by all people as a truth rooted in the ancient immemorial times (*in illud tempus*). The people of the land (natives, autochthonous people) had the strong belief that God placed them on their lands and that no authority except only God could take them out of their settlements. This is essentially the quality of the autochthony: the relationship with the land they take care of is how old the world is and has a root in the will of God directly. God made them the owners of these lands. They are owners with divine vestiture. They have been mentioned in these places, on their land, since immemorial times, from father to son. And the witness for this is directly God and their village entirely, from elders and ancestors to the nowadays' villagers.

COMMUNALIST CULTURE AND EMERGING INEQUALITY

Let's look at Stahl's sociology of communal society in the light of the cultural transmission theory of survival of a given structural trait. The *free villages* are the sample illustrating a more comprehending cradle of communal society. In 1864 the statistical data allows us to determine the number of totally free villages compared with the number of serf villages and mixed ones.

New cultural traits propagate as genetic mutations according to equation 1.1.14 of Cavalli-Sforza and Feldman,[22] (see description of symbols in Table 4.1):

$$\dot{p}(x) = M\left(\frac{\partial^2 p}{\partial x^2}\right) + \alpha p(1-p) \tag{4.1}$$

Throughout highlands of the Romanian rural area there emerged progressively a new social system. The aristocrats' exploitation was based not on "slaves or conquered people but on free village communities, by purely fiscal means, and only acquired property rights over the land and inhabitants much later."[23]

In the case of mixed system and even that of the former serf villages the evolution of communities followed a "polymorphic way."

The communalist culture and, therefore, the village communities survived until twentieth century which "was no longer the case in the rest of Eastern Europe," as Stahl underlines.[24]

Table 4.1 Description of Symbols of Cultural Trait of Equation (4.1)

Symbol	*Explanation*
$p(x)$	the prevalence of a cultural trait within a given area
$\dot{p}(x)$	The growth rate of $p(x)$ per unit of time
M	the rate of migration
$\left(\frac{\delta p}{\delta x}\right)$	Rate of change of p per kilometer along a path
$\left(\frac{\partial^2 p}{\partial x^2}\right)$	rate of change of $\left(\frac{\delta p}{\delta x}\right)$ per kilometer along the path
α	*Survival advantage* i.e., the difference between the *survival fitness* of two competing species, mutations, traits etc.

Source: Prepared by authors.

In Plains' areas, on the contrary, bondage prevailed; the villages fell into a second type of serfdom, so that, the penetration of capitalism in that area further stressed the serfdom.

Stahl offers an overview of the situation based on statistical data from 1864:

In the census of 1912 the number of villages with over 51% percentage of free population amount at about 70% from total number of mixed villages. In 70% of this type of villages the free population exceeds the number of the enserfed people so that we may conclude the communal prevailed one. The rural Law of 1864 has deepened the traits of the communalist culture in the Romanian villages. In 1912 the rural population lived in 5,822 formerly serf villages and 1,710 free villages, the number of mixed villages amounting to 1,462 villages (table 4.2). 1020 mixed villages were inhabited by an "absolute majority of free peasants (69.8% of such villages)."[25] By comparing two censuses of 1722[26] and 1912, Stahl concluded that in the last 200 years the number of free villages (those who had no lords) decreased in favor of a "trend toward enserfment of villages."[27] The most probable hypothesis is "that the free communal villages existed from the beginning of the state and that they were subjected over the course of history to a process of enserfment, which nevertheless did not succeed in enserfing all of them, even though the process began long ago."[28]

> The existence of these free village communities explains the forms that serfdom took in these regions and the special forms of serfdom explain, in turn, the particular ways in which capitalism made itself felt. A study of this social history is particularly apt in the Romanian provinces because nowhere in the Ponto-Baltic zone were the forms of village communities as recent or typical as in Romania, especially in Moldavia and Wallachia (which we will study almost exclusively). In these two Romanian provinces, the village communities were so alive that even in the mid twentieth century they could be found in large numbers and, in addition, many were still free, i.e. they had never had a local lord.[29]

Table 4.2 Number and Percentage of Villages Formerly Free, Serf, or Mixed

Hypothesis – α=survival advantage	Types of villages	number	percentage
$\alpha > 0$	free	1710	19%
$\alpha < 0$	serf	5822	64.8%
$\alpha = 0$	mixed	1462	16.2%
	Total	8999	100%

Source prepared by the author using information from H. H. Stahl, *Traditional Romanian Village Communities* p.10.
Note: α symbolizes the survival advantage of free villages.

A negative survival advantage of the communalist culture predicts its extinction. The communal power of individuals and of the community itself will decline and the resistance against external influences will weaken so that the members of the group will be attracted to other models and the group will enter a disintegration cycle caused by the force of imitation. The more negative the survival advantage of egalitarianism is, the faster communalism reaches extinction.[30]

Firstly we shall examine the idea that the social order of free villages is related to a special type of culture, called by Stahl communal culture. This type of culture survived to the greatest possible extent only within the free villages and has been progressively erased in the enserfed villages. Instead, in such areas the external influences have become gradually stronger so that the power of the village decreased in favor of the hierarchy of the state of occupation or conquest. Even in these situations, the old memory of the communal culture survived in the form of a strong resistance against the invader, occupant, and conqueror. Such a hypothesis is the only one allowing us to solve the issue of two opposed social types of villages within the same society and country: free and serf villages. By using the social map, Stahl highlights two completely distinct types of villages and zones:

> There are even "zones without lords," where the free peasants make up the absolute total. On the other hand, there are also "zones of serfdom," where free peasants do not exist or where, at most, they are but rare exceptions. And there are regions where free and serf villages co-exist. These diverse types of villages are sometimes so inter-mixed in the same geographical areas that any hypothesis of two civilizations confronting each other, giving birth to two distinct social histories, or of the decisive influence of geographic conditions, falls flat. The hypothesis of a difference in agricultural techniques could not be seriously considered either, for free and serf villages had the same agricultural level, the same economic occupations and the same work procedures, as we shall see.[31]

Therefore, we need another hypothesis and Stahl was reluctant to the idea of different types of cultural patterns underpinning different social organizations. As a matter of fact, the communal culture was the unique long-lasting type of culture in the villages before their splitting in two areas due to the establishment of an invading conquering state. As Stahl argues himself:

> We will then have to call upon other purely social circumstances to explain this phenomenon of the co-existence, in the same territories, in the same geographic and cultural conditions, of such contradictory social phenomena as those of the free and serf villages.[32]

So, the social phenomena are contradictory but the geographic and cultural conditions are the same. A cultural-focused explanation appears to be preferable to any other hypothesis when looking for a response to the communal trait shared by the villagers from different villages, either free or serf villages. This explanation is not sustainable when we look for a cause of the phenomenon of falling into serfdom (the emergence of the enserfed villages). If we want to explain the differences between the plains area villages and highland area villages, the factors which proved powerful enough to generate opposite social structures within a unique type of communalist culture must be considered. Two aspects are remarkable: the fact that

> the mass of free villages is found deep in the mountainous regions, the sub-Carpathian depressions and the hills where the earliest political States were born, This is proved by an act of 1247 and by the internal documents of the fourteenth century which indicate this as being the region where the state, properly called "the Romanian country," also called "Muntenia" (Land of the mountains), was founded.[33]

The serfdom of villages in the Danubian Plain can be explained by Tartar invasion countered by the action of Carpathian boyars who "threw themselves against the Tartars to reconquer the Danubian plain, a region of mostly serf villages," as Stahl mentions. For the paradox of encountering free villages where the state was born Stahl proposed his ingenious answer consisting in what will become his theory of a distinct type of communal society.

FROM COMMUNAL SOCIETY TO STATE-SOCIETY

The Village confederation and the Voivode-state show that the voivode-like state (*Viovodates*) did not eradicate the pre-state communal society (upholding that "old habits die hard").

> How was it possible, then, that the "free" villages dominate at the moment when the state was born? This problem would be insoluble if one committed the error of believing that there was only one way to exploit an agrarian population: the one known in the west, where the feudal lords were landowners, receiving as such the feudal dues in produce and labour. Lords can exploit village communities without owning them, by the simple imposition of a tribute, according to a state fiscal system. Thus, the central head of the warrior class could command a repressive state fiscal apparatus and distribute the "national revenue"—if one can call it such—to the members of the seigniorial class, / without owning the land, which continued as the patrimony of the / communal villages. A basis for the state could then be established by an ascendancy over the men without actual possession of the land.[34]

Concluding, the communal society in Romanian areas preserved its egalitarian profile due to *a mix of two factors*:

1. an *almighty communalist culture* entrenched on the land the natives lived on since immemorial time;
2. state's option (from the very moment it was born) of "exploiting the free villages by taxation" so that the land continued to be the "patrimony of the communal villages."

The inequality as a societal pattern operated from the outside of the communal society (as a burdensome casing) and the relation between the hierarchically built social system and the egalitarian communal society took over the form of the simple imposition of a tribute. The state evolved toward a "repressive state fiscal apparatus" outside of the local communal society. The two societal systems have coexisted laying so the foundation of a dual societal system. In such a system, the communal culture gains a leading role in the defensive strategy of the communal society. The social structures could be destroyed only if you had previously dismantled the *communalist culture* which is not easy at all, given that the old cultural pattern passed over into the written, literate culture, so that the communal village survived as a "village inside of an idea" ("village-idea"), as Stahl used to suggest. More surprising is to find out that the free villages, covering large and long strips in the mountain regions, the sub-Carpathian depressions and the hills, survived until the twentieth century, as Stahl proved by mapping the entire region, based on the census of 1912. And what is even more surprising is to discover that communalist culture and social organization survived where the state was born so that the two societal systems, a communal, egalitarian one and another hierarchical, ruler-based one, coexisted within the same mountain region, as the map regarding the genesis of Romanian feudal state unveils.[35]

Moreover, the Carpathian boyars threw themselves against Tartars in the Danubian Plain to reconquer the serf villages. This is another paradoxical aspect: the class of lords and free villages coexisted and supported each other. The Romanian case is but one example that allows us to speak of another face of the world where an evolutionary path prevailed distinct from the Western path. On this side of the line and on the other side, besides and beyond, two different social worlds have evolved: the village one that preserved a type of communal, egalitarian culture and a non-hierarchical, rankless societal organization, and, beyond the line, the other one, which has chosen a different way, toward a hierarchical, non-egalitarian culture and rank-based social organization. In the hither part of the world (eastern one), the (communal) culture appears to have been stronger than the social system, while, beyond the line, the social system proved stronger than the communalist culture and finally defeated it; and so over there what we call the "feudalism" (or, more precisely, feudal-capitalism) was born. Don't forget: the two sides of this world are rooted in the same Judeo-Christian culture. The fact that the two worlds followed diverging social ways does not mean they were spiritually separated from each other. On the contrary: the Judeo-Christian fundamentals of the European culture triumphed by the victory of the covenantal pattern in the process of constitutional building of all European societies. Finally, even in the Western area, the covenant society (and, therefore, communalist culture) reconquered the elites so that, the covenantal pattern has been generalized itself from bottom-up and top-down over the entire new world built on the cradle of covenantal culture. The new Christian era brought the triumph of covenantal culture, has generalized it as a mindset within the hierarchical society, putting thus the Judeo-Christian foundations for the evolutionary path of the whole Europe. Returning to the Romanian case, we hold over Stahl's finding about the way in which the alternative social system of serf villages expanded in the geography dominated by free village pattern and, therefore, by the communalist culture. It is an example of co-habitation of the two opposed societal system—a non-hierarchical, rankless one and a hierarchical, rank-based the other—within the same society. Such a process was not carried out by the dislocation of the free villages, on the contrary. This pattern survived next the serf-villages pattern (figure 4.1),

> [The] serf villages cross the mass of free mountain villages, as if the feudal lords, at first exploiting the free villages by taxation, had then pushed forward, making their way through the villages along the valleys leading to the Danube, hurrying toward the plain reconquered from the nomads, where they were able to take full ownership of villages seriously depopulated by the series of wars. The lords then repopulated these villages by colonizing them with peasants who were enserfed by the mere fact of settling on conquered lands.[36]

The state building process has not dismantled the alternative social system based on the non-hierarchical, communal organization, but, paradoxically, has strengthened it being that the lords and the Voivode relied on the free villages for a military purpose and as a source of income and financial support of wars and state military apparatus. Therefore, the way toward an alternative system, based on the coerced labor and serf villages, resulted almost exclusively from the military reconquest of former conquered villages (by invaders, who had enserfed the former free villages by the effect of military occupation) and by "colonizing them with peasants who were enserfed by the mere fact of settling on (former) conquered lands."[37] What is even more significant is that the system of free villages has organized itself in larger networking structures forming the so called quasi-autonomous "republics" some of them arising even near the center of the state, as it was the villages of *Campulung*, or, toward the south of Moldovia country where two other small "republic" survived, that of Vrancea and of Tigheciu.[38] Here, the pattern of state building is geographically reversed: the northern part of the country appeared to be the prevalent area of reconquest and of serfdom while the southern area was the free villages' area; the explanation is derived from the fact that the Moldavian state was formed by an act of reconquest from the Tartars executed by a group of Romanian warriors fromMaramureş on the other side of the Carpathians, not by local lords as in Wallachia. One can explain the nature of the serfdom in the villages of northern Moldavia precisely by the effect of this reconquest and repopulation of a profoundly devastated zone.[39]

The whole social history of Romanian society could be explained by the co-evolution of the two societal systems with a distinction for the Transylvanian country where, as Stahl underlined, "the Hungarians conquered all the Romanian villages. Two races were in conflict, the victorious race reducing to serfdom the vanquished one, leaving only a few free villages, for example, in the region of Făgăraş, which for a while was under the domination of the Wallachian State, and the military border zones where Maria Theresa and Joseph II later created the special Frontier's Regiments."[40]

We may understand why in this area, the clashes of the two systems took over a prevailing religious character and different judicial or legal acts and memoirs addressed to the emperor and the Court of Vienna adopted profoundly the covenantal spirit. The well-known Memorandum and *Supplex Libellus Valachorum* are examples of covenantal-minded documents. Such a peculiarity could explain why in the South-Eastern Romanian Principalities the social uprisings are so infrequent while in Transylvania the social uprisings (peasantry revolts) are extraordinary frequent and so violent. We must not forget that in Transylvania the societal organization was marked by the liquidation of the Romanian free villages system due to Hungarian conquest and peasants' enserfment while in Walachia and Moldavia other two forms of societal system prevailed, both of them preserving the communal system until the twentieth century next the hierarchical system of the state which itself was influenced profoundly by the communalist culture and relying on it whether it's taxation or direct military support by participating in the common army composed by free peasants with their own military equipment (lance and sword).

We must remember, therefore, that the three Romanian principalities followed three evolutionary societal lines (despite the fact that the three areas preserved their unitary Romanian spiritual identity, proving once more how important is the culture in the dynamic of history): in Transylvania, almost all free communal villages have been enserfed by Hungarian warrior people while, in the other Romanian Principalities prevailed "two other forms created by the *reconquest* of the nomads, Wallachia's being the work of a local class, Moldavia's that of a class of Romanian warriors from Transylvania. If our hypothesis corresponds to reality, we should find the symptoms of these three types of social development, which, later on, in spite of their different origins, will slowly unify, tending toward the same final stage of belated capitalist penetration."[41]

VILLAGE BOUNDARY AS THE GRID OF COMMUNAL LANDSCAPE CULTURE

The village landscape was originally the facet of the communalist culture and it may be invoked as an "archaeological testament enabling one to reconstruct past stages of man's social history."[42] As a matter of fact, people have always spoken of the "eternal order of the fields."[43] The geometry of rural landscape speaks about the most archaic and profound layer of social memory and the key-element of this memory is the straight line: "the territorial complexes of Romania are also formed by a series of long strips arranged parallel to each other."[44] This kind of memory is deeply encroached on the land so that such an arrangement worked as a method of communal thought and as a deepest layer of communal organization that explains the reproductive way of social evolution proper to the communal society. The social history memorizes three types of communal arrangements that are also three networking strategies of societal reproduction of this kind of communal organization. The first type is of the "communes under the same yoke" (sate *înjugate*); the second type is of the communes "related" (*însurărite*); and the third type is of the villages like "twin brothers" (*îngemănate*).[45] The three types of partitioning the territory cover a whole region witnessing so of the more profound layer of communalist culture and type of social organization encroached on the land enhancing so the conscience of autochthony to the natives. It was as if the covenant and, therefore, covenantal society was written directly on the land and people have shown themselves ready to die for the land. Of course, "this kind of partitioning of a whole region is not easily visible to the eye."[46] Figure 4.1 shows in a schematic form the two types of village boundaries as a framing thought of drawing the rural communal landscape at a regional scale.

This territorial grid working altogether as a system of territorial partitioning and as a social mindset has until now persisted in the Romanian area so that we may conclude that the country is laid on grid villages, rivers' and hills' lines and therefore on a covenantal territorial memory encroached on land. Figure 4.2 is "an actual example of an area with 'twin' territories and 'round' ones; free, mixed, and serf villages co-exist in the region of the Jiu and Gilort valleys in central Oltenia," as Stahl mapped it.[47] This geometry of strips has

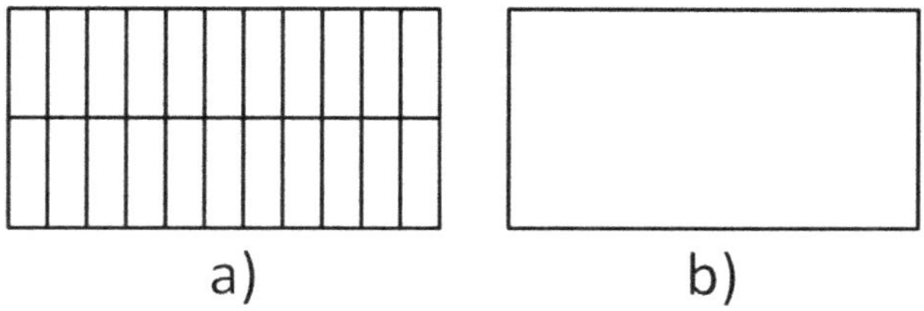

Figure 4.1 Types of Village Boundaries: (a) the "Related" Type; (b) the "Twin" Type. *Source*: Prepared by the author.

been encompassed, as a distinct socio-territorial communal system, in the state, hierarchical type of societal organization imbedding so durably the dual system in Romanian society composition. Studying the chronology of the communal village boundaries, which, as I have already mentioned, served as a pattern of territorial reproduction of the communal societal organization in a given territory, Stahl proved that the village boundaries have existed from "time immemorial if not forever." They, as a "vast operation of egalitarian inter-village partitioning, are parts of an *immemorial communalist culture* upon which the state itself has been constructed and remained definitely the foundational socio-territorial landscape of Romania. The clash between the two societal systems embraced therefore a form of territorial disputes and conflicts not only between individuals but also between social groups sharing different types of culture and/ or different ethnical belonging. As social memory is deeply encroached on land it might be rediscovered by generations, long run after the old memorizing people have passed away. I may call it *the memory of land* and it is an important part of the covenantal culture as the Country of the Holy Land has proved it. At the upper level, this culture is fixed under the territorial designation that, on the same time, played the role of administrative organization.

> The village commune is organized by a double (dichotomic) rule: the commune is split in two, lengthwise, the two halves named "upper part" and "lower part." For a whole group of old villages in Moldavia, where the reconquest of the territory from the nomads was more recent than in Wallachia and where the local social forms kept a more archaic nature than in other provinces, the documents mention also the existence of two rather enigmatic people called *knez* and *judec*. In other regions inhabited by Romanians, these prove to be village chiefs. In those villages with two *judeci,* the coupled halves of the village territory are designated by the term *judeci.* The names of the two *judeci* are sometimes used as geographic terms, based on their eponymous origin, while at the same time they are "socionyms," that is, collective names for all those in one half of the village.[48]

This system of social organization referring to the partitioning the land into village groups was kept in mind so that the village-minded thought and

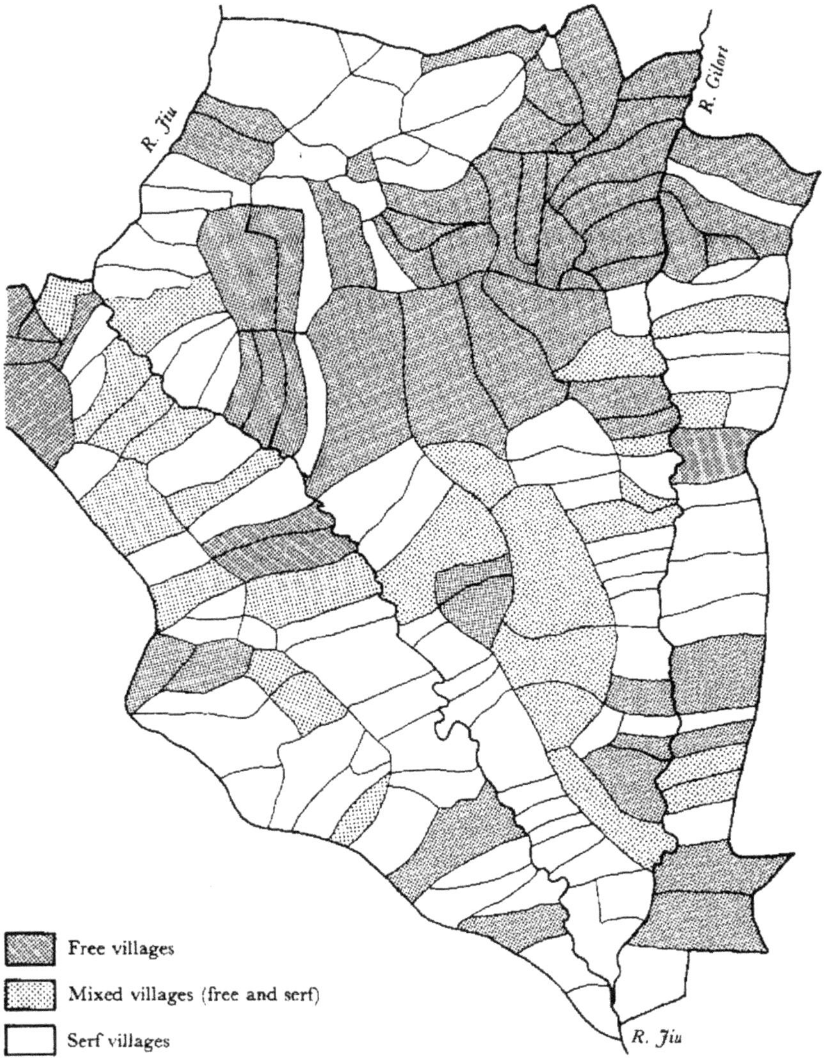

An actual example of an area with 'twin' territories and 'round' ones; free, mixed, and serf villages co-exist in the region of the Jiu and Gilort valleys in central Oltenia.

Figure 4.2 Map of the Region of the Jiu and Gilort Valleys in Central Oltenia with a Communal Landscape throughout an Area with "Twin" Territories and "Round" Ones, Where Free, Mixed, and Serf Villages Co-exist. *Source*: From Stahl, Traditional Romanian village communities, 18; Licence to use granted by Cambridge University Press on Oct. 18, 2022.

village pattern has been a profound layer of the communalist culture and it is preserved as such until nowadays. The country itself is, therefore, founded on the villages and through them on the communalist culture. The socio-territorial landscape is known and memorized as the most valuable covenant. Stahl's hypothesis is that such a memory could be dismantled after three to five generations. Probably, yes, but the memory of the land and, therefore, the remembrance of the Promised Land lives in the covenantal memory forever. This is another aspect which makes of the covenantal issue a permanent challenge for sociology and represents a facet of the actuality of such an approach. Its continuity is an imperative of sociology.

Therefore, "one must thus place this division into village communes before the birth of the state."[49] Of course, we may assume hypothetically a moment when the memory of the land itself will vanish in the sense that the land itself loses the encrusted signs of the old times and, therefore, of the ancient communalist culture. For instance, the organization based on the mound formations, arranged in a rigid geometrical pattern, might disappear being faded in time. But such an arrangement with a grid laid by the lines from a "central high mound, there is a whole line of lower mounds. Along this same line, on the map, one invariably finds other series of mounds, farther away and out of sight. These lines reveal a perfect knowledge of the terrain: they fit with the lines where streams separate land or where different geomorphic zones come together. (. . .) The peasants of today are perfectly aware of these things. They call the lines of mounds *măguri înşirate* (strung mounds) and the meeting point *crucea măgurilor* (cross of the mounds). And, even more importantly, these mounds still serve today, often enough, as reference points for the village communes, with the 4 corners of the communes coinciding with these mounds, as though the surveyors who measured out the village communes had taken these tribal triangles as their basis. It follows that at the time of the nomads, or just at the time of the reconquest of the territory by the indigenous people, a local population already existed, which took over, by groups of villages, these tribal 4 cells left by the riders of the steppe."[50]

We shall memorize that the land in such an organizational pattern was partitioned equally between villages so that they were "equal in rights" and that "this division took place before the formation of the autochthonous state."[51] Neither the Roman Empire nor any other state domination transformed totally the communal landscape and free communal villages continued to have and display a deeply communal character. "Not even the wave upon wave of invaders that swept across the region—Goths, Huns, Gepids, Avars, Slavs, Bulgars, Hungarians, Petchenegs, Cumans and Tartars—could ever wipe out the communal character of proto-Romanians areas."[52] During all this period of invasions there survived the same networking communal organization based on the *knez* in each village "and on the confederations of villages under the leadership of a voivode." It is only by assuming such an issue that we may answer the following question: "what were the forms of social organization that enabled the Romanians not only to survive in spite of the oppression of the migratory people, but also to evolve in such a way that there were, at the beginning of their written history, *Voivodates* and then 'states'?"[53]

The answer is one: the communal pattern of social organization based on the communal villages and on the regional networks called confederations of villages, wherefrom stemmed out Voivodates and then states, enabled the Romanians to survive and also to evolve throughout history until nowadays.[54] In the present time we assist to the most terrible collision of the two opposite societal and cultural systems sliding into a final battle between them, equating with a confrontation between the equality and inequality, between the covenantal pattern and artificial orderliness, imposed by a different, in-egalitarian societal system.

CULTURAL COMMUNITARIANISM AND HISTORICAL CHANGE

In Romanian culture there is a saying: *de la lume adunate si napoi la lume date* (*From people collected, to people returned*). This saying speaks about the way a communalist culture functions. H. H. Stahl called such a type of order, based on the sharing of cultural traits by the members of a communalist culture, the "order through diffuse tradition." This type of culture involves a permanent circulation of cultural traits from the communal group to individual and back from them to the entire group, in the form of the bivalent assumption: individual and collective. What is common to all is to me and vice versa, but by sharing, so that the individualization is not excluded, only that it is transparent and instantly assimilable. "The shared traits constitute a *communalist culture*;[55] its destruction leads to the disappearance of the collectivity explaining why communities don't hop models."[56] What stems from here is the idea that the power of a community does not equate with the ability to produce changes, but with the ability to eliminate them (when they are wrong, harmful) or, if someone from the outside has introduced some valuable changes, then, the community power can be attested by its capacity to assimilate them. Therefore, the power in the covenantal society equates with the capacity of refraining from any change, of not hopping between its own model and the alien one, from the traditional local model to a completely different one. The collision between religious congregations is an example of refusal to hop models, as Livni argues. "A functional community resists the innovation because it threatens its quasi-equilibrium."[57] The covenantal communalist culture (i.e., society) "resists any forced alteration" and he fights against anyone who tries to affect the way of life based on such a culture. It is legitimate to inquire about the outcome of such a conflict, through general approach[58] and by case studies as that about the village communities in Romania. The Biblical case of arising royalty in a covenantal society is a universal example of how such a phenomenon is occurring and on what happens to a covenantal/ communal society in such a transition from one type of organization to another. Does it take place, in this case, a hop from one model to another, or the new organization is adopted by still preserving the original model? The covenant in its form of the dialogue between God and "every member of the faith"[59] is a recurrent one, that is, it is occurring generationally, to each subsequent generation. "The 'you' in the 'Lord spoke to you' does not refer only to the generation of the Exodus but also to every subsequent generation (Deut. 5.3). This model of direct interaction between each faithful and divinity is recurring."[60]

The calendars, oral and written, themselves, stand apart as to the definition of the over-year traditional feasts that the village respects in the whole rural area: the oral (popular) calendar assumed the religious feasts; the written does not assume the popular (ethnographical) feats. The oral (ethnographic) calendar is more comprehensive than the official, written one. Communal village people "read" in the written calendar events, feasts signs and symbols which are not written in that calendar. And this was because the people of communalist culture knew to adjust them.

The communal culture is based on a system of signs, communally memorized and shared, largely distributed at all levels of existence. People of such a culture use a sign-language to communicate with each other and to memorize the structure of the world.

> In their practical relationships people manufacture their own signs—signs of notch, hierarchical signs, and signs of possession—and the community respects them, without questioning their origin. We will draw the conclusion that the sign is opaque for the rest of the world and bright for the one who uses it. The important thing is, in all cases, to respect the sign as such, the sign of the neighbor, the sign of another community, the dress sign, the sign of the boundary, the customary sign, even the sign of the devil, for the organization of the world to remain in accord with itself. Therefore, you have to defend the sign.[61]

The calendar is the densest spiritual concentration of cultural signs, names and symbols, thresholds and cycles. It is by itself a sort of condensed oral library, being that beneath any name of a day or of a feast a huge number of rituals and ceremonies, prescriptions, and prohibitions are treasured, suggesting an extraordinary communal memory. "We will not stop on those who have been laicized in the fairy tale—dragons, huge anacondas, Mother-of-forest, and so on—nor on the Saints in the Christian calendar (all with magical functions), but we will grasp the good and bad deities of the great magic primitive pantheon. The things we spoke about, but behold their secret name: The Fairies, the Saints, the Saints of Night, the Whispers, the Beauties, the Beloved, The Themselves, the Ladies, the Virgins, the Mercifully, the Empress, the Mighty, the Goddess, as the name with collective value (Zânele, Sfintele, Sfintele de noapte, Frumoasele, Mândrele, Dânsele, Doamnele, Iezmele, Fecioarele, Milostivele, Miluitele, Împărătesele, Puternicele, Zeiţele, Şoimanele, Măiestrele)."[62]

The days get extremely rich meanings and the oral calendar is like a memorizer of them all and they are transmitted through the oral diffuse tradition, meaning by oral memory, so that, man of the communal culture has always super-added a parallel time, a parallel realm, over the written calendar.

Taking an example, we will notice that the days of the week or the holy days evoke the concrete image of some women. If the moon or sun has a diffuse portrait, the temporal realities that are the days are perfectly incarnate. When someone escapes a misfortune, "a day has been made for him."[63] The days are responsible directly for the life and activity of the people; they are good-fated or ill-omened, insofar as the prescriptions are respected or violated. Moreover, they have personality, sympathies, and intolerances. So, on Mondays, do not sew, do not sweep, do not remove the trash from the house, do not bring land for soldering and do not take eggs from the nest. On Tuesdays do not start on the road, do not start various actions (although some are forbidden on Mondays!), do not spin "lest the Marţolea comes," the vengeful deity, a kind of foolish and crazy one, who "spoil the work of women, poke them with the spindle, even kill them," collaborating with bad guard (*piaza rea*) and bad watch. On Wednesday, no wool is scratched, no flocks, no leach is made, no salt is powdered, nothing is given from the house, the patron of the day being a pure saint, who claims to abstain from any temptation. Thursday is a day free for any activity, and *Joimita* is the deity of this great day, the woman worthy and fierce, with the mission to supervise the spinning of the hemp and punish lazy women. Friday is the most holy day, she is old and anchorite, a kind of pure grandmother, who helps clean people up to the extent that they respect her counsel with innocence. Like Saturday, it's a good-fated day, when the dragons can't hurt either, because they can't walk anymore, as they would get crippled. Sunday is the greatest day, respect for her is absolute. The Three holy days, Holy Wednesday, Holy Friday, and Holy Sunday, dominate the week. Of course, prescriptions and prohibitions are contradictory, often cancelling each other; the magical calendar is the most confusing calendar possible.[64]

The task of communal culture is therefore extremely difficult being that it has to synchronize different qualitatively calendars so that, while the common behavior is ordered on the basis of the *oral calendar* to also comply with the prescription of the written calendar. The names of the days possess magical powers so that the time is empowered with different predispositions from one day to the next. "To know how to name exactly, to know all the names under which a deity manifests itself means to get access to her powers, to use them or to neutralize them."[65]

The moments of oral calendar matched the successions of seasons so strict that when the reform of calendar was decided (the transition from the Julian to Gregorian calendar) the beat of activities did not match any more the periodical manifestations in the natural environment. Here are some reactions after changing the calendar:

> The old style is the good one: the trees still based on the old style come into leaf and into bloom and after the new will not . . . there was St. Elijah (new style) and apples did not bake; but on the old style they will be (will bake). . . And this is because time goes on after the old style. . . . It will be St. Nicholas tomorrow, but will you eat baked corn? All things are settled, with more righteousness, upon the old style.[66]

Year after year different manifestations in the world of nature occurred on approximately the same date. The man of the communal culture had projected on the written calendar the "name and the day" just because they were in possession of the previously more comprehensive oral, therefore, communal calendar. At the date of adopting Julian calendar, they held the reconciliation method to eliminate the risk of discrepancies between the two calendars. When the new Gregorian calendar was adopted, the discrepancies between solar succession of seasons, between written calendar and oral calendar had already and again emerged. The comprehensive power of the oral calendar and its universal share over a vast area, along with a social order based on the diffuse tradition and utilization of the same system of land measuring, the same pastoral and agricultural techniques, partially explain the survival fitness provided by the communal culture and, therefore, its triumph over the historical time. Through the oral calendar the whole community takes part to cosmic frames[67] like the life cycles or the phases of Moon, among others, so that different human events receive cosmogonic explanations. The wedding, for instance, is framed cosmically and liturgically, as in a mythic and religious scenario and everything in the communal life of villages is part of a profound synergism.[68] In a Bukovina legend it is stated that

> "The sun and the moon, not having heaven, walked on the Earth," among the people. So, people lived with the heavenly, celestial bodies on a perpetual day,

> in an equal regime of light, which represents not only a cosmogonic novelty, but also a support of the subsequent intimacy between people and the stars.[69]

The issue is that the "egalitarians" (the communal people) had a highly comprehensive way of life, very rich in mysterious meanings and anagogical interpretations. If you wish to transform such a communal society you have to deconstruct and dismantle a dense and harmonized culture, starting, obviously, with the system of beliefs centered on the profound feeling that one's way of living and behaving is in deep accordance with God's will and ordinance. To succeed in such a deconstructive process, you have to secularize firstly this world, to empty the universe of the divine, to remove the divinity from the soul and from the everyday life of the people. To fulfill such a task, you need to transform firstly the elite and so to create an ample room for disagreement between the elite and communalist culture and society. Such a task has been accomplished hardly and with reduced effects and extremely late so that in the twentieth century the traditional type of culture was still in full power and had deeply conquered the high culture, what allowed to literary critic Eugen Lovinescu to speak about the faulty line and, therefore, structural clash between culture and society, between what he used to call the reactionary rural-minded literature and modern urban-minded society. The two components of the dual society were diverging on the most aspect of social life and they haven't reconciled to each other even until now. That is one of the facets of what we may call the Eastern challenging issue, and this disagreement has not been eradicated until today nowhere in the East.

THE "NOVEL OF SOL" AND X-FACTOR OF COMMUNALIST MIND

The study of the communal culture includes the research of the mental system the man of this culture operates with. This system is reflected in the myths and legends of that culture. These narrative frames work as a mirror of reality by giving us the access key to a deeper social order. Let's consider an example: if A is the forest, B is the animal, C is a man whoever, we shall find out that in their mental and experiential combination a factor X interferes, which over-adds to those elements a new meaning, the value of a model, that is, the power to mediate the people's participation to a higher unity. This factor is transmitted by the vehicle of tradition but has its root in the primordial cosmogonic scenario, meaning the divine way of doing things in *illo tempore*, so that we can say: "That's how God did it. Let's do as God has done." In each thing is the call of God to respect his will and order he has established by his creation. The people who live in the communal society seek in each thing something like its divine reason and strive to repeat by fulfilling it into a model, a pattern. Such people are lingering after models as the only proof that by following a certain model you fulfill God's will. This is like an unwritten covenant with God, as if God has planted in each thing ways of doing and behaving that God calls humans to naturally respect. To live in a communal society equates with sharing a way of life we may call the communal strategy of life and so we can understand the odd fact that this way of living can survive in time, as if it had a special power to subsist, to last indefinitely. Such a strategy of life "stems from the direct, immediate, human's rapport with external forces, from the fact that the demarcations and hierarchies were not yet visible organized, neither within the society nor in nature, so that God Himself walks, travels here in the world, among men, mixing with them. The collectivity of the communal horizon is the "center of Existence," the "Centre of the world," and its horizon extends to the sky. The last visible borders are the stars. Blaga is right: "The village integrates itself into a cosmic destiny, in a totalitarian movement of life, beyond whose horizon there is nothing." The sacrament mixes with the profane, the celeste with the terrestrial, the real with the unreal, without any of the elements separating from the actual, understood as what is existing."[70] In the analysis I carried on Paul Anghel's book about the magic model in folklore, I have fixed some traits of communalist culture that I will resume here by excerpting some citations from various popular legends and from my own analysis including biblical studies.[71]

Here is an example offered by a legend from Dolj County:

> [T]he sky was very close to the Earth; but the man is careless by his nature, so he did not heed this godly goodness, because there was not little thing to man to have God around him, that he might ask his counsel as a good father, whenever he needed" (apud ibidem).[72]

And here it is another example from a legend of Valcea County:

> Before the time, the sky was near to the ground, so that you reached out to it when you were climbing on a stray, and God, with the saints, whenever they wanted, they came up and descended because they often walked on earth. . . . Not having heaven, the Sun and the moon walked on Earth [among men].[73]

Anghel notes:

> Therefore, people lived with the heavenly bodies on a perpetual day, an equal regime of light, which is not only a cosmogonic novelty, but also a support of the subsequent intimacy between people and the stars, as we will see. . . . The world seems to be a sui generis paradise."[74]

Indeed, we learn from the *Book of Genesis*, "in the beginning God made the heavens and the earth. And the earth was untraced and empty." St. Basil records that "the heavens and the earth were of equal rank (honor)" and both "incomplete," and St. Ambrose added, referring to the same issue: "Scripture stresses that things were first created and then put in order." And then God made the light. "And God said, let there be light; and it was light. And God saw that light was good." The settlement of man in the garden of Heaven is precisely the expression of the undivided world, and only sin brings to the separation, a very suggestive thing formulated in folklore, where the one who sins brings "the Rise of Heaven," the extraordinary revelatory metaphor for the banishment from heaven (and again, the evidence gathered by Paul Anghel is enlightening, as illustrated below):"[75] In the Legend of Valcea, an old aunt, "neither one nor two, throws away with muddiness in God." The consequence is the same "if he has seen so God, that men neither heaven can keep it clean, he lifted it higher." Or: "As punishment for the human race, (God) magnified the sky and lifted it up, up, where it is today with the moon with everything."[76]

As in the *Book of Genesis*, the sun and the moon had the rank of simple things of the earth, bathed in the light that was not owed to them. The popular narrator knew as Moses himself in the *Book of Genesis*, so, by means of the intercession of Revelation toward Moses, transmitted to the anonymous narrator through mysterious channels, that the regime of light is not due to the sun, neither to the moon, but to God directly, the first stage of creation, when the day and the night were not yet put apart from each other, and the evening still did not exist, because God made firstly the light and then separated the "light of darkness and called the Light Day and the darkness called him Night," "and it was evening and it was morning: first day."[77] The disturbing thing, referred to by Paul Anghel, refers to the distinction that the popular narrator knew to do, also based on the knowledge revealed, between the orderliness of things and their separation, as that of sky from earth, which do not hold to the orderliness of creation but to the consequences that human sin provokes in the orderliness of Creation:[78] "If God thus saw that men nor the heavens could keep him clean, he lifted him up."[79] The communalist culture is backed on three pillars:

1) The cosmogonic vision on the existence which is totally related to the biblical vision, and works as a mental mechanism so that the people of communalist culture see in everything a divine ordinance.
2) The cosmic vision that provided Proto-Romanians a standard time unit that helped people to see, in any events, in the happenings of the everyday life, a divine metric and to use it as a measure in all those

around him and his daily life. When somebody abates from this divine metric, the community supervenes directly, through diffuse tradition or by means of the "old and good men," communal institutions, in order to set matters straight. We may consider such a supervening as the root of restorative justice system. If someone was caught stealing, he was walked in front of the community, being determined to parade up and down, on the streets of village to be seen by everybody. If he stole a hen he would wear the stolen thing hanging around his body like a belt so that people could see that he was a chicken thief. This communal supervening meant to restore the divine orderliness of life when someone had harmed it has its source in what people knew: that God himself made when humans defaced the divine orderliness, as the legend says itself through the mythical communal memory. Here it is an example of such a legend known and upheld narratively by common people in Valcea County: "If God, so saw, that neither men nor the heavens could keep him clean, he lifted him up." Or: "As the punishment of the human race, (God) magnified the sky and lifted it up, up, where it is today with the moon with all. . . ." Or: "God was terrible angry (with fire) and has so far removed the sky from earth that not incidentally we say: far as the sky of the Earth." Or: "God fled with heaven all up; and now he sits backwards with his back to us."[80] These are conclusions of the cases A, B, C and D that exemplify different ways in which people defaced divine orderliness of the existence. "According to M. Eliade, this "retreat in heaven," this "removal of God," a theme with a capital role in the Romanian religious folklore, signifies the disengagement of Creator toward the evil in the world and the sinful world. The people of communal society dissociates themselves from such a defacing because God has done the same, and even applied the ultimate punishment: He has withdrawn from the world, and if man does not turn things, that is, he does not bring them to the divine orderliness, then God will leave him. The same is the denouement in the book of the Old Testament.

3) The communal society makes use also of the weekly feasts and of the cyclical feasts as the seasons or yearly feasts are, moments when people cast their minds back over the traditions and refresh the memory of the divine orderliness of the world. There are many arguments to conclude on the Judeo-Christian profile of the Romanian communalist culture, which appears to be, properly, the cradle of the Romanian people. In his study, Paul Anghel shares the idea of a difference between the folklore's popular vision and Biblical vision. As a matter of fact, in folklore, the mythic theme of *Deus otiosus*, of a God leaving the world, retreating from it, has the regime of a revelatory metaphor suggesting mythically but the idea of God's disengagement towards evil and sinful

humanity, as Mircea Eliade himself has noticed, and this vision is in total accordance with the Judeo-Christian view (as it was transmitted by Moses) from the *Book of Genesis*. On the other hand, the wording of "the exculpating of God," which appears in folklore through the theme of Divine reaction to the defacing act of man, noticed as such by Paul Anghel, clearly has metaphorical meaning, suggesting that the popular narrator did not understand to bind the imperfections of the world to the Creative act of God. Those imperfections are not due to the Creator, in the popular vision, but to His creature, from which the obsessive concern of the popular narrator on the matter that Paul Anghel frames thematically and metaphorically in the theme of "Creator's discharging" for the imperfections of the world. The world was created in unaltered light, but it was deformed by the sin of man, the evil of sin committed by man himself.

> Therefore, this is what the LORD, the God of Israel, says to the shepherds who tend my people: "Because you have scattered my flock and driven them away and have not bestowed care on them, I will bestow punishment on you for the evil you have done," declares the LORD.[81]

The two visions—the biblical one and the other prevailing in the communalist mind of the Romanian village—are similar and, in fact, are one.

NOTES

1. This paper follows a series of articles I dedicated to the sociological theory of H. H. Stahl about the communal society (one having been published in the Romanian Sociological Review) and it includes parts of them.

2. Joseph Livni and Ilie Bădescu, "The Battle of the Covenantal Society against Elitism - An Overlooked Chapter in The History of Social Inequality," *Romanian Journal of Sociological Studies, New Series* No 1 (2020), 2018 on the distinction between ahistorical society and historical society see: Mircea Eliade, *Myth and Reality* (Harper & Row, 1963), 18. The transition from covenantal, non-hierarchical, egalitarian society to a hierarchical, elitist, inequality-based society in Israel, overlapped with the shift from Proto-Israel to Historical Israel, was marked by "the conflict between Levites and the elders of the other tribes", the compete of the elitists with egalitarians ("battle of the Covenantal Society against the Elitism"). "(T)he Roman Commander Titus [son and heir of Emperor Vespasianus] marched with his army in 70 A.D. to the Temple. He destroyed it. . . ." 70 CE marked the end of Ancient Israel and of the battle between covenantal and elitist Judaism. Without Temple, the priesthood lost. The covenantal model survived not because it was superior but because in the conditions of diaspora it became the fittest"), p. 32.

3. On this issue and, therefore, on the definition of the communal structure see also: Steven J Mithen et al., "An 11 600 Year-Old Communal Structure from the Neolithic of Southern Jordan," *Antiquity* 85, no. 328 (2011). Presenting a "communal and monumental structure in Western Africa", the authors conclude that it is representative for a type of organization "in which community seems to take precedence over economy."

4. Idem.

5. See Livni and Bădescu, "The Battle of the Covenantal Society against Elitism - An Overlooked Chapter in The History of Social Inequality."

6. On the communal formations see H. H. Stahl, *Traditional Romanian Village Communities* (Cambridge University Press, 1977), 24 («Even in the province, during the high point of Roman domination, the slave or colonial latifundia existed only as an exception. It is true that the Roman domination created a flourishing urban life, imposing a general cultural influence that was decisive to the local population, without, however, being able to completely transform the villages, which remained as they had been: village communities of a deeply tribal character. After the Roman army left Dacia in 271, the cities fell into decay, drowned in the anonymous rural mass"). On very ancient social history and on this kind of formations see also: C. Daicoviciu, E. Petrovici, and G. Ştefan, *La formation du peuple roumain et de sa langue*, Bibliotheca Historica Romaniae, *Etudes* series, no. 1 (Bucharest, 1965). Also *Brlve Histoire de la Transylvanie*, Bibliotheca Historia Romaniae, *Monographies* series, no. 2 (Bucharest, 1965).

7. See Livni, "The Battle of the Covenantal Society against Elitism, An Overlooked Chapter in the History of Social Inequality" (chapter in this book): citations here are apud Livni from: Daniel J. Elazar and Stewart Cohen, *The Jewish Polity: Jewish Political Organization from Biblical Times to the Present* (Bloomington, IN: Indiana University Press, 1985); Daniel J. Elazar, *Covenant and Polity in Biblical Israel* (New Brunswick, NJ: Transaction Publishers, 1998); Daniel Judah Elazar, "The Almost-Covenanted Polity" (paper presented at the Workshop in the covenant idea and the Jewish political tradition, Ramat Gan, Israel, 1982).

8. See some relevant references in Livni's Introduction to Livni and Bădescu, "The Battle of the Covenantal Society against Elitism - An Overlooked Chapter in The History of Social Inequality."

e.g. Gary M Feinman, "The Emergence of Inequality," in *Foundations of social inequality* (Springer, 1995), 255, 56; Katherine I. Karen Wright, "Domestication and inequality? Households, corporate groups and food processing tools at Neolithic Çatalhöyük," *Journal of Anthropological Archaeology* 33 (2014); Benjamin P. Luley, "Equality, Inequality, and the Problem of "Elites" in Late Iron Age Eastern Languedoc (Mediterranean France), ca. 400–125 BC," ibid. 41 (2016); Stephen A. Dueppen, "Reinventing Equality: The Archaeology of Kirikongo, Burkina Faso" (University of Michigan, 2008).

9. *On the dual-system theory*" see: Daniel Kahneman, *Thinking, Fast and Slow* (Macmillan, 2011); Alain Samson and Benjamin G. Voyer, "Two Minds, Three Ways: Dual System and Dual Process Models in Consumer Psychology," *AMS Review* 2, no. 2 (2012).

10. See Henri H. Stahl, *Traditional Romanian Village Communities* (Cambridge: Cambridge University Press, 1980), 14.

11. As was the case in the transfer of pre-monarchic Israel to monarchy, see Avraham Faust, "The Rural Community in Ancient Israel during Iron Age I I," *Bulletin of the American Schools of Oriental Research* (2000). Apud Livni, Livni and Bădescu, "The Battle of the Covenantal Society against Elitism - An Overlooked Chapter in the History of Social Inequality," p. 12.

12. Stahl, *Traditional Romanian Village Communities*, 36.

13. Ibid.

14. Ibid., 35.

15. Ibid.

16. Ibid. 36; "Thus, although they are enserfed in the feudal manner, these villages remain communal as long as the common exploitation of the village territory is assured by the same primitive pastoral and agricultural techniques. This will remain the case as long as these communities do not make direct contact with a more developed market economy. In any case, the analysis of the village assemblies remains the keystone of the original system. Its breakdown begins the process of enserfment. For this it is useful to study its laws."

17. See Introduction by G.L. Ulmen and Carl Schmitt, "The Nomos of the Earth in the International Law of the Jus Publicum Europaeum" (Telos, 2006).

18. Here it is the retrieved document (Land title deed signed before Vasile Lupu ruler of Moldavia (1595–1661); note elders (oameni buni și bătrâni) are witnesses T. Codrescu, *Uricariul cuprinḑĕtoriŭ de hrisoave, anaforale si alte acte* (tip. Buciumului românu, 1887).:

Io Vasilie Voevoda, du mila lui D - zeu stăpânitor pământului Moldovei.

Eată că viind înaintea noastră şi înaintea a lor noştri moldovineşti boeri a mari şi mici, sluga noastră Ionaşco Dărman, cu femea lui Mărica şi cu copii lor, a ara : ạt înaintea noastră un zapis, ca mărturie de la *oameni buni și bătrăni*, anume : Ionaşco Băzăceanul şi Eremia Olăş de la Târgul Sucevei şi Toader Boul de la Nelipeşti și Ionaşco Boul, aşijdere şi Vasilie de la Bălşeaṇi și Isaia tot de acolo și Vasilie sin Căpitan, aşijdere, cum înaintea lor a vândut Gligorie de la Lipăeşti fratele lui Costandi, fiul Pătrăşcoaei, de a lui bună voe, de nime silit, nici asuprit şi a dat o jer bie, partea lui de la satul Lipăeştii, cu parte de loc pământ și sat și cu tot venitul, . . .

19. Cf. Nicolae Iorga, "Scrisori de Boieri Scrisori de Domni," in *Din publicațiile casei școalelor*, ed. Casa şcoalelor (Vălenii de Munte, Romania: Editura casei şcoalelor; Datina Românească, 1925), III.

20. Ibid., IV.

21. Ibid., V.

22. Luigi Luca Cavalli-Sforza and Marcus W. Feldman, *Cultural Transmission and Evolution* (Princeton, NJ: Princeton University Press, 1981).

23. Stahl, *Traditional Romanian Village Communities*, 7.

24. Ibid.. See also: Henri. H. Stahl, *Nerej, un village d'une région archaïque: monographie sociologique*, vol. V. 1 (Bucarest: Institut de sciences sociales de Roumanie, 1939). published by the Bibliotheque de Sociologie, Ethique et Politique under the guidance of D. Guşti), 3 volumes; Henri H. Stahl, "L'habitat humain et Ies

formes de la vie sociale," *Arhiva pentru ştiinţa şi reforma socială,* Year XII (1930).; "L'Organisation collective du village roumain," ibid.Year XIII (1931)"; Henri H. Stahl and Paul H Stahl, *Contribuţii la studiul satelor devălmaşe româneşti: Procesul de aservire feudală a satelor devălmaşe*, vol. 3 (Cartea Românească, 1998). 3 volumes (Bucharest, 1958-65).

25. Stahl, *Traditional Romanian Village Communities*, 11.

26. On the census of 1722 used by Stahl see Constantin C. Giurescu, *Materiale pentru istoria Olteniei supt austrieci* [Sources for the history of Oltenia under the Austrians], 3 vols., vol. 2 (Bucharest, 1909), 304–30. Apud Stahl, *Traditional Romanian Village Communities*, 11.

27. *Traditional Romanian Village Communities.*

28. Ibid.

29. Ibid., 8.

30. Livni and Bădescu, "The Battle of the Covenantal Society against Elitism - An Overlooked Chapter in The History of Social Inequality."

31. Stahl, *Traditional Romanian Village Communities*, 12.

32. Ibid.

33. Ibid., 13.

34. Ibid., 14.

35. (Source: ibid., 14).

36. Ibid., 14.

37. Ibid.

38. Ibid., 15.

39. Ibid.

40. Ibid.

41. Ibid., 16.

42. Ibid.

43. See also Roland Maspétiol, *L'ordre éternel des champs: essai sur l'histoire, l'économie et les vaeurs de la paysannerie* (Paris: Librairie de Médicis, 1946). On the same topic, H. H. Stahl cites also: Roger Dion, *Essai sur la formation du paysage rural français* (Paris: Arrault et cie, 1934); Gaston Roupnel, *Histoire de la campagne française* (Paris: B. Grasset, 1932); Georges Lizerand, *Le régime rural de l'ancienne France* (Paris: Presses Universitaires de France, 1942). Georges Lizerand, *Le regime rural de l'ancienne France* (Paris, 1942) (cf. Stahl, *Traditional Romanian Village Communities*, 16).

44. *Traditional Romanian Village Communities*, 16.

45. Ibid.

46. "Several remarks are in order here. It is hard to reproduce village boundaries on maps from the written description of the measurements found in the various documents. The peasant surveyors measured in 'lengths walking on the land', going over hills and through valleys in their own fashion without following the methods of modern surveying. There were no plumb lines and there was no way of sighting on a line with the horizon. Areas of equal size measured according to such 'lengths' can appear on a map as if they are unequal. It is just as important to note that measurement was not carried out on abstract surfaces but on real ones whose economic value

was unequal. Land of inferior quality had to be compensated with grants of more land since a larger amount was needed to be considered equal to a smaller amount of better land. Also, surfaces were not measured as such. Only the three 'lines' were measured in order to determine the location of the 'corners' of the land" (ibid.17–18).

47. See Henri H Stahl, *Sociologia satului devălmaş românesc* [Sociology of communal Romanian village], vol. 3 (Bucharest: Fundaţia Regele Mihai I, 1946); *Contribuţii la studiul satelor devălmaşe româneşti, vol. II, Structura internă a satelor devălmaşe libere*, 3 vols., vol. 2, Contributions to the Study of Romanian Joint-property Villages (Bucharest: Editura Academiei R.P.R., 1959). (three volumes edited between 1950-65). See also, Stahl, *Traditional Romanian Village Communities*, 18.

48. *Traditional Romanian Village Communities*, 22 ("All of the statistics and the texts of cited documents come from *Documente privind istoria României* (Documents relating to the history of Romania) published by the Romanian Academy, Bucharest, 1951-60. This includes twelve volumes plus a two volume place-name index for Wallachia from 1247 to 1627 and ten volumes for Moldavia from 1384 to 1620. For later documents we have used the collection *Documente privind relaţiile agrare în veacul al XVII-lea şi XVIII-lea* (Documents relating to agrarian relations in the seventeeth and eighteenth centuries), Bucharest, 1961 and 1966, note from Stahl citation in c.w., p. 22.

49. Ibid., 22.

50. Ibid., 23

51. Ibid.

52. Ibid.

53. Ibid., 25.

54. Ibid. ("The old blood ties, real or fictitious, which held the tribes together, were replaced by the ties of neighbourhood. Spaţial proximity replaced kinship as the main basis of social cohesion. This evolution was slow. Villages that were formerly a part of the tribe remained under a confederate authority which comprised a whole region. This tribal authority, having undertaken the work of partitioning the land which led to the territorialisation of villages, continued to safeguard the larger group. It thus fulfilled the duties of a quasi-state: to defend the area and settle disputes between villages".)

55. Menachem Topel, in *The Communal Idea in the 21st Century*, ed. E. Ben-Rafael, Y. Oved, and M. Topel (Leiden/Boston: Brill, 2012), 208.

56. Livni and Bădescu, "The Battle of the Covenantal Society against Elitism - An Overlooked Chapter in the History of Social Inequality."

57. Ibid.

58. Ibid., 6.

59. Ibid.

60. (e.g. Ex. 20:18, 20:22, Deut. 4.33).

61. Paul Anghel, *O istorie posibilă a literaturii române: modelul magic* [A possible history of the Romanian literature] (Timişoara: Augusta, 2002), 112. A comprehensive treatment of the issue of the sign, in the legal customary see Romulus Vulcănescu, *Etnologie juridică* (Bucharest: Editura Academiei Republicii Socialiste România, 1970), 117–61 (chapter: *Popular Legal Signs)*, 117–61.

62. Anghel, *O istorie posibilă a literaturii române: modelul magic.*

63. Ibid.

64. Ibid.

65. Ibid.

66. Ion Ghinoiu, *Calendarul țăranului român: zile şi mituri : 2018* [The Calendar of the Romanian Peasant. Days and Myths] (Bucharest: Univers Enciclopedic Gold, 2017), 11; see also, Richard Heinberg, *Celebrate the Solstice: Honoring the Earth's Seasonal Rhythms through Festival and Ceremony* (Wheaton, IL: Quest Books, 1993).

67. See Tudor Pamfilie, *Cerul și podoabele lui: după credințele poporului român* [The sky and his adornments] (Bucharest: Socec, P. Suru, C. Sfetea, 1915), 2–15 and I. Otescu, *Credințele țăranului român despre cer şi stele (Romanian Peasant's beliefs about heaven and stars)*, 44–60.

68. See E.N. Voronca, *Datinile şi credințele poporului roman (The traditions and beliefs of the Romanian people)*, Cernăuţi, 1903.

69. See Elena Niculiţă-Voronca, *Datinile şi credințele poporului Român: adunate şi aşezate în ordine mitologică* [The traditions and beliefs of the Romanian people] (Cernăuţi: Tip. Isidor Wiegler, 1903), 28, cited by Paul Anghel in Anghel, *O istorie posibilă a literaturii române: modelul magic.*

70. (Paul Anghel, *The Magic Pattern*, mss).

71. On a comparative analysis of Jewish and Romanian cultures (Biblical themes and folklore being included in analysis) see. Mădălina Măndiţă, *Compared Noology of Jewish and Romanian People: A Sociology of Communities* (Aachen: Shaker Verlag, 2017).

72. The legends cited here are from Pamfilie, *Cerul și podoabele lui: după credințele poporului român*; Ion Otescu, "Credinţele ţăranului român despre cer şi stele" (Bucharest: Analele A. R.,, 1907), 44–60.

73. Niculiţă-Voronca, *Datinile şi credințele poporului Român: adunate şi aşezate în ordine mitologică.*E.N. Voronca, *Datinile şi credințele poporului român (Traditions and beliefs of Romanian people)*, Cernăuţi, 1903, pag.28 (apud Anghel, *O istorie posibilă a literaturii române: modelul magic*, 189).

74. *O istorie posibilă a literaturii române: modelul magic*, 189.

75. Ilie Bădescu, *Paul Anghel – The Genial Wallach. The Eight Worlds of the Romanian Literature* (Bucharest: Walachia Press, 2018).

76. Anghel, *O istorie posibilă a literaturii române: modelul magic.*

77. (Genesis, I, 1–5).

78. apud Anghel in *O istorie posibilă a literaturii române: modelul magic.*

79. Ibid.

80. See P. Anghel, c.w, mss The examples are from Niculiţă-Voronca, *Datinile şi credinţele poporului Român: adunate şi aşezate în ordine mitologică*; Pamfilie, *Cerul și podoabele lui: după credințele poporului român*; Otescu, "Credinţele ţăranului român despre cer şi stele," 44–60.

81. (Jeremiah, 23, 2).

REFERENCES

Anghel, Paul. *O Istorie Posibilă a Literaturii Române: Modelul Magic* [in Romanian] [A Possible History of the Romanian Literature]. Timişoara: Augusta, 2002.

Bădescu, Ilie. *Paul Anghel – The Genial Wallach: The Eight Worlds of the Romanian Literature*. Bucharest: Walachia Press, 2018.

Cavalli-Sforza, Luigi Luca, and Marcus W. Feldman. *Cultural Transmission and Evolution*. Princeton, NJ: Princeton University Press, 1981.

Codrescu, T. *Uricariul Cuprinḑĕtoriŭ De Hrisoave, Anaforale Si Alte Acte*. tip. Buciumului românu, 1887.

Dion, Roger. *Essai Sur La Formation Du Paysage Rural Français*. Paris: Arrault et cie, 1934.

Dueppen, Stephen A. *Reinventing Equality: The Archaeology of Kirikongo, Burkina Faso*. University of Michigan, 2008.

Elazar, Daniel J. *Covenant and Polity in Biblical Israel*. New Brunswick, NJ: Transaction Publishers, 1998.

Elazar, Daniel J., and Stewart Cohen. *The Jewish Polity: Jewish Political Organization From Biblical Times to the Present*. Bloomington, IN: Indiana University Press, 1985.

Elazar, Daniel Judah. "The Almost-Covenanted Polity." Paper Presented at the Workshop in the Covenant Idea and the Jewish Political Tradition, Ramat Gan, Israel, 1982.

Eliade, Mircea. *Myth and Reality*. New York: Harper & Row, 1963.

Faust, Avraham. "The Israelite Village: Cultural Conservatism and Technological Innovation." *Tel Aviv* 32, no. 2 (2005): 204–19.

———. "The Rural Community in Ancient Israel During Iron Age I I." *Bulletin of the American Schools of Oriental Research* (2000): 17–39.

Feinman, Gary M. "The Emergence of Inequality." In *Foundations of Social Inequality*, 255–79. New York: Springer, 1995.

Ghinoiu, Ion. *Calendarul Ţăranului Român: Zile Şi Mituri: 2018* [The Calendar of the Romanian Peasant: Days and Myths]. Bucharest: Univers Enciclopedic Gold, 2017.

Giurescu, Constantin C. *Materiale Pentru Istoria Olteniei Supt Austrieci* [in Romanian] [Sources for the History of Oltenia Under the Austrians]. 3 Vols. Vol. 2. Bucharest, 1909.

Heinberg, Richard. *Celebrate the Solstice: Honoring the Earth's Seasonal Rhythms Through Festival and Ceremony*. Wheaton, IL: Quest Books, 1993.

Iorga, Nicolae. "Scrisori De Boieri Scrisori De Domni." In *Din publicațiile casei școalelor*, edited by Casa şcoalelor. Vălenii de Munte, Romania: Editura casei şcoalelor; Datina Românească, 1925.

Kahneman, Daniel. *Thinking, Fast and Slow*. New York: Macmillan, 2011.

Livni, Joseph, and Ilie Bădescu. "The Battle of the Covenantal Society Against Elitism - An Overlooked Chapter in the History of Social Inequality." *Romanian Journal of Sociological Studies, New Series*, No. 1 (2020): 3–36.

Lizerand, Georges. *Le Régime Rural De L'ancienne France*. Paris: Presses Universitaires de France, 1942.

Luley, Benjamin P. "Equality, Inequality, and the Problem of "Elites" in Late Iron Age Eastern Languedoc (Mediterranean France), Ca. 400–125 BC." *Journal of Anthropological Archaeology* 41 (2016): 33–54.

Măndiţă, Mădălina. *Compared Noology of Jewish and Romanian People: A Sociology of Communities*. Aachen: Shaker Verlag, 2017.

Maspétiol, Roland. *L'ordre Éternel Des Champs: Essai Sur L'histoire, L'économie Et Les Vaeurs De La Paysannerie*. Paris: Librairie de Médicis, 1946.

Mithen, Steven J., Bill Finlayson, Sam Smith, Emma Jenkins, Mohammed Najjar, and Darko Maričević. "An 11 600 Year-Old Communal Structure From the Neolithic of Southern Jordan." *Antiquity* 85, no. 328 (2011): 350–64.

Niculiţă-Voronca, Elena. *Datinile Şi Credinţele Poporului Român: Adunate Şi Aşezate În Ordine Mitologică* [in Romanian] [The Traditions and Beliefs of the Romanian People]. Cernăuţi: Tip. Isidor Wiegler, 1903.

Otescu, Ion. *Credinţele Ţăranului Român Despre Cer Şi Stele*. Bucharest: Analele A. R., 1907.

Pamfilie, Tudor. *Cerul Şi Podoabele Lui: După Credinţele Poporului Român* [in Romanian] [The Sky and His Adornments]. Bucharest: Socec, P. Suru, C. Sfetea, 1915.

Roupnel, Gaston. *Histoire De La Campagne Française*. Paris: B. Grasset, 1932.

Samson, Alain, and Benjamin G. Voyer. "Two Minds, Three Ways: Dual System and Dual Process Models in Consumer Psychology." *AMS Review* 2, no. 2 (2012): 48–71.

Stahl, Henri H. *Contribuţii La Studiul Satelor Devălmaşe Româneşti, Vol. Ii, Structura Internă a Satelor Devălmaşe Libere*. Contributions to the Study of Romanian Joint-Property Villages. 3 Vols. Vol. 2. Bucharest: Editura Academiei R.P.R., 1959.

———. "L'habitat Humain Et Ies Formes De La Vie Sociale." *Arhiva pentru ştiinţa şi reforma socială,* Year XII (1930).

———. "L'organisation Collective Du Village Roumain." *Arhiva pentru ştiinţa şi reforma socială,* Year XIII (1931).

———. *Nerej, Un Village D'une Région Archaïque: Monographie Sociologique* [in French]. Vol. V. 1, Bucarest: Institut de sciences sociales de Roumanie, 1939.

———. *Sociologia Satului Devălmaş Românesc* [in Romanian] [Sociology of Communal Romanian Village]. Vol. 3. Bucharest: Fundaţia Regele Mihai I, 1946.

———. *Traditional Romanian Village Communities*. Cambridge: Cambridge University Press, 1980.

Stahl, Henri H., and Paul H. Stahl. *Contribuții La Studiul Satelor Devălmașe Românești: Procesul De Aservire Feudală a Satelor Devălmașe*, Vol. 3. Cartea Românească, 1998.

Topel, Menachem. *In the Communal Idea in the 21st Century*, edited by E. Ben-Rafael, Y. Oved, and M. Topel. Leiden, Boston: Brill, 2012.

Ulmen, G. L., and Carl Schmitt. "The Nomos of the Earth in the International Law of the Jus Publicum Europaeum." *Telos*, 2006.

Vulcănescu, Romulus. *Etnologie Juridică*. Bucharest: Editura Academiei Republicii Socialiste România, 1970.

Wright, Katherine I. Karen. "Domestication and Inequality? Households, Corporate Groups and Food Processing Tools at Neolithic Çatalhöyük." *Journal of Anthropological Archaeology* 33 (2014): 1–33.

Chapter 5

The Covenant as Ideal Type

A Sociological Study of a Covenanted Community Model

Mădălina Mândiță

The *verstehen* of Jewish people always represented a very intriguing subject for humanities, especially for sociology. Considering that religion constituted the central dimension through which sociologists tried to study and explain society, the question of Jewish religion poses challenges in understanding the fundamentals of social existence. The angle through which we view the constitutive point of this people is the question of Covenant, a theophany considered to be the beginning of a long and troubled history, from different perspectives—social, political, and economic. The premise of this chapter is that the Covenant is the constitutive framework of the Jewish people, one with a deep impact on all social dimensions, building a resilient people.

Thus, we overview the main sociological understanding of the importance of Judaism with different theories in explaining the uniqueness of Jewish people. Max Weber set the constitutive frame for a social relevance that marked the rationality of the Western world; the functional-structuralist model of Emile Durkheim explained the equivalences between society (community) and religion; from an evolutionist perspective, Antonin Causse identified the changes from primitive mentality toward rational and individualistic ethic. From this sociological framing, we introduce the contributions from the theology of the Old Testament centered on the Covenant. With the help of the *sociology of spiritual order*, noological sociology, represented by I. Bădescu, we discover the importance of actualizing the spiritual latency, in the form of *togetherness*, properly revealed by the Covenant. Building on these contributions, of *togetherness* as it is lived by the covenanted people, we propose an ideal-typical definition of the *covenant community*, trying to delineate the Jewish Covenant people and other societies in which we find covenantal-type like characteristics. Having in mind that *togetherness* represents an essence of sociality, this *being-together* acquires special meaning for Jewish people due to the Covenant made with God, a tremendous formative event, creating history and resilience in time. For understanding the uniqueness of the covenanted people, it is necessary to present the different types of Covenants and their impact on social interactions, essentially the complex interwinding of religion and society. Sociology of covenant represents sociology of *togetherness*, of a particular type of sociality, one that creates order endowed with meaning from the highest transcendental value, from God.

THE COVENANT IN CLASSICAL SOCIOLOGY

From a sociological perspective religion represents a key dimension as a motive for action in creating economic and social ethics (Weber), as a mirror of society, revealing the power of cultic manifestation (Durkheim), or as a change of primitive mentality toward ethical individualism (Causse). Whatever the perspective would be, classical sociology acknowledged the power of religion in creating identities, bringing social change, and preserving communities' identities. We review the key elements of a sociology of religion applied to this *major social event, the Covenant with God*, starting from the premise that the *covenant* is a prototype for understanding and defining sociality, the relation between society and individual, and the specific identity of a particular community.

Covenant as a Society: Durkheim—"Don't forget I am the son of a rabbi"[1]

The sociology of David Emile Durkheim has been recently placed in the larger context of his cultural heritage, as the heir of a long line of rabbis.[2] A new reading of his major sociological contribution is made appealing to a specific style of thought. Using the *rabbinic lens* Winfield frames his thinking by "drawing attention to how he employs the same system of classifications, hierarchies, examples, terminology, and argument styles as the Talmud and influential historical and contemporaneous rabbis." The focus on law, moral action, social and individual security during disorders or anomie, and social solidarity all were influenced by his Judaic setting. The social facts, the object of sociology, are derived from visible manifestations, actions, and laws that manifest according to specific rules which can be scientifically studied. Using Weberian terminology, the focus of Durkheimian sociology is on the innerworldly manifestations of ideas and values, measured and visible in social facts which have their specific laws.

Thus, Winfield recalls the importance of actual manifestation of ideas, exemplified by the demand of God for Abraham to sacrifice his son, explained by a rabbi as a test of Abraham's emotions which were only internal, but needed to be actualized, transposed in action, as *lived-experiences*.[3] This is why, affirms Winfield, "his deed allowed his latent fear to emerge into actuality, and then his merit was complete and could be rewarded.[4] Deeds, 'bring out the thing from ability to actuality, giving a reward for a good action and not just a reward for a good heart' (22:1). Jewish philosophers from the Middle Ages onwards recognized outward observance of rituals as a signal of internal religiosity.[5]

Morality is to be found in law and action, as Durkheim writes in *Moral Education* (1925),[6] where he presented morality as a "system of commandments" and a "comprehensive system of prohibitions" (p. 42). Fixed and specific rituals and rules act to "determine conduct, to fix it, to eliminate the element of individual arbitrariness" (p. 27). Durkheim distanced his moral system from those that rely on beliefs and emotions, the "spiritualistic philosophy [that] continues the work of Protestantism" (p. 7). The principal duty of a Christian toward God is emotional—"to love his neighbor"; in this theology, ritual duties toward the divine diminish in number and importance (p. 7).[7]

This reality means a diminished cultic manifestation, a diminished unity brought by rituals, and a weak religious reality of manifesting community. The author underlines the precepts of Judaism toward the Jewish law, Halakha, which is "thought of as a path that teaches practitioners how to walk through life."[8] Thus, the laws and rules of social facts are the object of sociological explanation, the main source of actualized morality in Durkheimian sociology.

For Durkheim religion is a social fact (it binds people in cultic and ritual manifestations, creating solidarity), and religious representations are collective in their essence. Here too, action is the key to religion, which is more than a system of beliefs; religious action is the mechanism that leads to religious beliefs. Without group-specific actions, the group will lose its group-specific beliefs.[9] Durkheim analyzes the positive and negative cult, rituals that move between sacred and profane, all manifesting in concrete actions, remembering that these "positive and negative cult practices correspond with the rabbinic system of positive and negative commandments. There are 613 commandments that can be divided between 248 'positive commandments' [mitzvot aseh, lit. 'commandments to do'], and 365 'negative commandments' [mitzvot lo taaseh, lit. 'commandments not to do']."[10]

This is how social action and religion are profoundly interconnected, as Weberian and Durkheimian sociologies proved, moving from religious beliefs toward building society, and communities, in a dialectic of sacred and profane, with an impact on all social dimensions.

The crux of religion for Durkheim, according to Winfield, is reflected by the tenets of Kodesh [holy] and chol [profane/mundane] in Judaism. In the words of Lindenthal, "there is probably no other religion which possesses as extensive a literature concerned with the dichotomy between the sacred and the secular in every sphere of human endeavor as Judaism." The categories of pure and impure are also connected with the rabbinic teachings, because "for Durkheim, the Torah, and the Talmud, sacredness, and profanity, purity and impurity are states that emerge from certain actions and bodily states — not belief."[11]

Religion means society/community, and Durkheim rejected the position to view religion as a personal, psychological phenomenon. For him, underlines Winfield, the community is the central point of religion which manifests itself as a gathering because it is united by what is sacred and relates to the profane in common practice and representation, creating something that is above and transcends it. This coming-together, based on shared values and manifested behavior, defines rituals and keeps individuals in the meaning of their gathering. This contribution helps understand society, covenantal or covenantal type-like communities, as it will be developed in the second part of this chapter.

The main point of Winfield, according to which Durkheim's communal practice mirrors the community in Jewish law, culminates in the equivalence made by Durkheim between society and God. Even though this is blasphemy, we could say that Durkheim set society as above and beyond the individual, from a scientific point of view, just like God is Above and Beyond man, from a religious point of view. Durkheim spoke in sociology as a social scientist.

Relevant also to his sociology was the social context in which he lived, in a time when Jewish communities were in the process of accommodation to modernity, of integration into larger societies. Discussing Durkheim and his response to modernity, Deborah Moore also considers that his conception of religion "did not contradict the experience of Jews. Traditionally, a Jew cannot be a Jew alone; the community provides the context of Jewishness."[12] The social medium in which Durkheim wrote was marked by the integration of French Jews. His sociology of religion was not meant to attack any religion, but to establish "the reality of the object of faith without accepting the intellectual content of traditional religions."[13] Ultimately, emancipation meant a choice between society and God, but Durkheim considered himself "quite indifferent to this choice since I see in the Divinity only society transfigured and symbolically expressed."[14] This is why the Durkheimian theory of religion is considered by this author as a synthesis of his Jewish French thinking.

The role of the cult in constructing communities, the prevalence of action over belief, the group's power to validate the reality of beliefs, and the relation between God and man are all found reflection in the Jewish tradition, reminds Moore. Durkheim acknowledged that divinity is real only in human consciousness, underlines Moore, along the reciprocal relationship between God and man, elements which reflect a Jewish point of view found especially in the covenant relationship, a type of special dialogue/interaction that defined this people.

The Covenant of God to his people irradiates the entire Jewish history, becomes the foundation of their national life, "the cornerstone of Jewish political and interpersonal relationships. In essence, it is a contractual agreement between God and Abraham, and between God and the Jewish nation. It is this contractual feature of ancient Israelite life which made justice—not charity—the dominant value of that society."[15]

The characteristic of justice is found in the contractual relation analyzed by Durkheim when considering the moral relationship between the two parties, underline the authors. The contractual relation is important for the whole social system, and justice is the norm that guides its fairness. Accordingly, the contract is not derived from individuals, it is a collective product endowed with "sacredness," and "justice" exists as a social force and a social fact that is independent of human will and the individual. Justice is not the agreement between two or more individuals in the sense of being a personal contract. Like the Torah and the law in general, justice is external to the individual. Durkheim argues clearly that justice is the norm that specifies that the contractual relationship is between units in the social system that do not have the same degree of power.[16]

Just as God, part of Covenant, has obligations toward his people, Durkheim connects God with society precisely along these lines: society must meet certain obligations toward its members, including the regulation of their desires. When it fails in these obligations, it is unjust. Like the prophets and other charismatic leaders who are the symbols of the Jewish collective conscience and who stand as guardians of Tzedek, the moral imperative in the covenant, so society must oversee all contractual relationships and must insist that the parties obey the norm of justice. The role of the prophets is to ensure that those in power do not disregard Tzedek and use their position to exploit those who are powerless. In this role, the prophets have become the moral conscience of the nation and exercise the community's right to be critical of their leaders. It is this social condition which, we propose, made justice the pinnacle of the moral order.[17]

Compared with the ancient prophets, it is highlighted that Durkheim too was critical, preoccupied with the abuses against the weak, the deficiencies of modern political directions, and Western culture "when he felt that they failed to promote justice or promoted its obverse, anomie."[18] His focus on justice and the search for a science of moral facts enabled Durkheim to be the moralist that his father was and the scientist that his father wanted to be. It allowed him to keep his Judaic heritage alive yet assimilate into the French republic. It wed fact and value, object and subject, science and morality, phenomena which have often been understood as being poles apart. Justice, as Durkheim conceived it, would lead to subjective contentment in the lives of individuals, and yet was also a social fact.[19]

Thus, religion is a social fact, justice is the purpose of the contractual relationship, the actualization of beliefs is the manifestation that validates the created reality, and the power of ritual and cultic organization testifies to the existence of society, all are the pillars in Durkheimian sociology. Along these, it must be mentioned the question of solidarity and its mechanical and organic types that Durkheim also analyzed. All these are elements in creating the *ideal types* constructed for the *verstehen* of *covenantal community* differentiating them from the *covenantal type-like societies*.

Social solidarity, or *being together*, is an essence that builds history. The entire social reality has two forms of actualized reality, community, and society, considering the study of solidarity as the object of Durkheimian sociology through the social manifestations, in social facts.[20]

Mechanical solidarity, according to Durkheim, is characterized by the resemblance of people, common feelings and values, repressive rights, an individual consciousness that depends on the collective type, solidarity derived from similarities, with an individual that belongs to the community and is at its disposal, with personality absorbed by the community. On the other way, *organic solidarity* is characterized by the differentiation of personalities, with separate functions that bind individuals in society, with a restitutive law and a division of labor, thus society is moving in concert, according to Durkheim. In history, from an evolutionary perspective, mechanical solidarity decreases permitting organic solidarity to develop.

About the ancient Jewish people, Durkheim affirms that mechanical solidarity is very strong, and here "religion pervades the whole of social life."[21] Discussing the repressive character of mechanical solidarity, Durkheim views Exodus, Leviticus, Numbers, and Deuteronomy as examples. Out "of the 4,000–5,000 verses there is only a relatively tiny number in which are expressed rules that might conceivably pass as not being repressive."[22] All these rules have a religious character, "they all likewise emanate from the Godhead; to violate them is to offend him, and such offenses are sins that must be expiated. The Book does not distinguish between this kind of commandment and another, for they are all divine words that cannot be disobeyed with impunity."[23] This is why the whole Hebrew law bears the stamp of repression, underlines Durkheim, because all the expressions contained in the Pentateuch are the commandments of God, sealed, so to speak, with his direct guarantee, from this origin they all derive an extraordinary prestige that renders them sacrosanct. Thus, when they are violated, the public conscience is not content with mere reparation but insists upon an expiation—one of vengeance. Since what is peculiar to the nature of the penal law is the extraordinary authority of the rules that it sanctions, and since men have never known or imagined any higher authority than that which the believer attributes to his God, a law deemed to be the word of God Himself cannot fail to be essentially repressive. We could even say that every penal law is more or less religious, for what lies at its heart is the feeling of respect for a force superior to that of the individual, for a power in some way transcendental, regardless of the particular symbol whereby it impinges upon the consciousness, and this sentiment is at the basis of all religious feeling. This is why, in a general fashion, repression dominates the entire corpus of law in lower societies: it is because religion permeates all legal activity, just as, moreover, it does all social life.[24]

Durkheim, with his cultural background and his efforts to identify the laws of social facts, establishes the power of law as the manifestation of social solidarity. If in mechanical solidarity the law is repressive (penal), in organic solidarity the law becomes more restitutive (civil, procedural law).

The challenge for researching the covenant type of a social structure is to see how the prevalence of repressive or restitutive laws substantiates a community. The uniqueness of the Jewish people is that it maintained its mechanical solidarity amid expanding organic solidarity, and this group identity is explained only by the Covenant with God, which created a covenanted community in a continuously differentiated world. We may say that only in the type of *covenantal community*, the organic and mechanical solidarity strongly interwound, favored by specific social conditions, such as being a minority, in Diaspora, and having a powerful religious identity.

These are the main guidelines that Durkheimian sociology brings to understand society as the manifestation of social facts. The question of the covenant is understood as an actualization/lived relationship of God to his people, established laws characterized by justice, solidarity (sociality), punishments, and ways to survival in case of social perils, such as anomy. The social solidarity, mechanical and organic, can be used to understand the Covenant as a *social event* par excellence. Even though Durkheim identifies a passing from mechanical to organic solidarity, these are two states useful in understanding the Covenant, especially for Jewish people and not only. This chapter attempts to construct an *ideal type* of *covenantal community* and one for the *covenantal type-like society*. The intriguing question is to explain how the powerful forces of mechanical solidarity survived and manifested amidst organic solidarity in an increased modern social division of labor. The key answer is in the *Covenant* with God, in the social prototype of what was called *covenant community*.

Covenant as a Prophetic Power

Ancient Judaism[25] represents "a model of Weberian empirical research, certainly a better model than the narrower and more speculative *The Protestant Ethic and the Spirit of Capitalism* ([1904] 1958)."[26] Weberian sociology was developed as an effort to understand the peculiarities of Western culture, and his study of Judaism was the way to access the uniqueness of changes that marked the entire Occidental religiosity and culture. In this chapter the focus is on the *berith* with Yahweh, analyzed in its specific social context, which developed social structures that evolved, changed, or reacted to political and economic events. This specific event represents, for sociology, the formation of a people, the bond that formed the *covenanted community* of Jewish people, with specific characteristics. The main legal forms developed since were researched by Weber, with an attention on the revisions made after the Exile, starting with the *berith* that changed social structures. The novelty of this oath was that it was made with God, its "peculiarity consists in the first place in the extensive employment of the religious *berith* as the actual (or construed) basis of the most varied legal and moral relations. Above all, Israel itself as a political community was conceived as an oathbound confederation."[27] The stability of the social organization for this covenanted community was guaranteed by God, not as a guarantor of the oath, but as a part of it. Thus, Weber finds that this event "provided a solid basis for permanent political and military structures,"[28] with Yahweh as a God of union, of specifically social and legal order.

The power of the Covenant was tested amidst social, political, and military troubles by the advent of prophets. Now, the prophecy was "absolutely religious, oriented toward the fulfillment of Yahweh's commandments."[29] Political or military alliances alone offered little assurance in times of danger. Deliverance comes from God because the covenanted people "stood in the berith with Yahweh. Nothing must enter the competition with the berith, especially not trust in human help, which would bespeak of godless disbelief and evoke Yahweh's wrath."[30] This brought a type of salvation that concentrates on the law, on the teachings of Yahweh, a "special promise of salvation held out to Israel made morally correct action and the abidance by everyday ethic all important. However banal and self-evident this may seem, here alone it was made the basis of religious prophecy."[31] The mission of the prophet was to fight against sin, to reveal and explain the correct social behavior, to obey the law, there was no thought of metaphysical gnosis and interpretation of the world. The nature of Yahweh contained nothing supernatural in the sense of something extending beyond human understanding. His motives were not concealed from human comprehension. On the contrary, the task of the prophet as well as the Torah teacher was, indeed, to understand Yahweh's counsels in terms of justifiable motives.[32]

Here Weber identified a type of rational understanding that built the specific rationalization found only in the Western world. The world becomes intelligible, the motivation/meaning of everything that is happening can be discovered, and the manifestations of God have reasons that can be met by human understanding; thus, the world becomes rational. This is a construction of a powerful ethic with a tremendous possibility for social actions, and social change, in the construction and preservation of collective identity.

Along with obeying the law, another characteristic is underlined, the question of faith, which "signified only the unconditional trust in Yahweh's omnipotence and the sincerity of his word and conviction in its fulfillment despite all external probabilities to the contrary."[33] This total trust requested by the omnipotence of God was best tested in times of political chaos, or social disintegration, paradigmatically set by the time of Exile. Religious unity in the face of political and social destruction was the way to keep identity, organize social behavior to survive, and not lose hope in God's plan.

Weber sociologically analyzed the impact of this religious ethic on the social, political, and economic manifestations, revealing the profound interdependence of religion and social structures. The Covenant proved to be a free and assumed bound, one with God, the construction and survival of a people, a *covenanted community*, with specific characteristics.

Political and military catastrophes, the collapse of the monarchy, the prophetic phenomenon, the Babylonian captivity, and the dispersion of Jews are all key events that illuminate the history of the covenanted Jewish people.[34]

The Babylonian captivity marked the beginning of the Diaspora, "the Exile was also the great turning point of Western civilization."[35] The prophets appeared during a great political crisis, which was preceded by the rise of urban culture, the liberation of Philistines, a grandeur that was never forgotten, recalls Bendix. Thus, the prophets attacked the innovations brought by the kingship, voiced the people's sufferings, calling for justice. Their "basic ideal is the time-honored 'law' of the ancient Israelite confederacy; the basic evil is the transformation of this good society of the past into an Egyptian 'house of bondage.' However, this is not an opposition to the monarchy as such, since during the wars of liberation the monarchy had enormous prestige."[36] They opposed the political alliances, idolatry, and despotism in a troubled international context; they were spokesmen of the traditional Judaic morality. The prophet's mission lay basically in his moral exhortation of the people and in his thundering oracles of doom for all those who did evil. His accent was on retribution in the here and now, not on salvation in the beyond, for Israel had a special duty to adhere unswervingly to the binding law of its God. The great contribution of the Biblical prophets was to make the *morally correct actions of everyday life into a special duty of a people chosen by the mightiest God.*[37]

If in the past the prophecy was directed toward political and military events, now the focus was on obeying the Law. Yahweh made a covenant with his people, and the effects of breaking it meant violation of his Law. The peculiarity is that "the demands for charity and religious purity were not unique in Israel. But in Israel these demands were enjoined upon the people as a whole, not merely upon the rulers, because under the covenant the people were jointly responsible for one another."[38]

The evils over his people were explained as depending on man's acts, and "the God of the prophets assumed a majesty that was incomparably greater than that envisaged in the old God of the confederacy or the teachings of Deuteronomy. In the prophetic image, God instantly changed nature and history to achieve His designs; He moved kings and empires at will to punish His sinning."[39] Even when the Temple was destroyed the glory of Yahweh increased, becoming the god of historical universalism, underlines Bendix. Thus, "this theodicy of the prophets became the central religious mentality of ancient Judaism. Though Yahweh is the majestic ruler of the cosmos, His ancient promises to Israel remain entirely concrete. The people will prosper in the here and now, if they obey His commandments."[40] The Exile was seen as "the place of all hope and future welfare"[41] although people disobeyed the Law. After the Exile the meaning of suffering was directed toward salvation, here was the final culmination, "Israel in exile now appears as the champion, the object of salvation, glorifying the endurance and suffering of the people before God by giving their fate the meaning of a world-historical mission."[42] Devotion to the law, hoping for a better future, "the prophets established a religion of faith that subjected man's daily life to the imperatives of a divinely ordained moral law. In this way, ancient Judaism helped create the moral rationalism of Western civilization."[43]

Covenant as an Ethical Community

In 1937 A. Causse published *Du groupe ethniques a la communaute religieuse. Le Probleme de la religion d'Israel*,[44] recognizing the contribution of Max Weber in *Ancient Judaism*, his main critique was that Weber did not pay sufficient attention to the primitive mentality and its evolution toward the rational and individualistic ethic that characterized this religion. Causse recognized the organic solidarity of the clan, tribe, and family as the main sources, the ones that were affected by the dissolution under the impact of monarchy, and urbanization, bringing a deep social crisis, in a time when "the covenant lost its primitive force, this mystique connection, stronger than any other physical connection between men, with sworn fidelity, respect for the contractual law, and a spiritual connection between allies."[45] The social crisis meant also a religious crisis, bringing the prophetic phenomenon, a new reactivation of the covenant, given the problems that political realities brought a detachment from Yahweh. As Weber, Causse too acknowledged the power of ethical development, of the moral behavior of people to unite the Jewish community, to reinforce the solidarity brought by the Covenant. In the prophetic event, Causse finds the passing from primitive collectivism, of natural connection, toward moral individualism, of a personal dimension of people to God, accountability, and responsibility, of rationality in the cult. He considers that these changes are expressed by the Deuteronomy, "a book of reform and teaching, which represent the beginning of a new religious conception, the religion of Torah,"[46] a voluntary, assumed, and lived brotherhood. He views the prophets of exile as the *great wakening of Israel*, bringing not a new social life, but a "new sociological formation, one which will not be a confederation of clans, not a people, but a religious community with a life that will no longer be tied to the realities of an ethnic group with the destiny of a nation."[47] We could say that this profound religious crisis brought a new social reality, helping in time communities around the world to be one community, to organize accordingly to the same law, to be a *covenanted community* founded on the re-actualization of the Covenant. The shock of the Exile, the consolidation of the Torah, and this new type of self-perception were based on the reinstatement of a foundational event, a social and religious fact, the Covenant. This piety rediscovered after the social and political crisis brought also a type of universalism, a "particular social evolution in which the religious community tends to organize itself outside of political institution and territory."[48]

His analysis of the monarchy brings Causse to draw the same conclusion as Weber, meaning that "a social question becomes a religious question."[49] The accent is put by Causse on the Deuteronomy, on the personal responsibility of the individual, without entering in conflict with the institutional forms of the religious community, "since Torah was seen as means of propagating the personal presence of Yahweh in the presence of his worshipers."[50] This transition toward personal accountability and responsibility *in the community* of believers is owed to the Law, a deep connection formed by the Covenant. For this sociologist, Torah represents the *national country* of the Jewish community, all standing on the Moses Covenant, a religious as well as a *social event*, with tremendous impact in time, attested by the history of Jewish communities around the world.

TYPES OF COVENANTS

The first part of this chapter reviewed a sociological contribution focusing on the Jewish Covenant. This helps circle the formation of the ideal type of *covenantal community*, with the premise of Covenant as a decisive socio-religious event, which formed Jewish people and impacted many social structures, and brought social change. The social phenomenon of the covenant acquired different forms of expression, manifestation, and interpretation, contributing to a peculiarity that will be addressed in the last part of this research, defining the Jewish community as a covenantal one.

More types of covenants point to the most decisive elements in Jewish history, from a religious perspective, but most importantly from a sociological understanding indicative of a unique community. Here we appeal to the work of Bernhard W. Anderson, *Contours of Old Testament Theology*, which focused on different types of Covenants and their prevalence under the impact of changing social conditions.

The first, the *Noahic Covenant*, an everlasting one, is based on the promise of God to humankind to never destroy the world; it is unconditional, universal, and not dependent on human behavior. The *Abrahamic Covenant* is one made by God with Israel, concerns the future, the promise for prosperity, and the land of Canaan, offering promises, not laws. The *Mosaic Covenant*, an everlasting one, is a liberating one, conditioned on people's behavior which must obey the given Law. The rainbow, the circumcision, and the Sabbath are their signs. The *Davidic Covenant* brought a new type of theology, which reflected the social and monarchical reality of the Jewish people.

With the Mosaic Covenant starts the cultic form of religiosity, remembering the relevance of the cult as actual religiosity in community, meaning "the establishment of Israel as a worshiping community."[51] This is a conditioned covenant depending on people's behavior; it can be revoked and not obeying its commandments could break it. There have been made parallels between the Mosaic Covenant and the Hittite form of suzerainty treaty, between a higher power and its vassal. The form of suzerainty treaty is similar to the one made by Moses with God, but the most striking affinity would be the one which deals with curses and blessings, argues Anderson. Israel, upon his liberation from Egypt, is to obey the laws, as a vassal to God, otherwise, punishments will follow. Israel "is to conduct their social life according to the agreement made at Sinai, and that means to pursue justice and to recognize the rights of every member of the community, including the alien one."[52]

Here the author draws attention to the liberation theology, which sometimes is used in an incomplete comprehension of the Sinai event. This means that freedom is not self-determination or used to enter under another power, but it was offered so that the liberated people transform themselves into a worshiping community, serving God, the only true leader. "God's liberating work began in rescuing slaves from the misery and suffering of imperial bondage; it was completed in shaping those slaves into a community regulated by 'statutes and ordinance.' Israel freedom was not freedom *from* but freedom *for*."[53]

Linking Abrahamic Covenant with the Mosaic one, the unconditional with the conditional, the Deuteronomic theologians "relativized the land promise that is to make the possession contingent on the behavior of the people on the land. If the people are unfaithful to the covenant, the result will be that God will bring judgment on them, scattering them among the nations, where they will worship worthless idols (Deut. 4:25–29)."[54]

The Davidic Covenant, the royal covenant, brings a *new theology* underlines Anderson, because it had to reconcile the sacred kingship with the image of Yahweh as king. Thus, the task of David's theologians was to adapt these two institutions that originally were alien to Israelite experience—dynastic kingship and sacramental temple—to Israel's faith so that they could become symbols for expressing the relationship between God and people, indeed, between God and the world. Their success is evidenced in the fact that David escorted the ark—the Mosaic symbol of Yahweh's presence in the midst of the people, into Jerusalem.[55]

Some view the Davidic covenant as an ideology, a type of practice that justifies a political program, a legitimization of monarchic power, "emphasizing order at the expense of freedom. The Davidic covenant, according to some scholars, was a kind of *fall from grace*,"[56] it was in contrast with the times of tribal confederacy marked by freedom and egalitarian ways of living. The monarchy period was a challenging time and triggered the prophetic movements, an important social phenomenon that impacted Western rational thought, as Weber proved. For sure, this period was a decisive moment, following a troubled political, social, and religious time.

The sociological understanding of the relation of God with his people is useful also in understanding the theological (new) meanings attributed, actualized, and lived by the people. But, according to this author, these meanings must reveal that above sociological reality they are concerned with the relation between God and people, transcending the level of immanence.

In the Davidic covenant, Yahweh is bound to David and its line forever, in contrast with the Mosaic Covenant, in which entering into the covenant was made voluntarily. Here the king is responsible for justice, the subject in which Torah is revealed, the covenant becoming "the basis for social stability, which is rooted not in the authority of the king but in the cosmic role of God mediated through the anointed one."[57] This covenant has different symbolizing patterns of the relationships between God and Israel, and God and the world, underlines Anderson, not conditioned by humans, assuring stability and hope for the future troubles of history. The covenant as a social and religious reality proves its tremendous power when Israel is confronted with social and national trauma, following the Exile and their loss of national independence.

In the postexilic reality, the covenant finds its centrality, reinstatement, and revival in the efforts to assure the survival of the people of Israel.

Re-actualizing the Sinai Covenant in Postexilic Times

The Exile brought a powerful need to understand the destruction of Jerusalem by the Babylonian empire, and to reaffirm the covenants, meaning the identity as a covenanted community. If the Sinai Covenant depended on hearing the voice of God and obeying his commandments, the Davidic one required obedience toward the king, even though the king makes mistakes, being based on *steadfast love*, recalls R. J. Bautch. This is why "one covenantal type, associated with Sinai, is conditional in its ideology, northern in its provenance, and historical in its discourse, while the Davidic type is unconditional, southern, and oriented to creation."[58] Living the Exile meant a reevaluation of the community's identity, this crisis reaffirming the centrality of a social and religious total event—the *Covenant.*

The focus for rebuilding the people was on the consequences of forgetting the Laws of God, as well as on the promise of a better future despite the crisis brought by this major social trauma. This meant also a remembering of Abraham's Covenant. In the author's words it was

> an idealized promise of land and progeny, but as a postexilic paradigm of relationship, it retains traces of human obligation. Thus, the renovation of the covenant in the postexilic era involves a synthesis of Abrahamic and Sinai traditions, in effect a kind of dialogical relationship between concepts of conditional and unconditional covenants.[59]

These Covenants were powerfully lived in postexilic times, the writings "exhibit a religious and societal choice for continuity with the pre-exilic period through the retention of a venerable Covenant that hinges upon an objective set of obligations, namely, the laws from Sinai."[60]

Confession of sins and new impetus toward creation are considered by Bautch as keys to approach this re-actualization of the Sinai Covenant. The breach of the Sinai Covenant that brought the Exile was used to restore its Laws in postexilic times, collective acknowledgment of sins was coupled with God's forgiveness, argues Bautch. This renewal is like creation, recalling the power of the Creator to renew the Sinai Covenant. There has been also a reevaluation of kingship, clan, and family, Bautch identifying a new level of analysis relevant from a sociological view. Tribes, clans, and houses represent a concentric structure, together with the monarchy, influencing the conception of the covenant with God, states the author. The monarchic times changed the perspectives on kingship:

> The Deuteronomic reform consolidated and stabilized the concept of Israel as "a people," thereby laying the theological groundwork for a robust understanding of covenant. To an unprecedented degree, the concept of an Israelite people became linked to the motifs of covenant and land late in the monarchic period.[61]

Thus, in the postexilic times, the institution of kingship influenced the attitudes relating to the Covenant, and despite the destruction of political and religious institutions, the family became the center of lived/actualized religiosity, manifesting in customs, "markers of identity in a foreign land while supplying group cohesion."[62] Now, "family and covenant became the operative terms for social formation, with kinship playing a significant role in these deliberations and writings."[63] Marriage and covenant, two powerful and old institutions, are again strongly connected following the writings of Ezra bringing "nonconformity to the way of the world, allegiance to Torah, and greater solidarity within the postexilic community."[64] This meant a new type of solidarity, based on kinship groups, clans, and ethnic fraternity, bringing a new "social cohesion, just as Ezra's campaign against intermarriage is designed to make the clans and their members see themselves as "Israel." Indeed, Nehemiah's lending reforms are clearly designed to inculcate a sense of fraternity and common agreement.[65] The elites, adopting a more correct behavior, the conception of Jews as brothers, assuming social awareness, facilitated a "sense of social equity," social interdependence between elites and people, reaffirming the Sinai Covenant as an ideal of an Israel to which all Jews may belong equally.[66]

Therefore, the covenant and Torah are reevaluated in postexilic times, points out Bautch, toward active human participation, relevant for identity formation, with kinship and family as a model for a larger social structure, creating a national identity, "from Ezra–Nehemiah generating large social entities with centralized authority which constitutes an exercise in Jewish nationalism."[67] The author concludes that "appealing to kinship as the basis of broad Jewish unity, the Covenants inculcate a sense of communal descent and culture. Requiring adherence to Torah in its breadth and its particularity, the covenants remind the people of their relationship to their God, the God of history. Covering over the scars of exile, the Covenants posit a broad collective that claims the legacy of Israel and possesses remarkable potential for forming a national Jewish identity."[68]

God and Its Covenanted People

The relationship between individual and society/community is a very complex one in the history of human sciences. Here, we try to enable an understanding of covenant by how an individual is formed by the community, and how the community enforces/empowers an individual, in a very special relationship, the one with God. David Novak, while discussing the rights and duties in this context, underlines that "right must now be seen as being exercised by both God and the community as well as by individual persons.[69] For recognizing the institution of rights, Novak appeals to returning to the theocratic principles of the Jewish covenantal system. And by "theocracy," I do not mean its usual connotation today as basically the dictatorship of clerics, but, rather, its original denotation as "the rule of God." The Jewish people has always considered itself to be under the ultimate rule of God who has made a unique and everlasting covenant with it, but the forms of polity it has been able to appropriate have often been borrowed from its historical surroundings.[70]

The most important element in understanding the Covenant is the relation between God and the community elected, "the covenant is what lies between God and us,"[71] making this event a sociological one with tremendous consequences. In the author's words "there is no higher relationship with God possible than the relation of the word,"[72] in a discursive community that defines human life. This is the reason that the law is central to the covenant, underlines the author, seeing covenantal theology as a political theory, because "the deepest religious concerns are public before they are private."[73] Community mediates between God and the individual, having the role of helping the communal discourse with transcendent meaning. Otherwise, the institutions of that society become hollow. Individual Jews, warns Novak, cannot forget that "God has elected the whole people of Israel for the covenant. To forget that is to commit the basic modern distortion of the covenant, which has asserted in one way or another that it is not God who elects Israel but Israel who elects God."[74]

The Noachite Covenant is for humankind, a precondition of the one made with Abraham, which refers to a transformed future world. The Covenant entails claims of God on all people, but especially on Israel, the covenanted elected people. The Sinai Covenant, through God's manifestation and the ritual bound of the two parties, entails the voluntary decision of the community toward the Law, either obeying or breaking it. This covenant transformed the people into a worshiping community pending upon the correct behavior claimed by God.

One such claim is Justice, along with kindness and humility, but justice as God wants for the world, recalls the author, without forgetting that the final justice is delivered by God alone. Human prayers for justice are happening in the covenanted community, therefore "the greatest indictment of this community and its institutions by the prophets was their condemnation of the perversion of the rights of the most helpless members of the community by those with the societal power to do otherwise."[75] If it fails, political destruction is delivered. The equality in the covenanted community is "because of the superiority of the divine member, the founder and sustainer of the covenant to whom they are all equally related."[76]

Torah is the greatest gift of God for people, becoming their laws on earth, it must be interpreted and applied, with God's blessing, must be accepted voluntarily, not forced, only in this way the covenant becomes practically operative, underlines Novak. The right to interpret the Law is made by the means of reason, "for it is human reason that discovers the purposes of the Torah and understands how they correspond to authentic human desires. The exercise of that reason is rooted in the people's desire to be in covenant with God, and it leads to their assurance that God desires to be in covenant with the people."[77]

The question of rights and duties in Judaism is the purpose of Novak's book, illuminating the importance of divine Law with its application in relations between individuals, as a community tied to God, revealing the force of covenant as "the highest purpose of created human existence."[78] This is why the regulation between individuals and communities, with the foundation of Covenant with God, acquires a very important position for the political theory in general, and in the end "political theory must become political theology to be authentically Jewish," considering that the "the fullness of human rights, for Jews, must be finally seen in the ontologically prior covenantal relationship between God and Israel, which makes even interhuman rights a matter of cosmic significance. Ethics must be finally grounded in ontology."[79]

Regarding the claims of the community on his members, Novak reminds the judicial and legislative aspects of governing the community; at this level "the community (Gemeinschaft) is a society (Gesellschaft), functioning impersonally through its formal political and legal institutions."[80] But the authentic needs of the community have precedents over the individual ones, this being an important element in Jewish tradition, according to Novak, because "the relationship between God and individual persons is still one between God and the members of the covenanted community."[81]

In a conclusion of Novak's book, it can be said that tradition has a central meaning for community, especially regarding the covenanted community with God, because every individual within the community as a totality is directly connected with God, the only truly sovereign. Even Spinoza was impressed by this powerful connection, recalls Novak, because he saw in this characteristic the only defense against political tyranny. If in the theory of social contract, the key is the agreement among individuals,

In the covenant the essence of the polity is a relationship between God and the community, one that is initiated by God's election of the community and fulfilled by the community's positive acceptance of that election and the law from God that gives it both structure and content. Even when individuals act alone, they are still very much communal beings in covenant with God.[82]

All these authors recognized the political impact of the Covenant, and its influence on other institutions to lead communities, having God as absolute power and with equal members of the covenanted community. In Novak's analysis, the theocratic principles are imbued with administrative and political aspects, and political theory becomes political theology regarding the Jewish people, the covenanted community. This is also the position of Daniel Elazar, who considers the biblical model of ancient Israel as the ultimate covenantal community. These contributions are decisive in the conceptualization of an *ideal type* for the *covenantal community*, compared to the *covenantal-type like societies*.

COVENANTAL COMMUNITY: COVENANT AS A POLITICAL FORCE

The socio-political aspect of *covenant* is analyzed by Daniel Elazar, also as a key to understanding the main developments in the Western civilization, with a focus on the political impact of institutions. His vast research led him to elaborate on the characteristics of *covenantal society*, seeing politics as the participation of a community in social life with the scope of a good life, in a dialectic of justice–injustice. Here, the sociological concept of covenant acquires a political prevalence, becoming "less a theological concept than a theo-political one."[83] As we saw above, the covenant means *togetherness*, a congregation of "equal humans who consent with one other through a morally binding pact supported by a transcendent power, establishing with the partners a new framework or setting them on the road to a new task, that can only be dissolved by mutual agreement of all the parties to it."[84] If for Weber rationality is the peculiarity of Western civilization, for Elazar the covenant represents its founding pillars. Established God–human relations as well as interhuman relations, made Elazar affirm that the covenant "must be understood as being political far more than theological in character, designed to establish lines of authority, distributions of power, bodies politic, and systems of law."[85] According to Elazar, the genius of this idea is that it legitimizes political life and establishes a right way to connect people and develop institutions. The author sees the covenant as a social and political reality, which imposes limitations on the power between parties, involving voluntary concessions and freedom, all under "the covenantal authority to reward or punish the consequences of that freedom at some future date."[86] Thus, for Elazar, the covenant has the seeds of modern constitutionalism, deriving from here the idea of limited government.

Considering covenant as a theo-political reality, he acknowledged: the need to limit the manifestation of power; the distinction between those who are part of the covenant and those who are not; the intracommunity relations; the need to manage the conflicts and demands. All form the political aspect of social life, within the lines of power manifestation and practice of justice.

These dimensions of the biblical covenants—social, political, and moral—bind parties together in the pact that God made with the Jewish people, and the moral aspect, the religious one, brings distinction between the covenant form and other forms of contract—oath or social bindings. The moral aspect of covenant, especially the collapse of the moral order, as it was in the events that precluded the Exile, triggered the prophetic movement and contributed to the resilience of the Diaspora of Jewish people. The justice and injustices toward the Law of God became the spiritual frame for the community's profile, as a covenantal community.

Elazar's contribution, in four volumes, is focused on the political dimension, up to modern constitutionalism and American federalism. He examines the political systems, institutions, and social and political behaviors linked to the covenant tradition as a political concept. He compared the covenantal society (egalitarian) with hierarchical and organic types. He assumes a moderate position concerning these three types, considering that "there are gradations of covenantalism to be found in-between."[87] In other words, the distance or the closeness from the *ideal type*, from a sociological perspective, is assumed in this chapter.

The covenant, for Elazar, is to be understood under the moral aspect, assuring the right way to live and interact, and from this reason "no human system and especially no political system can afford not to be under judgment"[88] making individuals humans in relation with a higher power, God, and building many (different) institutions accordingly.

The survey of other forms of vassal treaties or oaths found in ancient Western Asian civilizations leads him to conclude that the covenant of Jewish people with God is "the only record we have of a fully covenantal civilization, that of ancient Israel as portrayed in Scripture."[89] For Elazar, the whole cultural, ideological, behavioral, and institutional reality is attested by this covenantal aspect, a total social event, which influenced Western history.

For a better understanding of the covenantal form of constructing society, Elazar makes the difference between covenants, compacts, and contracts. Compacts and covenants differ from contracts in being more public, reciprocal, flexible, perpetual, and for an unlimited duration, and in need of mutual agreement to abrogate them. Contracts are more private, unilateral, and subjected to abrogation under specific conditions. What is more specific to the covenant, differentiating it from compact, is its moral force, God, as part of the covenant or guarantor. The compact is a secular form of covenant, affirms Elazar. Covenant "is the oldest of several terms that deal with the formation of the political order through consent as manifested in a pact or an appropriate level of mutual binding"[90] under *God*'s authority, we must underline.

The organization is different in the hierarchical, organic, and covenantal forms. The hierarchy is based on force, conquest, with power in the form of a pyramid, with a leader at the top, with levels of authority and administration. The organic form of organization is more natural, with a center and a periphery from which the power is transmitted toward the periphery. The covenantal form is like a matrix, of equal cells, which are bound by common institutions, with laws that are in agreement with everyone. It has "multiple centers, each constitutionally protected. Its apotheosis is a federal system in which the constituent units are represented in the framing government and also preserve their existence, authority, and powers in those areas which are not delegated to the framing institutions."[91]

There are degrees of covenant forms and manifestation. But in minorities Elazar finds the majority of covenantal forms and strength in generating historical movements, "it is the key minorities that do, and if they are covenantal, then the societies become covenantal."[92]

At the end of his research, Elazar concludes that the covenantal tradition found expression in political realities such as: (1) the political organization is a construct established by man, founding civil society in the form of the social contract, pact, covenant; (2) it transforms constitutionalism in new practical constitutional design; (3) the idea of popular sovereignty (under God), people covenanting with each other and forming their constitutions; and (4) when it was not strong enough, people developed cooperative models of the organization even in hierarchical structures.[93]

Thus, founding Western political ideas on the covenant tradition means for Elazar that political systems will become more humane and freedom-seeking, with the potential to be self-governing.[94] Starting from equality, negotiation, consent, and freedom, "covenantal systems have emphasized the sharing of power and authority among institutions and offices rather than its concentration and thereby have promoted notions of federalism that recognize that power emanates from the people upward and is properly distributed and shared."[95] Affirming that the whole world is under divine Law, the "the goal of the Bible is the development of the holy commonwealth, a people organized into a body politic, and the commonwealth is essential for the good life. So understood, the people and the polity are necessary for God's plan for Jewish and human salvation and redemption, and full achievement of the goals of political activity is dependent upon God's intervention to redeem humanity."[96]

For Elazar, the Jewish political tradition and history are marked by the covenant phenomenon, a social, political, and religious *total social reality*. His effort was to identify elements of the covenantal organization in history, providing "the promise of building states and societies upon proper relationships among the members of societies, a proper balancing or ordering of power, a proper sense of justice that would guide the use of power, and institutions, traditions, and behaviors rooted in culture and established upon morally and operationally sound footing."[97]

If sociology viewed religious, economic, and political dimensions separated, in Elazar's perspective these are not differentiated, but are taken together "as a bundle of grounded institutions that emerge over history, presided over by the idea of an Invisible God Almighty."[98] The blending of theo-political perspective is a duality, and if it represents "a pathway to a modern federalism and a decentralized communitarianism, as Elazar claims, is another matter, for it must be said in a frankness that while he was willing to suspend judgment about the federalist future of the United States, he was unshakable in his commitment to the covenantal past as the source of Western civilization."[99] Elazar does not analyze conflicts, or the differences between Judaism and Christianity, and even the celebration of democracy founded in seeds in the covenant is difficult to attest to, concludes Horowitz. The problem, for this author, is the unification of the sacred covenant with the secular state, which can be successful in a certain country, but not in all.

Horowitz considers that the federalist ideal combined with covenant could function in Israel, a small country, but not in the United States, a pluralized and Protestant country. He finds "the concept of the covenantal tradition, linked as it is with the idea of federalism, to be more ideal than real,"[100] in a context of intensified central authority and state power, when secularization works against theology, against a theo-political orientation.

Following Elazar in his endeavor to prove the covenantal form of social organization, J. Livni adopted the covenantal premise and analyzed the covenantal structure within the categories: opposition to hierarchy, federative network, justice administration, assembly government, office holders, and institutions.

I. Bădescu and J. Livni focused on the covenantal forms of social organization, characterized by egalitarian values, compared with the hierarchical form which promotes inequality. I. Bădescu describes covenantal order as one which "makes of social memory a mirror of time and of all that are passing in the world, mighty or minor, great or insignificant, the powerful of history and the humble of fate. And that is what covenantal equality is about."[101] Following Elazar, J. Livni affirms that the covenantal form begins with proto-Israel, with its nomadic social structure that brought to Canaan the egalitarian ethos of Covenantal communities. This theme is substantiated in more details in chapter 1 of this volume. Deep social changes occur during the time of the monarchy, and "history marched from the period of the Judges to that of the Kings, that is, from equality to hierarchy and inequality. Clashes between old and new, between local and central, between elders and crown, were inevitable."[102] J. Livni compares the covenantal, egalitarian communities, with the one of the Waldensians and with the Romanians of the Carpathians. These were small, remote communities, threatened by extinction under the pressure of larger social changes, but survived isolated on the periphery. In the same article, I. Bădescu is analyzing the Romanian rural communities, organized similar to covenantal ones, in which prevails a communal life, with a self-sustaining system, "to culminate in their first form of state organization, the so-called Voivodates."[103]

I. Bădescu also finds the progressive movement from a covenantal, egalitarian form of a social organization toward inequality, toward hierarchical social structures, at the same time resisting communal societies which survived, although in a small number. The "two systems of societal organization, a hierarchical and a rankless one, co-existed and periodically collided with each other,"[104] and their contraction or expansion is of particular sociological relevance for the health of people. I. Bădescu underlines that these communal structures manifested a "non-hierarchical social order which relies on the genealogy going up to its spiritual origin confirmed and empowered in the form of a covenant demanding the observance of its spiritual teachings."[105]

In understanding this phenomenon, we cannot make abstraction of the changes and consolidation of political power, and centralized power structures, as it was the monarchy time for Jewish people, or in the time of consolidation of the modern state in Romania for the case of these rural communal structures.

The two authors concluded that even if the Temple was destroyed, the covenantal system regained power in the case of Jewish people, and as Rome fell, its hierarchical system grew, although "covenantal Christianity resisted extinction in some remote regions because they were less accessible because covenantal systems are locally managed by the community."[106]

So far there is an agreement about the political implications of the covenant, due to the administrative power in managing interhuman relations, under the divine Law, in the name of justice and for a struggle against injustices in the world. The characteristics of Elazar's covenantal communities help to establish the components of the proposed *ideal type* for comparison purposes. To complete the sociological image of the community as a social unit, we appeal to the noological theory of I. Bădescu, which can include both covenantal and covenantal type-like forms of social organization. The noological theory can explain communities that can function as *covenantal* (even secular, unrelated, or opposed to religious values), as well as *covenantal type-like communities*, both under the perspective of the sociology of spiritual order.

NOOLOGICAL COMMUNITY: COVENANT AS LIVED-COMMUNITY

The specific characteristic of man is its spiritual dimension, with its consciousness and creative power. Within this spiritual dimension, it is recognized the prevalence of religion as one primordial field of manifestation. The noological theory of society[107] is focused on the spiritual foundation of society and has three categories of analysis, where prevails the religious experience as the main field in examining social reality. The first is *spiritual latencies* (inner experiences, a sublayer of individual and collective spirit, having a communion nature manifested in spiritual interaction, customs, symbols, and mythic or artistic actions). The second category is one of the *spiritual frames* of manifesting latencies. Here the inner experiences are actualized and lived, and receive their social expression, forming *places of noological gathering* of people with the same latencies.[108] Considered "strengthened fortresses of the collective soul,"[109] spiritual frames are the most relevant for sociological analysis, permitting to measure the power or weakness of a community concerning the actualization or decrease of spiritual latencies. The third category is one of *spiritual teachings*, the pillars of every people in what regards their values, norms, religious beliefs, customs, and ways of life. Applied specifically to the field of the religious dimension, the noological theory helps reveal the strength of society by the way of its actual lived beliefs. The author considers the belief in God as a total and complete spiritual place, from which irradiates "the spiritual power of a people, of a society in general, materialized in the totality of the 'spiritual places' in which and through which one experiences the growth of social interactions in number and intensity, to embrace the entirety and unity of existence in full."[110]

According to I. Bădescu, the spiritual power includes culture, and values, manifested at an individual level through character, personal evolution, and at a collective level through genius, cultural creations, great characters, and exemplary persons. In researching the spiritual order of society, I. Bădescu is distinguishing spiritual teachings from other sorts of teachings. The ones that consider the individual in its fullness, uniting him with the world in a superior meaning, transcending the purely immanent existence, and connecting him with higher powers. The strength of this spiritual power is evident also in the cultural unity, and especially in one with special cohesion, in the religion of a people, and its identity.

The spiritual latencies are latent, they need to be actualized, lived, and expressed, taking social and cultural forms which create identity, and assure power, and resilience in history. They can also be forgotten, weaken, or not lived at a collective level sufficient enough to assure the correct compliance to the spiritual teachings. Here, the easiest example is also the prophetic movement, which determined a reevaluation and reactivation of the most important spiritual teachings, as we saw above, through the reactivation of the Covenant with its power to reinstate a people, even after the Exile, on the correct path stressed by the Law.

These are the most important elements in the theory of the noological order of society established by I. Bădescu. From a noological perspective, the Covenant of Jewish people is a dialogue between man and God, representing the actualization of a latency, manifested in specific spiritual frames, determining a tremendous spiritual power in the most difficult circumstances, such as the Exile.

Seeing the Covenant as a prototype of communion in its full manifestation in Jewish history, this *total social event* can be measured according to the actualization or de-actualization (distance from it). The history of Jewish people can be analyzed as an actualized lived community, founded on the teachings of Covenant, in its fullness of spiritual manifestation as well as a distance from the Law. Both ways (actualized and de-actualized) determined specific social and political behavior; however, not menacing the pillars of identity sustained by the Law. Jewish people are manifesting as a truly covenantal-lived community from a noological view.

The noological communities are all human groups, especially if we see them through the cultural and spiritual manifestations (religiously, artistic). What differentiates them are the social systems built in history, the different identities, and history. The studies of I. Bădescu attested to the power of the religious dimension in society, especially of Christianity,[111] creating the possibility to apply this system of sociology to other people and communities, offering comparative potentiality. If we see Jewish people as a noological community, as a people created by the Covenant event, there is also the possibility to compare to other social, political, and economic structures of other religions, evaluating the close or distance from the constructed ideal type. The manifested inner lived experiences, in frames of social reality according to a series of values, represent the path of noological sociology to access the meanings of an actualized, lived reality, as well as a prognosis over the spiritual strength of a people in a challenging world.

THE COVENANT AS IDEAL TYPE: COVENANTAL COMMUNITY AND COVENANTAL TYPE-LIKE SOCIETIES

Two Ideal Types of Sociological Understanding

The *Verstehen* sociology, founded by the tremendous contribution of Max Weber, is a very fruitful research path for understanding apparently irrational and challenging social phenomena. The provocative task of explaining the uniqueness of Western systems of beliefs was addressed in Weberian sociology. Understanding the rationality (reasons) of irrationality was the purpose of his sociology.[112]

The taken path consisted of the construction of pure types, an *ideal type* as a mental device, analytical concept, logical and rational, useful to compare empirical social behaviors and measuring their distance or closeness from this pure type. By comparing the social and often irrational social behaviors (or difficult to explain) with this logical instrument, we bring to a rational understanding of the social reality. *Verstehen* is the goal of Weberian sociology in the effort to reveal the meanings of social action in creating identities and different paths in history.

An ideal type aims to reflect the uniqueness of a phenomenon in different historical conditions, the particular social manifestations, based on its explanatory capacity of social facts. In Weber's words, "the goal of ideal-typical concept-construction is always to make clearly explicit not the class or average character but rather the unique individual character of cultural phenomena."[113] Many sociological concepts, such as organic and mechanical solidarity, salvation, asceticism, and prophets, are ideal types that help to understand rationally many irrational and challenging social realities. The ideal type is made by exaggerating one element of reality and selecting relevant aspects which are synthesized to form a construct for comparing empirical facts to see differences and reveal causes for this deviation.

The Covenant of God with Jewish people is seen in this chapter as an *ideal type*, with a series of characteristics and consequences that formed and conducted this people over a long and troubled history. The Covenant was presented using the most important sociological perspectives as a *total social fact*, with the ways it was lived by the Jewish people during profound social changes, such as monarchy, prophetic reaction, the Exile, and survival of postexilic communities, all in dialectic of closeness or distance from its laws. The four forms of Covenants had different degrees of responsibilities, conditionality, and effects. The prototype of these covenants is the Covenant with Moses, the conditional one which brings specific Laws, with regard to which God judges the following or breach by his people.

The power of the Covenant made researchers define the Jewish people as a *covenantal people*, a *covenanted community*. It also impacted other peoples and specific religious, political, and social developments, up to consider the modern constitutionalism having seeds of this ancient social organization. By establishing the main characteristics of the Jewish Covenant, as the ideal type of *covenantal community*, one can compare it with other communities, especially with the *covenantal type-like societies*, which approach the pure type, but also differentiate from it.

Following the contributions used in this chapter, the main lines which help to construct the ideal type of *covenantal community* are:

Durkheimian sociology attested to the importance of the law, of moral action as a concrete manifestation of belief, underlining the weight of solidarity as *togetherness*, community not only as a religious congregation. Halakha (The Law), as an example of establishing the correct social and individual behavior, creates the cultic manifestation, the religious community as a full society, becoming a fundamental key for a *covenantal community*. Cultic action, as a concrete manifestation of beliefs, is of particular importance for sociology, with its collective religious manifestations forming the identity of a group. For Durkheim, religion means essentially community, society on a larger scale, one coming-together binding the social unit. The Covenant of Jewish people made with God means applied justice, as opposed to anomie (disorganized and weak sociality, lack of norms), precepts within strictly delimitated sacred and profane realms. With regard to the mechanical and organic solidarity of Jewish people, the two types are strongly wound together because of the characteristics of the *covenantal community*, unlike Durkheim's characterization of complex, stratified, and specialized societies where mechanical solidarity decreases in favor of the organic one. The strongly connected types of solidarity are expressed and uniquely manifested by the Jewish people. United by the Law, irrespective of land or territorial spreading, they manifest a communion with the past generations, empowering present ones, in the perspective of a future pledged to them by God.

Weberian sociology guided the *verstehen* of the Jewish Covenant revealing the power of *berith* to create a *people* and its profound social and political structures as a consequence of having God as a partner. Weber analyzed the prophetic movement as one particular event which influenced Western thought, even the rationality of modern times. Deliverance from social and political perils comes only from Yahweh, from obeying Torah, and from returning and re-actualizing the Covenant if forgotten. Re-actualized and affirmed *covenantal community*, and trust in God as a partner in the most difficult social realities are the characteristics that define this people, according to Weber. The lived and continuously actualized Exile does not separate the covenanted people from God but it intensifies the trust in national salvation.

The Torah became the supreme *locus* of Jewish people when confronted with the social changes brought by monarchy and Exile, when the Covenant had to be remembered and re-lived, creating a powerful ethical community, as attested by Causse. The power of Covenant, after the Exile, lived on a social and political dimension, allowed the Jewish people to survive and to return to the ancient values of family, laws, and solidarity.

Without forgetting that God elected a community to give the divine Law by which the people should live, it is important to acknowledge the administrative, and political, implications, the governing of the community, and the relations between its members and other communities. The political implications are underlined by Elazar who views the *Covenant* more as a theo-political reality than a theological event. This is a key point in delimitating between *covenantal community* and *covenantal type-like societies*, especially in secular times, having in mind the risks of the equation of society with religion, as was in the case of Durkheim. It is important to specify elements of the *two ideal types* of community and society by reference to the Covenant as a social, political, and religious reality.

COVENANTAL COMMUNITY

From a sociological and political perspective, the Jewish people are the prototype of the *covenantal community*. This *total social event* (without addressing here the theophanic element) created a people with a unique identity, by the means of specific and elaborated commandments revealed by God. The power of the divine Law was often tested by the distance or approach from the Covenant, creating the history of this people, like in the times of monarchy, Exile. No other people experienced history in these specific parameters. The essence is the Torah, the only one which is perennial, only here the true identity of the people is affirmed and recognized, its immutability presenting challenges in the interactions with human-made laws. An argument for the absolute character of divine Law, based on the covenant, might be, as Novak underlined, the difficulties in arriving at a constitution in the state of Israel. This could be an argument in favor of the Jewish people as a truly covenanted community even in the modern times of secular states. A truly *covenantal community* is a religious community based on divine precepts, from which derive all other necessary human rules and organization, but in the frame of the Jewish Covenant. Thus, we can view the differences between contract and covenant as becoming most revealing with regard to *covenantal type-like societies*, predominantly secular, unlike the *covenantal community*, which is decisively religious.

The social power of *covenantal community* is manifested also in the winding together of mechanical and organic solidarity, as described by Durkheim, and explained by the strength of intragroup social relation, specific rituals, and the extensive elaboration of divine-inspired commandments. The impact of Exile determined a drive toward the preservation of identity and religion as the only paths for resilience. Sustained by the covenant, as a unifying force, the scattered Jewish communities survived in small communities, as minorities, consolidating their identity even more.

A community that covenanted directly to God was radically transformed by this encounter and developed a particular type of sociality, based on a comprehensive and total system of divine laws, a community which is subjected to promissory deliverance or divine punishment, according to the God's laws as they are lived by community or, on the contrary, broken by community. This is a proposed sociological definition of the covenantal community, used for comparison purposes, following the methodological implication of the constructed ideal type. The definition was inspired by the prototype of the Jewish Covenant, as attested above; however, it could be applied and used to research other types of communities in which we could find similar characteristics (the following elements of the proposed ideal type), including them in the covenantal type of social organization. The elements of the ideal type for covenantal community are:

Covenantal parts

- God, supreme leader (vertical orientation, monohierarchic, with only one pole of recognized power)
- Elected community (chosen people, a community of believers, all equal before God, with mechanic solidarity strongly intertwined with the organic one due to the mission promised by God)

God's given laws (perpetual, unconditional, conditional, promissory, immutable)

- Commandments from which derive all the following norms:
- Social rules
- Political organization
- Justice administration
- Economic tradition
- Family regulations

God delivered consequences (through worldly events)

- Punishments
- Salvation, survival—either worldly or messianic salvation

For Jewish people, as the one created by the Covenant, there were times when even this people distanced itself from this ideal type, faced consequences but returned to this foundational event. Even this prototype of the covenantal community had periods when approached more the *covenantal type-like society*, as attested above, exemplified by the prophetic movements or by the monarchy time. The uniqueness stands in the revival of the covenant and its developed power to understand the motives (as Weberian sociology finds) for sufferings and punishments, as the consequences of breaking the laws of the covenant. What was unique is that the people did not astray from God in troubled times, but approached him even more, delivering a very peculiar rationality which influenced the Western world and other religions. And this can be an example of irrationality which is made rational and understood by revealing the motives of social action, as Weber attested.

COVENANTAL TYPE-LIKE SOCIETY

These are more similar to a contractual organization than the above covenantal religious-inspired form. Here the political (as administration of social relations) aspect takes prevalence over the religious dimension. Even though the legitimization of political power by religion was/is largely practiced, this should not equate the two forms of social organization, one has God as supreme leader, the other one human powers. If the covenantal forms are more likely for small groups, and minorities, *the covenantal type-like society* is adequate for larger groups, as was analyzed by Elazar in the case of modern constitutionalism concerning American federal organization. This form is a secularized version of the covenantal type, without the purpose or motive of transcendental reason, but managed for the benefit of people in the immanence. The *covenantal community* is driven by religious and transcendental mission and meanings, was beneficial for political organization and survival, manifesting in the immanence. The *covenantal type-like society* is driven by secular meanings and mission, is also beneficial for social and political organization, is manifesting in the immanence, without a religious motivation. The elements of the ideal type for *covenantal type-like society* are:

Contractual parts

- State powers, administrations (with or without religious legitimization, multiple poles of power)
- Society of citizens, equals before human laws, predominantly with organic social solidarity

Humans made laws for all social dimensions, with evolving and changing character

- Separation of religious norms from the secular ones
- Social rules according to each historical tradition
- Political organization
- Justice administration
- Economic organization
- Family regulations etc.

Human delivered consequences (through worldly institutions)

- Compliance—immanent survival without transcendental motivation
- Rejection/breach of contract (civil and penal laws)

A covenantal type-like society *refers to the administrative, worldly powers in a larger society, based on the compliance of values, laws, and ways of life, with a social identity of people as citizens (specific group identity), without transcendental salvation, but with immanent purposes of identity preservation*. This is the proposed sociological definition for the covenantal type-like society, used for comparison purposes, following the methodological implication of the constructed ideal type. The covenantal characteristic found in this type of social organization refers to the importance of consolidating community relations and identity (common traditions, destiny, values) which sustain the necessary social solidarity. The religious legitimization of human leadership should not make the superposition or unification of divine powers with human powers, even though this type of legitimization was used and proved its fruitfulness for social organization, mobilization, and preservation of identity in history. This is the case especially in secular modern times, when the separated realms, of sacred and profane, are well established and distinctive. The covenantal forms of communion remain highly beneficial for use in the larger society, with great potential for social solidarity and manifested strong identity, and here are the reasons that this type of sociality uses some elements of the covenantal type of community.

Between these two opposed types of social organization, we could have an intermediary level. The small and isolated communities, rural sects, religious groups, or with other profiles, could share many similarities with the covenantal form, but we should remember the characteristics of the proposed *ideal type*, based on the prototype of ancient Jewish people that covenanted with God, as the only truly covenantal civilization. This intermediary level refers to communities with specific characteristics determined by the medium in which they live, by local culture or specific religion, similar more to the organic type as classified by Elazar.

PERSPECTIVES

The covenant represents a very intriguing question from a sociological point of view, as attested by the vast literature in classical sociology concerning the specific characteristics of the Jewish people which influenced the world history and especially its Western part. Considering the covenant as a fundamental pact in organizing communities and society, due to its rules for relations between individuals and with the divine absolute power, this *total social fact* of Jewish Covenant is the prototype of social organization, which impacted all dimensions of society. The political character was prevalent for Elazar, which analyzed *the covenantal type of community* through the political (administrative) aspect of social organization. We proposed the ideal type of a *covenantal type-like society*, making a distinction for the larger societies, with different religions and traditions, in secular times, when the theological and political dimensions are separated regarding conduct and organized state power in different political traditions. Warning against the unification of religious and political dimensions in the Elazar approach, Horowitz also draws attention to their differentiation from a sociological perspective, reminding us that Elazar did not analyze the differences between Judaism and Christianity, ignoring the secularization as well as the Protestant tradition in the case of American federalism.

This chapter attested to the tremendous power of the prototype of the Jewish Covenant, its sociological and political impact, becoming a source of a unique type of community and sociality. As a total social, political, and religious event the ideal type of the covenanted community is introduced by the Jewish people. If we look back to the times of ancient Israel, when covenant and community merged in a particular type of sociality, we arrive at the starting point of a process that formed and influenced world history and Western thought.

NOTES

1. Taylor Paige Winfield, "Rereading Durkheim in Light of Jewish Law: How a Traditional Rabbinic Thought-Model Shapes His Scholarship," *Theory and Society* (2020): 563–595.
2. Ibid.
3. See noological theory with tree stages of understanding spiritual realities: spiritual latency, actualized/de-actualized spiritual manifestations and spiritual teachings. Ilie Badescu, *Noology. System of Noological Sociology. The Spiritual Order of the World* (Manchester: Expert Academic Press, 2021).
4. M. Ben Nahman, *Ramban on Genesis* (New York: Metsudah Publications, 2009 [1246–1286]).
5. Winfield, "Rereading Durkheim in Light of Jewish Law: How a Traditional Rabbinic Thought-Model Shapes His Scholarship," 573; Heinemann, I. "Thereasons for the commandments in Jewish thought from the bible to the renaissance," (Boston: Academic Studies Pres, 2008 [1953), 174.
6. É. Durkheim, *Moral Education: A Study in the Theory and Application of the Sociology of Education* (New York: Free Press of Glencoe, 1961 [1925]).
7. Ibid., 573.

8. Id.
9. Ibid., 577.
10. Id.
11. Id.
12. Deborah Dash Moore, "David Emile Durkheim and the Jewish Response to Modernity," *Modern Judaism - A Journal of Jewish Ideas and Experience* 6, no. 3 (October 1986): 295.
13. Ibid., p. 297, R. Aron as cited by Moore, "David Emile Durkheim and the Jewish Response to Modernity."
14. Ibid., 298.
15. Eugen Schoenfeld and Stjepan G. Mestrovic, "Durkheim's Concept of Justice and Its Relationship with Social Solidarity," *Sociological Analysis* (1989): 111–127, 123.
16. Ibid., 124.
17. Ibid., 124–125.
18. Ibid., 125.
19. Ibid., 125–126.
20. Ilie Bădescu, *Istoria Sociologiei - Marile Sisteme* (Galați: Porto Franco, 1994).
21. Emile Durkheim, *The Division of Labour in Society* (Macmillan, 1984).
22. Ibid., 93.
23. Id.
24. Ibid., 94.
25. Max Weber, *Ancient Judaism* (New York & London: Free Press, 2010).
26. Tony Fahey, "Max Weber's Ancient Judaism," *The American Journal of Sociology* 88, no. 1 (July 1982): 62–87, 63.
27. Weber, *Ancient Judaism*, 75.
28. Ibid., 79.
29. Ibid., 275.
30. Ibid., 281–282.
31. Ibid., 296.
32. Ibid., 314.
33. Ibid., 318.
34. Reinhard Bendix, *Max Weber, Classic Monographs, Vol. Ii: Max Weber, an Intellectual Portrait* (London & New York: Routledge, 1960).
35. Ibid., 246.
36. Ibid., 248.
37. Ibid., 256.
38. Ibid., 258.
39. Ibid., 259.
40. Ibid., 260–261.
41. Ibid., 262.
42. Ibid., 263.
43. Ibid., 264.
44. Antonin Causse, *Du groupe ethnique a la communaute religieuse* (Libr. Felix Alcan, 1983).

45. Ibid., 53.
46. Ibid., 137.
47. Ibid., 195.
48. Ibid., 306.
49. S. T. Kimbrough, "A Non-Weberian Sociological Approach to Israelite Religion," *Journal of Near Eastern Studies* 31, no. 3 (July 1972): 195–202, 200.
50. Ibid., 202.
51. Bernhard W. Anderson, *Contours of Old Testament Theology* (Minneapolis: Fortress Press, 1999), 107.
52. Ibid., 143–144.
53. Ibid., 148.
54. Ibid., 152.
55. Ibid., 196.
56. Ibid., 197.
57. Ibid., 206.
58. Richard J. Bautch, *Glory and Power, Ritual and Relationship. The Sinai Covenant in Postexilic Times* (New York & London: T&T Clark, 2009), 13.
59. Ibid., 45.
60. Id.
61. Ibid., 93.
62. Ibid., 94.
63. Id.
64. Ibid., 102.
65. Ibid., 106.
66. Ibid., 108.
67. Ibid., 117.
68. Ibid., 118.
69. David Novak, *Covenantal Rights, A study in Jewish Political Theory* (New Jersey: Princeton University Press, 2000), 12.
70. Ibid., 30.
71. Ibid., 78.
72. Ibid., 80.
73. Ibid., 82.
74. Ibid., 83.
75. Ibid., 89.
76. Ibid., 93.
77. Ibid., 114.
78. Ibid., 115.
79. Ibid., 116.
80. Ibid., 153.
81. Ibid., 157.
82. Ibid., 216–217.
83. Daniel J. Elazar, *Covenant and Polity in Biblical Israel* (New Brunswick, NJ: Transaction Publishers, 1998), Introduction.
84. Ibid.
85. Ibid.

86. Ibid.
87. Ibid.
88. Ibid.
89. Ibid.
90. Daniel J. Elazar, "Introduction," in *Covenant & Commonwealth: From Christian Separation through the Protestant Reformation, The Covenant Tradition in Politics, vol. 2*, 1996. https://www.jcpa.org/dje/books/ct-vol2-int.htm.
91. "Introduction," in *Covenant and Constitutionalism: The Great Frontier and the Matrix of Federal Democracy, The Covenant Tradition in Politics, vol. 3*, 1998. https://www.jcpa.org/dje/books/ct-vol3-int.htm.
92. Ibid.
93. Daniel J. Elazar, "Preface," in *Covenant and Civil Society: The Constitutional Matrix of Modern Democracy, the Covenant Tradition in Politics, Vol. 4*, 1998b. http://www.jcpa.org/dje/books/ct-vol4-pref.htm.
94. Michael J. DeBoer, "Review," *Journal of Law and Religion* 16, no. 2: 805–811.
95. Ibid., 808.
96. Ibid., 809.
97. Ibid., 810.
98. Irving Louis Horowitz, "Daniel J. Elazar and the Covenant. Tradition in Politics," *Publius: The Journal of Federalism* 31, no. 1 (Winter 2001): 3.
99. Ibid., 4.
100. Ibid., 6.
101. Joseph Livni and Ilie Bădescu, "The Battle of the Covenantal Society against Elitism - An Overlooked Chapter in the History of Social Inequality," *Romanian Journal of Sociological Studies, New Series* no. 1 (2020): 6.
102. Ibid., 11.
103. Ibid., 28.
104. Ibid., 29.
105. Ibid., 30.
106. Ibid., 35.
107. See *Noologia. Cunoașterea Ordinii Spirituale a Lumii: Sistem De Sociologie Noologică* (București: Mica Valahie, 2002); Ilie Bădescu, *Noopolitics, The Theory of Asyncronous Phenomena* (Bucharest: Mica Valahie, 2006); *Noology. System of Noological Sociology, The Spiritual Order of the World* (Manchester: Expert Academic Press, 2021).
108. Ilie Bădescu, *Noologia. Cunoașterea Ordinii Spirituale a Lumii*, 239.
109. Ibid., 246.
110. Ibid., 167.
111. See Bădescu, *Noopolitics, The Theory of Asyncronous Phenomena*; *Noology. System of Noological Sociology, The Spiritual Order of the World.*
112. Anton C. Zijderveld, "Ideal Type," in *Encyclopedia of Social Theory, Vol. I*, 389–390 (Thousand Oaks, CA: Sage Publications, 2005).
113. *On the Methodology of the Social Sciences* (Illinois: The Free Press of Glencoe, 1949), 101.

REFERENCES

Anderson, Bernhard W. *Contours of Old Testament Theology*. Minneapolis: Fortress Press, 1999.

Bădescu, Ilie. *Istoria Sociologiei - Marile Sisteme*. Galați: Porto Franco, 1994.

———. *Noologia. Cunoașterea Ordinii Spirituale a Lumii: Sistem De Sociologie Noologică*. București: Mica Valahie, 2002.

———. *Noology. System of Noological Sociology, the Spiritual Order of the World.* Manchester: Expert Academic Press, 2021.

———. *Noopolitics, the Theory of Asyncronous Phenomena* [in Romanian]. Bucharest: Mica Valahie, 2006.

Bautch, Richard J. *Glory and Power, Ritual and Relationship: The Sinai Covenant in Postexilic Times*. New York, London: T&T Clark, 2009.

Bendix, Reinhard. *Max Weber, Classic Monographs, Vol. II: Max Weber, an Intellectual Portrait*. London and New York: Routledge, 1960.

Causse, Antonin. *Du Groupe Ethnique a La Communaute Religieuse. Le Probleme Sociologique De La Religion D'israel*. Paris: Felix Alcan, 1937.

DeBoer, Michael J. "Review." *Journal of Law and Religion*, Vol. 16, No. 2 (2001), pp. 805–11.

Durkheim, Emile. *The Division of Labour in Society*. New York, London, Toronto, New Delhi: Macmillan, 1984.

Elazar, Daniel J. "Introduction." In *Covenant and Constitutionalism: The Great Frontier and the Matrix of Federal Democracy, the Covenant Tradition in Politics*, Vol. 3. https://www.jcpa.org/dje/books/ct-vol3-int.htm, 1998.

———. "Introduction." In *Covenant & Commonwealth: From Christian Separation Through the Protestant Reformation, the Covenant Tradition in Politics*, Vol. 2. https://www.jcpa.org/dje/books/ct-vol2-int.htm, 1996.

———. "Introduction." In *Covenant & Polity in Biblical Israel: Biblical Foundations & Jewish Expressions*, Vol. I. https://www.jcpa.org/dje/books/ct-vol1-int.htm, 1995.

———. "Preface." In *Covenant and Civil Society: The Constitutional Matrix of Modern Democracy, the Covenant Tradition in Politics*, Vol. 4. http://www.jcpa.org/dje/books/ct-vol4-pref.htm, 1998.

Fahey, Tony. "Max Weber's Ancient Judaism." *The American Journal of Sociology*, Vol. 88, No. 1 (July 1982), pp. 62–87.

Heinemann, I. *The reasons for the commandments in Jewish thought: from the Bible to the Renaissance*. Boston: Academic Studies Press, 2008.

Horowitz, Irving Louis. "Daniel J. Elazar and the Covenant: Tradition in Politics." *Publius: The Journal of Federalism*, Vol. 31, No. 1 (Winter 2001), pp. 1–7.

Kimbrough, S. T. "A Non-Weberian Sociological Approach to Israelite Religion." *Journal of Near Eastern Studies*, Vol. 31, No. 3 (July 1972), pp. 195–202.

Livni, Joseph, and Ilie Bădescu. "The Battle of the Covenantal Society Against Elitism - An Overlooked Chapter in the History of Social Inequality." *Romanian Journal of Sociological Studies, New Series,* No. 1 (2020), pp. 3–36.

Moore, Deborah Dash. "David Emile Durkheim and the Jewish Response to Modernity." *Modern Judaism - A Journal of Jewish Ideas and Experience*, Vol. 6, No. 3 (October 1986), pp. 287–300.

Novak, David. *Covenantal Rights, a Study in Jewish Political Theory*. New Jersey: Princeton University Press, 2000.

Schoenfeld, Eugen, and Stjepan G. Mestrovic. "Durkheim's Concept of Justice and Its Relationship With Social Solidarity." *Sociological Analysis*, Vol. 50 (1989): 111–27.

Weber, Max. *Ancient Judaism*. New York & London: Free Press, 2010.

———. *Ancient Judaism*. New York: The Free Press, 1967.

———. *On the Methodology of the Social Sciences*. Illinois: The Free Press of Glencoe, 1949.

———. *The Protestant Ethic and the Spirit of Capitalism*. Mineola, NY: Dover Publications, 2012.Winfield, Taylor Paige. "Rereading Durkheim in Light of Jewish Law: How a Traditional Rabbinic Thought-Model Shapes His Scholarship." *Theory and Society*, Vol. 49 (2020), pp. 563–95.

Zijderveld, Anton C. "Ideal Type." In *Encyclopedia of Social Theory*, Vol. I, 389–90. Thousand Oaks, CA: Sage Publications, 2005.

Chapter 6

Romanian Traditional Society

Social Control and Social Order

Adela Şerban

BRIEF THEORETICAL PERSPECTIVE ON TRADITIONAL SOCIETY

What we call *traditional society* refers to a social system[1] generalized before the modern era, characterized by a regime of collective life organized exclusively by community institutional resorts.[2] Within its framework, the social realm was organized in autonomous socio-territorial villages, similarly configured, each of them fully including all the social institutions needed for the community existence. The traditional society system is by its nature polycentric. Each village is a complete social world in small, designed to meet all the needs of its members within their innate constitutive nature, incorporating the entire diversity of structures, institutions, and types of social groups that can be developed in natural living conditions.

Traditional villages coexist systemically, maintaining between them a fabric of orderly connections, of interchanges, a cultural and material wiring which enables to consolidate a territorial unitary social and cultural identity. The element that holds the whole ensemble together, both at intra- and inter-village level, is a cultural semantic-ritual system, representing a corpus of cultural codes, deep-seated, preserved, and transmitted in the form of an unitary interconnected chain of experiences and ritualized manifestations, known as the "system of traditional customs."[3] Since the socio-cultural semantics is transmitted through language, inter-village systems are built within linguistic units. They form territorial social structures, with a united system of social reaction and response, capable of sustainably maintaining a natural ecosystem of communities. These identity and linguistic networks of traditional communities constitute, in their essence, the reality we are indicating by the concept *ethnicity*.

Emerging from an inherent social morphology,[4] the traditional society is not simply a past social system, but also the substance from which the contemporary social structures are built. Deepening the knowledge on its normative and institutional system provides us important clues of understanding about the functioning of our own contemporary societies and about a set of essential social realities, which, despite their epistemological importance for the theoretical corpus of sociology, remain yet confusedly conceptualized (*community*, *identity*, *ethnicity* are just a few of them).

The archaic traditional village represents the closest known social structure to the community archetype. It is an interpersonal environment with an absolutely special profile: its human composition is stable, there are no significant migratory fluctuations, and the renewal of generations is done almost exclusively through biological continuity. Inside it, the weight of non-existing social ties between members is zero, and all the strong social ties developed by the members are necessarily localized inside. All members know each other and are all connected to each other through personal social networks (direct connections between people or direct connections established by their close or trusted people). The spheres of social connections of community members converge and intersect, allowing a concentration of psychic life among the same people. All people are interconnected through an enormous network of interpersonal channels, developed for various aspects and necessities of life. The traditional village is practically the densest and most complex human psychic concentration that can be generated by putting people together.[5]

The researchers who carried out extensive and intensive studies on modern communities found that the decay of the community environment in modernity is not only an urban phenomenon, but also a rural one, the contemporary villages facing strong degradation of their institutional and normative background. The community as a reality does not sustain itself only through the small size of the village and through the quasi-stable human base, but it depends on a collective regime of social life, culturally and institutionally capable of preserving the social order and structure.

The polycentric format of the traditional society was maintained through a shared social system, which imposed the same rules, restrictions, and prohibitions on a large group of villages regarding territory, family property, food, housing, clothing, sexuality, parenthood, work, kinship, movement of people and groups inside and outside the village, their displacement from one village to another, the conduct of foreigners and their behavior toward them, the special regime of some institutional groups, and so on, allowing a synchronized organization of people within a territory with the preservation of societal conditions necessary for the social system to work.

Unlike modern social system (which we experience today), traditional social systems do not exert coercion through the action or pressure of visible organized institutional groups and are not subject of changes imposed by the will of different influent social groups, but instead the social order is generated, controlled, and regulated through internal cultural-institutional processes, without the deliberate involvement of any particular group. This is a defining characteristic. Beyond a certain flexibility of their display, traditional social systems do not differ substantially from each other, due to the fact they are based on a similar social and cultural conditions and conditionalities.

Along with the increase of the state intervention capacity and the imbalance of territorial power between the natural (traditional) social system of these connected free villages and the political-military authority (always external to the polycentric system of communities), the traditional social system underwent a gradually process of alterations, with already a strong degradation in the period in which the first intensive researches began.

Because the same reality gives a large variety of "damaged" types, and we, as researchers and observers, have direct access only to the latter, the methodological and theoretical challenge is to reconstruct the initial design of the traditional social system via a complex process of extracting the ideal-type from the clues hidden in historical documents and from exploring the semantic of traditional socio-cultural system as it is reflected in the folkloric oral cultures documents. The model presented in this chapter is based on the results of a research conducted by the author for twelve years on social morphology in Romanian traditional society. Romania had started the transition to the modernity rather late; in the first decades of the twentieth century more than three quarters of Romanian population lived in a still very archaic form of rural villages and the semantic of the oral socio-cultural systems was still in use. The amount of the information collected by ethnologists, folklorists, and sociologists in the second part of the nineteenth century and the first second of the twentieth century helped us to give a proper insight on a now extinct social system, originated in archaic times.

THE SOCIAL SYSTEM IN ROMANIAN TRADITIONAL SOCIETY: AN OVERVIEW

The first essential principle of the Romanian traditional social system is the total decentralization of power. The traditional regime of collective life was socially leveling, not allowing individuals or social groups to achieve and preserve social power, nor the emergence of social polarities based on major differences in capabilities, prestige, or resources. Traditional Romanian communities have no chiefs or central authority. (Consequently, neither do the villages in a territory.) Each member of the community had held authority in one/some particular aspect(s) related to the life of the group, which, in most cases, changed in time, depending on their life experiences. Women and men, of all age groups, whatever their role in the community, could come to hold equivalent positions of influence and moral authority in different social and ritual contexts. Between institutions or their active groups there are no hierarchies of power and authority in relation to the community, but they are redefined depending on the context. The Romanian traditional community was organized in such a way that none of the internal groups could accumulate enough power, authority, or prestige to impose their own vision of social organization or to intervene in the existing social structure.

An important feature of the Romanian traditional system was its democratic character. In traditional villages the decisions on issues concerning the whole community[6] were made by general consensus, in accordance with the confirmed values of the community. The design of the social structure of the archaic village is optimized to arrive at functioning and effective democratic mechanisms. Democracy calls for partners with common values and interests, equal in authority and equally exposed to the problems that affect the group and it needs a collective response or a collective solution.[7] People can hardly be like that, but the families from traditional villages were, that's why the partners summoned to take collective decisions in the village were not the individuals separately (as we understand democracy today), but the families. In the Romanian archaic village the status of all families was equal. Each family managed its household autonomously, in accordance with the rules of social conduct accepted in common; each exercised the same responsibility and was directly facing the effects of the problems affecting the community.

The Romanian social traditional system was meritocratic, a prestigious position being a direct result of collective confirmation of competences. In a small community, with small institutional groups, everyone's performance and abilities were visible, and everyone could directly see them. In the case of ritual providers, the whole village was literate in the ritual code in order to be able to correctly evaluate the performance. And in the case of specialized skills, the abusive granting of institutional prerogatives to incompetent individuals would have implied effects immediately felt by everyone. If the medicine man, the midwife, the soldier, the member of the elders' council, among others, did not master their jobs, the village was endangered. Since every institutional competence is vital for the functioning of the community, in the condition of a general leveling of power, meritocracy is a survival necessity recognized through consensus by everyone. At the same time, since there are no hierarchies of power between families and groups, their capacity to sabotage the meritocratic selection process is practically impossible.

The second fundamental principle of the Romanian social system was self-sufficiency, subsistence through one's own powers, without external dependence. All free villages were socially and economically autonomous. The people of the Romanian traditional communities have all the necessary data and techniques to be able to ensure all their fundamental needs within their village. Foreign exchanges are made only to vary the range of food products and consumer goods, not to cover vital needs.

In Romanian traditional villages ownership of the land was collective, and the property as we understand it today did not existed. The land was jointly owned undivided by the whole community and exploited by agreement between the families.[8] This social system survived in different parts of Romania until the first decades of the twentieth century, especially in the territories where in the past the so-called *peasant republics* were recorded.[9] The land loss was equal for the traditional communities with the losing of internal autonomy of the village; fact confirmed by the social condition established in the vassal villages. The people's relationship with the land occupies a central place in the traditional community axiological system, the land being understood as an ally, as a supporting element, not as a good. The land sustains people's lives and it mediates the connection with the past, with the ancestry—this was the reason why it was valued and had an inalienable character. Whether we are talking about the agricultural land of the village or the infield of the households, the property is only understood as the right of use and inheritance, not as a tradable good, the sale and purchase of houses and land between villagers and foreigners did not exist. Moreover, the house and the yard were the subject of a legacy with very deep implications. The cemetery as a specially delimitated place is a late reality in the Romanian social space, in the traditional villages the ancestors being buried in the house yard, in a special place with a sacred character, often indicated in oral folkloric texts as the "flower garden." Giving up the house would be equivalent to abandoning the ancestors and committing a sacrilege. In modern times, in the south part of the country, after the law prohibited burials elsewhere than in specially arranged places, the locals established the practice of attaching mortuary plaques on the houses, through which the observers were informed about who lived and died in that house, symbolically and ritually marking the place. Even if in the last decades the practice is starting to fade away, the mortuary plaques can still be seen today attached on the exterior walls of the old houses.

The Romanian traditional social systems drastically discourage migration from one place to another, both in groups and individual. Moving from the village was allowed only through marriage, because in this case there is a "guarantor" of the "human quality" of the newcomer.[10] Foreign refugees had a discouraging status—the process of erasing the stigma of being a foreigner was long and arduous, spanning several generations, during which they were excluded from collective decisions and from relationships of trust and prestige. The customary penal system used by the Romanian traditional communities included two major punishments: death or exclusion; this was why on a newcomer always hover the suspicion that another community found him inadequate to the commonly accepted code of conduct, so he was not a "good person," worthy of being integrated in their community. The Romanian traditional community can be described as a social bastion, nothing that comes from the outside (physical or informational) had to be assimilated before it had been checked or verified for a long time, but only until it passed the test of the life together.

The Romanian archaic villages were part of the natural ecosystem, the traditional social system sustaining through a complex web of customs and rituals the harmony between man and nature, inducing and globally maintaining this balanced behavior. Through that aspect, we could say, without the risk of mistake, that the Romanian traditional village was a model of ecologically friendly community. The system of rituals and celebrations was organized to be respectful of the life cycle and circulation of animals. Killing animals without reason and unjustified cruelty toward them were elements drastically sanctioned by the community through its axiological system. The low population density and the limitation of the production volume to the needs of the families from small communities made it impossible to exhaust the local resources provided by nature. Natural products were used throughout the domestic production system (pottery, weaving, tools), in the kitchen and in the pharmacopoeia. The system of social values was built around the consideration of the forest and the rivers as essential elements for survival, cultivating their cultural assimilation as supporting entities, invested with the role of personal friends of the community and people.

In the corpus of the cultural content of the Romanian orality there is a folkloric formula that essentially mirrors traditional community life and the socio-psychological condition of its members, in the form of defining the cruelest fate possible for a human being in that type of society: "To die without a tallow candle and without someone from your village."[11] The non-community state is given by the absence of the world of belonging and of the ritual that supports it and makes it possible, ritual systems being the creative vectors of local identity.

In Romanian traditional social system, ordering schemes are always accompanied by forms of ritual manifestation. Ritual allows incomparably more than the simple transfer of cultural meanings, because it makes it possible to imprint human life with them, to impregnate the mind and the soul with the imprint of a complex vibration (of a "rhythm" of collective life) associated with a cultural content. The repetition of that content produces the deepening of a meaning but also of an experience, inducing a connection between the act and its meaning.

THE FAMILY SYSTEM

Among all the institutions of Romanian traditional society, the family occupies a special place in the morphology and functional composition of the traditional community. Its internal structure is inextricably linked to the family, the traditional village being in its essence a family fraternity, built from a complex fabric of kinship relationships. The common approach to family realities found in today's branch sociologies is to operate with them as if they were independent units, independent of the community referential to which they belong. The family, however, unlike the community, is not a reality with an autonomous existence, but it exists and subsists only in a network of families functioning interlinked and assisted by a group of cultural-educational institutions, which complete and fulfill each family functions. The truly new phenomenon that modernity brings in terms of family life consists neither of the reduced average number of children, nor of the increase of the age of marriage, nor of the emphasis on the couple or any other phenomena noted by the specialists, but of the fact that, for the first time in the historical evolution of humanity, on a large scale, families are "detached," functioning in partial and anemic community networks—all the phenomena mentioned above actually representing effects of this fundamental change of status and state that the modernity processes brought with them.

The community is a dense inter-personal environment characterized by a preponderance of medium-close ties; through these ties the community exercises its control over its component groups. Close ties are strongly affective; they mobilize psychological loads that, in the case of conflicts of interest between the community members (frequent in the everyday life), can fuel socially toxic situations. In contrast to these, the medium-close ties are rational, allowing a lucid management of the challenges and crises that affect the daily life of the small groups. In the absence of this community leverage of control, strong family ties would become predominant and uncontrollable. Almost all the anarchic phenomena of urban modernity (corruption, influence peddling, excessive accumulation of money and goods, overturning of meritocratic selections, among others) have their roots in the "individualization" of the family and in the expansion of family interest to the disadvantage of a collective balance of interest.

In the traditional society, the essential function of the family is to ensure a complete transfer of the collective culture between generations, without damage or alteration. The family can be considered a self-regenerating organ of the village, the internal adjustment of the family to the entire traditional institutional system; this system actually is the source of the high performance of traditional community sustainably perpetuating a defined socio-cultural design. In Romanian traditional society, the family education process is focused on the transfer of values and cultural languages, the man not being considered "complete" until this process of cultural assimilation had finished. Normally, the processes of physical and psycho-cultural maturity are reached at once. In Romanian popular culture, the expression "with a black beard and with all the mind" designates a man who has gone through both development processes: bio-physiological and psycho-cultural. If the process of cultural transfer is partially blocked or if something does not work well and the socio-cultural semantics is not internalized, the man is seen by the traditional community as not being developed correctly and spiritual malformations are expected to appear. The result is, in this case, a man with psycho-cultural disabilities, unable to function properly in his community. In the Romanian cultural system, that person is designated by the word *unfinished* (*neisprăvit*), a word with a strong pejorative meaning indicating the level of collective rejection on this social outcome. Another process associated with the dys-functional cultural transfer, different from the first but related, consists in the subsequent deletion of parts of the cultural code or the mutilation of the schemes of this code by personal option. For Romanian traditional society the man resulting from this process is essentially socio-cultural damaged, incompatible with the social order of the community system, and consequently banished, sent to live "in his law" (which is no longer shared with the rest of the people). The traditional community acted prophylactically in relation to the risk of "cultural defects." If the "unfinished" doesn't represent a threat to the community order (if his cultural disabilities did not interfere with his community functioning, case in which he would be expelled from the village) he was tolerated. However, he was isolated and turned into "teaching material," being a negative example at hand. None of the two types of psycho-cultural disabilities (evaluated by the community as dangerous for internal order or not) were allowed to transfer their "deficiency" through paternity or influence.

The modern family preserves both the function, the reflex and the pattern of operation, what it has lost is the systemic cultural ensemble held in common with a social sphere of interaction.

One of the main sources of the inner weakening of the family (especially the vulnerability of the marital bond and the inability to exercise family authority in the relations between parents and children) is the de-ritualization of social life (and together with it that of family life) and the breaking of the rhythms of living together. Functioning in a strongly ritualistic environment, as the traditional village society was, had induced a balanced and unitary rhythm in the life routine, which exercised repeated actions of harmonizing the members of the same community and the members of the same family.

EDUCATIONAL SYSTEM IN THE TRADITIONAL SOCIETY

The Romanian traditional society educational system covers a diverse and complex set of training packages, institutions, and educational schemes extended in modernity largely by means of what we call today *informal education*, or, in a more accurate formulation, the *non-formalized education*, an educational system without an organizational display. Although this system is little known and researched today, an important part of the traditional institutions of education, training, and control have strongly influenced known modern institutions, through a transfer of practices, relational models, and educational techniques.

As Mihai Pop pointed out in his essay dedicated to the educational system in oral cultures, in traditional environments "education was and is still done, for the most part, by habit, not by training, [. . .] the informational data necessary for the formation of the personality were not communicated from the outside to be learned, but accumulated gradually according to the need to face each step of the social hierarchy, each new situation."[12] Traditional cultural languages, he points out, "were not learned, but acquired like the mother tongue, without being explained, which also explains the similarities between folklore and language noted by P. Bogatârev and R. Jakobson."[13] The specificity of traditional education is the gradual master of social codes (linguistic, behavioral, ritual, gestural,among others) through inter-personal transfer of skills, experience, knowledge, and meanings, in accordance with the person's age and the social functions it is expected to exercise, the results of this acquisition being especially evident in contexts or in situations of *passing*, when the person is subject of the exam of the quality and completeness of the status he achieved. "In oral environments"—explained M. Pop—"each age category, each step of the social hierarchy required the acquisition of different languages, a certain standard of knowledge. A certain personality model corresponded to each of them. The transition from one category to another was marked, if not by an 'initiation rite,' in any case by a ceremonial act, by a custom. The acquisition of the standard was strictly necessary to be able to cross the threshold from one category to another. Education was therefore done according to this. The functional character of education ensured everyone the opportunity to fully use their own language to communicate with others, to establish contacts on different levels, it offered them sufficient capacity of argumentation to deal with different situations that happened within the community he lived in. Just as the one who did not know the traditions of the place could not integrate and was considered a stranger, the one who did not reach the standards required by the community could not move from one category to another, because he would not be able to communicate fully with the members of the category to which he was to pass."[14]

In the traditional society, the entire complex system of relations established within the family and the community participated directly and actively in the formation of each young person in accordance with his place and social role, so that, at the end of the transition to adulthood, each person came to fully master the fundamental information and codes for survival in the social and natural context of which it was a part. The articulation of this system has seriously deteriorated with the de-structuring of community system and with the contemporary social transformations that have anarchized the family environment by making it autonomous in relation to a given community. In certain modern institutions, however, which were born through similarity with counterpart traditional institutions, the structural principles of the traditional educational system experienced greater inertia, surviving until now, although often in partial or altered forms. This is the case, for example, of the craftsman apprenticeship, liberal professions, and higher academic institutions, but also to an extended set of applied professions which require qualifications certified by skill, exercise, and practice. Some institutions were taken over and transferred almost intact, such as the case of the institution of the *troop child*, a traditional institution par excellence.

The traditional apprenticeship model involves periods of training resorting to a hierarchical personal relationship with a master, who acts not only (and not even primarily) as a teacher for transferring the necessary information to practice the profession or to acquire a higher level of training, but especially as a facilitator of the person's integration into the social environment associated with the professional role for the full internalization of the new social status. The two fundamental principles that tacitly and implicitly regulated the traditional institution of apprenticeship were the sovereignty of the master (or trainer) authority and the public test, the collective confirmation of the performance and training of the apprentice in accordance with the requirements of the beneficiary community. If the first principle, that of the sovereignty of the training authority, has been partially preserved in most forms of professional apprenticeship in contemporary society, even in the formalized systems, the resort of traditional testing, which imposed the professional qualities of the person in the community's consciousness, was largely abandoned and replaced with mechanistic-standardized verification and confirmation forms. Today, the person first acquires the status and only later confirms himself within a given community. The situation is not only specific to professional environments, but also to current social situations (age, marital, among others). This state of affairs is not the consequence of a distinct social logic of the modern system, but rather of an impossibility to compensate in the context of a massive, impersonal social environment, the role and complex function exercised by the social control system specific to traditional communities.

The efficiency of collective social control resides in the polysemantic character of traditional education, which ensures not only the transmission of separate social and cultural codes, but also a correlation of all these languages, so that any "defect" or any training deviation became immediately perceptible as a stridency of each member of the community and to the community as a whole. The ultra-specialization and detachment of the person from the community disharmonizes, lags, and, sometimes, even damages the process of correlated acquisition of social languages; as a consequence, the effectiveness of training and education mechanisms in accordance with the complex needs of a community can only be inevitably lower.

THE SOCIAL CONTROL IN ROMANIAN TRADITIONAL SOCIETY

A characteristic of the traditional Romanian social system is the strong emphasis on the decentralization of power, authority, and capacity of social influence. Within the archaic Romanian village, the sources of generating community solidarity were systemic, and the internal unity was maintained and fueled through a quasi-unanimous attending to various celebrations and ritual moments. The social world in the traditional society was already preconfigured, with carefully ordered structuring and social behavior patterns, where the association of individuals and families took place in given institutional frameworks, with very little space for new associative forms to could emerge. The associative capital from Romanian traditional communities didn't generate an active involvement in forms of economic, civic, or political enterprises, but usually remained almost exclusively a systemic defensive associative capital.

The traditional normative and institutional system equipped the community with a strong and unitary capacity to react to what we could call the systemic "offense." The priority toward which the community response is channeled (at group, family, and individual level) is not the need felt individually or as a member of certain social groups, but the impact brought to the ordering system as a whole. This trait generates deep consequences and can be traced not only in population's involuntary reaction but also in its social imagology and in the conceptualization of collective problems.

A particularity of the traditional Romanian social system, which derives from the structuring of its internal morphology, is the differentiation of the patterns of associative involvement according to gender. If the male social potential of involvement was dissipated in a high number of groups and relatively small forms of association, the female community constitutes a block. The functional distribution is also inhomogeneous in the traditional Romanian system: the management of the cultural and spiritual life of the community is an almost exclusively a female territory, while the corpus of household and defense activities is distributed almost equally between men and women (of course, with a precise specialization and a clear division of competences).

If the military defense reaction of the community required a general mobilization only at certain moments, the monitoring and psycho-mental control against semantically foreign cultural schemes demanded a permanent mobilization, the community control in this aspect being ensured by a large female network capable of triggering collective mobilizations of the entire community through prophylactic and punitive mechanisms. Intra-community control is a complex social mechanism involving specialized bodies for identifying *weak cultural-behavioral signals*. The social system allows them to stimulate the injection of aggressive psychic concentrations to stimulate an extraordinary mobilization against the targeted person using the pressure exerted on his groups of strong ties to extirpate the non-conforming scheme. The control mechanisms in Romanian traditional society constitute an informal institutional package maintained in the modern context through transfer and adaptation, which continues to largely capture the Romanian associative energies.

From the traditional social control system, the modern contemporary counterpart took mainly the external component, the public order; we refer here not only to the operational units of the army or police, whose organization, composition, and structure retain significant similarities with the defense units from the traditional natural system, but also to the community institution of the council of elders, which served as a basis of inspiration for the institution of state justice. The council's function was to resolve internal imbalances and dysfunctions by impartially judging conflicts between the parties and resolving them justly. Their prerogatives were quasi-similar to those performed today by judicial bodies: mediation (defuse a conflict between individuals or families), restitution (when there is damage to the patrimonial rights of individuals or families), or punitive (in the case of an offense against the community order, that is, a serious breach of the general code of conducts or value system).

The traditional community, in addition to external social control, had also a cultural and psycho-social control system, implemented by a large female social network. The system has survived partially by inertia until present time through informal levers mainly in rural areas and in urban slums (see figure 6.1). The institution, unnamed by the ethnographers or by the ethnologists who identified it, represents a network of "signalers" or "hunters" or social behavior, structured on several levels, whose role is to monitor the community to

Figure 6.1 In Rural Areas Culture and Education Has Been Traditionally Managed by Female Networks. *Source*: Courtesy of Dafna Leonard.

identify signs that betray behavioral deviations, that is, functional faults in the system. The operating mode follows an established pattern: Once a deviant element is identified in a person, it is first flagged. The control group (usually made up of elderly women) informs the respective community member that the element has been seen and must be removed from the system, giving them a grace period (not exactly defined) to self-recover. As a rule, communication takes place first gesturally, then verbally indirectly (by insinuation) and finally explicitly. During this period, the person is constantly monitored. If the problem is not solved, but extends over time, it inevitably deepens, because the structure of the human psyche is consonant and the deviant element generates more offenses. The control group then activates a social mechanism similar with "phagocytosis" upon the foreign cultural scheme. Through the internal communication system, the network informs the entire community about the problem, the news circulating by mouth to mouth and producing aggressive mental concentrations within the community. These, in a first phase, only inflame the person's social strong ties, causing psychological suffering and thus stimulating an extraordinary mobilization of the person and his intimate group to extirpate the non-compliant behavioral scheme. If the effect does not occur, and the man proves that he is "contaminated" definitively, the person is subject to the reproach of the whole community, publicly punished by the elder council, and deprived of the community membership status. Practically, the community acts as a giant social "macrophage" that devours the psychic being of the "outcast," the Romanian expression "to enter in the mouth of the village" precisely and explicitly describes the nature of the process. The targeted person can never, under any circumstances, return to the status from which he was expelled.

The awareness of this scary path and the desire to avoid it triggers in each person a mechanism of self-monitoring and psychic self-devouring of non-compliant elements. If this personal control mechanism fails, the closest social circle takes over and exercises the function. First the intimate group, the narrow circle of the very close people. Then, if it also fails, successively more distant social spheres intervene, until, in the last instance, the community itself steps in. And if the community also fails to destroy the foreign cultural and behavioral element, the man is thrown out of the village, which in traditional societal conditions was equivalent to death, because no other village received unknown fugitives and the interstitial spaces between villages were places where a single man could not survive. But rarely the thing got here, because the whole process left deep wounds in the community from which the convicted was expelled, in the overwhelming majority of cases the intimate social group acted effectively on the person and repaired the "defect" before the process became irreversible. As things returns to normal, the "macro-phagocytic" process of the community is gradually inhibited, returning to the initial monitoring phase.

In modern societies, with weak community structures, this process is reproduced partially and truncated, limited to the family and neighborhood network, the failure of the maximum pressure phase resulting in family ruptures by removing the person from his circle of belonging. But we find in contemporaneity the reflex mobilized as a public resource, often translated into the public space to give weight to media lynching campaigns.

If the systemic social control intervention of the traditional community could not be reproduced contemporaneously in an equivalent system, some of the specific institutions have their modern counterparts, with interesting development and evolution. Mainly two of these, personified and exemplified in two Romanian traditional customs: *Shouting across the village* and *Fool's days*, show a strong functional similarity with modern forms, their analysis offering an explanation for the contemporary popularity of the latter. "Shouting across the village" can be considered the community ancestor of modern investigative or scandalous media, of public disclosures that can harm a person's reputation. Of course, there are also numerous differences between the two, derived from the social context of use and from the role of the institution in relation to the referential system to which it belongs, but indisputably, the first influenced and shaped the later institution of the press. In this context, the punishable defects of the community members were made public by a ceremonial crowd that shouted them out. It is no coincidence that the ritual moment of this "divulging" of the secrets was Maundy Thursday in Easter

Lent, the day of the slanderous judgment of Jesus Christ, the ritual having both the function of deepening the understanding of the reality of betrayal, as well as the function of compensation, the unworthy earthlings enduring rightfully the humiliation of their mistakes and deeds. In contrast to contemporary media public exposures, the ritual manifestation was fully controlled, so as not to degenerate into abuse or slander. Also, a certain dosage of this resort of social control, concentrated in a single annual moment, must be noted.[15]

Another source of social control in traditional society was the persuasion and combating of inappropriate social behavior through specific institutions active only in ritual moments. One of the manifestation of these unnamed institutions is the ancient *Days of Fools*, which reveals a social mechanism of control through collective education regarding the danger of altering the cultural code and identity of the community. The custom involves staging a show that can last up to a week and that satirically brings to the community the experience of encountering a dissolving otherness. Beyond the many variants of this custom, their common element consists in a set of public manifestations performed by a ritual group, which does not respect the social and cultural codes of the community, with the function of defusing through humor and satire the fear of dissimilar people, but also the installation of a reflex of symbolic rejection of the temptation for cultural borrow. Ritual performers, always men, usually wear feminine clothes, ragged and inappropriately fitting (to suggest the overthrow of order and normality), disturb the collective activities of the village, and make "nerds, fools and jokes, [. . .]sing some songs or shouts of humorous content, through which they persecute and fighting against such things foreign to the community, or things that do not correspond to the nature of the Romanian people, but those who are in contact with other nations want to introduce them into the village, either in the apparel, or in the house, or in the what other respect would it be."[16] Nevertheless, this way of social control by ridiculing the cultural "adversary" has a high degree of persistence and topicality in contemporary Romanian society. At the same time, this educational and preventive resort influenced the institution of educational entertainment, pamphlets, and satire, contributing to its wide acceptance and popularity among the Romanian public of today.

SHORT INSIGHT INTO THE INTERACTIONS BETWEEN THE STATE AND THE TRADITIONAL SOCIETY

The traditional imagological corpus evokes a deep state of socio-anthropological cleavage between the traditional society based on a peasant civilization and the macro-organizational world (of the aristocracy, the civil service and the professional guilds developed by their needs), indicating an insurmountable incompatibility between the two social ordering systems. The contemporary social reality preserves this state of affairs, the Romanian society being marked by this cultural cleavage, somewhat unexpected and unusually historically resistant. To understand the social processes behind it (and its often unintended implications) one needs a simultaneous learning of the contemporary phenomenon and its underlying archaic roots.

The vast majority of royal chancellery documents from the centuries in which took place the statehood consolidation in Romania attests a fundamentally violent and abusive approach of the state political-military apparatus toward local communities. A large majority of the consulted documents evoke the situation of the "gifting" of the right to rule over villages enslaved by force to those close to the reign, indicating a form of authority imposed by rapture and not by an organic growth due to the enlivening of some local institutions. The practice continued in later centuries, being a common fact that the Phanariot lords gave villages as a "gift" to their clienteles, the last explicit cases of this kind was recorded in the very first half of the nineteenth century by Ion Diaconu in his work dedicated to Vrancea County, where during the reign of Constantin Ipsilanti in Moldova, in 1801, four villages were offered to the boyar Iordache Roset Rosnovanu with the "right of ownership." The communities in question, along with ten others from their vicinity, had reacted, seeking justice in court. Only sixteen years later, during the Phanariot ruler Scarlat Callimachi, the villages won their case, after a costly judgment borne financially in common.[17]

The princely and imperial documents (in the case of Transylvania) from the seventeenth—eighteenth centuries record numerous disputes and requests for intervention in case of rebellions, attesting the status of the villages as tradable goods or objects of inheritance like any property, without any differentiation from material properties. Quite a lot has been written about the status of Gypsy slaves in these centuries in Romanian territories, which are recorded in documents together with household goods and animals. The similar status had also the "Rumanian" villages, which were listed alongside them too, as property.

Indisputably, the practice of selling some communities in their entirety retains a similarity with slavery practices and is a form of slavery, even if it is carried out at a completely different level of social intervention. This form of slavery, insufficiently addressed in specialized literature, includes a corpus of attitudes and institutional practices that shaped the modern decision makers' patterns in relation with the population in the Romanian contemporaneity. Perhaps the most significant of these is the reflex of not considering the community a partner, but an arena for the exercise of discretionary power, to disregard and undermine the community's right to be an active participant in the decision-making process, therefore, implicitly, by blocking the civil public control.

CONCLUSIVE REMARKS

Traditional societies in general, and Romanian traditional society in particular, are underlying social structures and institutional systems with parallel functioning from the official state ones, which even if sometimes the latter extracts its organizing pattern and operating principles from the first, they remain distinct and, from certain points of view, even competing. The traditional social system is a complex wiring of cultural schemes that enable a social community regime of life with several defining characteristics: poly-centricity, complete decentralization of power within the communities and between them, collective life regulated exclusively through collectively assimilated cultural norms, social intervention using spread networks of people spontaneously coordinated one with another through cultural inputs.

The traditional social system collectively imposes itself with a power of a covenant. Its internalizing is transforming people, giving them a strong sense of identity, a complete and deep mark of recognition. Its continuity and preserving stems from communities' and peoples' faith in its matching with the structure of human nature and with the collective and individual needs of communities. It exists as an internal reality, as long as people are connected through it. By replacing the old social world with a new one, the traditional social system does not fade away completely, but continues to make its voice heard in the ways its people react and assimilate the changes, bringing its "face" into the structures and actions of the new world and creating a new version of any alternative social order.

NOTES

1. By *social system* we understand a collective life regime established and maintained on a large group of people through a system of indirect and diffuse pressures that are exerted in a sustainable, stable and organized manner through accepted norms and institutions.

2. The reader will make the distinction between the notion of *traditional society* as a socio-political system build on state traditions and integrating in its public symbolism axiological and customary repertoire inspired by the community social system, and the community social systems itself. This chapter uses the notion as it was operationalised by Robert Redfield, *Peasant Society and Culture: An Anthropological Approach to Civilization* (Chicago: Chicago University Press, 1956). There is a huge literature on the matter, for the readers interested in approaching the distinctions.

3. Among the first sociologists who pointed out the importance of ritual in the configuration of traditional societies was E. Durkheim, who even called them "ritual societies", to emphasize the character and nature of their social system.

4. For the detailed argumentation see Adela Şerban, *Securitate si Insecuritate Societală* [Societal Security and Insecurity] (Bucharest: Romanian Academy Publishing House, 2013).

5. Ibid.

6. Related to the village property, the community's response to a threat or just an external challenge, the acceptance of some families from neighboring villages or the exclusion of wrongdoers from community, etc.

7. Since there are no concentrations of power, the problems of a traditional community produces consequences borne equally and directly by all the members.

8. This system of manage community land property is called "devalmăşie". Henri .H. Stahl, *Contribuţii la studiul satelor devălmaşe romineşti: Confederaţii de ocol, structuri teritoriale şi tehnici agricole* (Bucharest: Editura Academiei Republicii Populare Romine, 1958); Henri H Stahl, *Contribuţii la studiul satelor devălmaşe româneşti, vol. II, Structura internă a satelor devălmaşe libere*, 3 vols., vol. 2, Contributions to the Study of Romanian Joint-property Villages (Bucharest: Editura Academiei R.P.R., 1959).

9. For details, *Sociologia satului devălmaş românesc* [Sociology of communal Romanian village], vol. 3 (Bucharest: Fundaţia Regele Mihai I, 1946)..

10. Territorial densification of the family networks was a rule in Romanian traditional social system. Most of the young people married people from the same village or from immediately neighboring villages (via the social contacts of the families) and only a very small percentage (generally shepherds) with people from villages located at greater distances (positioned on transhumance routes).

11. See Ovidiu Bârlea, *Folclor românesc (Folklore roumain), vol. I. Bucureşti. Ed* (Bucharest: Minerva, 1981).

12. See Mihai Pop, "Rolul educaţional al limbajului culturii populare," in *Educaţie şi limbaj [education and Language]*, ed. Sorin Stati (Bucharest: Editura Didactică şi Pedagogică, 1972), 139.

13. Ibid.. The author refers to the study Petr Grigorevič Bogatyrev and Roman Jakobson, *Die Folklore als eine besondere Form des Schaffens* (Nijmegen-Utrecht: Domum Natalicium Schrijnen, 1929). (N.a.)

14. Pop, "Rolul educaţional al limbajului culturii populare," 140.

15. See Simion Florea Marian, *Sărbătorile la români: studiu etnografic* [Romanian Celebrations], vol. 2 (Bucharest: Editura Grai şi Suflet, 1994), 105–108.

16. See *Sărbătorile la români: studiu etnografic*, vol. 1 (Bucharest: Editura Grai şi Suflet, 1994), 234.

17. See Ion Diaconu, *Ţinutul Vrancei*, vol. 1 (Bucharest: Socec&Co, 1930), XXII–XXIII.

REFERENCES

Bârlea, Ovidiu. *Folclor Românesc (Folklore Roumain)*, Vol. I. Bucureşti Ed. Bucharest: Minerva, 1981.

Bogatyrev, Petr Grigorevič, and Roman Jakobson. *Die Folklore Als Eine Besondere Form Des Schaffens*. Nijmegen-Utrecht: Domum Natalicium Schrijnen, 1929.

Diaconu, Ion. *Ţinutul Vrancei*. Vol. 1. Bucharest: Socec & Co, 1930.

Marian, Simion Florea. *Sărbătorile La Români: Studiu Etnografic* [in Romanian] [Romanian Celebrations]. Vol. 2. Bucharest: Editura Grai şi Suflet, 1994.

———. *Sărbătorile La Români: Studiu Etnografic*. Vol. 1. Bucharest: Editura Grai şi Suflet, 1994.

Pop, Mihai. "Rolul Educaţional Al Limbajului Culturii Populare." In *Educaţie Şi Limbaj [Education and Language]*, edited by Sorin Stati, 139–44. Bucharest: Editura Didactică şi Pedagogică, 1972.

Redfield, Robert. *Peasant Society and Culture: An Anthropological Approach to Civilization*. Chicago, IL: Chicago University Press, 1956.

Şerban, Adela. *Securitate Si Insecuritate Societală* [in Romanian] [Societal Security and Insecurity]. Bucharest: Romanian Academy Publishing House, 2013.

Stahl, Henri H. *Contribuţii La Studiul Satelor Devālmaşe Romineşti: Confederaţii De Ocol, Structuri Teritoriale Şi Tehnici Agricole*. Bucharest: Editura Academiei Republicii Populare Romine, 1958.

———. *Contribuţii La Studiul Satelor Devălmaşe Româneşti, Vol. II, Structura Internă a Satelor Devălmaşe Libere*. Contributions to the Study of Romanian Joint-Property Villages. 3 Vols. Vol. 2. Bucharest: Editura Academiei R.P.R., 1959.

———. *Sociologia Satului Devălmaş Românesc* [in Romanian] [Sociology of Communal Romanian Village]. Vol. 3. Bucharest: Fundaţia Regele Mihai I, 1946.

Ursache, Petru. *Etnosofia* [*Ethnosophy*]. Edited by Paideea. Bucharest, 2006.

Vulcănescu, Mircea. *Prolegomene sociologice la satul românesc* [*Sociological Prolegomena to the Romanian Village*]. Bucharest: Editura Eminescu, 1997.

Vulcănescu, Romulus. *Etnologie juridică* [*Juridical Ethnology*]. Bucharest: Editura Academiei, 1970.

———. *Mitologie română* [*Romanian Mithology*]. Bucharest: Editura Academiei, 1987.

Chapter 7

From Covenant to Compact to Contract

The Legal Transplantation of Puritan Jurisprudence to America

Peter J. Mazzacano

A common theme in the academic literature on legal transplantations is that rules, institutions, legal concepts, and systems of law are moved from one country to another or from one group of people to another.[1] To put it in simple terms, the laws of one country are "borrowed" from another.[2] The phenomena of legal transplants have been common since the beginning of recorded history. This should not be surprising, but at the risk of sounding like a cliché, imitating the laws of another country is thought to be the highest form of legal flattery. However, the process of legal transplantation on the legal culture of the recipient country is not always consistent or uniform. Indeed, the imitation can be incremental and messy, and in the new land the transplant can change and transform itself and develop into its own, unique form. Imitation has its risks. The transplantation process is rarely neat or linear and it may not operate as expected in the recipient country.

As this chapter argues, the Puritans in America are a case in point: Their theology, social thought, and practical wisdom about law formed the basis of their legal order—this theory or philosophy of law was Puritan jurisprudence. However, the transplantation of English common law in the form of Puritan jurisprudence to America was never their objective. Yet the Puritan creed and their concomitant practices unintentionally shaped and facilitated the later development of a democratic political culture and reinforced republican ideals in a way that the colonial Puritans would have found troubling. This development did not happen quickly. Indeed, the entire process developed over the course of many centuries, beginning with John Calvin and his European followers in the sixteenth century, then by John Winthrop during the American colonization, and culminating with John Adams and the American Revolution. These three periods mark progressive stages in the development of law, and its transplantation, in Puritan lands: the early European covenantal epoch associated with Calvin; the godly community and social compact envisioned by Winthrop in Massachusetts Bay; and the rise of John Adams's legalistic contractual constitutionalism following the Revolutionary War. Each stage, imperfect and muddled as it was, was an incremental step from jurisprudential notions of a covenant to the social compact to a legal contract, ultimately shaping the American Constitution.

THE FIRST EPOCH: THE DIVINE COVENANT

The word "covenant," and its derivations, is key to Puritan thought. It signifies all of humankind's worldly relationships with God. The Lord has covenanted with His people with these words: "I will be your God and you shall be My people" (Leviticus 26:12). In this sense, the term "covenant" is infused with the idea of a contract or agreement between two parties and this idea came to permeate Puritan thought. "We are by nature covenant creatures," one Puritan leader wrote in 1624, "bound together by covenants innumerable and together bound by covenant to our God. Such is our human condition. Such is this earthly life. Such is God's good creation. Blest be the ties that bind us."[3]

The original term in the Bible is *berith* which is usually translated as "covenant."[4] While the words "covenant" and "contract" are often used interchangeably, this is a mistake. A contract is a lower form of covenant, but this is not to suggest that a covenant is just a glorified contract. They are distinct forms. A contract is a mutually beneficial agreement between men, and it is legally binding between them, and enforceable by the sovereign. It can be honored, and it can be broken. By contrast, a covenant is a solemn, spiritual agreement in the form of a perpetual pledge or promise. Strictly speaking, the Biblical covenant is not an agreement, contract, or compact. It cannot be canceled or breached. With a covenant, both parties agree to honor their promises regardless of whether the other party keeps their part of the agreement.

The idea of a divine covenant between God and man has been a part of Western religious thought from the very beginning. Indeed, the word "covenant" (originally, *berith* or *diatheke*) is referred to 310 times in the Bible.[5] The term *diatheke* is significant. The translators of the Bible did not use the more common Greek word *suntheke*, which is used when the parties are equal. Instead, they deliberately chose *diatheke* to emphasize that the provisions of the covenant were dictated by one party only, in the form of a unilateral covenant.[6] Mutual agreement plays no role in a divine covenant. One example of many is found in Deuteronomy 7:9: "Know therefore that the Lord thy God, he is God, the faithful God, which keepeth covenant and mercy with them that love him and keep his commandments to a thousand generations."[7] Here, God assures humankind that His unilateral promise and faithfulness goes beyond the imperfect ways of men. He has bound Himself to His covenant with man, regardless of the actions of men.

The Puritan religious movement, beginning with John Calvin, was rooted in this biblical covenantal thinking. Thus, covenant theology was a development of theological thought and construction within the Calvinistic tradition. However, this is not to suggest that Calvin founded covenant theology. Most likely, covenant theology appears to have been founded by Calvin's predecessor, Zwingli, and then taken up by him and other later Reformed theologians, such as Bullinger, Ursinus, Olevianus, and Junius.[8] In England, it goes back to Tyndale and John Frith but was best articulated by Bullinger as follows: "God, in making leagues, as he doth in all things, applied himself to our capacities. . . . And therefore, when God's mind was to declare the favour and good-will that he bare to mankind . . . it pleased him to make a league or covenant with mankind."[9]

Covenant theology developed among the Puritans in England in parallel to its development on the Continent. To Bullinger and his kind, the first covenant was made with Adam after the Fall, and then later with Noah and Moses. On God's side He made the promise of His Son, and through Him humankind would receive the benefits of reconciliation and heavenly blessings; in turn, man was obliged to honor God with faith and obedience.[10] This is also how Ursinus saw the covenant: not as a decree, but rather in terms of a beneficial agreement between God and man. In his words, the Christian covenant can be defined as:

> a mutual promise and agreement, between God and men, in which God gives assurance to men that he will be merciful to them, remit their sins, grant unto them a new righteousness, the Holy Spirit, and eternal life by and for the sake of his Son, our Mediator. And, on the other side, men bind themselves to God in this covenant that they will exercise repentance and faith, or that they will receive with a true faith this great benefit which God offers, and render such obedience as will be acceptable to him. This mutual engagement between God and man is confirmed by those outward signs which we call sacraments, which are holy signs, declaring and sealing unto us God's good will, and our thankfulness and obedience.[11]

The Biblical covenant was a unique feature of Puritanism and in its highly developed form it became a cornerstone for its model community. The Puritan concept of the covenant, which was to eventually swell into the popular idea of the social contract in the eighteenth century, was an obsession with the Puritans. They found the covenant throughout the Old Testament. Abraham had entered into a covenant with God in order to be the "father of many nations."[12] In turn, Abraham's family had entered into a "church estate" by a covenant with Abraham; and Moses led a "church in the wilderness" which was founded by a covenant.[13]

With these biblical precedents in mind, John Winthrop was to later write, "[i]t is of the nature and essence of every society to be knit together by some covenant, either expressed or implied."[14] Similarly, John Cotton stated, "[i]t is evident by the light of nature that all civil relations are founded in covenant."[15] The Puritans read their bibles in light of man's covenant with God and from this abstracted and derived therefrom a pervasive political philosophy. In the words of Cotton:

> When Jehovah made a covenant between the King and the people, that covenant was but a branch of the Lord's covenant with them all, both King and people: for the King promised but to rule the people righteously, according to the will of God: and the people to be subject to the King so ruling. Now these duties of the King to them, and of them to the King, were such as God required in his covenant, both of him and them.[16]

This unification of theology and political theory had its origins in England when the Puritans were becoming more deeply entangled in the constitutional struggle with the king. This belief in a higher law, which could be appealed to against the arbitrariness of rulers, led, irresistibly, into a developing political creed. With increasing earnestness, the Puritans advanced the thesis that government originated in a compact of the people and was to be limited by the terms of the agreement. As Cotton was to later note, "[l]ook what a King requires of his people, or the people of a king, the very same doth God require of his people, and the people of God [. . .] this is, a governor, a provider for, and a protector of his people."[17] To Cotton and other Puritans, limiting the rulers' power by a higher law was a divine ordinance to restrain the innate sinfulness of man. However, it also served a second function: it was a device to avoid political oppression and despotism.

The Puritans had an immense preoccupation with Biblical notions of the divine covenant and saw it as an everlasting contractual bond between God and humanity. But to the Puritans the divine covenant went beyond man's relationship with God; it extended to relationships between persons in church, state, and civil society as well. They countered the organically hierarchical conception of society, including the divine right of monarchs that prevailed in the medieval Catholic world. If no one, whether pope or monarch, had divine authority to interpret the Bible for others or to rule others, then a covenant was a logical alternative for organizing human relationships. Not surprisingly, for example, reformed Protestants redefined marriage as a covenant rather than a sacrament. Individuals and families covenanted to form religious congregations. No ecclesiastical hierarchy existed to impose priests on them; instead, congregations called ministers or pastors to serve the community. This congregational structure was not an episcopal polity but a federal polity. Indeed, the word *federal* itself originated from the Latin *foedus*, meaning covenant or agreement, and the Puritans' theology was similarly called *covenant* or *federal theology*.

In this way, the Puritans brought to America a sub-variety of English Puritanism known as "covenant theology." There was little difficulty in translating and transplanting a theological doctrine of the covenant into a concept of human community and social organization. It was a small logical leap from covenant to social compact, a "city upon a hill."[18]

On their way to the new world, Winthrop could, thus, preach to the settlers that they were obliged to act in godly ways because they had established a covenant with God. Having accepted the obligation to live in a Christian way, their new community was to be relatively free from the corruptions of the world. Thus, Winthrop spoke of the settlers as having "entered into a covenant with Him for this work."[19] By virtue of their having committed themselves to God's protection on the voyage and in the new world, He had "ratified this covenant and sealed our commission [and] will expect a strict performance of the articles contained in it."[20]

Having agreed to be God's people and to live in a godly fashion, Winthrop said little about government, except that providence had provided them with an opportunity "to seek out a place of cohabitation and consortship under a due form of government both civil and ecclesiastical."[21] Although Winthrop did not define these terms, their meaning was already implicit. In the godly city, the natural leaders were to rule in the best interests of the community, seeking "their welfare in all things."[22] In turn, the people were to accept the government because of their God-ordained duty to "faith, patience, obedience."[23]

It was not until 1637 that Winthrop elaborated on the political aspects of the covenantal relationship between the rulers and the ruled. Before the General Court, Winthrop set forth the unified theory of the Puritan community. As Winthrop explained it, the political theory, upon which the community was based, was part of Puritan theological doctrine, and the binding idea was the notion of the covenant: "The essential form of the commonweal[th] or body politic such as this is [. . .] I take to be this—the consent of a certain company of people to cohabit together under one government for their mutual safety and welfare."[24] The Puritan belief that the covenant was the central instrument that allowed men to live together in religious harmony, even though the relationship occasionally caused problems, led Winthrop to reach the following conclusions:

1. No commonwealth can be founded but by free consent.

2. The persons so incorporating have a public and relative interest each in other, and in the place of their cohabitation and goods and laws, etc., and in all means of their welfare so as none can claim privilege with them but by free consent.
3. The nature of such an incorporation ties every member thereof to seek out and entertain all means that may conduce to the welfare of the body and to keep off whatsoever doth appear to tend to their damage.
4. The welfare of the whole is not to be put to hazard for the advantage of any particular members.[25]

To Winthrop, individuals, in a natural, graceless state, were at liberty to do as they please. However, when these same individuals became infused with the godly spirit, they were then at liberty to do only what God commanded. This was one of the essential terms of God's covenant with man. The regenerates, therefore, came together and formed churches and a state upon explicit agreements, in which they all promised to live with one another according to the laws and for the purposes of God. The government was created by an act of the people.

But this was not any type of government; it was to be a government which God had circumscribed, as discerned from the Bible. The rulers were not self-appointed, therefore, but were God-appointed through the people and elected to an office which had been established by God. Winthrop states that "It is yourselves who have called us to this office, and being called by you, we have our authority from God, in a way of ordinance."[26] Such beliefs were also echoed by other Puritans. John Cotton stated to Roger Williams that no magistrate had power over the bodies or property of the people, except by their free consent. However, because regenerate men were only "stewards" of their bodies and property, in order to improve them for God's glory, "they may not give their free consents to any magistrate to dispose of their bodies, goods, lands, liberties at large as themselves please, but as God (the sovereign Lord of all) alone [pleases]."[27]

Similarly, John Eliot noted that in both church and state, the godly willingly submitted to His regiment. The regenerates were eager to "enter into covenant with the Lord to become His people, even in their civil society, as well as their church society."[28]

In the godly Puritan community, therefore, men thrice committed themselves to the rule of law and the control of authority: first with God, then with each other in the church, and again in the state. With such regulated relationships, Winthrop could insist that though the government of Massachusetts Bay was bound by law and received its authority through God and the people's elected officials, the people were nevertheless at "liberty to that only which is good, just and honest."[29] By entering into a covenant with God, and then with each other, the citizens were to renounce their natural lusts, and retain only the freedom that "is maintained and exercised in a way of subjection to authority."[30]

Thus far, it is evident from this analysis of the theoretical basis of Puritan religious thought that one outcome of the Puritan attempt to create a godly community arose from the notion of God's covenant with man. In Puritan thought, this community was a covenantal, authoritarian theocracy only insofar as God was the absolute sovereign, whereby His fiats were law, and the magistrates and ministers were His officials, but were chosen by the people. Although both church and state were conceived to have derived their authority from God, and both sought to do God's will, their functions were separated. However, this division was not always absolute. The functions of church and state differed, and their powers were distinct, but both were a part of an organic community whose goal was to serve God. The state's primary concern was the rule of law; men's souls were the responsibility of the church. While church and state were committed to the welfare of the entire community, the church was to guide it in the way of God's truth; the state, in turn, was to preserve order in the community. The "ultimate and supreme" goal of both was that "the common good of the society, state or kingdom" be preserved and "God in all things [. . .] glorified."[31]

The Puritans believed that a covenant existed between God and man, and unlike a compact or contract, it had a moral dimension, religious in nature, requiring the consenting parties to go beyond its black letter so as to observe its spirit, under the watchful eye of God. As such, the covenant was of a higher order than a compact or contract, as it contained a morally binding element in the form of an oath or promise.

THE SECOND EPOCH: THE SOCIAL COMPACT

Developing out of the Puritan notion of its covenant with God came a lower form of agreement: the social compact between men. It was an easy and logical transition: the idea of a covenant could also apply to the formation of communities and governments between men. Individuals, families, and congregations could covenant together to form towns, and towns could covenant to form larger confederations or unions. As they developed these arrangements, the colonists adopted and coined a variety of related secular words to describe and distinguish between their instruments of governance, such as *compact*, *contract*, *combination*, *agreement*, *charter*, *frame*, *fundamentals*, *patent*, *ordinance*, and eventually *constitution*. For example, what is today called the Mayflower Compact (1620) was known by its contemporaries as the Plymouth Combination, or "agreement among the settlers at New Plymouth."

The primary intent of Winthrop and other members of the Massachusetts Bay Colony to leave England and to go to Massachusetts Bay was not only to build a "city upon a hill" to serve as an example to the unenlightened. Their other goal was to also establish their own in situ godly community that was to be distinct, separate, and apart from that of England, and one that was to be held together by a social compact. While the parties to the covenant with God swore an oath before and to God, but where these same men formed a body politic, they believed themselves bound by God to keep the promises they made in constituting their community.

The Puritan community that Winthrop and the Puritans envisioned in the New World would be much more than that depicted in the Gospel of Matthew, from which the phrase was borrowed. In Matthew 5:14 the regenerates "are the light of the world. A city that is set on a hill cannot be hid."[32] But to Winthrop, the phrase in his address reflected the core of his thinking concerning the type of society that he and his fellow passengers sought to establish. It would be a city in the literal sense, for the leaders of the Winthrop fleet planned to settle in one, centralized community. The community itself would be an urban center, the place of church and government.

It would also be a city in the biblical sense, as God's city. Like Saint Augustine's medieval notion of the organic town, as depicted in his *The City of God*, Winthrop's image of the city was somewhat metaphorical, and the term "city upon a hill" denoted more of a community of saints than a physical urban area. The basis of the city was its religious ideals. While the foundation of a physical city was selfishness, the city Winthrop envisioned was to be based on the love of God. Here men would serve God in the ways that He demanded. In the church, men would worship God and His word in its purest form, which would be heard by all. But most importantly, men would fit into a society in such a way that would contribute to the glory of God and His son, Jesus Christ.

The Puritan theory of the organic, godly community demanded that members of the community unite. There was, therefore, no room for the lone dissenter, who was sometimes persecuted—this despite the Puritan migration for the very reason that their beliefs differed from that of their bishops. In New England, they moved in and established communal groups, and maintained firm control over this united entity. They believed they were establishing a community in which the one and only truth would reign forever, and for that reason, unanimous acceptance of the majority consensus was essential. This was a key component in the social compact. Relatively broad political participation, therefore, was not to facilitate the expression of divergent viewpoints, and not to foster democracy, but rather to provide the broadest base possible for community consensus. And with having participated in the political process in some manner, however loose and unstructured, community members usually felt obliged to accept the results of the majority.

While it was a simple and logical development to move from the concept of a divine covenant to a theory on a compact between men, the idea of the social compact was not a Puritan invention. The concept of the social contract or compact developed during the Age of Enlightenment out of concern for the legitimacy of the authority of the state over the individual. Although the antecedents of social contract theory are found in antiquity, specifically in Greek and Stoic philosophy and Roman and Canon Law, the heyday of the social contract was the mid-seventeenth to early nineteenth centuries, when it emerged as the leading doctrine of political legitimacy. The covenant idea also was secularized by Hobbes, who used covenant in his *Leviathan* (1651) to describe the creation of a body politic; John Locke (1632–1704), who used compact for this purpose in his *Two Treatises of Government* (1689); and other English political philosophers, such as John Milton (1608–1674) and David Hume (1711–1776). Later, in 1762, Jean-Jacques Rousseau (1712–1778) used the term *social contract*. While each of these thinkers approached the concept of political authority differently, the common thread among them was that law and political order were not natural, but rather human creations. However, the Puritans imbued the social compact with religious and godly notions, and the descendants of the Puritans increasingly turned to compacts and other secular instruments to describe their political foundings and developments.

The non-arbitrary, participatory conception of government was the Puritan cornerstone upon which the political institutions of the commonwealth, and later, the American republic, were built. Religious beliefs had united with political theory and provided the main strands which held together the communal fabric of the colony—in the form of a social compact. But while the Puritan experiment led to a panoply of political innovations in the New World, it did some borrowing, with adaptations, from what the colonists had known in England. Indeed, the Puritans also drew on the Bible as a source of law; modifying or ignoring its provisions was necessary to suit local circumstances. There may also have been a conscious or unconscious rejection of many of the characteristics which had shaped the English common law, such as the central role of the crown, inequalities of land tenure, access to justice, and the power conferred in the hands of judges. Of course, it is arguable whether the application of English common law to Puritan America can really be described as a legal transplant. After all, there was no "host" body onto which laws could be transplanted, and while English legal concepts were moved to foreign soil, they were transported in the ideas of the Puritans who traveled there. Clearly, English law was influential to some degree: the movement and transmigration of legal ideas and institutions across borders is a natural phase in the legal development of any nation.[33]

Specifically, when common Puritans began to participate more directly in the government of the colony, they worked to ensure that their elected rulers abided by established and published laws even though there was a dearth of written legal authorities. As early as 1635, Winthrop recorded in his journal:

> The deputies having conceived great danger to our state, in regard that our magistrates, for want of positive laws, in many cases, might proceed according to their discretions, it was agreed that some men should be appointed to frame a body of grounds of laws, in resemblance to a Magna Carta, which, being allowed by some of the ministers, and the general courts should be received for fundamental laws.[34]

Thus, while certain Puritans enjoyed the franchise, codified political rights for all inhabitants were to be established in order to destroy any lingering vestige of arbitrary government.

The Puritan concern with written laws was unprecedented for that time. They reduced their laws to codes, although this term may have meant no more than a collection of compilation of written laws. Thus, Massachusetts began to codify its laws in 1634 and Pennsylvania in 1682. In some cases, these codifications may have been made to overcome the scarcity of written legal sources, nevertheless, the act of codification was also directed at curtailing the power of magistrates, judges, and those in power.

The *Body of Liberties*, a document originally published in 1641, is the first legal code established by the European colonists in New England and was composed of a list of liberties, rather than restrictions, and was intended for use as guidance for the General Court of the time. Like elsewhere in the godly community, democracy and theocracy were to be synthesized in a mode that had the semblance of a social compact. The resulting *Body of Liberties* did its best to balance religious orthodoxy with popular rights. While it recognized that all law originates with God, like the covenant, the selection was carefully based on universal morality, rather than on the harsh ordinances of the Bible. Moreover, as Winthrop noted, the real basis for the final product was not so much the Bible, but English common law.[35] This was evident in the preamble of the *Body of Liberties*, which illustrated the blending of liberty and authority in an organic godly community:

> The free fruition of such liberties, immunities, and privileges as humanity, civility, and Christianity call for as due to every man in his place and proportion without impeachment and infringement hath ever been and ever will be the tranquility and stability of Churches and Commonwealths. And the denial or deprival thereof, the disturbance if not the ruin of both.

We hold it, therefore, our duty and safety whilst we are about the further establishing of this Government to collect and express all such freedoms as for present we foresee may concern us, and our posterity after us, and to ratify them with our solemn consent.

We do, therefore, this day religiously and unanimously decree and confirm these following rights, liberties, and privileges concerning our Churches and Civil state to be respectively, impartially, and inviolably enjoyed and observed throughout our jurisdiction forever.

> 1. No man's life shall be taken away, no man's honor or good name shall be stained, no man's person shall be arrested, restrained, banished, dismembered, nor any ways punished, no man shall be deprived of his wife or children, no man's goods or estate shall be taken away from him, nor any way damaged under color of law or countenance of authority, unless it be by virtue of equity of some express law of the Country warranting the same, established by a general court and sufficiently published, or in case of the defect of a law in any particular case by the word of God.[36]

With the *Body of Liberties* came the culmination of the establishment of fundamental rights for the inhabitants of Massachusetts Bay. With its passage, the Puritans put an end to their fear of arbitrary government. The rulers, for their part, had reduced the possibility of the formation of a pure democracy or rule by the "mob."

Just as importantly, the *Body of Liberties* was a departure from the relative limits placed on authority in England during this same period. It constituted a truly democratic innovation primarily by championing civil rights and limited judicial powers through a written constitution. For example, in general, many of the provisions in the *Body of Liberties* were more humane than those in English common law. The rights of servants were humanitarian in character; lashes inflicted for punishment were limited to forty; and the capital laws were more lenient than the contemporary practice in England.[37]

Furthermore, theft was not punishable by death, although in England robbery, burglary, and larceny over the value of one shilling were capital felonies.[38] Cruel and barbarous punishments were forbidden, as was torture, except on a convict for a capital offense to discover accomplices, in which case the torture was not to be "barbarous and inhumane."[39]

Feudal dues were also prohibited, complete testamentary liberty was guaranteed, and foreigners were assured the equal protection of the laws. Indeed, the *Body of Liberties* provided that "every man shall have liberty to complain to the General Court of any injustice done him in any [judicial] Court."[40] Whether a man be "[i]nhabitant or foreigner, free or not free," he was allowed to attend any court, council, or town meeting and propose consideration of his case "in convenient time, due order, and respectful manner."[41] In all such cases, the defendant was given the privilege "to put himself on the court" to avoid a jury verdict.[42]

Penalties were not fixed except for capital laws; indeed, penalties were very rare in the early laws of Massachusetts Bay. This was in accordance with the Puritan belief that justice could best be secured by considering each case on its own merits, as well as on the grounds that the Bible prescribed few fixed penalties except for capital crimes.[43]

Other features of the *Body of Liberties* were also peculiar to the Puritans of Massachusetts Bay, and unknown in England. Payments for legal defense were forbidden; crops or vegetables in the field or garden could not be taken from someone in distress; and taxes could not be levied on a man for property that "he hath in England, or in any foreign parts."[44]

The *Body of Liberties* was also well ahead of its time in the area of women and animal rights. While the common law authorized a man to chastise his wife with a "reasonable instrument," the *Body of Liberties* declared that "Every married woman shall be free from bodily correction or stripes by her husband, unless it be in his own defense upon her assault."[45] And, although animals received no protection under English law, "The Brute Creature" was given a section of its own. Clearly, the Puritan compilation of fundamental laws was so enlightened that it would have done credit to any Commonwealth in the seventeenth century.

As for theocracy, the *Body of Liberties* clarified what had already been practiced.[46] Massachusetts Bay was established as a model godly community and not as a theocracy. On this point, the *Body of Liberties* was emphatic. Law 58 stated that "Civil authority hath power and liberty to see the Peace, ordinances and rules of Christ observed in every church according to his word, so it be done in a civil and not in an ecclesiastical way."[47] A subsequent section limited church authority by decreeing: "All churches have liberty to deal with any of their members in a church way," but the church has no power to "retard or hinder" the course of civil authority.[48] To ensure this absence of ecclesiastical interference, the *Body of Liberties* also boldly stated that "No church censure shall degrade or depose any man from any Civil dignity, office or authority he shall have in the Commonwealth."[49] In the case of a jurisdictional dispute, the General Court would have the sole power to interpret the matter.

Thus, by the end of the first decade, a fine balance had been struck between the ruling authorities, the ministers, and a godly democracy. In this model community, the line between church and state had been drawn to the extent that the community selected rulers and shared in the making of laws, while the officials usually retained power through entrenched concepts relating to Puritan theology, stemming from the covenant and progressing to a social compact. Government rule was to be limited, and the rights of the ruled, now codified in law, were not to be arbitrarily threatened.

Indeed, by the terms of the social compact, there was to be a limitation on the power of all officials, as based on the rule of law. As Cotton stated, neither magistrates nor ministers should "affect more liberty and authority then will do them good, and the people good," so it became necessary "that all power that is on earth be limited."[50] Although the people were not to rebel at every minor injustice, when they discovered that their rulers "have broken the fundamental articles of the covenant," they were to be released from their oaths of obedience.[51] Anticipating Locke and the ideas that were to become so popular in the eighteenth century, one Puritan leader went so far as to assert the then novel and revolutionary idea that when rulers violate "the way of justice and happiness, which they are sworn to maintain [. . .] it is lawful to take up arms of defence."[52]

When the Massachusetts Bay Puritans planned to create their state, the influence of their English experience came to the fore. In reaction to this experience, they developed a number of novel and innovative institutional features. The new state was English, but only in a negative respect: it was created in order to limit the king's prerogative by migrating beyond his reach and by establishing covenantal rights as a protection against absolutism and arbitrariness. On a more local level, the congregational format of church polity in New England was based somewhat on the English model of the Parish. Indeed, many of the first settlers were drawn from country villages and had participated in local government by serving on the vestries which controlled parish activity.[53] However, the numbers of those participating had been extremely limited as local government in England had been relatively oligarchic.[54]

In contrast to English traditions, the Puritan state was constructed upon a foundation of reason and democratic godliness in which men came together to form churches and a state with an explicit agreement, the social compact. Together they promised to live with one another according to the laws and for the purposes of God. Thus, the government of the godly community was democratic in that it was brought into being by an act of the people. In turn, God guided the society by acting through the people. The collective will of the godly, bound together at first by the covenant, and later by the social compact, projected and continued the will of God into the state. John Davenport expressed it as "In regular actions of the creature, God is the first Agent; there are not two several and distinct actings, one of God, another of the People: but in one and the same action, God, by the People suffrages, makes such a one Governor, or Magistrate, and not another."[55] As Davenport suggested, actions were not disjointed in a godly community. All outcomes were part of a coherent divine plan. This resulted from the terms of the agreement between the people and God, where they had compacted to form a godly state in which His ordinances were to be practiced.

Thus, in Puritan thought, the holy society to be erected was extremely voluntaristic and here lay the potential for fostering democratic and republican values. The godly community was to be created by men through their own free choice. Church and state institutions were to be made up of "visible saints," drawn from all ranks of society who migrated because of a desire to participate in the creation and direction of a godly community, and not because they were of noble birth or were forced to participate in community affairs. The leaders, therefore, were not to be of a specific economic class, but were drawn from the holy and regenerate, which, in theory, transcended class lines. One example, noted by Winthrop, revealed that a Black servant woman was admitted to the Dorchester church because of her "sound knowledge and true godliness."[56]

Though every resident in the community was obliged to attend and pay taxes for the support of the church, no one became a member unless she or he signified this strong desire. The visible saints were expected to act positively because they had in them a spirit of God that made them capable of every exertion. When persecuted in one state, for example, they imitated the apostle and fled, not to escape government, but to establish a better government, formed on the basis of a social compact. They maintained, however, that any government into which men did not voluntarily enter was not worthy of the name.

Paradoxically, in a world with limits on social action, Puritan theory relied heavily upon voluntarism. This was possible because when a man received the spirit of God, he availed himself of his liberty to enter a compact with God, promising to abide by His laws. In return, God guaranteed redemption. A regenerate man was, thus, committed to God's cause not only in his personal life, but also in church and community affairs. In other words, when a man became regenerate, he was to volunteer his liberty, and do only what God commanded. And God commanded certain acts from the entire community of saints as well as from each individual saint. This was the foundation of the social compact.

Consequently, voluntarism within the social theory of Puritanism was based upon the law of God and it required the willing submission of citizens. As men exist in nature, stated Thomas Hooker, no one person had any power over another: "there must of necessity be a mutual engagement, each of the other, by their free consent, before by any rule of God they have any right or power, or can exercise either, each towards the other."[57] He continued: "All relations which are neither natural nor violent, but voluntary, are by virtue of some covenant," like a social compact.[58] But the fact that social relations originated with "free" consent did not compromise the order God had ordained; it indicated only that this order was not to be one of caste.

However, as already noted, the quest for a godly community did not translate into a theocratic polity for the towns of the Puritans. There was to be a division of labor between magistrates and ministers, so Puritan communities were never theocracies in the sense of rule by the clergy. In the organic Puritan community, both church and state had a duty to govern for godly ends. The Puritan desire to create a holy polis did not immediately translate into a democracy any more than it translated into a theocracy, or oligarchy; nor did it simply mirror English political institutions and practices. All that can be stated with any degree of certainty is that soon after the arrival of the Puritans, their community of visible saints quickly evolved into a cohesive political unit and unintentionally centered itself around democratic precepts.

In this way, Puritan godliness became compatible with democratic ideals. But there is an essential difference. Godliness led to the acceptance and development of certain democratic and republican practices within the context of a relatively closed, corporate, religious community, where deference to authority was usually tolerated. Godliness, thus, helps to explain the emergence of democracy, therefore, only as an indirect or secondary product of Puritanism, needing time to develop.

It now remains to be seen to what extent these Puritan ideals, which focused on godliness, cross-fertilized into a legal culture that ultimately permeated the institutions and practices of colony and town as the land developed into a constitutional republic.

THE THIRD EPOCH: CONTRACTUAL CONSTITUTIONALISM

To the Puritans, a godly or virtuous person might be borne by either a poor or rich family. This godly ideal of the equality of souls had imparted to the Puritans a deep moral fiber which became evident in the political affairs of Massachusetts Bay, and later, in the American republic. In such an environment, even a certain degree of imposed authority never bred subservience, nor was it ever incompatible with a large degree of essential equality and individual self-respect.

Perhaps it was this Puritan humanism which lay at the heart of their godly ideal. From their recorded statements it seems clear that they tended to accentuate the element of rationalism and sought to enlarge the sphere of competence of natural reason even to those not inspired by God's special grace. As John Cotton noted, man learns much by experience and education, "yet there is also an essential wisdom in us, namely, our Reason which is natural."[59]

Like Cotton, most Puritans believed that man, however depraved by sin and passion, was essentially a rational and responsible being, capable of learning, and requiring only godliness to bring him to ultimate salvation. Every man, regardless of his material worth, was, therefore, considered competent to judge based on his innate reason, free to choose between good and evil, and naturally imbued with at least a semblance of some higher moral principles. Translated into the political sphere, such a conception of man lent itself easily to democratic ideals.

However, if the Puritans have been hailed as the forerunners of American democracy because of their attitudes toward religion and political participation, this was not their intention. To interpret an event by what it ultimately became is a dangerous reading of history. Preconceptions about Puritanism which have been established in later times must be discarded, and Puritanism must be approached with a view to its own context.

While an understanding of New England Puritanism may be conceded to have some significance for the understanding of America's later political culture, the unqualified use of such terms as "democratic," "oligarchic," or "theocratic' is inadequate. If the Puritans were "democratic," there is a failure to explain why only the godly were allowed the suffrage franchise, to the exclusion of others. If Massachusetts Bay was a "theocracy," why was there a division between the functions of church and state, as well as between magistrate and minister? As for Puritan Massachusetts being an "oligarchy," this fails to account for the electoral responsibility of the Commonwealths' ruling officials and the limitations placed on their possessing broad, discretionary powers. Finally, if Puritan Massachusetts simply imitated English legal precedents, in the sense of the wholesale transplantation of jurisprudence from the old world, it does not explain the rise of unique political and ecclesiastical institutions in New England, especially the revolutionary Puritan conception of the franchise, based, not on property, but on godliness.

Puritanism and its component parts, particularly its focus on godliness, amounted to a formative ideology in the new world. Because their convictions had consequences in an ideologically free environment, Puritan ideals and practices were of primary importance in the shaping and perpetuation of a coherent set of political ideas and practices. Consider that scholars have documented how established value systems can persist for generations, even through revolutionary change.[60] Indeed, that Puritan values may have been transmitted, to some extent, is plausible when note is taken, for example, that all U.S. Founding Fathers were reared either in Massachusetts or Virginia.[61]

Indeed, the rise of contractual constitutionalism after the Revolutionary War in America was the logical outcome of Puritan thought regarding the divine covenant and the social compact. As Bernard Bailyn noted, Puritan thought provided "the Revolutionary generation" with a "major source of ideas and attitudes."[62] To Bailyn, the elaborate system of Puritan thought, erected in New England beginning in 1630, had been "consolidated and amplified" by numerous writers throughout the seventeenth century, and was "channelled into the main stream of eighteenth century political and social thinking."[63] In this sense, it is possible that Americans became products of their history, where ideology and institutions were neither entirely lost nor entirely new. In the words of Samuel Eliot Morison: "The institutions that the Puritans founded, Church, Commonwealth, Town, College, were so firmly established as to outlast the purposes for which they were intended. Church and College and Commonwealth have been patched and altered again and again, without losing all their original character."[64]

To Bailyn and Morison, as well as others, Puritanism was clearly a formative ideology that was perpetuated for generations, if not centuries. And in the founding of the American nation, Puritanism was a formative ideology that contributed to the shaping of distinctive political and ecclesiastical institutions. Clearly, the colony lived by a legal order that was distinctive by the standards of contemporary England the other British colonies.

Indeed, key historical political thinkers believed that Puritanism clearly left a mark on the character of U.S. political institutions. It is not surprising, therefore, that some studies on colonial America have tended to focus on the homogeneity of that American society.[65] Thus, Alexis de Tocqueville could write that "the whole destiny of America is contained in the first Puritan who landed on these shores," because "Puritanism was almost as much a political theory as a religious doctrine."[66] He also noted that religious and political conflicts in England drove dissenters to America. It was from this "Puritan movement" and the English "middle classes" from which most of the emigrants sprang, hence, "the colony came more and more to present the novel phenomenon of a society homogeneous in all its parts."[67] But as we have seen, economically, the Puritans of Massachusetts Bay came from all walks of life.

John Jay had enunciated a similar sentiment two generations before Tocqueville's statement. In *The Federalist Papers*, Jay discussed the common heritage of American immigrants: "Providence has been pleased to give this one connected country to one united People—a People descended from the same ancestors, speaking the same language, professing the same religion, attached to the same principles of government, very similar in their manners and customs."[68]

More recently, Louis Hartz developed the controversial "fragment theory." He believed that the colonial beginnings of America shaped its political culture well into the twentieth century. To Hartz there was a dissenting, liberal fragment that migrated to America: this fragment "detaches itself from the whole [. . .] and the part develops without inhibition."[69] Detached, it became for the first time the "master of a whole region."[70] Thus, "the fragmented British Puritan can make Calvin universal in New England, simply by virtue of his migration."[71]

A variation of Hartz's fragment theory is Seymour Lipset's theory of formative events. To Lipset, "Countries, like people, are not handed identities at birth" as Hartz's theory contended, "but acquire them through the arduous process of 'growing up.'"[72] To extrapolate from this view, the impact of legal transplants is limited. Once grafted on a new land, laws and legal concepts can develop in unexpected ways. However, early events favored certain outcomes over others. In Lipset's view, "historical events establish values and predispositions, and these in turn determine later events."[73] That is, certain historical "formative" events served to fix certain values in the public mind, largely by embodying these values in institutions and patterns of behavior that would endure.

Although it may be difficult to quantify the ideas expounded above by Tocqueville, Jay, Hartz, and Lipset, it must be noted that Massachusetts Bay was only a part of New England, and by extension, the New England way was not necessarily the American way.[74] But the New England Puritans helped to cultivate several constitutional ideas that would later prove influential for the United States after the American Revolution. As we have seen, among the most novel were their ideas of social, political, and ecclesiastical covenants, rooted in biblical covenant thinking but prescient to later notions of contractual constitutionalism. Also influential were Puritan ideas of natural rights and liberties and their necessary protection by church and state authorities alike. But the Puritans' most prescient and enduring contribution lay in their theory of godliness and the need to create constitutional safeguards against tyranny. This led them to develop early doctrines of separation of church and state, separation of powers within church and state, checks and balances among these powers, and federalist layers of authority. From these circumstances there eventually developed, in the most rudimentary form, the proposition for a more representative government and the beginnings of a native contractual constitutionalism.

The connection between the influence of the Puritans and the discontent that led to the Revolutionary War in America could not be more direct. The connection is evidenced in the words of John Adams. Writing in 1765, Adams defended the "sensible" New England Puritans against those "many modern Gentlemen" of his day who dismissed them as bigoted, narrow, "enthusiastical, superstitious and republican."[75] Such "ridicule" and "ribaldry" of the Puritans, proffered mainly by the fashionable "new lights" of philosophy and politics, are "grossly injurious and false," Adams retorted.[76] Far from being narrow bigots, the Puritans were "illustrious patriots," for they were the first "to establish a government of the church more consistent with the scriptures, and a government of the state more agreeable to the dignity of human nature than any other seen in Europe: and to transmit such a government down to their posterity."[77]

On the eve of the American Revolution, in an essay Adams invoked Winthrop, reviewing the history of the Massachusetts Bay original charter and the determination of Winthrop and his fellow Puritans to preserve their liberties. Seeking to dismiss the charge that those who opposed tyranny were rabble at an early age and rabble at the time he was writing, Adams stressed the fact that Isaac Johnson, Winthrop, and Thomas Dudley—all early leaders of the Massachusetts colonial experiment—were "not the rascally Rabble of Romulus, but Gentlemen of Family, Fortune, Education, and Figure."[78] In 1780 Adams again found cause to praise Winthrop and the other "first Planters of New England" as great men who struggled with the dangers of the wilderness to enjoy "superior liberty for themselves, and the prospect of it for their children."[79]

Only after the success of the Revolution, when New Englanders such as George Bancroft began to write histories of the new nation, did Americans outside Massachusetts learn that they too owed much to the Puritan founders. Not surprisingly, later in life, Adams would recognize Winthrop as an honorary Founding Father, a view shared by many prominent Americans in the nineteenth century. And key to Winthrop's thinking was the concept of a higher law, not natural law per se, but rather its pious kindred spirit, godliness, which, once translated into the political realm, led to limited government. The notion of natural law that provided a limitation upon government was seized upon by Adams and other American revolutionaries, resulting in the rise of contractual constitutionalism.

Indeed, starting with Puritan ideals of godliness, the influence of natural law became the cornerstone of American constitutionalism. Its influence on American legal thinking in the seventeenth and first half of the eighteenth centuries was particularly profound, and natural law was the key weapon used in the revolutionary arguments against the supremacy of government. The more prominent opponents of legislative supremacy included not only John Adams, but also James Otis, Sam Adams, Patrick Henry, John Dickinson, Thomas Jefferson, Oliver Ellsworth, John Rutledge, James Wilson, Luther Martin, William Patterson, George Wythe, James Madison, and Alexander Hamilton. There were also many laymen such as Benjamin Franklin and George Mason, and especially the clergymen who were proponents of the doctrine of natural law.

The legal battle destined to end in revolution and the establishment of American contractual constitutionalism was initiated by James Otis in the *Paxton's Case of the Writ of Assistance*.[80] In this case, Otis challenged Massachusetts's authority to issue writs of assistance, general search warrants that empowered local sheriffs to enter private homes and businesses to seize smuggled goods. Otis told the colonial court that he objected to such writs, which were created by a parliamentary act in 1662, because they violated natural law principles. According to John Adams, Otis "as also a great master of the law of nature and nations. He had read Pufendorf, Grotius, Barbeyrac, Burlamqui, Vattel, Heineccius [. . .] It was a maxim which he inculcated in his pupils [. . .] that a lawyer ought never to be without a volume of natural or public law, or moral philosophy, on his table or in his pocket."[81] According to Otis in *Paxton's Case*: "As to acts of Parliament. An act against the constitution is void: an act against natural equity is void; and if an act of Parliament should be made, in the very words of the petition, it would be void. The Executive Courts must pass such acts into disuse."[82] Adams added to this statement: "Then and there the child Independence was born."[83]

In these brief quotations is found the essence of what would later evolve into American contractual constitutionalism: (1) the inalienable rights of man and the basis of the bills of rights; (2) the doctrine of delegated powers; (3) the contract theory of the state; (4) popular sovereignty; (5) the right of altering, changing, or abolishing government; and (6) by implication, the doctrine of judicial review inherent in a fundamental law based on the consent of the governed. These were legal notions taken up by later prominent Americans, including James Wilson and Thomas Jefferson. While Wilson was probably the most able expounder of contractual constitutionalism, it was Thomas Jefferson who gave immortality to the rights of man in the Declaration of Independence. Jefferson's classic and almost poetic phrasing of the doctrine of natural law has become a universal inspiration to man to assert his natural rights of freedom and independence and to assume the prerogative of establishing his own political institutions. "We held these truths to be self-evident," states the Declaration,

> that all men are created equal, that they are endowed by their creator with certain inalienable rights, that among these are life, liberty and the pursuit of happiness. That to secure these rights, Governments are instituted among men, deriving their just powers from the consent of the governed. That whenever any Form of Government becomes destructive of these ends, it is the Right of the People to alter or to abolish it, and to substitute new Government laying its foundation on such principles and organizing its powers in such form, as to them shall seem the most likely to effect their safety and Happiness.[84]

CONCLUSION

From Winthrop and his Puritan followers to Adams, Jefferson and the American revolutionaries, Puritanism was clearly a formative ideology that was perpetuated for generations, if not centuries. James Bryce wrote in his landmark study on the American commonwealth that "Someone has said that the American Government and Constitution are based on the theology of Calvin and the philosophy of Hobbes. This at least is true, that there is a hearty Puritanism in the view of human nature which pervades the instrument of 1787. It is the work of men who believed in original sin, and were resolved to leave open for transgressors no door which they could possibly shut."[85]

There is no doubt that Puritanism did, indeed, contribute to the genesis and genius of the American experiment in ordered liberty and orderly pluralism. But the importance of Puritanism lies not in generalizations drawn from a broad historical situation, but in the comprehension of the complex practices, ideals, and institutions of Puritan society, as elucidated through a narrow focus, beginning with the ideal of a godly community that pervaded Puritan jurisprudence. For it is only with a micro perspective that one can begin to discover the very essence of Puritanism as it affected the political culture of early Massachusetts Bay and its divine covenantal notions that later transformed into social compact ideals, ultimately crystallizing into legalistic constitutionalism following the Revolutionary War. Each stage, flawed and disorderly as it was, was a small step that ultimately helped to create and shape the American Constitution and legal system and the American nation as we know it today.

NOTES

1. See generally, Alan Watson, *Legal Transplants: An Approach to Comparative Law* (Athens: University of Georgia Press, 1993).
2. Watson, *Legal Transplants.*
3. William Perkins, "Sermon of 1624," quoted in A. Kuyper, Jr., *Die Vastigheid Des Verbonds* 104 (2nd ed., 1913).
4. David Novak, "Law: Religious or Secular?," *Virginia Law Review* 86, no. 3 (April 2000): 584.
5. According to John Witte, Jr., "Puritan Sources of Enlightenment Liberty," in John M. Owen IV and J. Judd Owen, eds., *Religion, the Enlightenment, and the New Global Order* (New York: Columbia University Press, 2011), 141. More specifically, "covenant" is referred to 286 times in the Old Testament and 24 additional times in the New Testament.
6. Dinu Moga, "John Murray and James B. Torrance on Covenant Theology," *Perichoresis* 17, supp. 1 (Spring 2019): 95.
7. King James edition.
8. Everett H. Emerson, "Calvin and Covenant Theology," *Church History* 25, no. 2 (June 1956): 136.
9. Emerson, "Calvin," 137.
10. Emerson, "Calvin," 137.

11. Zacharias Ursinus, *Catechism* (Heidelberg, 1612), 199–200 (translation by G.W. Williard (Cincinnati: Elm Street Printing Co., 1888).

12. Genesis 17:4.

13. Everett H. Emerson, *Puritanism in America, 1620-1750* (Boston: Twayne Publishers, 1977), 49.

14. Emerson, *Puritanism*, 52.

15. Emerson, *Puritanism*, 49.

16. Perry Miller, *The New England Mind* (Cambridge: Harvard University Press, 1982), 415.

17. Miller, *The New England Mind*, 413.

18. John Winthrop, "A Model of Christian Charity," in a speech delivered aboard the *Arbella* on the voyage to New England (1630), in Perry Miller and Thomas Johnson, eds., *The Puritans—A Sourcebook of their Writings*, Vol. I (New York: Harper and Row, 1963), 199.

19. John Winthrop, *The Winthrop Papers*, 5 vols., Allyn B. Forbes, ed. (Boston: Massachusetts Historical Society, 1931-1947), vol. 2, 292 [hereinafter, *The Winthrop Papers*].

20. Winthrop, *The Winthrop Papers*, vol. 2, 292.

21. Winthrop, *The Winthrop Papers*, vol. 2, 290.

22. Quoted in Darrett B. Rutman, "The Mirror of Puritan Authority," in George M. Waller, ed., *Puritanism in Early America* (Lexington: D.C. Heath. & Co., 1973), 12.

23. Winthrop, *The Winthrop Papers*, vol. 2, 282.

24. Winthrop, "*The Winthrop Papers*, vol. 3, 422–423.

25. Winthrop, "*The Winthrop Papers*, vol. 3, 423.

26. John Winthrop, *Winthrop's Journal, History of New England, 1630 to 1649*, 2 vols. (New York: Charles Scribner's Sons, 1908), vol. II, 238 [hereinafter, *Winthrop's Journal*].

27. Miller, *The New England Mind*, 420.

28. Miller, *The New England Mind*, 420.

29. Perry Miller, *Errand into the Wilderness* (Cambridge: Harvard University Press, 1981), 149.

30. Miller, *Errand*, 149.

31. Rutman, "The Mirror of Puritan Authority," 81.

32. King James edition.

33. Esin Orucu, "Law as Transposition," *International and Comparative Law Quarterly* 51, no. 2 (April 2002): 205.

34. *Winthrop's Journal*, vol. I, 191.

35. *Winthrop's Journal*, vol. II, 65–66.

36. Samuel Elist Morison, *Builders of the Bay Colony* (Boston: Northeastern University Press, 1981), 231.

37. Morison, *Builders,* 232.

38. Morison, *Builders,* 232.

39. Morison, *Builders*, 232.

40. Rutman, "The Mirror of Puritan Authority," 236.

41. Rutman, "The Mirror of Puritan Authority," 160.

42. Morison, *Builders*, 233.

43. George Lee Haskins, "The Government of the Massachusetts Bay Colony, 1630-1650," in Sydney V. James, ed., *The New England Puritans* (New York: Harper and Row, 1968), 82.

44. Morison, *Builders*, 233.

45. Morison, *Builders*, 234.

46. John Cotton, for example, recognized that Massachusetts Bay was not a theocracy in his letter to Lord Say and Seal. He stated: "that magistrates are neither chosen to office in church, nor do govern by directions from the church, but by civil laws". See Perry Miller and Thomas Johnson, eds., *The Puritans—A Sourcebook of their Writings*, vol. I (New York: Harper and Row, 1963), 210. Evidence of this separation between church and state is also contained in Winthrop's "Model of Christian Charity" where the settlers sought "to seek out a place of cohabitation and consortship under a due form of government *both civil and ecclesiastical*" [emphasis added]. See Alan Heimert and Andrew Delbanco, eds., *The Puritans in America* (Cambridge: Harvard University Press, 1985), 89.

47. Aaron B. Seidman, "Church and State in the Early Years of the Massachusetts Bay Colony," *New England Quarterly* 18, no. 2 (June 1945): 216.

48. Seidman, "Church and State," 216.

49. Seidman, "Church and State," 216–217.

50. Miller, *The New England Mind*, 416.

51. Miller, *The New England Mind*, 410.

52. Miller, *The New England Mind*, 410.

53. Rutman, "The Mirror of Puritan Authority," 59.

54. Rutman, "The Mirror of Puritan Authority," 59.

55. Miller and Johnson, *The Puritans*, 190.

56. Digby E. Baltzell, *Puritan Boston and Quaker Philadelphia* (Boston: Beacon Press, 1982), 124–125.

57. Miller and Johnson, *The Puritans*, 188.

58. Edmund S. Morgan, *The Puritan Family* (New York: Harper and Row, 1966), 26.

59. Miller and Johnson, *The Puritans*, 24.

60. Timothy H. Breen, *Puritans and Adventurers* (New York: Oxford University Press, 1980), xvi.

61. Baltzell, *Puritan Boston*, 4.

62. Bernard Bailyn, *The Ideological Origins of the American Revolution* (Cambridge: Harvard University Press, 1980), 32–33.

63. Bailyn, *Ideological Origins*, 32.

64. Quoted in Baltzell, *Puritan Boston*, 7.

65. See, for example, T.H. Breen, *Puritans and Adventurers* (New York: Oxford University Press, 1980), xi–xviii.

66. Alexis De Tocqueville, *Democracy in America*, George Lawrence, trans., J.P. Mayer, ed. (New York: Doubleday & Co., 1969), 38, 279.

67. De Tocqueville, *Democracy in America*, 39.

68. Alexander Hamilton, James Madison, and John Jay, *The Federalist Papers* (New York: Bantam Books, 1982), no. 2, 7 (John Jay).

69. Louis Hartz et al., *The Founding of New Societies* (New York: Harcourt Brace, 1964), 7.

70. Louis Hartz et al., *The Founding of New Societies*, 5.

71. Louis Hartz et al., *The Founding of New Societies*, 11.

72. Seymour M. Lipset, *The First New Nation: The United States in Historical and Comparative Perspective* (New York: W.W. Norton and Co., 1979), 16.

73. Seymour M. Lipset, *The First New Nation*, 7.

74. Richard P. Gildrie, *Salem, Massachusetts 1626-1683* (Charlottesville: University Press of Virginia, 1975), ix.

75. R. Taylor, M. Kline and G. Lint, eds., *Papers of John Adams*, 2 vols. (Cambridge: Belknap Press, 1977), 1:114–116.

76. Taylor, Kline and Lint, *Papers of John Adams*, 1:114–116.

77. Taylor, Kline and Lint, *Papers of John Adams*, 1:114–116.

78. Francis J. Bremer, "Would John Adams have called John Winthrop a 'Founding Father?'" *Common Place: The Journal of Early American Life* 4, no. 3 (April 2004), http://commonplace.online/article/would-john-adams.

79. Francis Bremer, "Would John Adams".

80. Quincy 51 (Mass. 1761); 8 Viner 118 (1761).

81. John Adams, *The Works of John Adams*, 10 vols., vol. 10, Charles Francis Adams, ed. (Boston: Little, Brown and Co., 1865), 275.

82. Quincy 51 (Mass. 1761); 8 Viner 118 (1761).

83. John Adams, *The Works of John Adams*, vol. 10, 248.

84. Thomas Jefferson et al., *The Declaration of Independence* (Jackson: Applewood Books, 1997), 3–4.

85. James Bryce, *The American Commonwealth*, 2 vols., vol. 1 (Boston: Little, Brown and Co, 1889), 299.

REFERENCES

Adams, John. *Papers of John Adams*. Edited by Robert Taylor and Mary-Jo Kline Gregg L. Lint. Cambridge: Belknap Press of Harvard University Press, 1977.

———. *The Works of John Adams, Second President of the United States*. Boston: Little, Brown, 1865.

Bailyn, Bernard. *The Ideological Origins of the American Revolution*. Cambridge, MA: Harvard University Press, 1980.

Baltzell, E. Digby. *Puritan Boston & Quaker Philadelphia*. Boston: Beacon Press, 1982.

Breen, Timothy H. Puritans and Adventurers. *Change and Persistence in Early America*. New York: Oxford University Press, 1980.

Bremer, Francis J. "Would John Adams Have Called John Winthrop A 'Founding Father'?" *Common Place: The Journal of Early American Life* 4, no. 3 (2004).

Bryce, James Bryce. *The American Commonwealth*. Boston: Little, Brown and Co, 1889.

de Tocqueville, Alexis. *Democracy in America*. Translated by George Lawrence. Edited by J. P. Mayer. New York: Doubleday & Co, 1969.

Emerson, Everett H. "Calvin and Covenant Theology." *Church History* 25, no. 2 (1956): 136–44.

———. *Puritanism in America 1620–1750*. Vol. 71. Boston: Twayne Publ., 1977.

Gildrie, Richard P. *Salem, Massachusetts, 1626–1683: A Covenant Community*. Charlottesville: University of Virginia Press, 1975.

Hamilton, Alexander, James Madison, and John Jay. *The Federalist Papers*. New York: Bantam Books, 1982.

Hartz, Louis. *The Founding of New Societies*. New York: Harcourt Brace, 1964.

Haskins, George Lee. "The Government of the Massachusetts Bay Colony." In *The New England Puritans*, edited by Sydney V. James. New York: Harper and Row, 1968.

Heimert, Alan, and Andrew Delbanco. *The Puritans in America: A Narrative Anthology*. Cambridge, MA: Harvard University Press, 1985.

Jefferson, Thomas. *The Declaration of Independence*. Jackson: Applewood Books, 1997.

Kuyper, Abraham, Jr. *De Vastigheid Des Verbond*. 2nd ed. Amsterdam Kirchner, 1913.

Lipset, Seymour M. *The First New Nation: The United States in Historical and Comparative Perspective*. New York: W.W. Norton and Co, 1979.

Miller, Perry. *Errand into the Wilderness*. Cambridge, MA: Harvard University Press, 1981.

———. *The New England Mind: The Seventeenth Century*. Cambridge, MA: Harvard University Press, 1982.

Miller, Perry, and Thomas H. Johnson. *The Puritans: A Sourcebook of Their Writings*. New York: Harper and Row, 1963.

Moga, Dinu. "John Murray and James B. Torrance on Covenant Theology." *Perichoresis* 17, no. s1 (2019): 91–117.

Morgan, Edmund S. *The Puritan Family*. New York: Harper and Row, 1966.

Morison, Samuel Eliot. *Builders of the Bay Colony*. Boston: Northeastern University Press, 1981.

Novak, David. "Law: Religious or Secular." *Virginia Law Review* 86 (2000): 569.

Örücü, Esin. "Law as Transposition." *International & Comparative Law Quarterly* 51, no. 2 (2002): 205–23.

Rutman, Darrett B. "The Mirror of Puritan Authority." In *Puritanism in Early America*, edited by George M. Waller, 65–79. Lexington: D.C. Heath. & Co, 1973.

Seidman, Aaron B. "Church and State in the Early Years of the Massachusetts Bay Colony." *New England Quarterly* (1945): 211–33.

Ursinus, Zacharias. *Commentary on the Heidelberg Catechism*. Translated by G. W. Williard. Cincinnati: Elm Street Printing Co, 1888.

Watson, Alan. *Legal Transplants: An Approach to Comparative Law*. Georgia: University of Georgia Press, 1993.

Winthrop, John. "A Model of Christian Charity." In *The Puritans—A Sourcebook of Their Writings*, edited by Perry Miller and Thomas Johnson, 199. New York: Harper and Row, 1963.

———. "Winthrop Papers, 5 Vols." In *Massachusetts Historical Society*, edited by Allyn B. Forbes. Boston, 1931–1947.

———. *Winthrop's Journal History of New England, 1630–1649.* Vol. 2. New York: C. Scribner's Sons, 1908.

Witte, John. "6. Puritan Sources of Enlightenment Liberty." In *Religion, the Enlightenment, and the New Global Order*, edited by John M. Owen IV and J. Judd Owen, 140–73. New York: Columbia University Press, 2011.

Chapter 8

The Salem Witch Trials and the Decay of the Great Puritan Experiment

Rachel Christ-Doane

On a dry and windy day in early February 1693, the proceedings of the Massachusetts Supreme Court of Judicature were violently interrupted. Chief Justice William Stoughton stormed from the session having just been informed eight condemned witches had been given personal reprieves by the governor himself.[1] This dramatic scene marked the conclusion of the Salem witch trials. Over the course of the year 1692, nineteen people were hanged, one man tortured to death, at least five people died in prison, and approximately 200 people were accused of witchcraft, arrested and jailed.

The witchcraft trials of 1692 took place at a pivotal moment for the Massachusetts Bay Colony, as Puritan dominance waned and reluctantly gave way to a more inclusive Protestant government. In an environment of ever-growing fear and uncertainty, as worries about the safety and rights of the colonists, as well as the fate of the Great Puritan experiment, continued to grow, a witchcraft panic was ignited. Though witchcraft suspicions were common in New England, they rarely escalated to trial, and even less frequently resulted in conviction. However, for one terrible year, the order that previously governed this society, one predicated on personal responsibility and moral leadership, broke down. These events were not only the last major series of witchcraft trials in the English colonies, but effectively signaled the end of Puritan dominance in America.

There are many explanations as to what drove the strange and terrible events that overtook Essex County in the year 1692. The complexity of these events requires a diverse array of methodologies. Early scholarship often focused on the accusers, arguing these events were the result of wicked adolescent girls who accused others to deflect their own guilt after dabbling in forbidden fortune telling.[2] In 1974, historians Paul Boyer and Stephen Nissenbaum forged a new trail, instead arguing the trials could be best understood through the socio-economic and political divisions within the local population. As a result of this work, scholars began delving deeper into the Salem story. Some, such as Dr. Linnda Caporael, focused on medical and environmental factors that may have triggered the accusations.[3] Others, such as John Demos and Mary Beth Norton, explored the influence of social and physiological pressures.[4] More recently, Emerson Baker highlighted the convergence of political, religious, and environmental events, creating a calamitous "perfect storm" in 1692.[5]

This chapter will consider how the breakdown of two essential facets of Puritan society, the role of self-administered justice and the importance of elder (particularly ministerial) leadership, resulted in the Salem catastrophe. Though a successful covenant society had existed in New England for the better part of a century, the decline of Puritan dominance, signaled by the arrival of a new colonial charter in 1692, resulted in a breakdown of order during the late seventeenth century.[6]

Ever vigilant in their duty to uphold their covenant with God, residents of New England naturally harbored suspicions and personal misgivings against their neighbors' potentially sinful behavior. Though normally restrained by both the ministry and the law, these stopgaps were disrupted in 1692, first in Salem Village due to actions of local minister Samuel Parris, and then in the greater colony, as a result of the reckless choices by the judges who oversaw the witchcraft trials. Decades of distrust, anxiety, and gossip quickly mutated into witchcraft accusations, as the powerful fire of suspicion and terror burned throughout Essex County. Hundreds of people, from all levels of society, were sent to jail. Though this breakdown in order was eventually reversed, and stability restored, these were the largest and deadliest witchcraft trials to ever take place in North America.

A CITY UPON A HILL

In 1630, John Winthrop, future governor of Plymouth Colony, gave a speech to his fellow pilgrims aboard the ship *Arabella*. These travelers were part of the Great Puritan migration, a period between 1620 and 1640 when pilgrims made the dangerous voyage across the Atlantic in hope of creating a new world where they could practice religion as they saw fit, free from the corrupting influence of the Church of England. Emphasizing the stakes at hand, Winthrop reminded his fellow passengers of their obligations to one another, as this new world would be "a City upon a Hill, the eyes of all people are upon us." As he outlined the significance of this expedition, Winthrop cautioned his fellow passengers, reminding them "if we shall deal falsely with our God in his work we have undertaken and so cause him to withdraw his present help from us, we shall be made a story and a byword through the world."[7]

Arriving in a new and foreign land, these settlers saw themselves as the chosen people, who, having entered into a covenant with God, had an opportunity to create a society that would honor and fulfill the expectations of this special relationship. As Calvinists, the Puritans believed in pre-destination. This notion held that from the time a person was born they were either destined for heaven or for hell. Over the course of one's life, each person was expected to examine their soul to determine if they were possibly one of the chosen few—known as Visible Saints. Rather than describing a location of worship, a Church referred to a gathering of Visible Saints. It was these individuals who were entrusted to govern the community, and colony.

Every institution, from the government to the family, was intended to strengthen moral reform and encourage each person to live up to their covenantal responsibilities. Internalized authority was paramount; whether destined for heaven or for hell, every person was expected to submit to God's will, as expressed by the Bible. Rather than establishing a theocracy, the New England colonists created Bible commonwealths. In these communities, all were expected to uphold the covenant, a task that required constant vigilance so as to identify and correct those who failed to live up to this shared responsibility.

Though not every person was destined for heaven, it was believed the actions of each person affected the greater community. Misfortune could be interpreted as either a sign of God's displeasure or as a judgment against the imperfections of one among them. "Everyone shared the consequences of wrong acts. The recommended response to ill-fortune was to search one's fallible soul for defect or compliancy and amend the fault, whether as an individual or, if necessary, as a community," notes historian Marilynne Roach.[8] As John Winthrop underscored in his address on the *Arabella*, the community would thrive or fail *together*. In this environment, neighbors watched neighbors, and gossip spread like wildfire.

THE PERFECT STORM

Founded in 1626, Salem was one of the first settlements in Massachusetts Bay Colony. When Salem's church was founded three years later, a covenant was publicly read and signed by thirty settlers. In this oath, church members affirmed their commitment to "Covenant with the Lord and one with another" and vowed to "bind ourselves in the presence of God, to walk together in all his ways."[9] The covenant of this church, composed by Reverend Francis Higginson, echoed the ambitions of the greater settlement, to work together as a community to create the Kingdom of God on this earth, to be a "city upon a hill." The Salem Church is regarded by many historians as the "prototype of the Massachusetts Bay Colony churches."[10]

Despite the passion of the first generation of settlers, fears about the fate of this Great Puritan Experiment emerged by mid-century. Rather than seeing a significant increase in church membership, a sure signal of the colony's success, doubts about their salvation plagued the second generation. "Many lacked the zeal of their parents and had failed to experience the personal conversion experience wherein God let them know they were among the elect, the saints destined for salvation in heaven," observes Emerson Baker.[11] As fewer people were eligible to receive the sacraments, including baptism for their children, spiritual leaders worried about the fate of the colony should they fail to live up to their covenantal responsibilities.

To make matters worse, as fears were growing about the spiritual state of the colony, a string of ostensibly never-ending misfortune plagued the colonists throughout the second half of the seventeenth century. By the late 1670s, the colonists were fighting a bloody and escalating conflict with Indigenous tribes and their French allies. As highlighted by Mary Beth Norton, these wars not only resulted in massive loss of life, but in economic devastation, both in terms of inflation and loss of property.[12] To make matters worse still, smallpox, a deadly and highly infectious disease, was spreading through the colony. Even Mother Nature seemed to oppose the young settlement, as the worst of the Little Ice Age hit New England in the last decades of the century, resulting in unusually cold winters and extremely dry, hot summers.[13]

Perhaps worst of all, in 1684, King Charles II revoked all charters under English dominion, only renewing them after a demonstration of loyalty to the crown. As the original colonial charter had been modified from a commercial charter, Massachusetts Bay had been remarkably independent for decades, more so than any other colony. Without this important document, the settlement lost considerable autonomy, including the ability to elect its own governing officials. Concerns over land ownership emerged, as the removal of the charter voided existing land titles. Most significantly, without the charter, the colony was no longer dominated exclusively by Puritan ideology.

When a royal governor, Sir Edmund Andros, arrived to assume authority of the provisional government in 1686, the colony was plunged into further distress. A highly unpopular official, Governor Andros altered laws, passed new taxes, and enforced toleration for all Protestant religions. Public scorn and resentment of his government festered throughout the colony. Back in England, as distinguished Boston minister Increase Mather attempted to negotiate a new charter, one ideally favorable to Puritan interests, the Glorious Revolution erupted, resulting in the rule of William and Mary.[14] Negotiations began all over again.

When the new charter was finally issued in 1691, many felt Reverend Mather had not pushed hard enough to retain Puritan control. Under the new charter, Massachusetts Bay Colony was expanded to include Maine and Plymouth Colony, creating the Dominion of Massachusetts Province. Though they now had the freedom to elect most of their own governing officials, the legal toleration of all Protestant religions was also permanently enforced. As Baker notes, "the charter confirmed the change already made by the provisional government—freemen of the colony no longer needed to be members of the Puritan church."[15] Though issued in 1691, this new charter would not land in the colony until May 1692, arriving with a new governor in the midst of an ever-worsening witchcraft panic.

THE WOES OF SAMUEL PARRIS

Amidst the difficulties of the greater colony, there were mounting troubles in Salem. For decades inhabitants of a rural, inland section of Salem known as "Salem Village," had hoped to gain independence. Despite having a minimal voice in local governance, the villagers were required to pay taxes to Salem Town. They also had to travel miles each week, in all manner of weather, to attend religious services, as the village had no meetinghouse of its own. After years of struggle, in 1672 the General Court finally granted Salem Village the right to form their own parish.[16] Through the first step toward future independence, factional divides quickly emerged as the village searched for an appropriate ministerial candidate, resulting in a decades-long dispute.

In June 1688, Reverend Parris arrived in Salem Village. He was the fourth ministerial candidate in just sixteen years. In his youth, Parris had failed as a merchant, and now found himself the minister of a contentious rural community. To make matters worse, he appears to have been a difficult man to please. Before his ordination, he issued a list of requests, including an annual allotment of firewood and title rights to the parsonage. Though eventually an agreement was made, many prickled at his unwavering insistence. Far from bringing the community together, existing fissures deepened, as factions sided for and against the new minister.

At the ordination of Samuel Parris, a covenant for the newly formed Salem Village church was read aloud and signed by twenty-five men and women. With the signing of this covenant, parishioners vowed to "submit to the order, Discipline, and Government of Christ in this his Church" as well as to the "ministerial teaching, guidance, and oversight of the Elder, (or Elders) thereof" and agreed to engage in "mutual brotherly watchfulness according to Gospel Rules."[17] By 1690, only fifty-three people had signed the covenant, equating to about one-quarter of the village's adult population.[18] Though technically having assumed the role of the village's moral leader, expected to guide the path of righteous behavior, Samuel Parris began his term as a minister in the midst of controversy, without the trust of many of his new parishioners.

UNDER AN EVIL HAND

Through the winter of 1691, trouble plagued the village's newest minister. Those who had opposed his ordination made their displeasure known by refusing to contribute to his salary. As historian Richard Trask notes, "A good portion of the inhabitants were unwilling to give Parris, both as to his personal comfort among them and in their acknowledgment of him as their spiritual guide, either their generosity of spirit or of purse."[19] Months went by with no resolve. Over the course of the winter, Parris's sermons emphasized the watchfulness of the Church over sinners, perhaps a pointed reminder to those who opposed him.

To make matters worse, by January 1692, Reverend Parris's 9-year-old daughter, Betty Parris, and 11-year-old niece, Abigail Williams, began showing symptoms of a strange and disturbing illness. The girls twitched and moaned, screamed and flung themselves about the room. They clutched their heads and made animal sounds. The alarmed parents tried the usual remedies— various medicinal concoctions, fasting, prayer, all to no avail. After weeks with no improvement a local doctor examined the girls, and made an alarming diagnosis—the children, he said, were "under an evil hand." They were tormented by witchcraft.

In the seventeenth century, the witch was the antithesis of the Puritan saint. A witch was believed to be a person who had forsaken God and covenanted with the Devil. From time to time, colonists believed themselves to be confronted with these accomplices of Satan's hellish crusade— though suspicions rarely resulted in a trial. While witchcraft was often suspected following personal misfortune, English law required a strict standard of evidence to prove an accusation. As Marilynne Roach observes, "for the most part, communities held uneasy truces with resident suspects against whom they could prove nothing definite. They suspected more individuals than they ever took to court, where magistrates were usually reluctant to convict and where the accused might well sue them for slander."[20]

By 1692, however, the colonists had good reason to fear the Devil's servants were at work. The loss of the charter, ongoing wars to the North, recent smallpox outbreaks, and severe weather could easily be interpreted as demonic. In his 1684 book *An Essay for the Recording of Illustrious Providences*, Increase Mather predicted God would serve judgment on New England if the colony remained on its current course. His son, Cotton Mather, a young minister poised to follow in the steps of his father, added more credence to this anxiety when he published an account of a recent case of bewitchment in Boston. This 1689 work *Memorable Providences Relating to Witchcrafts and Possessions* described the bewitchment of the Goodwin children, a case which resulted in the colony's first witchcraft execution in decades. The younger Mather reminded his readers it was dangerous to doubt the existence of witchcraft, and that "no age passes without some apparent demonstration of it."[21] A member of the third generation of New England's ministers, Cotton Mather and his contemporaries were aware of the precarious position of the colony. It was of the utmost importance that the covenant remained intact, and disturbing to conceive it might be in grave danger on their watch.

In Salem Village, word quickly spread that witchcraft was at work in Reverend's own home. Toward the end of February, on a day when Samuel Parris and his wife were away, neighbor Mary Sibley arrived with a solution. Why not try folk magic? Sibley directed John Indian and Tituba, enslaved people owned by Samuel Parris, to create a witch cake. Derived from English folk tradition, this cake was a mixture of rye meal and the urine of the bewitched girls. This odious concoction was then formed into a loaf, baked in hot ashes, and fed to a dog. It was believed the person responsible for the bewitchment would hopefully be wounded as a result and possibly reveal themselves in turn. Though magic was discouraged, considered a dangerous invitation to the Devil, many New Englanders continued to utilize these older traditions. It was not uncommon to resort to such a practice, particularly if bewitchment was feared.

Reverend Parris was enraged to find magic had been attempted in his house. Far from curing the illness, around the time of the witch cake experiment, two more girls reported similar torment; 12-year-old Ann Putnam Jr, a neighbor, and Elizabeth Hubbard, the 17-year-old niece of William Griggs, a local physician (likely the doctor who pronounced the girls bewitched). They too, it was believed, were now tormented by witchcraft.

After admonishing Mary Sibley in private, Reverend Parris brought the matter to the congregation. When faced with the threat of witchcraft in the community, "ministers generally recommended caution, and often concealed the names of suspects to protect them," notes Roach.[22] Though local ministers advised Parris to "sit still and wait upon the Providence of God to see what time might discover," in late March the Reverend informed his congregation that as a result of this blasphemous act of folk magic "the Devil hath been raised among us, and his rage is vehement and terrible, and when he shall be silenced, the Lord only knows."[23] Far from offering measured leadership in a time of crisis, Samuel Parris stoked the fear quickly engulfing his congregation.

At this time, some believed a witch could project a spectral version of themselves beyond the bounds of their physical body to harm unwitting victims, and this apparition could potentially be correctly identified by the victim. Faced with a growing crisis, the afflicted girls were asked to identify those who tormented them. Eventually, they claimed to recognize specters of three witches—Tituba, the enslaved woman owned by the Parris family, and two local women, Sarah Good and Sarah Osborne. By February 29, Thomas Putnam, father of the afflicted Ann, along with three other village residents, brought the matter to the Salem magistrates and arrest warrants were issued.

At this point, these events were not yet atypical for the colony. Reports of young people tormented by witchcraft, as was the case of the Goodwin children, surfaced from time to time. However, the environment of heightened fear combined with the colony's precarious legal situation, would now lead to several unusual procedural decisions. Contrary to custom, the first arrests came without the requirement of providing bond. At this time, a criminal complaint required the person making the accusation to post bond, an assurance the case was significant enough to warrant legal action and that they intended to see the complaint through. As Bernard Rosenthal observes, this departure from English law now "made charges of witchcraft easier to lodge, and by the time the law began to be followed, as it eventually did, matters may have spread too far."[24] Moreover, evidence was also gathered from all four of the afflicted witnesses, despite the fact that three of the four were under the age of 14. In the 1690s, English jurists typically required children to be above the age of 14 if they were to testify in a capital felony case.[25] As such, of the first four individuals to be afflicted in 1692, only one, 17-year-old Elizabeth Hubbard, was technically of age to provide admissible evidence.

On March 1, Sarah Good, Sarah Osborne, and Tituba were examined before local magistrates Jonathan Corwin and John Hathorne in the Salem Village meetinghouse. Notably, the magistrates had elected to conduct these preliminary examinations publicly, rather than in private (as was tradition). This would result in explosive and shocking scenes, as the afflicted fainted, screamed, and thrashed before a sizable crowd of alarmed onlookers. The entire village was thus well aware of, and likely terrified by, these accusations.

The first to be examined was Sarah Good. Contemporary accounts indicate Goody Good fit the typical description of a colonial witch. Marilynne Roach astutely notes, "A witch's nature was turbulent, and women, then as later, needed to do far less than men to seem so."[26] At the age of 38, Sarah Good was homeless with two young children and an indigent husband. Relatives and neighbors would later testify that she was an unwelcome houseguest, and that misfortune often followed if and when she was turned away. Though she fervently maintained her innocence, records from this initial examination suggest her guilt was presumed by many in the community.

The second to be examined was Sarah Osborne. Like Sarah Good, Goody Osborne maintained her innocence, stating "she was more like to be bewitched than that she was a witch."[27] She too was evidently already suspected by some within the community, as during her examination members of the crowd, including her own husband, added that she had not been to church for over a year, though she claimed this was due to illness. Norton observes these early examinations established a pattern that would soon be repeated again and again, "The magistrates, assuming guilt; the accused, struggling to respond to the charges, the afflicted, demonstrating their torments; and the audience, actively involving themselves in the exchanges by offering information and commentaries."[28]

Tituba was the last to face the magistrates. Though her origins are unknown, it is possible she was an Arawak Indian from South America and was purchased by Samuel Parris while he lived in Barbados.[29] Though she initially maintained her innocence, eventually Tituba was forced to confess. As an enslaved person who lived in the home where the affliction began, she was certainly aware of her extreme vulnerability— she was the perfect scapegoat for such a crime. Over the course of several examinations in the days to come, both in public and private, Tituba followed the magistrates leading questions, spinning an elaborate tale. Contemporary author and critic of the witchcraft trials, Robert Calef, notes that Tituba may have been beaten by Samuel Parris to force her to confess. "Her master did beat her, and otherways abuse her, to make her confesse and accuse (such as he called) her sister-witches," says Calef.[30] If Calef is to be believed, Samuel Parris was at least in part responsible for the escalation that followed.

Tituba told the magistrates the Devil had threatened to kill her if she did not hurt the children. She told tales of animals who came to her, telling her to serve the Devil, and flying through the night on a stick. In addition to herself, she told the magistrates there were four women and one man, including Sarah Good and Sarah Osborn, who tormented the children as well.[31] This particular revelation was beyond alarming. Not only did the magistrates have a witch in their midst, but Tituba's confession suggested there was a much larger conspiracy at hand.

All three women were held in prison to await trial. The community was left to reflect on the severity of the situation. Perhaps the warnings of Increase Mather were coming to fruition—the Devil had indeed arrived to wage war in New England.

STOKING THE FIRE

Though Betty Parris, Abigail Williams, and Elizabeth Hubbard temporarily recovered after these arrests, the torment of young Ann Putnam Jr. continued.

Ann soon claimed to be tormented by other local witches. In short order, Ann Putnam Jr. would become one of the most active of the afflicted witnesses. In 1867, Salem historian Charles Upham referred to this 12-year-old girl as "the leading agent in all the mischief that followed."[32]

While the story that Ann Jr. was part of a circle of girls who met at the parsonage to learn forbidden magic (first described by Charles Upham and further popularized by Arthur Miller's 1950 play *The Crucible*) has been definitively refuted, Ann certainly would have known Betty Parris and Abigail Williams. These girls lived in the same general area and were close in age. When Betty and Abigail first became ill in January, Ann Jr. would likely have heard about, or even possibly seen, the affliction firsthand.

Among the first specters named by Ann Jr. following the initial arrests was Martha Corey. Although not without an unblemished past (having given birth c. 1677 to an illegitimate son, later described as "mulatto"), unlike the other suspects, Goody Corey was a member of the Salem Village Church. Having been accepted to the church only a few years prior, Martha Corey was now among the Visible Saints of the community. The naming of Goodwife Corey marked a notable shift in the pattern of accusation. If the Devil had in fact recruited a church member, this situation was even more dangerous than previously imagined. Given her status, Edward Putnam (Ann's uncle) and Salem Village resident Ezekiel Cheever visited Goodwife Corey at home, allowing her to address the charges before lodging a formal accusation. On the way they stopped at Thomas Putnam's home to ask Ann Putnam Jr. what Goodwife Corey's specter was wearing that day—a test hoped to perhaps validate the identity of the invisible witch. When confronted with this question, Ann claimed she was struck blind by the specter, and could not see her clothing.

When the men arrived at Martha Corey's home, she remarked that she knew why they had come and that they would want to see what clothing she wore. Despite her declarations of innocence, Martha's predication of the clothing test was considered suspicious. Two days later, Ann's father invited Goodwife Corey to his home to face the child directly. Upon her arrival, both Ann and Mercy Lewis (a 17-year-old servant employed by the Putnams) became visibly anguished. Ann claimed to see a vision of a man being roasted on a spit in her parents' hearth and said, "Goody Corey, you be a turning of it."[33] From this point onward, both Ann Putnam Jr. and Mercy Lewis would regularly report spectral torment.

Both as the head of a household and a member of the Salem Village Church, Thomas Putnam was yet another village elder, a Visible Saint, whose actions were far from reassuring. In the weeks and months that followed, Thomas Putnam would appear repeatedly before local magistrates to lodge accusations. Putnam only ceased to bring forth new accusations in July when magistrates once again began demanding bond. The motivations of

Thomas Putnam have been the subject of considerable scholarship. In 1974, Paul Boyer and Stephen Nissenbaum's seminal work *Salem Possessed: The Social Origins of Witchcraft* highlighted the socio-economic divisions and political tension among the inhabitants of Salem, which they argue contributed to the pattern of accusation in 1692. Though in recent years some have argued the divisions drawn by Boyer and Nissenbaum are not as influential as once believed, the impact of the political and socio-economic struggle within Salem Village cannot be discounted.[34]

The behavior of Thomas Putnam, for example, must be placed within this framework. Thomas was a third-generation member of the Putnam family in Salem Village. While this family had long been among the most powerful in the village, their influence was waning in the decades leading up to 1692. The Putnam family owned land away from the water, and as a result were cut off from the markets and opportunities of Salem Town. As time went on, the Putnam clan became increasingly confined to in-land property that was ever more stretched to accommodate the growing family. To make matters worse, in 1666, Thomas's father, Thomas Putnam Sr., remarried and four years later, another son, Joseph Putnam, was born. With the birth of this child came complications for Thomas and his brothers. In his will, Thomas Sr. left his second wife and their son the prime parts of his homestead—an arrangement which evidently left the sons from his first marriage feeling slighted. To make matters worse, when his father-in-law, George Carr, died in 1682, he too left behind a controversial will. Yet again, Thomas went to court, along with his two brothers-in-law, to dispute the will. And yet again, he failed to acquire his wife's expected inheritance. Although still a member of an established and affluent family, by the 1690s, Thomas Putnam Jr. was seeing his prospects diminish.

Throughout the year 1692, Thomas's daughter, wife, and servant would accuse dozens of people of practicing witchcraft, some of whom had clashed with the Putnam family in the past, and others chosen seemingly at random. While determining the cause of the affliction of these members of the Putnam household is outside the scope of this chapter, it is significant to note the driving role Thomas Jr. played in the events of 1692. Beyond bringing forward accusations from his household, Thomas Putnam also served the proceedings as a secretary of the court. In recent years, historians have detected noticeable consistency in Putnam's descriptions of the afflicted and accused. According to Emerson Baker, this consistency is significant, as "Putnam's depositions had a very high success rate in getting grand juries to return indictments against the accused."[35] While the actions of Thomas Putnam could be interpreted as driven by paternal concern for the health and safety of his family and community, rather than as insidiously based in his own self-interest, his actions directly resulted in the arrests of dozens of people in 1692.

With prominent church members such as Thomas Putnam in the lead, more and more accusations were brought before the magistrates, and a growing number were committed to jail to await trial. The mysterious affliction had now crept well beyond the parsonage neighborhood. Maids accused their mistresses of signing the Devil's book. Refugees from the Native Wars told horrifying stories of spectral torment, perhaps conflating past trauma with present danger. Church members with an unblemished past, such as 71-year-old Rebecca Nurse, were accused of witchcraft, brought before the magistrates, and jailed. Even Reverend George Burroughs, former minister of Salem Village, was sighted in spectral form by the afflicted. By late April, matters had escalated far beyond what was ordinary.

THE SPECTRAL EVIDENCE DILEMMA

Though arrests and pre-trial examinations had been going on for months, formal trials could not yet be held in Massachusetts, as the colony was still without its charter. Even when the charter finally arrived in May, accompanied by a new Royal Governor, Sir William Phips, there was still much to be done before business could resume as usual. The new charter required colonial law to be rewritten and approved by the English parliament. As a result, Massachusetts law was still uncertain until elections could be held and laws formally rewritten and approved. Boyer and Nissenbaum make note of the unhappy irony, as "the most severe challenge to confront the judicial system of Massachusetts during the entire colonial period came at the moment when the system was nearly immobilized."[36]

Immediately upon arrival, Governor Phips was faced not only with the ongoing war to the North, but with a witchcraft crisis unlike anything previously experienced in the English colonies. By this time, the chain of accusation had been allowed to run wild, largely unchecked. A small group of adult women, and a few men, had now joined the ranks of the afflicted witnesses. The inclusion of complaints from grown, married women, some of whom were full church members, surely increased anxiety. Something needed to be done.

Given that jails in Salem, Boston, Ipswich, and Cambridge were quickly filling with witchcraft suspects, the newly appointed governor moved swiftly. A fortnight after his arrival, with freshly appointed officials in place, a temporary court was established. Due to the present circumstances, a Court of Oyer and Terminer (meaning to hear and to determine) was created, rather than a Superior Court. While this court would oversee various criminal hearings in Suffolk, Essex, and Middlesex counties, its most pressing function was to address the growing body of witchcraft cases.

Lieutenant Governor William Stoughton was appointed Chief Justice over eight judges, several of whom had overseen the recent witchcraft examinations in Salem. Though well-educated, none of these magistrates had formal legal training. This was not an uncommon occurrence in colonial New England, where properly trained lawyers were still sparse among the settlers. However, that is not to say these men were unqualified by the standards of the day. They had all worked as county magistrates under the old charter, and several had even sat on witchcraft cases in the past (none of which had resulted in a conviction).[37] As Emerson Baker notes, despite their lack of formal legal training, "for a generation magistrates had in fact been an important brake on the general public's eagerness to prosecute witches."[38] In this society, careful and cautious judgment was expected in a witchcraft case.

As this new court prepared to face its substantial docket, the magistrates considered the most pressing challenge posed by this particular type of criminal offense— the problem of evidence. Typically, English courts required either a confession or two eye witnesses able and willing to testify to the use of black magic in order to pass a guilty verdict in a witchcraft trial. This strict evidentiary requirement was the reason why conviction rates were typically low in the English colonies.[39] This posed a particular challenge in 1692, as the most significant complaint was of spectral attack.

The business of differentiating between disease and bewitchment, and then further correctly identifying the Devil's agents, was no simple matter in the latter half of the seventeenth century. A crime fixed at the crossroad of religious and legal authority, colonial ministers were trusted to provide sound guidance and moral leadership and were often able to de-escalate matters before they went to court. Most of New England's ministers believed that discerning between the illusions of the Devil and intentional, malevolent magic was not a task to be taken lightly. In his 1684 *An Essay for the Recording of the Illustrious Providences*, Increase Mather expounded upon this matter. This text included reference to the case of 16-year-old Elizabeth Knapp in Groton, Massachusetts. In this case, Knapp reportedly experienced a similar affliction to what was experienced in 1692— she cried, screamed, twitched, and spoke with (what appeared to be) a demonic voice.[40] Though Elizabeth accused her neighbor of bewitching her, her minister, Samuel Willard, was skeptical of the claim. In a stark contrast to the actions of Samuel Parris, Reverend Willard did not seek legal action against the neighbor. Instead, the accused person was brought forward to pray with the tormented girl, "after which [Elizabeth] confessed that Satan had deluded her; making her believe evil of her good Neighbour without any cause."[41] It is true that Samuel Parris, as the father and uncle of the first two afflicted girls, may have been more emotionally entwined and thus less capable of the rational action exhibited by Reverend Samuel Willard. However, Reverend Parris was not the only minister who failed to redirect the panic in 1692.

In fact, Increase Mather's son, Reverend Cotton Mather of Boston, was one such religious leader. Shortly after his appointment to the Court of Oyer and Terminer, Judge John Richards appealed to his minister for advice on the use of spectral evidence. In his response, Reverend Cotton Mather outlined several points for consideration. Notably, he advised "that in the management of the affair in your most worthy hands, you do not lay more stress upon pure specter testimony than it will bear." He went on to say, "it is very certain that the Devils have sometimes represented the shapes of persons not only innocent, but also very virtuous."[42] He states the best way to be certain of guilt is through a credible confession. Beyond that, supernatural knowledge or feats of physical strength, a witch's mark (a deformity or abnormality on a witch's body, given to them by Satan himself), a wound on an accused person that matched the description of the afflicted, or evidence of the creation of poppets *could* indicate guilt. He also added that it was possible for a discontented person to be lured in by the Devil, and in this case advised these "lesser criminals be only scourged with lesser punishments, and also put upon some solemn, open, public, and explicit renunciation of the Devil? I am apt to think the Devils would then cease afflicting the neighborhood."[43] Though this advice was for the most part consistent with previous ministerial leadership, Mather's letter concluded by stating he left the "thorny affair before you," trusting the magistrates would exercise their best judgment. Perhaps Mather could not have been expected to intervene any further, as he trusted these elite men, each of them Visible Saints, to act in the best interests of the colony and heed his words of caution. However, by the time he, along with his father, did more to directly involve themselves in the proceedings, it was far too late.

THE TRIALS BEGIN

Faced with an ever-worsening situation, the Court of Oyer and Terminer met in early June. The first person to be tried before this new court was Bridget Bishop, a resident of Salem Town. Her case was carefully selected by Attorney General Thomas Newton (the only official with formal legal training), as hers' had the most substantial evidence beyond complaints of spectral torment. Goodwife Bishop had been suspected of witchcraft in the past, and had even been brought before the court once before (though on that occasion she was not convicted). There was no short supply of neighbors willing to testify against her. Ten witnesses came forward to recount years of suspicion and mysterious happenings, including reports of poppets (a form of English folk magic) in her home, objects disappearing, and acts of misfortune following confrontations with Goodwife Bishop.

In addition to this evidence, the afflicted added their own claims, alleging Goodwife Bishop had attempted to force them to sign the Devil's book, thus agreeing to a Satanic covenant. Finally, a physical search of Bridget's body was conducted to determine if there was evidence of the Devil's mark. A group of nine women and one male doctor conducted the examination, finding evidence of a "preternatural excrescence of flesh between the pudendum and anus much like teats and not usual in women."[44] Altogether, the evidence was overwhelming. Bridget Bishop was found guilty. On June 10, just over a week after her trial, Bridget Bishop was taken from jail to the edge of town and hanged.

In the immediate aftermath of this first execution, it became apparent that John Richards was not the only judge with questions about proper evidence. Nathaniel Saltonstall quit the court shortly after Bridget Bishop's death. Though the reasons behind his resignation went unrecorded, it is thought he objected to the outcome of the court's first session.[45] Historian Sarah Rivett has argued the Salem trials can best be understood when placed in the context of the wider, trans-Atlantic developments, as these events straddled the emergence of the Enlightenment and Scientific Revolution. The late seventeenth century is frequently framed within popular culture as a brutish, uneducated world. Not only is this an inaccurate representation, but it was, at least in part, the struggle to overcome the contradictions between empiricism and Puritan theology that led to the deadly evidentiary mistakes made during Salem's witchcraft trials. As Rivett observes, in the years leading up to the Salem witch trials, the Puritans "struggled to live contentedly in a world that was certain of divine existence yet faced with the increasing awareness that the invisible was essentially unknowable."[46] How were the magistrates to proceed, when faced with such extensive scenes of visible torment? Could this torment provide empirical evidence of spectral attack?

Three days after the first execution, the Governor's Council asked a group of ministers for additional advice, particularly with regard to the use of spectral evidence. In their response, the ministers, like Reverend Cotton Mather, cautioned that "in the prosecution of these, and all such witchcrafts, there is need of a very critical and exquisite caution, lest by too much credulity for things received only upon the Devil's authority, there by a door opened for a long train of miserable consequences." Though they advised caution, particularly with regard to spectral testimony, the letter again concluded by acknowledging the difficult task at hand and wishing for "the speedy and vigorous prosecution."[47] Though these ministers warned there was danger in relying on spectral evidence, they also made clear that they trusted the justices' judgment to resolve the dangerous matter at hand as quickly as possible.

NEIGHBORS SPEAK OUT

The court met three more times over the coming months. Despite the warning against the use of spectral visions from the ministers in June, this form of evidence continued to hold a significant place in the court's proceedings. The imperative need to resolve matters quickly seems to have encouraged the use of this controversial evidence. When combined with local gossip, this proved to be a deadly combination.

On June 28, the next session of the Court of Oyer and Terminer began with the cases of five women, Rebecca Nurse, Sarah Good, Elizabeth How, Susannah Martin, and Sarah Wildes. Past conflicts with neighbors and relatives were once again brought forward as evidence of their Satanic allegiances. Some of these women had been suspected of witchcraft in the past. The court heard tales of sickness, misfortunes, sudden tragedies (most occurring after an argument or conflict with the accused), all of which were believed to be preternatural.

Samuel and Ruth Perley submitted a deposition describing the illness of their daughter Hannah, who over a period of two years "pined away to skin and bone" until she succumbed to her illness and passed away.[48] According to Samuel Perley, the child named Elizabeth How during her fits, claiming she was the one responsible for the illness. As previously noted, though suspicions of witchcraft (particularly following sudden or severe illness), were common, they did not usually escalate to action, thanks in large part to the intervention of local ministers. This had been the experience of Elizabeth How. During her trial in 1692, Rowley minister Samuel Phillips spoke in Elizabeth's defense, offering a contrasting account of the illness of Hannah Perley. He confirmed the child named Goodwife How during her illness, but informed the court once her fit was over, she no longer remembered naming How. Reverend Phillips also recalled witnessing Hannah's brother call to his sister from his chamber window "Goodwife How is a witch, say she is a witch."[49] In this instance, the Reverend had "rebuked him for his boldness to stir up his sister to accuse the said Goodwife How" and added "no wonder that the child in her fits did mention Goodwife How, when her nearest relations were so frequent in expressing their suspicions in the child's hearing when she was out of her fits."[50] Though the illness of Hannah Perley was enough to spark witchcraft rumors that shadowed Elizabeth How for years, gossip, rumor, and trivial accidents perceived to be preternatural had not been enough to convict someone for witchcraft. That is, not until 1692.

The supremely unusual progression of these trials, however, is best illustrated by the trial of Rebecca Nurse. Goodwife Nurse was a 71-year-old resident of Salem Village. She had raised eight children to adulthood, was a member of the Salem Town Church, and was known to be hardworking and responsible. Rebecca was no ordinary witchcraft suspect. After her arrest in late March, the Nurse family quickly rallied to her defense. In the weeks before her trial, a petition was circulated in support, signed by thirty-nine people. During her trial, numerous friends, neighbors, and relatives came forward to speak on behalf of Rebeca Nurse, attesting to a life of charity, hard work, and faith in God.

Initially, the jury found Rebecca Nurse innocent. In an apt illustration of the raucous displays experienced by the Court of Oyer and Terminer, upon pronouncement of this verdict, the afflicted witnesses immediately dissolved into a display of violent torment. The outburst was enough to cause Chief Justice Stoughton to recall the jury, asking them to reconsider the verdict in light of this new evidence. Once recalled, Justice Stoughton also instructed the jury to consider a specific statement made by Nurse during her examination. Deliverance Hobbs, another accused witch, had given evidence against Goodwife Nurse. When she entered the courtroom, Rebecca asked "But she's one of us?" The magistrates wondered at the statement, did she mean a *witch* like us? Goodwife Nurse was brought back to the court to explain her remark. Possibly due to exhaustion caused by the strain of the day's ordeal, or perhaps because she was hard-of-hearing, Goodwife Nurse made no response. Her silence was taken as a sign of guilt. When the jury returned with the new verdict, they found Rebecca Nurse guilty. Though her family later explained she had meant a *prisoner* like us, it was already too late. As Baker notes, "Rebecca's religious, economic, and political standing normally would have protected her from charges, or at least kept them from being taken seriously. Her conviction demonstrated that almost no one in the colony was safe."[51]

All five women were found guilty during this session of the Court of Oyer and Terminer and sentenced to death by hanging. On July 19, Rebecca Nurse, Sarah Good, Susannah Martin, Elizabeth How, and Sarah Wildes were brought to Proctor's Ledge at Gallows Hill and executed. Six people had now been hanged, and the trials were far from over.

AFFLICTION SPREADS LIKE FIRE

Following the July executions, the epicenter of the crisis shifted away from Salem. Once again, beginning with a local mysterious illness, the town of Andover would now take the lead in the witchcraft crisis. The witch hysteria first reached Andover in May, though it was initially limited to the accusation of just one local woman. Martha Carrier was an unsurprising target for a witchcraft accusation. She was an outspoken woman, known to argue with her neighbors. To make matters worse, her family was also blamed by many for beginning the smallpox epidemic that killed thirteen Andover residents in 1690. Following Goodwife Carrier's arrest, accusations halted in Andover for six weeks. However, having invited two of the afflicted girls from Salem to determine if his wife's debilitating illness was the result of bewitchment, Joseph Ballard inadvertently sparked a new phase in the witchcraft panic. Andover would soon experience a recording-breaking number of confessions. Ultimately, more people were accused of witchcraft in Andover than any other town in Essex County. By the end of the witch panic, sixty-three Andover residents had been accused, forty-five jailed, and three executed.

Why Andover became so engulfed in the witchcraft trials by mid-summer has only recently been the subject of considerable study. In his 2018 book *In the Shadow of Salem: The Andover Witch-Hunt of 1692*, historian Richard Hite examined the web of accusation that spread across Andover. Like Salem, local tensions surrounding the ministerial post had been simmering for years. In 1692, the Andover pulpit was shared between two men, the elder Reverend Francis Dane, who had ministered in Andover for forty-three years, and the younger Reverend Thomas Bernard, invited to join as a second minister in 1682. Though not an uncommon arrangement, the fact that the two men were splitting a salary, and that Reverend Dane appeared in no hurry to retire, certainly caused friction. It is interesting to note that the family of Francis Dane was targeted at an alarming rate in 1692—five of his grandchildren, two of his daughters, and one of his daughters-in-law were accused. Hite argues that the ministerial quarrel in Andover was not as central to the eruption of witchcraft accusations as has previously been suggested, and that the Dane family was possibly targeted because of a familial relationship to Martha Carrier, rather than because of their connection to the aged minister.[52] Either way, in the years leading up to 1692, this community was certainly tense and internally divided. Andover, like Salem, was a powder keg about to explode.

Once the Salem accusers were summoned to Andover to diagnose an ailment as the effect of bewitchment (in and of itself a very unique circumstance, as the afflicted now effectively stepped into a role reserved for medical professionals) a spark was ignited.[53] Upon their arrival, the girls soon suggested that Goody Ballard's affliction was caused by Ann Foster, a local widow in her mid-70s, described by Hite as "quite frail physically."[54] Goodwife Foster was questioned extensively, facing the magistrates on at least four occasions. Though she confessed during her first examination, the interrogations continued. It is unclear what drove such excessive questioning of an elderly woman. Perhaps, by this time, tensions were running too high to be calmed by a simple confession. Whatever the cause, by her fourth session, Goody Foster went far beyond any other story yet spun in 1692. Not only did she confess to attending a meeting of witches, led by none other than Salem's previous minister George Burroughs, but Goody Foster claimed *305 witches* were in the country at that very moment!

In short order, Mary Foster Lacey and Mary Lacey Jr. (the daughter and granddaughter of Ann Foster, respectively) were arrested as well. This chain is not unsurprising, as witchcraft was thought to run in families, most commonly through the female line. Both women quickly confessed, and went on to implicate others, including Martha Carrier (whom Mary Lacy Jr. termed the future "Queen in Hell"), as well as several of Goody Carrier's children. As Hite observes, "Once the witch hunters saw Andover as the home of the future 'Queen in Hell,' it was no great leap for them to conclude that this leader of the coven had actively and effectively solicited her neighbors."[55]

By this time, the actions of the court had a faint ring of desperation. Over the next several weeks, increasingly severe measures were taken by the court to root out the colony's witches. As noted by fellow prisoner John Proctor, when the Carrier boys were brought to Salem for examination and refused to confess, "they tied them neck and heels till the blood was ready to come out of their noises."[56] Under torture, the boys confessed, and confirmed for the court that their mother was a witch. Over the next several weeks, confessions poured out of Andover. As Hite aptly observes, "For a time, the atmosphere in Andover reached the stage where confessing one's guilt seemed a reasonable strategy for avoiding the hangman's noose."[57]

THE THIRD HANGING DAY

The Court of Oyer and Terminer met for a third time in August. Notably, during this session, the court heard the cases against four *men* and one woman, a significant shift in the proceedings thus far. Even more sensationally, a minister, Reverend George Burroughs, was among those tried before the court.

The trial of George Burroughs was yet another extraordinary moment in these already unusual events. In 1680, Reverend Burroughs had become the second candidate to fill the role as minister of Salem Village. Burroughs had lived on the frontier in Maine, survived devastating Native raids, and returned to Essex County, all before the age of 28. As a parsonage had not yet been built when he first arrived in Salem, the minister and his family resided with Captain John Putnam Sr., the uncle of Thomas Putnam. It was while living with Captain John and his family that gossip began to swirl around young Burroughs. According to the Putnams, Burroughs was unusually strict with his wife, and reportedly asked her to keep his "secrets." Tales of supernatural strength and knowledge were whispered as well. When his first wife died in childbirth, Reverend Burroughs was forced to borrow money from Captain Putnam to cover her funeral costs—an act that would eventually cause friction between the two men. To make matters worse, Burroughs remarried soon after the death of his first wife, a bit *too* quickly, said some members of the community.

By 1683, Burroughs had tired of the rumors and never-ending factional divides in Salem Village and returned to the Maine Coast. When Reverend Burroughs returned two months later to settle his accounts, old disputes arose, and Captain Putnam had him arrested for his first wife's funeral debt. Eventually, the monetary disputes were settled, but when Burroughs left for good, he did so on less then favorable terms, particularly with the Putnam family.

On April 20, 1692, two months after her affliction began, Ann Putnam Jr. was the first to claim to be tormented by the specter of their former minister. The following day, Thomas Putnam wrote a letter to Judges Hathorne and Corwin, detailing the torment of his daughter by this new specter. Others soon joined in, complaining of the minister's spectral attack. In a deposition given on May 9, Ann testified that the apparition of George Burroughs had attempted to force her to sign the Devil's book. She stated there also appeared to her "Two women in winding sheets and napkins about their heads"—the ghosts of Burroughs wives, whom she claimed he had murdered.[58] Thomas Putnam Jr. and his brother Edward added their own statements in two depositions attesting to the truth of the claims of the afflicted and underscoring the severity of their torment. Though it will never be known with certainty, perhaps these accusations were the result of the soured relations between the Putnam family and Reverend Burroughs.

When the Court of Oyer and Terminer met for a third session in August, the accused were now *far* beyond the ordinary witchcraft suspects. During this session Martha Carrier, the alleged "Queen in Hell," was tried along with four men, John Proctor, John Willard, George Jacobs Sr., and Reverend George Burroughs. By this time, George Burroughs was described as the leader of Satan's earthly forces, ruling alongside Martha Carrier. The trials had reached a kind of fever pitch, as they purportedly now included the captured leaders of Hell itself.

As was made evident by several of these cases, those who were bold enough to openly challenge the proceedings could find themselves in grave danger. Though John Willard had initially been in favor of the witchcraft proceedings, even assisting with arrests as a deputy constable, his opinion soon changed after interacting more extensively with both the accusers and accused. Shortly after his support shifted, his specter was sighted by the young Ann Putnam Jr. Though initially able to avoid arrest, Willard was eventually discovered working on land he owned 40 miles to the west, and was arrested. John Proctor also experienced the consequences of speaking out against the proceedings. Skeptical from the start, Goodman Proctor had openly and unapologetically questioned the authenticity of the afflictions. When his own servant, Mary Warren, had reported spectral torment, he managed to keep her afflictions at bay by keeping her occupied with household chores. The day after the trial of Rebecca Nurse, John Proctor told a neighbor, Samuel Sibley, that he planned to "thrash the Devil" out of Mary Warren, a statement that would soon come back to haunt him. As had been the case for Rebecca Nurse, on this day petitions were once again brought forward, this time attesting to the good character of John Proctor and his wife, Elizabeth. Though fifty-one friends, relatives, and neighbors signed the petitions, they evidently held little sway for the Salem magistrates.

On the last day of the court's August session, a huge crowd gathered to attend the trial of George Burroughs. Onlookers included Reverends Increase Mather, Deodat Lawson (former minister of Salem Village), and Reverend John Hale from neighboring Beverly. In a courtesy not extended to many, the first part of this examination was conducted privately, away from the screams of the afflicted witnesses. Reverend Burroughs was questioned about various rumors, many of which centered on his failings as a minister. Did he take communion? Were his children unbaptized? When he was brought into the courtroom to face the afflicted, the witnesses fell into a display of violent torment. They claimed to see the ghosts of his wives and deceased children, whom they again claimed had been murdered by Burroughs. Maintaining his innocence to the very last, Burroughs attempted to refute the accusations and offered a letter to the court in his own defense. As noted by Roach, in this unusual document, Burroughs lifted an argument from Thomas Ady's book *A Candle in the Dark*, claiming "it was impossible for one to make an actual contract with the Devil, much less send Devils to do one's will."[59] The judges were unmoved, finding him guilty as charged. All five suspects were convicted and sentenced for execution.[60]

On August 19, a sizeable crowed gathered to watch the execution, drawn, no doubt, by the presence of a minister among the condemned. Even Reverend Cotton Mather made his first trip to Salem that year to witness the hanging. When Reverend Burroughs stepped up to the gallows, he made one final attempt to demonstrate his innocence. During this period, many believed witches were unable to recite the Lord's Prayer without error. Several of the accused had attempted this folk test during the 1692 trials. Most were unable to recite the prayer perfectly, either due to a lack of study or the incredible pressure in the courtroom. However, while standing on the gallows facing certain death, Reverend Burroughs perfectly recited the prayer before an incredulous crowd. Writing in the year 1700, Robert Calef described this dramatic scene:

> When [George Burroughs] was upon the ladder, he made a speech for the clearing of his innocency, with such solemn and serious expressions, as were to the admiration of all present: his prayer (which he concluded by repeating

> the Lord's prayer) was so well worded, and uttered with such composedness, and such (at least seeming) fervency of spirit, as was very affecting, and drew tears from many, so that it seemed to some that the spectators would hinder the execution.[61]

In light of this upset, Cotton Mather came forward, reminding the crowd that the Devil could disguise himself as an angel of light. This was consistent with his previous stance, despite the fact that the court had on several occasions freely used this folk test as proof of guilt. Caught between support for the magistrates, as esteemed members of the colony, and disagreement with some of their methods, the young Mather now found himself in a tangled position. Thanks in part to the reassurances of Reverend Mather, the execution was ultimately carried out. Contemporary accounts indicate that many left this day with a feeling of considerable unease.

THE APEX

By September, public unrest was becoming increasingly difficult to ignore. Letters and petitions, authored by relatives of the accused, as well as by those languishing in prison, appeared throughout the summer and into the fall. These petitions begged the court to reconsider its current course, plainly stating that justice was not being administered. On September 9, Mary Esty and Sarah Cloyce, the sisters of Rebecca Nurse, submitted a petition to the court from jail. This appeal is truly remarkable, particularly considering the condition of the women who authored it. They asked that, "The testimony of witches, or such as are afflicted, as is supposed, by witches may not be improved to condemn us without other legal evidence concurring" and further begged not to be condemned "without a fair and equal hearing of what may be said for us as well as against us."[62] Facing execution, Mary Esty would soon write a second petition, where she poignantly wrote, "I petition to your honors not for my own life for I know I must die and my appointed time is set but the Lord he knows it is that if it be possible no more innocent blood may be shed which undoubtedly cannot be avoided in the way and course you in."[63] Others, including several elite men of the colony, voiced their own concerns in private letters to the magistrates. Shocked by the accusation of his neighbor, elderly Salisbury resident Mary Bradbury, Robert Pike, a militia leader and justice of the peace also wrote a letter, sending it directly to Jonathan Corwin. He too argued against the legality and practicality of the use of spectral evidence.

In addition to these written appeals, one man articulated his discontentment through his actions at trial. Though not without controversy in his past, Giles Corey was 73 years old and a member of the Salem Town church. His wife,

Martha, had been accused of witchcraft in March and also stood trial in September. The Court of Oyer and Terminer resumed on September 6, for what would be a two-week session. Six cases, all ending with a guilty verdict, were heard in the first week. Mary Bradbury, whom Pike had hoped to save and for whom 118 people signed a petition in support, was among those found guilty. The following week, nine more people were tried before the court, resulting in yet another 100 percent conviction rate. Though Goodman Corey pled not guilty, in order for a trial to move forward the suspect was expected to answer the question, "How will you be tried?" with the answer, "By God and my country." By this time, Corey had been held in jail for five months, he had seen those who attempted to plead or argue for their innocence convicted, no matter their background, social rank, or the number of friends and neighbors willing to testify to their good character. He knew those who maintained their innocence were the ones being executed.

As a result, he elected to "stand mute," refusing to answer the traditional question. After three chances to reply with no progress, the court decided to use an old legal procedure called *peine forte et dure* (French for hard and forceful punishment). This form of torture involved a suspect lying on the ground with more and more stones placed upon their chest so as to force them to speak. While legal by English Common Law, this method of torture had never before been used in the colonies, despite a recent occasion where it could have been invoked. Just two years before, Judges Corwin, Hathorne, Richards, and Sewall, who all now sat on the Court of Oyer and Terminer, had been on the Court of Assistants tasked with trying a pirate who stood mute. In this case, despite his silence, the trial moved on, resulting in conviction and execution.[64] However, at this stage in the proceedings, the court perhaps felt it could not accept a challenge to its authority, and elected to use this extreme form of torture. On September 19, Giles Corey was brought to an open field, laid on the ground under a board, and heavy stones were piled on his chest. He was dead by noon.

Despite the growing popular unrest, made worse still by the gruesome death of Giles Corey, another date of execution was set for late September. On September 22, Martha Corey, Mary Esty, Alice Parker, Ann Pudeator, Margaret Scott, Wilmot Redd, Mary Parker, and Samuel Wardwell were brought to Proctor's Ledge and hanged. This was the largest group execution yet in 1692. Thankfully, it was also the last.

THE MINISTER'S PROTEST

Though the afflicted continued to complain of spectral torment, by early October protests against the proceedings could no longer be ignored. As was demonstrated by the fate of the unfortunate Giles Corey, it was impossible to prove, at least by logic or reasoned argument, one's innocence before the Court of Oyer and Terminer. No one was safe from accusation, as those of greater and greater affluence were named by the afflicted—though, as in the case of Mary Bradbury, these were in most cases the lucky few able to avoid arrest or flee from jail, quietly seeking refuge elsewhere until the trials came to an end.[65]

By early October, the ministry's position was finally no longer one of respectful deference. Having conferred with local ministers on the matter since August, Reverend Increase Mather was finally ready to take a definitive stand. Reverend Samuel Willard, who had been vocally skeptical of the proceedings for months, and had himself been cried out upon by the afflicted (though in this case the afflicted had been chastised not to lie, and sent from the room—an unusual move proving that the court could and did choose who to believe and when) also published a criticism of the trials. In the writings of both Mather and Willard, the ministers clearly and forcefully called for an end of the use of spectral evidence. Though they both affirmed the existence of the Devil, they resolutely stated the Devil could take the shape of an innocent person. Mather went so far as to assert, "It were better that ten suspected witches should escape, than that one innocent person should be condemned." Mather's essay was read aloud before a group of ministers gathered at Harvard College on October 3. Fourteen ministers added their signatures to the publication, indicating their full support. Though this document alone would not halt the proceedings, the influence of this chorus of voices from the local ministry was powerful. Boyer and Nissenbaum have gone so far as to assert, "What finally put a stop to the whole process was the direct and organized intervention of the principal ministers of eastern Massachusetts."[66]

Around this same time, a group of Andover residents submitted a petition on behalf of their imprisoned neighbors. Twenty-six people added their names to this document, which was submitted directly to the governor on October 18, 1692. The first two signatures were those of Francis Dane and Thomas Bernard, the ministers of Andover. Whatever friction may have existed between these men, they now came together to protest on behalf of their parishioners. Those who signed this petition must have been acutely aware of the considerable risk involved; not only did they ask the court to reconsider the imprisonment of their neighbors, but their petition argued the charges brought against their fellow residents were made by "distempered persons." The petition acknowledged the large number of confessions made by Andover residents, while also noting that these confessors may have been frightened into condemning themselves, and some of them, such as Samuel Wardwell, had in fact eventually denied the truth of their confessions.

To add further credence to these objections, around this same time Lady Phips, the wife of the governor himself, was accused of witchcraft. Though Lady Phips was never arrested or formally charged, the fact that his wife's specter was allegedly sighted certainly impacted the governor. On October 12, Phips wrote to the clerk of the Privy Council in England stating he had elected to cease arrests for witchcraft "without unavoidable necessity."[67] This letter signaled his decision to halt the proceedings of the Court of Oyer and Terminer, a choice he would publicly reveal on October 29.[68]

Though the Court of Oyer and Terminer was dismissed, the witch trials were not yet at an end. There were still witchcraft cases that needed to be tried, and people languishing in jail. These cases would not be dealt with for another two months. At this point, following in the wake of the Andover petition, more and more people demanded the release of prisoners as the winter approached.

A special session of the Superior Court was set to meet in Salem on January 3, 1693, to oversee the remaining cases. Most significantly, this court no longer accepted the much-contested spectral evidence. With the removal of the contested procedures adopted by the previous court, the conviction rate dropped. Only three people were convicted by the new court, each indicted by other evidence beyond spectral torment. Though another hanging was scheduled for February, for the remaining convictions issued by Oyer and Terminer as well as the few recent indictments, this execution never took place. By late January, Governor Phips stepped in once more, and issued reprieves for all of those convicted, both by the original and new court—

much to the displeasure of Chief Justice William Stoughton, who would go to his grave maintaining the court had acted in the best interest of the colony. Slowly, the jails began to empty. The Salem witch trials were finally at an end.

THE AFTERMATH

In the years that followed, the inhabitants of New England resumed the routine of colonial life. Farmers returned to their neglected fields. Wars continued with the Indigenous tribes to the North. Taxes were reassessed by the newly reestablished government. Life went on, though forever shadowed by the experiences of 1692. In Salem Village, earlier disputes continued, chiefly those involving the minister's salary. Much to the chagrin of the families of the witchcraft victims, Parris remained minister of Salem Village. However, the experiences of 1692 were not soon forgotten. For many of the inhabitants, the sanctity of the Salem Village covenant had been irreparably violated, and many found themselves unable to forgive Parris for his actions. For months several relatives of witchcraft victims refused to attend Church, eventually abstaining from taking the sacrament as well.[69] These objections to Reverend Parris persisted for years. Though in May 1695 Thomas Putnam, along with 105 other villagers, submitted a petition asking Reverend Parris to remain as their minister, the following April, Samuel Parris announced his intention to leave Salem Village for good.

In 1697, the Massachusetts General Court ordered a day of fasting and prayer in atonement for errors made by the colony, including the witchcraft trials. Sermons were read across the colony. Roach observes, "Unfortunately, how that service proceeded in Salem Village—with Ann and [Ann Jr.] and the other once-afflicted folk present in the congregation, Thomas who had been so busy writing the testimony, and Parris sitting among the rest as a private inhabitant while someone else substituted in the pulpit—passed unrecorded." Though the majority of the magistrates from the Court of Oyer and Terminer never publicly acknowledged wrongdoing, on this day of public fast, Samuel Sewall stood before his congregation in Boston with his head bowed. His minister, Samuel Willard, read a statement aloud on his behalf. Sewall acknowledged his failings in the year 1692 and asked forgiveness for his involvement. He would continue to observe this day of penance for the remainder of his life. In addition to Sewall, twelve members of the jury issued a statement of apology acknowledging they had been "sadly deluded and mistaken."[70]

The later lives of the afflicted witnesses are sparsely documented, as was common for most women during this period. Some appear in court records, having committed a sin or criminal offense. Others, like Betty Parris, married, raised children, and had seemingly normal lives.[71] In 1706, Ann Putnam Jr. became the only previously afflicted person to acknowledge wrongdoing in 1692. At the age of 27 she sought to become a full member of the Salem Village church. By this time the requirements for church membership had become more lenient, requiring "a strong heartfelt desire for the sacraments and a generally good Christian life rather than a conviction that one was elect," though Salem Village still required a public statement of faith and confession of past sins.[72] Samuel Parris had since been replaced by a new minister, 22-year-old Joseph Green. The young Reverend Green brought a much-needed spirit of reconciliation to this divided community. He had already reorganized the meeting house, sitting the families of accused and accusers next to one another. Perhaps he hoped Ann's confession of faith would further mend broken fences. It was he who assisted Ann Jr. with this important task. Before accepting her confession of faith, the Reverend went so far as to seek the approval of Samuel Nurse (son of Rebecca), who read and accepted the statement.

On August 25, 1706, Ann Putnam Jr. stood before her congregation, made up of the relatives and individuals who had been both accusers and accused, while Reverend Green read her confession of faith aloud. In this statement, she told the congregation: "I desire to be humbled before god for that sad and humbling providence that befell my father's family in the year 92" even specifically noting that because she "was a chief instrument of accusing Goodwife Nurse and her two sisters, I desire to lie in the dust, and to be humbled for it, in that I was a cause, with others, of so sad a calamity to them and their families."[73] No existing records indicate how this statement was received by the community, though perhaps some wondered if this young woman, who had been at the center of such tragedy, was indeed worthy of admittance to the church.

THE COVENANT UNDER ATTACK

For all intents and purposes, the Great Puritan experiment was over by the last decade of the seventeenth century. Change had come to New England, solidified by the arrival of the new charter and pushed further still by the enormous, inescapable mistakes made during the witchcraft trials of 1692. Though Governor Phips enacted a publication ban after dissolving the Court of Oyer and Terminer, allowing only the court-sanctioned account of the trials, composed by Cotton Mather and published in the fall of 1692, he could not hide what had happened in Salem. In his October letter to the clerk of the Privy Council, Phips articulated the logic behind this ban, stating he hoped to limit "the needless disputes of people upon this occasion," and that he feared further discussion may ignite "an inextinguishable flame."[74] Baker argues this was largely a response to fear for the future of the colony, one which, having lost its charter, was already understood to be in considerable danger. He notes, "collectively the concerns raised about the trials changed people's views of their government and helped bring an end to the Puritan theocracy."[75] Despite the publication ban, critical discussions of the trials were circulated in the 1690s, and Robert Calef published his visceral attack of the whole affair by 1700.

The successful mechanisms that once sustained this Puritan colony were shattered in 1692. Self-administrative justice, a system that had been successful when checked within strict legal confines, temporarily collapsed. As a result, decades of gossip and suspicion fed a staggering number of accusations. Local ministers failed to temper fears within the community, instead allowing a hastily assembled court to manage mounting public pressure. Though the eventual intervention of the ministers contributed to the conclusion of these tragic events, their lack of leadership in the heat of the crisis was inescapable. In some ways, the Salem witch trials were the last gasp of an old world order, one where the supernatural was legally regulated and proof of the paranormal was a point of political contention.

When the American Revolution began, the lessons of the Salem witch trials had not been forgotten. In fact, these events became a powerful and popular metaphor, used on both sides of the political spectrum, invoked to criticize behavior deemed to be irrational, superstitious, or fanatical—a comparison that continues in American public discourse to this day. Though the Salem witch trials signaled the end of the New England covenant society, its fundamental basis can still be gleaned in the American democratic federative government, formed nearly a century after the witchcraft trials.[76] The Salem witch trials may have signaled the end of the Great Puritan experiment, but they also made way for a new world, one no longer based solely on a special covenant with God, but still inarguably molded from the efforts of the devoted men and women who sought to be a "city upon a hill."

NOTES

1. Marilynne Roach, *The Salem Witch Trials: A Day-By-Day Chronicle of a Community Under Siege* (New York: Cooper Square Press, 2002), 373, 536.
2. Charles Upham, *Salem Witchcraft* (Mineloa: Dover Publications, 2000); Marion Starkey, *The Devil in Massachusetts: A Modern Inquiry into the Salem Witch Trials* (New York: Alfred Knop, 1950); Chadwick Hansen, *Witchcraft at Salem* (New York: George Braziller Inc, 1950).
3. Linnda R. Caporael, "Ergotism: The Satan Loosed in Salem?" *Science*, 192 (April 2, 1976): 21–26. In this article, Dr. Caporael notoriously proposed that ergotism may have caused the behavior of the afflicted witnesses in 1692. Though this theory was quickly discreated as improbable by scholars of the Salem witch trials, it became a popular news story, sweeping across the United States. For this reason, it has remained popular in media to this day.
4. Mary Beth Norton, *In the Devil's Snare: The Salem Witchcraft Crisis of 1692* (New York: Vintage Books, 2002); John Demos, *Entertaining Satan: Witchcraft and the Culture of Early New England* (New York: Oxford University Press, 1982).
5. Emerson Baker, *A Storm of Witchcraft: The Salem Witch Trials and the American Experience* (New York: Oxford University Press, 2015).
6. Though the charter was officially issued in 1691, it did not arrive in the colony until May of 1692. As such, it did not begin to go into effect until one year after it was decreed.
7. John Winthrop, "A Model of Christian Charity," Digital History, https://www.digitalhistory.uh.edu/disp_textbook.cfm?smtID=3&psid=3918
8. Roach, *The Salem Witch Trials*, xix.
9. Francis Higginson, June 6, 1626, Records of the First Church of Salem, Archives: Record Books, First Church of Salem.
10. Edmund Morgan, *Visible Saints: The History of a Puritan Idea* (London: Cornell University Press Ltd, 1963), 82.
11. Baker, *A Storm of Witchcraft,* 49.
12. Norton, *In the Devil's Snare.*

13. Ibid, 58.

14. In 1688, popular resentment towards Catholic King James II, ruler of England, Scotland, and Ireland, culminates in the invasion of Dutch Prince William of Orange, known as the Glorious Revolution. After successfully overthrowing King James II, William and his wife Mary take the throne, ruling as joint monarchs. They are known as King William III and Queen Mary II.

15. Ibid 67.

16. For more see: Paul Boyer Boyer and Stephen Nissenbaum, "In Quest of Community 1639-1687," in *Salem Possessed: The Social Origins of Witchcraft* (New York: MJF Books, 1974), 36–59.

17. Samuel Parris, November 19, 1689, Church Book Belonging to Salem Village, Records of the Salem-Village Church from November 1689 to October 1696, University of Virginia Library.

18. Boyer and Nissenbaum, *Salem Possessed.*

19. Richard Trask, "Introduction," in *The Devil Hath Been Raised: A Documentary History of the Salem Village Witchcraft Outbreak of March 1692* (Danvers: Yeoman Press, 1997), xiv.

20. Roach, *The Salem Witch Trials*, xxv.

21. Cotton Mather, *Memorable Providences Relating to Witchcraft and Possessions a Faithful Account of Many Wonderful and Surprising Things that Have Befallen Several Bewitched and Possessed Persons in New England* (Boston: R.P, 1689).

22. Roach, *The Salem Witch Trials*, xxii.

23. Samuel Parris, "27 March, Sab, 1692, Sacrament Day," in *The Salem Witch Trials Reader*, ed. Francis Hill (Boston: DaCapo Press, 2000), 123.

24. Bernard Rosenthal, "General Introduction," in *Records of the Salem Witch-Hunt*, ed. Bernard Rosenthal (New York: Cambridge University Press, 2009), 17.

25. Norton, *In the Devil's Snare,* 21.

26. Roach, *The Salem Witch Trials*, xxii.

27. "Examination of Sarah Good, Sarah Osburn, & Tituba," in *Records of the Salem Witch-Hunt*, 127.

28. Norton, *In the Devil's Snare*, 27.

29. Elaine Breslaw, *Tituba, Reluctant Witch of Salem* (New York: New York University Press, 1996).

30. Robert Calef, *More Wonders of the Invisible World or Wonders of the Invisible World Displayed in Five Parts* (Salem: Reprinted by John D. and T.C. Cushing Jr. for Cushing and Appleton, 1823), 189. https://archive.org/details/morewondersofinv01cale/page/188/mode/2up?q=Tituba

31. "Two Examinations of Tituba, as Recorded by Jonathan Corwin," in *Records of the Salem Witch-Hunt*, 133.

32. Upham, *Salem Witchcraft*, 633.

33. "Deposition of Edward Putnam v. Martha Corey," in *Records of the Salem Witch Hunt*, 152.

34. Jane Kamensky, "Salem Obsessed; Or, 'Plus Ça Change': An Introduction," *The William and Mary Quarterly* 65, no. 3 (2008): 391–400.

35. Baker, A *Storm of Witchcraft*, 121.

36. Boyer and Nissenbaum, *Salem Possessed*, 7.

37. Baker, *A Storm of Witchcraft*, 17.
38. Ibid, 164.
39. Though England did experience several large witchcraft trials, these did not result in the enormous execution rates experienced in other European countries during the early modern period. For example, in 1675, over the course of just one day, 71 people were executed for witchcraft in Torsåker, Sweden. For more on the larger phenomenon of witch-hunting in Europe see Julian Goodare, *The European Witch-Hunt* (Oxon: Routledge, 2016).
40. Increase Mather, *An Essay for the Recording of the Illustrious Providences: Wherin, an account is given of many remarkable and very memorable events, which have happened in the last age; especially in New England* (Boston: Samuel Green, 1684), 140, https://quod.lib.umich.edu/e/evans/N00296.0001.001?rgn=main;view=fulltext
41. Ibid, 141.
42. Cotton Mather, May 31, 1692, "To John Richards," Collect 8, Levin/Massachusetts Historical Society, Salem Witch Trials Documentary Archive and Transcription Project.
43. Ibid.
44. "Physical Examination No. 1 & No. 2 of Bridget Bishop, Rebecca Nurse, Elizabeth Procter, Alice Parker, Susannah Martin, & Sarah Good," in *Records of the Salem Witch-Hunt*, 362.
45. Saltonstall himself would later be named as a witch by gossip, though legal action was never taken against him
46. Rivett notes that the problem of spectral evidence was not exclusive to the English colonies, this matter was of concern to many of the prolific thinkers of the time, including John Webster and Balthasar Bekker. Sarah Rivett, "Our Salem, Our Selves." *The William and Mary Quarterly*, no. 3 (2008): 500.
47. Increase Mather, *The Return of several Ministers, Consulted by His Excellency, and the Honorable Council, upon the Present Witchcrafts in Salem Village* (London: J. Dunton, 1693), https://quod.lib.umich.edu/e/eebo/A70086.0001.001/1:9.1?rgn=div2;view=fulltext
48. "Deposition of Samuel Perley & Ruth Perley v. Elizabeth How," in *Records of the Salem-Witch Hunt*, 351.
49. "Testimony of Samuel Phillips & Edward Payson for Elizabeth How," in *Records of the Salem-Witch Hunt*, 373.
50. Ibid.
51. Baker, *A Storm of Witchcraft*, 32.
52. Richard Hite, "Prelude to Witchcraft," in *In the Shadow of Salem: The Andover Witch-Hunt of 1692* (Yardley: Westholme, 2018).
53. The identities of the two girls who traveled to Andover is unclear. Richard Hite notes that subsequent events indicate one of these girls may have been Mary Warren. It has also been suggested Ann Putnam Jr. may have been the other girl, though this is speculation. Hite, *In the Shadow of Salem*, 70; Marilynne Roach, *The Salem Witch Trials*, 198.
54. Hite, *In the Shadow of Salem* 71.
55. Ibid, 84.

56. Marilynne Roach, *The Salem Witch Trials*, 209.
57. Hite, *In the Shadow of Salem*, XVI.
58. "Deposition of Ann Putnam Jr. v. George Burroughs and Statement of Edward Putnam & Thomas Putnam v George Burroughs," in *Records of the Salem Witch-Hunt*, 245–246.
59. Roach, *The Salem Witch Trials*, 360.
60. Though tried alongside her husband, Elizabeth Proctor was not sentenced to execution in August as she was pregnant. The court granted her a stay of execution until she could deliver her child. Elizabeth Proctor was scheduled to be executed in February of 1693, but her life was sparred thanks to the reprieves issued by Governor Phips in late January.
61. Upham, *Salem Witchcraft*, 518.
62. "Petitions of Sarah Cloyce & Mary Esty," in *Records of the Salem Witch Trials,* 620.
63. "Petition of Mary Easty," in *Records of the Salem Witch Hunt*, 658.
64. Baker, *A Storm of Witchcraft*, 190.
65. Mary Bradbury, Philip and Mary English, and Elizabeth Cary are notable examples of the impact of affluence once imprisoned for witchcraft. Those with the financial means were in most cases able to flee to safety.
66. Boyer and Nissenbaum, *Salem Possessed*, 9.
67. William Phips, "Letters of Governor Phipps," in *Narratives of Witchcraft Cases: 1648-1706*, ed. George Lincoln Burr (Mineola: Dover Publication, 2002), 197.
68. Roach, *The Salem Witch Trials*, 286.
69. Termed by Marilynne Roach as the "dissenting brethren," these men included Thomas Wilkins, Samuel Nurse, John Tarbell, and Peter Cloyce. Roach, *The Salem Witch Trials*, 397.
70. "The Apology of the Salem Jury," in *The Penguin Book of Witches*, ed. Katherine Howe (New York: Penguin Books, 2014), 197.
71. Norton, *In the Devil's Snare*, 310; Baker, *A Storm of Witchcraft*, 234.
72. Ibid.
73. Upham, *Salem Witchcraft*, 672.
74. William Phips, "Letters of Governor Phipps," in *Narratives of Witchcraft Cases,* 197.
75. Baker, *A Storm of Witchcraft*, 195.
76. Daniel J. Elazar, *Covenant and Constitutionalism: The Great Frontier and the Matrix of Federal Democracy*, Volume 3 (New York: Routledge, 2017), 2.

REFERENCES

Adams, Gretchen. *The Specter of Salem: Remembering the Salem Witch Trials in Nineteenth-Century America.* Chicago: University of Chicago Press, 2008.

Baker, Emerson. *A Storm of Witchcraft: The Salem Witch Trials and the American Experience.* New York: Oxford University Press, 2015.

Breslaw, Elaine. *Tituba, Reluctant Witch of Salem*. New York: New York University Press, 1996.

Calef, Robert *More Wonders of the Invisible World or Wonders of the Invisible World Displayed in Five Parts*. Salem: Reprinted by John D. and T.C. Cushing Jr. for Cushing and Appleton, 1823. https://archive.org/details/morewondersofinv01cale/page/188/mode/2up?q=Tituba.

Caporael, Linnda R. "Ergotism: The Satan Loosed in Salem?" *Science* 192 (April 2, 1976): 21–26.

Demos, John. *Entertaining Satan: Witchcraft and the Culture of Early New England*. New York: Oxford University Press, 1982.

Elazar, Daniel J. *Covenant and Constitutionalism: The Great Frontier and the Matrix of Federal Democracy*, Vol. 3. New York: Routledge, 2017.

Hansen, Chadwick. *Witchcraft at Salem*. New York: George Braziller Inc, 1950.

Higginson, Francis. June 6, 1626. "Records of the First Church of Salem." Archives: Record Books, First Church of Salem.

Hite, Richard. *In the Shadow of Salem: The Andover Witch-Hunt of 1692*. Yardley: Westholme, 2018.

Kamensky, Jane. "Salem Obsessed; Or, 'Plus Ça Change': An Introduction." *The William and Mary Quarterly* 65, no. 3 (2008): 391–400.

Mather, Cotton. *Memorable Providences Relating to Witchcraft and Possessions a Faithful Account of Many Wonderful and Surprising Things That Have Befallen Several Bewitched and Possessed Persons in New England*. Boston: R.P., 1689. https://quod.lib.umich.edu/e/eebo/A50139.0001.001?rgn=main;view=fulltext.

———. May 31, 1692. "To John Richards." Collection 8, Levin/Massachusetts Historical Society, Salem Witch Trials Documentary Archive and Transcription Project.

Mather, Increase. *An Essay for the Recording of the Illustrious Providences: Wherin, an Account is Given of Many Remarkable and Very Memorable Events, Which Have Happened in the Last Age; Especially in New England*. Boston: Samuel Green, 1684. https://quod.lib.umich.edu/e/evans/N00296.0001.001?rgn=main;view=fulltext.

———. *The Return of Several Ministers, Consulted by His Excellency, and the Honorable Council, Upon the Present Witchcrafts in Salem Village*. London: J. Dunton, 1693. https://quod.lib.umich.edu/e/eebo/A70086.0001.001/1:9.1?rgn=div2;view=fulltext.

Morgan, Edmund. *Visible Saints: The History of a Puritan Idea*. London: Cornell University Press, 1963.

Norton, Mary Beth. *In the Devil's Snare: The Salem Witchcraft Crisis of 1692*. New York: Vintage Books, 2002.

Parris, Samuel. "27 March, Sab, 1692, Sacrament Day." In *The Salem Witch Trials Reader*, edited by Francis Hill, 123–124. Boston: DaCapo Press, 2000.

———. November 19, 1689. "Church Book Belonging to Salem Village." Records of the Salem-Village Church from November 1689 to October 1696, University of Virginia Library.

Phips, William. "Letters of Governor Phipps." In *Narratives of Witchcraft Cases: 1648–1706*, edited by George Lincoln Burr, 196–202. Mineola: Dover Publications, 2002.

Rivett, Sarah. "Our Salem, Our Selves." *The William and Mary Quarterly* 65, no. 3 (2008): 495–502.

Roach, Marilynne. *The Salem Witch Trials: A Day-By-Day Chronicle of a Community Under Siege*. New York: Cooper Square Press, 2002.

Rosenthal, Bernard, ed. *Records of the Salem Witch-Hunt*. New York: Cambridge University Press, 2009.

Starkey, Marion. *The Devil in Massachusetts: A Modern Inquiry into the Salem Witch Trials*. New York: Alfred Knop, 1950.

"The Apology of the Salem Jury." *The Penguin Book of Witches*, edited by Katherine Howe, 197–198. New York: Penguin Books, 2014.

Trask, Richard. *The Devil Hath Been Raised: A Documentary History of the Salem Village Witchcraft Outbreak of March 1692*. Danvers: Yeoman Press, 1997.

Upham, Charles. *Salem Witchcraft*. Mineloa: Dover Publications, 2000.

Winthrop, John. "A Model of Christian Charity." *Digital History*. https://www.digitalhistory.uh.edu/disp_textbook.cfm?smtID=3&psid=3918.

Chapter 9

The Catholic Hierarchy and Clerical Sexual Abuse

Jo Renee Formicola

Nothing conjures up more conspiracy theories than stories about the internal workings of the Catholic Church. Speculation about the wealth of the Vatican bank, its real estate holdings, and art treasures are the stuff of documentaries. Investigations into pontifical secrets, organizations such as "the Knights" as well as the Mafia, and corruption among Popes and their illegitimate children abound. Violations of celibacy, rampant homosexuality, and priestly pedophilia all add to rumors of grave clerical relationships and sins. But even with continuous investigations and unsolved mysteries, the Catholic Church continues to pursue its religious mission to bring souls to Christ. Adherents, and skeptics alike, increasingly ask how can such a hierarchical institution continue to function and still play a role as a moral advocate in the world, especially during the clerical sexual abuse crisis.

The Church's beginnings help to answer this question. Historically, the Bible recounts the founding of Jesus's Church, its leadership, and purpose. In Matthew 16:18 for example, Jesus tells his Apostle:

> [T]hou art Peter and upon this rock I will build my Church and the gates of hell shall not prevail against it. And I will give you the keys of the kingdom of heaven. And whatever you shall bind on earth shall be bound, even in heaven. And whatever you shall loose on earth shall be loosed, even in heaven.

This statement has traditionally been used by the leaders of the Catholic Church to justify a) the legitimate, temporal founding of Jesus's Church on earth, b) the establishment of its religious leadership structure, and c) its obligation to implement the institution's spiritual mission to bring salvation to Jesus's followers.[1] Thus, even to the present, the Catholic Church considers itself a divinely mandated organization; one with a unique structure and spiritual purpose. As a result, it develops its own processes, rules, and sanctions for the institution's existence in the world.

The Church survives, then as now, even during the current clerical sexual abuse tragedy, due to its ability to adapt to social, legal, and moral challenges. This is evidenced by the resilient governance of its hierarchy, as well as the relevant pastoral and canonical responses it employs.

THE DEVELOPMENT OF THE HIERARCHY AND ITS GOVERNANCE POWER

The development of the Catholic hierarchy into a religious institution with significant governance power is unique and different from the pattern of leadership that emerged in modern civil governments. These dissimilar sacred and civil structures have evolved due to the diverse nature, scope, and authority of their organizations. Thus, there have historically been challenges to Catholic Church-State governance, as evidenced today in the crisis of clerical sexual abuse.

Daniel Elazar, the eminent American political scientist, known for his seminal studies on political culture, provides a paradigm that can be used to see the contrast between the beginnings of religious and civil hierarchies. He argues that the traditional covenant between Abraham and God became the critical component of a moral consensus; one that eventually established sacred laws based on personal obligations and then led people to develop political compacts and constitutions. He contends that these religious efforts led to the institutionalization of rights, individual freedom, and the rise of modern democratic institutions.[2]

The Catholic, sacred governance structure is somewhat like Elazar's model of the evolution of secular government. It is similar, in so far as it, too, was developed as the result of a moral consensus. But, beyond that, Catholic theologians[3] also interpret Jesus's divine mandate as a *new* covenant, a fulfillment of the Mosaic one that Elazar posited. Citing St. Mark's gospel, where Jesus says that "This is my blood of the covenant,"[4] they claim that this statement supports a catechesis that respects the Old Testament, but also one that is central to an acceptance of Christ as the savior of mankind. By casuistry, the new covenant between Jesus and his Apostles has also been used to justify the hierarchical, unified interpretation of Scripture and a conduit to interpret personal religious obligations.

The greatest difference between Elazar's theories about the evolution of secular hierarchies and the reality of the Catholic sacred one can be seen in the development of the governance structure of the Church. It is a type of organization that never officially allowed the election of its leadership by non-religious personnel, but instead instituted ecclesiastical laws that were based on a "holy ordering" of authority. It was composed of bishops and priests, and exercised in both religious and civil contexts, as needed, with the assistance of deacons.

Bishops, who have always been considered the successors of the Apostles, were, thus, at the top of the Church leadership structure, where the most important bishop-leader was the Bishop of Rome, and usually recognized as the "Pope" or "Pontiff."[5] Unlike secular regimes, then, the Catholic hierarchy relied on its divine mandate to create a closed, religious, and pragmatic governance model that led to the development of its own legal system and enforcement mechanisms.

Bishops have always had the primary responsibility for the pastoral care of those within their "dioceses" or territorial jurisdictions.[6] Traditionally, Church laws that dealt with religious responsibilities, such as tithing and sacramental obligations, were imposed by a bishop's fiat. Codified, consistent, or national civil laws did not exist during the developing years of the Church, nor did nascent governments have the political power to challenge a bishop's authority during much of the first millennium. Many infant civil territories lacked strong rulers, legal structures, governments, ideologies, and economic systems that could question the established spheres of Church organization and power.

Early Christian history recounts the travels and evangelization of St. Paul who wrote epistles about the role of the Church, the basis of the powers of its leaders, and the obligations of the laity. The *Acts of the Apostles* in the Bible also give a glimpse of Church authority, but it was not until the end of the first century that *The Didache* or *The Lord's Teaching Through the Twelve Apostles to the Nations* emerged and included for the first time sections on Christian ethics. It described the virtuous "Way of Life" as well as the wicked "Way of Death."

Bishops, often appointed and supported by wealthy families or other powerful bishops, then, could interpret early sporadic, conflicting, or unclear religious rules. In their positions, bishops were expected and designated to implement the Church's growing religious rules and eventually even carry out civil responsibilities in environments with large numbers of Christian converts. Thus, inconsistent temporal and spiritual laws were often subject to various hierarchical understandings of Church authority, behavior, and rituals.

In 325 CE, the Emperor Constantine called a meeting of the bishops at Nicea to regulate Catholic religious practices, standardize theology, and unify the Roman Empire. But his attempts at a religious-political symbiosis failed, thus allowing various bishops to continue to use the title "pope" until the sixth century. At that time, however, Pope Gregory the Great (540–604 CE) claimed sole authority to appoint bishops and heads of monasteries. Thus, there remained a continuing source of contention and confusion among early church leaders and civil authorities on the nature and scope of papal authority.

In 1079 CE, a body of "electors," later to be known as the College of Cardinals, was established to vote for the Pope, but a questionable vote among them led to a schism and two men claiming the position. A century later, the Third Vatican Council (1179 CE) recognized the need to develop a clearer hierarchical consensus about how popes were to gain their positions and incorporated specific rules regarding papal accession into an embryonic Church legal system. Only cardinals[7] had the right to elect a pope with a two-thirds majority, and any candidate who declared himself pope without receiving the appropriate number of votes would be excommunicated from the Church.

As a system for papal succession was finally beginning to develop, other questions about the hierarchical governance structure of the Church were also coming into question. In response, subsequent Church councils declared the primacy of the Pope over the hierarchy and the entire world. He was declared as the "Vicar of Christ" at the Council of Trent (1545 CE) with the power to ordain priests and carry out his pastoral functions without the consent of the laity. Most importantly, the bishops also declared, at this time, that Holy Orders, the sacrament of priestly ordination, inculcated and imprinted an indelible, or special, character on the soul of a priest. This doctrine was later referred to as "clericalism" by its detractors and has impacted the entire debate over the punishment of the clergy during the sexual abuse scandal more than 500 years later.

In modern times, a General Council, known as Vatican I (1869), proclaimed that the Roman Pontiff was infallible when speaking *ex cathedra*, that is, as a pastor and teacher with supreme Apostolic authority. This meant that in the papal position, the head of the Church could define a doctrine of faith or morals, and that it would be irrefutable and unchangeable even by Church consent. At another synod, Vatican II (1962–1965) the assembled bishops reenforced the doctrine that the Pope is the divinely appointed head of the entire episcopate, that he can exercise authority over the faithful, and may do so without the bishop's mediation.[8]

Even with all these historical attempts to clarify the role of the Pope as well as the Church's relationship to society, the broad term "hierarchy" today goes beyond just the persona of the Pope as the Bishop of Rome and his governance powers. While he is the head of the Catholic hierarchical structure, the term, hierarchy, includes and refers to other Church authorities who carry out papal directives and agendas, specifically bishops.

A bishop, therefore, acts alone in his specific diocese or in solidarity with a group of his fellow bishops. In the first instance, each individual bishop is appointed by the Pope as the pastoral leader of his diocese, and is expected to tender his resignation at age 75. This means that a bishop is specifically responsible for teaching and evangelizing for the salvific purpose of the Church: to save souls and bring them to Christ.

There are, however, other aspects to a bishop's pastoral role. Besides preaching and writing, he is responsible for establishing and maintaining schools for the education of the faithful; raising funds to pay for the operations of buildings and grounds; running seminaries; managing the clergy and Church employees; and often serving as the corporate liaison with civil authorities on matters of real estate, finances, and civil law.

From a hierarchical perspective, then, a bishop is above all other religious authorities in his own diocese and can act as representative of the Church in temporal matters as well. His power over the management and supervision of clerical affairs is historically and definitively within his purview. As the administrator of a seminary in his diocese, he deals with its faculty and students, and the education of the young men who are preparing for the priesthood. He appoints pastors and priests in his parishes. He is the manager and the keeper of personnel and medical records of priests. He hires and fires teachers and other personnel in Catholic schools and other Church organizations. Most importantly, he also appoints and oversees all religious managers of the episcopal bureaucracy, the diocese.

On another level, the assembled bishops at Vatican II (1962–1965) affirmed the collegial nature and authority of the hierarchy acting in fraternal solidarity with their fellow bishops. They asserted the right to create regional conferences to deal with religious and policy problems in their regional, geographic areas as united organizations, but also affirmed that they could not exercise such power without the consent of the Pope due to his prerogative and power as the Roman Pontiff or supreme leader of the Church.

This later became a problem as regional hierarchical organizations tried to enact religious policies with civil implications that, to them, threatened the salvation of those in their pastoral care. In Latin America, for example, at the 1968 Conference of Latin American Bishops (CELAM) in Medellin, the Church leaders, aware of growing oppression and inequality, adopted a declaration that essentially rejected the principles of the political left or the right, and based its political support on the principles of Jesus Christ—peace, justice, and love.[9] They supported social doctrines such as an "option for the poor," and called on the Church to challenge the autocratic regimes in their part of the world. In response, a decade later with the growth of "liberation theology," and the election of a new Pope, John Paul II modified their political policies and replaced them with his own. He called on priests to be pastors, not politicians,[10] and used his papal power to outlaw liberation theology in 1984, claiming that its narrative of Jesus did not meet with the Church's catechesis.

This, again, began to lead to modern theological questions about hierarchical authority and canonical power. In 1998, Pope John Paul narrowed the authority of the bishops by issuing two directives. In an Apostolic Letter,[11] he clarified that bishops' regional organizations developed after Vatican II operated as a collegial union rather than as a canonical one. That meant that such associations did not have universal legal status in canon law, and thus could not create public policies, or require any of their fellow bishops in local or global conferences, to accept the policies that they adopted. Bishops could ask for an exception or a consideration of a policy, but this could only be accommodated in instances where a policy was approved unanimously by their hierarchical conference. It would, however, still require a two-third approval or "recognitio" from a Vatican commission. In another Apostolic Letter,[12] he required that those who were to enter in ecclesiastical leadership take an oath of obedience to the doctrines of the Church and the canon law.

This tightened hierarchical power reflected and affected the centralized governance of the Vatican in the United States, as well. When the United States Conference of Catholic Bishops (USCCB) attempted to set policies to sanction priests accused of clerical sexual abuse, the organization was denied that outright authority by the Vatican. Religious authorities at the Holy See considered such actions as an attempt to force their national policies on global members of the hierarchy. Thus, the hierarchy's decision to place a proposed zero-tolerance policy for clerical sexual abusers required a joint USCCB-Vatican commission to review the bishops' policies. They were told that the recommendations of the U.S. bishops' organization had to revolve around theology, recognize that predatory priestly behavior was a sin, based on the mandates of the Ten Commandments and canon law, and that it had to be adjudicated from that perspective.[13] Thus, the USCCB's recommendations to deal with clerical sexual abuse could only require the bishops in the United States to comply with them and accept the legal limitations set by the office of religious orthodoxy, that is, the Congregation for the Doctrine of the Faith (CDF).

THE CATHOLIC HIERARCHY RESPONDS TO CLERICAL SEXUAL ABUSE

The treatment of clergy for predatory behavior by the Pope and bishops has evolved, but their right to impose religious sanctions has always been based on the Church's theological view that such deviant behavior is a *sin*, that is, a violation of the Sixth Commandment that forbids adultery and implies other violations of sexual impurity. Bishops, therefore, have historically prescribed their own, specific religious penalties as a part of their right to punish moral transgressions. Recognized as their spiritual responsibility by civil rulers, the hierarchy's legitimacy to mete out sanctions went unchallenged by those who did not see sin as being within their secular purview.

Instead, Church rules were accepted during the early days of Christianity as the civil standard for punishing clerical sexual abuse. Broad rules found in the Epistles of St. Paul and St. Barnabas forbade corrupting boys or bedding males. Examples of these sins can be seen in *The Didache*, mentioned earlier, particularly in the section on the "Way of Death." It decried adultery, fornication, pedophilia, murder, witchcraft, abortion, and infanticide.

Clergy were expected to be known by their morals and expected to carry out their religious tasks. In 177 CE, Bishop Athenagoras called for the excommunication of sodomites and pedophiliacs from the Church. At a council of bishops at Ancyra (314 CE) religious authorities set out the strict penance and excommunication punishments for homosexuality. *The Penitential Book of St. Bede* in the eighth century called for various sanctions from confession and repentance to public flogging and the shaving of a cleric's hair for rape, bestiality, and sodomy. He also maintained that the higher the position of the perpetrator of the crime, the higher his punishment should be. In 1051 CE, St. Peter Damien wrote *The Book of Gammorah*. A Benedictine reformer, he called for changes arising from sodomy and other sins of impurity calling for the sinners be "foully besmeared with spit . . . and be bound in iron chains."[14]

Despite these early sanctions of priests for crimes against the Ten Commandments and the sacraments, members of the clergy and even the hierarchy were often involved in what some have simply called the "dark side" of the priestly behavior. Their punishments were inconsistent and based on the interpretation of the severity of the moral transgressions according to their superiors.

The differences in the various religious perceptions of the culpability of clerical sexual abusers stood at the center of a long-standing and larger dispute over the Church's right to supervise and sanction the clergy for spiritual failings versus the demands of civil authorities to punish priests for civil crimes. Indeed, the official Catholic view of clerical sexual abuse historically has been that it constitutes a "delict" or a grave religious "sin," and therefore, is to be adjudicated only by Church leaders who have legitimate authority to sanction and forgive moral transgressions.

The justification for this ecclesiastical interpretation and power is based on two major Catholic theological tenets. The first is that each person is created in the image and likeness of God. This means that a person is born with a dual nature that reflects both a temporal and spiritual dimension. Thus, as a human being, a person is born with free will, that is, with the ability to choose good or evil. As a spiritual being, however, that same person is also worthy of dignity and respect, able to repent sins, and rise above human nature. Second, in relation to priests, traditional doctrine holds that clerics, who also have a spiritual and temporal dimension, can make free moral choices but additionally also have a special gift from God due to their ordination in the sacrament of Holy Orders. That gift is "grace," which provides priests with the ability to confess their sins, repent, and reconcile with God even if their moral choices were grave transgressions.

These theological beliefs gave rise to a system of ecclesiastical or church law designed for the institutional governance of the Church and the management of the clergy. There are essentially two aspects of this religious law. The first is ad hoc and responsive, that is, it is characterized by a series of individual directives or policies that have evolved due to religious, political, or social challenges during the 2,000 years of the Church's existence.

In sociological terms, these hierarchical actions can be interpreted as "living law," a definition used by Eugen Ehrlich who analyzed the coexistence as well as the tensions between social and legal structures. In his seminal work,[15] Ehrlich maintained that due to the daily social associations within society, people outside the established order create peaceful customs and stable interactions, which in turn develop social change and regulations. Thus, they enable shifts in norms as defined by hierarchical organizations as well as provide the often needed external pressures to augment and update the status quo.

This is evident even today as both Church and State hierarchical governance structures continue to grapple with the rights and responsibilities of each to confront clerical sexual abuse. The responsive orders of the Catholic leadership, therefore, can be understood as having been designed to reply to specific moral challenges, transitory civil statutes, secular demands for changes in society, and the need to establish more contemporary religious laws. Historically, they generated sanctions that evolved into precedents through papal writings, dictates, and reforms. Supplemented with changing hierarchical policies, practices, and procedures, this type of law enabled the management of clerical personnel, the maintenance of the structures of the Church, and the advocacy for moral-political issues such as social justice, human rights, and peace. Within these broad categories, examples of related responses by the popes facing the crisis of clerical sexual abuse include the actions of Popes John Paul II, Benedict XVI, and Francis.

The early papacy of John Paul II was characterized by contemporary concerns: supporting a pro-life global agenda as well as pursuing religious engagement in Eastern Europe that could lead to a change in the Communist political system in that part of the world. But, also during his papacy, growing public allegations of clerical sexual abuse emerged, leading to civil investigations, demands for clerical personnel records, and secular supervisory oversight of Church authorities. They became a matter of major litigation between state and canon lawyers and occurred first in the United States and subsequently led to a crisis in almost every country where the Church had religious personnel.

In the United States, there were hints of such abusive priestly behavior, early warnings by Church insiders who monitored early cases of clerical abuse, and reports of this tragedy to high-ranking Church officials.[16] But, these concerns went unheeded for many reasons: partially by authorities in Rome concerned with other matters, individual bishops who refused to acknowledge such allegations, and limitations on the national organization, the United States Conference of Catholic Bishops (USCCB). None seemed to understand the meaning and depth of the crisis and thus insisted on their traditional right to manage the clergy on their own terms in their own dioceses.

Pope John Paul, himself, blamed American society and its "hyper-inflated sexuality," homosexuality, and a "cultural chasm" for the tragedy of clerical sexual abuse.[17] After his death, Pope John Paul's official spokesman, Joaquin Navarro- Valls, reportedly said that John Paul did not immediately understand the gravity of the sexual abuse crisis. "I don't think Pope John Paul understood the 'cancer' of clergy sexual abuse immediately," and added, "I don't think anyone did," until he became aware of the accusations against clergy in the Boston archdiocese in 2002.[18]

This is evidenced by Pope John Paul's surprised reaction to the scope of the scandal. He called all the U.S. Cardinals to Rome along with the leadership of the USCCB to discuss the issue, to communicate the Church's theological principles for handling such predatory behavior, and to assure a unified response of the hierarchy in the crisis.

These responses, agreed on by all, were an admission that clerical sexual abuse was a crime and a sin, that the church must provide solidarity and assistance to the victims and accept the gravity of the abuse regardless of the number of cases. Together, the Church leaders stressed that there was no relationship between celibacy and pedophilia and that Church leaders should promote correct moral teaching about sexual abuse. But the most critical principle was the unified support that the Church recognized the power of Christian conversion and the ability of a sinner [even a priest] to return to God.[19] Thus, even though an admission of clerical sexual abuse as a crime was noted, the special theological position and religious treatment of a priest were protected by his "clericalism." No official Church offer of institutional co-operation with civil authorities was promised at that time—nor for almost two decades later.

Instead, these pronouncements by Pope John Paul with the American hierarchy stressed theological responses to the crisis rather than pragmatic ways to address the sociological implications of them for children and their families. Realizing that this approach could prove to be insufficient to American Catholics and the public, the head of the USCCB tried to defend the papal leadership of Pope John Paul immediately after the meeting. "He gets it," he said, while trying to explain that the Church does not do crime; it does sin.[20]

The USCCB, however, dissatisfied after the papal meeting and feeling public pressure, moved quickly on its own to pass a strong policy statement that would set out serious sanctions for predatory priestly actions. Its national organization issued a "Charter to Protect Children"[21] in 2002 that called for a zero-tolerance policy for clerical sexual abusers and mandatory punishments for them. It gave civil authorities the right to prosecute priests for predatory behavior, required bishops to report such crimes to civil authorities, and called for publicly releasing the names of those who had been sanctioned for pedophilia in the past.

Even with the near unanimous vote of its membership, however, some of the USCCB policies were different from those in canon law and meant that a joint commission at the Vatican had to approve their mandates. Four years later, it did so, but with the caveat that the policies of the organization could apply only to the American hierarchy and did not have canonical or universal status.

Nevertheless, the American Bishops, as a national organization, continued to deal with the tragedy of clerical sexual abuse while they waited for official approval for their charter from Rome. They set up norms for bishops and other Church leaders to deal with allegations of sexual abuse in the United States that did not require Vatican approval, and established a review board to gather data and advice from experts about how to deal with the crisis.[22] They also took part in many civil cases even though some members of the hierarchy tried to protect religious freedom and preserve their right to manage the clergy in abuse matters. Eventually, however, most bishops understood their civil responsibilities and agreed to give depositions, turn over personnel files to state authorities, and even succumb to state oversight of some of their facilities and personnel that dealt with children.[23]

With the death of Pope John Paul in 2005 and the election of Joseph Cardinal Ratzinger as Pope Benedict XVI, a more forceful approach to clerical sexual abuse appeared at the Vatican. As a world-class theologian, Ratzinger served as the prefect of the CDF for twenty-five years and thus knew, from his experience, its doctrinal strengths and institutional weaknesses. He was in a position, then, to control and reform the internal workings of its judiciary. His appointment to that position by John Paul was almost as a co-equal in his power to protect Church orthodoxy and enforce canon law at the Vatican.

As prefect of the CDF, Ratzinger sought to bring greater attention and accountability to the problem of predatory priestly behavior by requiring bishops to report allegations of sexual abuse to Rome, centralizing the adjudication of clerical sexual abuse cases within the CDF, and assuring uniform treatment of all those who would be tried at the Vatican.[24] Working closely with John Paul, Ratzinger adjudicated cases of clerical sexual abuse and admitted after being elected Pope that he was aware of the "filth"[25] that existed within the Church.

As Benedict XVI, then, the new pope who was a theologian, was also a pragmatist, and *the* religious enforcer of the Church's doctrines; a person who was concerned with reform based on holiness.[26] While he did not make major revisions to canon law as pope, Benedict imposed stricter *moto proprios*, or papal directives, that impacted Church processes to deal with clerical sexual abuse. He made changes in seminary education, the religious preparation of men for the priesthood, and forbade those with homosexual tendencies to attend seminaries.[27] He publicly castigated the hierarchy in Ireland to reform itself after a civil investigation revealed its lack of appropriately dealing with clerical sexual abuse. Later, he also made an official apology to the people of Ireland and their victims of clerical sexual abuse.[28] He also prosecuted Father Marcial Maciel in 2006, a notorious abuser of seminarians; removed him from public ministry and ordered him to spend the rest of his life in prayer and penance.

Benedict XVI continued to carry out reforms of the CDF and the prosecution of clerical sexual abusers, but decided to retire at age 85, overwhelmed by other papal tasks at his advanced age. He was the first pope to leave office in 600 years, but as rumors swirled about his ill health and inability to deal with crises any longer, it could have been expected.

He adopted the title "Pope Emeritus" and intended to lead a simple life. However, in 2020, Benedict was found to have been involved in a cover-up of clerical sexual abuse by an investigation led by the German bishops' conference. It revealed that the malfeasance occurred when Benedict was Archbishop of Munich and Freising, the time before he came to the Vatican, the CDF, and the papacy. Once found out, Benedict admitted his wrongdoing, apologized for his past behavior,[29] and was left with a serious stain on his commitment to fight clerical sexual abuse.

An understanding of some of the disparate and unsuccessful responsive actions of the hierarchy, then, helps to explain the increasing use of the second kind of the Catholic ecclesiastical legal system: canon law. It provides insights about the ability and weaknesses of the Church's governance structure to develop unified and pragmatic policies to deal with clerical sexual abuse as well as the reasons for the conflict over Church demands to manage the clergy for grave sins versus global civil challenges to investigate and punish clerics for criminal acts.

Canon law, then, is the *formal* system of statutes promulgated by the leader of the Catholic Church, the pope, and enforced by various religious authorities and agencies below him known as the Roman Curia, or Church administration. It was through a codification of this type of law that the Church legalized how it would organize and govern itself.

These precepts can be found today in the books that comprise the current Code of Canon Law. It consists of over a 1,000 "canons," or laws that cover the general norms of clerical behavior, religious obligations and rights, the teaching and sanctifying functions of the Church, regulations concerning Church property, religious sanctions, and the judicial procedures for violations of ecclesiastical precepts. The Code applies to the entire Church—its institutions and personnel. Throughout Church history, it has been considered as universal law, enlarged, and finally revised in whole or in parts in 1917, 1983, and 2021.

In the Code of 1917, four significant canons dealt with the sins of sexual abuse. The first, Canon 2359, maintained that impure involvement with a minor *below* the age of 16 or participation with adults in debauchery, bestiality, sodomy, pandering, adultery, or incest with blood relatives would result in the suspension of a cleric, who could also possibly be deposed, declared infamous, and deprived of any office, benefice, dignity, and responsibility, in the Church. The second canon gave *bishops* the discretion to impose a punishment or treatment for a priest found guilty of a delict or a grave religious crime. The third justified a bishop's power to provide religious sanctions based on his *informed conscience*, that is, based on traditional religious teachings and his personal education. This meant that bishops could handle delicts of a sexual nature themselves, and bypass a canonical investigation or trial. Thus, ecclesiastical law maintained that there was no need for the accused to provide witnesses and no right of the priest to defend himself. The fourth principle maintained that a priest could be defrocked for grave sins, that is, deprived of his religious function and ministry by the bishop. He could also be laicized or returned to the secular life and freed from religious control by the CDF in Rome.

The Revised Code of 1983 set up even more specific judicial procedures to deal with the grave sin of clerical sexual abuse. It dealt with ecclesiastical procedures for accusations; revisited the age of the minor victim; and whether force, threats, or public actions were perpetrated on the young person. However, the new code also required that an investigation into such allegations were to be started at the diocesan level. Individuals were to be appointed by the bishop in the case of sexual delicts; the accused cleric would be allowed to have a lawyer and witnesses, be confronted by his accusers, and allowed to hear the sexual allegations against him. Only then could the bishop decide if there was enough evidence to proceed with further action that could include sanctions as serious as excommunication from the Church. This expulsion could occur only if a priest was involved in a scandal and considered to be beyond correction, reproof, reform, or pastoral care. These new canonical practices included several civil rights like those in state courts: a grand jury hearing, requiring an indictment, and moving a case to an appropriate court. The major difference, however, was that the jury would be appointed by the bishop. If a cleric was found guilty, he could no longer carry out his ministry or administer the sacraments. He could be defrocked and remain a priest in name only. He had the right of appeal, but generally the time it took to hear the case in Rome resulted in the bishop imposing the final sentence on a priest.

In 2021, Pope Francis took a major step to bring about a judicial recognition and revision of the hierarchy's responsibilities for sanctioning clerical sexual abuse. Through an Apostolic Constitution, that is a public solemn declaration, entitled *Pascite gregem Dei*,[30] he declared that the obligation to punish clerics was "to be carried out as a concrete and essential requirement of charity, not only towards the Church, the Christian community and potential injured parties, but also towards those who commit crimes and are themselves in need of the Church's mercy and correction."[31] As a universal mandate required of all the hierarchy, Francis reminded the hierarchy that disciplinary sanctions were part of charity, and went further by saying that tolerating immoral conduct with exhortations or suggestions are "insufficient remedies." He wrote:

> For this reason, it becomes necessary for bishops and superiors to inflict penalties. Negligence on the part of a bishop in resorting to the penal system is a sign that he has failed to carry out his duties honestly and faithfully. . . . Charity thus demands that the Church's pastors resort to the penal system whenever it is required, keeping in mind the three aims that make it necessary in the ecclesial community: the restoration of the demands of justice, the correction of the guilty party and the repair of scandals.[32]

Thus, the Pope officially required the hierarchy to send cases of clerical sexual abuse to criminal prosecutors when required by civil law. This was the first time such a requirement was placed on the entire hierarchy.

In 2022, Pope Francis continued his policy of demanding structural reforms within the Church's judicial processes to deal with clerical sexual abuse. He issued another Apostolic Constitution at that time entitled *Praedicate evangelium*.[33] It was a directive that built on his previous revision of canon law and impacted the constitutional reorganization of the Church's entire bureaucracy, that is, the Holy See.

Pragmatically, the document discusses the intricacies of the Church's judicial workings, the individual tribunals that deal with the administration of justice, and the responsibilities of each agency in judging religious disputes, appeals, and discipline as well as its role in protecting the rights of the

Church.[34] From a governance perspective, this reform was designed to bring about a major change in the service component of the Church bureaucracy. It emphasized modern principles and the criteria needed to carry out a more and focused service to the Pope, bishops, hierarchical conferences, communities, and the world.[35] New operating principles with revised rules and reformed structures were to impact the entire administration of the Church, specifically the Secretariat of State and other offices that serve the Pope. Insisting on competence, Pope Francis outlined changes in procedures and regulations for relations with states and international organizations as well as those of Church diplomats who carry out Church-State relations.

This internal reorganization is significant because as civil investigations into many aspects of the Church's authority have increased in cases of clerical sexual abuse, they have also revealed some of its antiquated internal mismanagement as well as corruption within the Church's infrastructure. They have exposed the need to reform the type and expectations of the leadership and Church judicial processes. What is significant here is that this specific reform offers the Church an opportunity to regain trust in its authority and its commitment to transparent policies for competent accountability, especially in its continuing attempts to deal with clerical sexual abuse.

In the past *civil* investigations took the lead in scrutinizing the Church infrastructure and providing evidence for those who argued for more vigorous papal oversight, external investigations, and major attempts at internal administrative reforms. They showed that such actions were necessary to bring a sense of credibility back to the institutional Church. Now, however, Pope Francis has recognized this weakness, responded, and re-visited the Church's religious and governance responsibilities.

Theologically, Francis's actions and reforms are also intended to provide strong Christian witness that in turn would "foster a more effective evangelization to promote a more fruitful ecumenical spirit and . . . encourage a more constructive dialogue with all."[36] Evangelization, then, will still be placed at the service of the Church for its growth and collaboration with other religious institutions.[37] It follows Pope Francis's credo: evangelization is a task to be accomplished by charity and inter-religious dialogue[38] that is focused on the laity and the family and life.[39]

POPE FRANCIS, THEOLOGY, AND CLERICAL SEXUAL ABUSE

Both types of ecclesiastical law, ad hoc responsive orders and codified canons, are directly or indirectly based on Scriptural law and natural law, and are the foundations for the diverse executive, legislative, and judicial powers of the leader of the Church, the Pope. They are the legal manifestations of his religious agenda, social doctrines, and the basis of his moral political guidance. Considered together, responsive orders and codified canons, today, deal with both the substance of the day-to-day religious functioning of the institutional Church as well as the processes of its government and universal authority. In tandem, these two aspects of the Catholic legal system are controlled by the Pope who initiates, implements, and enforces the internal actions of the Holy See, or bureaucracy of the Church, as well as the external relations of this complex legal system.

Theological tenets serve as the underpinning of the Church's social doctrines as well as its ecclesiastical law. They are crucial to understanding hierarchical responses to secular challenges, especially those posed by the clerical sexual abuse crisis.

The primary religious principle that explains actions to protect all life is the tenet of *Imago Dei*. It is the belief that each person is created in the image and likeness of God and therefore has dignity and worth. Thus, the Church has translated this tenet into social doctrines that support human rights around the world, the centrality of the right to life, religious freedom, the family, marriage, children, education, work, and labor unions. It incorporates the Church's commitment to end sex trafficking and sexual abuse.

Imago Dei also justifies prioritizing the option for the poor and marginalized as well as the Church's advocacy for the economic involvement of all in society, the right to immigration, and a just policy of globalization. Finally, the Church also supports a social doctrine that is a political commitment to the common good that employs evangelization for the principle of subsidiarity or personal participation in democratic governance as well as the principle of solidarity or unity that leads the Church to ally itself with those seeking the values of truth, freedom, justice, love, and peace.[40]

Further, these theological beliefs are buttressed by the two types of Catholic, ecclesiastical law that assure the continued existence of Jesus's Church and its salvific mission. While Elazar's theories deserve repeating, it is also important to reiterate that unlike secular regimes, the Catholic hierarchical structure has created its own unique leadership model, one that has existed for more than 2,000 years. To this must be added, that it has also developed a religious legal system and enforcement mechanisms based on theologically based social doctrines. These have not evolved due to a social consensus, but rather a *moral* one that enables the Church to continue its existence.

The ecclesiastical law of the Church, therefore, is an outcome of that moral consensus. It is significant in so far as it has historically been considered as the independent, legitimate, and unquestioned religious means to carry out the Church's spiritual mission to bring souls to Christ.

Pope Francis, the Bishop of Rome, and elected leader of the Catholic Church, is the man who is now tasked with dealing with the liabilities and problems that have emerged and escalated during the two-decades-old global clerical sexual abuse crisis. Following John Paul, who was simply ignorant of the scope and nature of the crisis for most of his papacy, and Pope Benedict who was overwhelmed by it all, Pope Francis has stepped into a policy quagmire and has been attempting to bring order into chaos in dealing with predatory priestly behavior.

Individual scholars and researchers, however, have been justified in their critiques of the Church's governance structure and mismanagement since the findings by numerous civil agencies around the world have been made public. A general pattern can be seen in these government-led investigations of clerical sexual abuse: cover-ups of accusations by Church leaders, forced signings of non-disclosure agreements to silence victims, priority policies to protect the reputation of the Church, reassignments of predator priests, a lack of truthfulness about the movement of clergy to new parishes, and poor communications between local bishops with officials at the Vatican. They have resulted in political and social challenges to former religious exemptions and understandings of religious freedom that have led to subpoenas of Church leaders, the incarceration of clerics, worldwide financial bankruptcies of dioceses, oversight of Church institutions and employees dealing with children, and even legal challenges to the Pope.

Most significantly, the Church has responded, and in certain situations, continues to use, canon law as the primary means to sanction clerical sexual abusers. However, the ecclesiastical norms imposed by the Church are different from the civil and criminal standards. In the past, religious superiors often reassigned or retired clerics; they sent them to "hospitals" to be "fixed" or monasteries to "repent." Other priests left the priesthood voluntarily and were thus unpunished by canon law. If clerics chose to remain, they could not say mass or perform the sacraments. In rare cases, they faced excommunication. Now, the Church has increasingly reformed canon law, but still maintains the right to prosecute and sanction priests for religious crimes and with religious punishments.

The criminal prosecution of priests, however, is different. It was historically considered as part of the responsibility of Church officials. They had argued that to reveal predatory priestly behavior to civil authorities would be a violation of religious freedom and traditional civil exemptions as well as being outside the sphere of civil authority. But recently, new and continuing civil demands for information about clerical sexual abuse have resulted in major legal challenges and societal demands for change.

The most critical challenges are civil, legal demands for the Vatican to accept responsibility for the actions of its hierarchy and clergy, as well as social pressures for the Church to co-operate in creating solutions to end the victimization of children. They are now being acted on by Church authorities, led by Pope Francis.

He has re-visited Pope John Paul's admission in 2002 with the American hierarchy in Rome, that clerical sexual abuse was a crime as well as a sin. Unfortunately, the actual means to move from that principle to the development of new global processes and policies to eliminate the crisis were not approved by Church authorities since that time. Now Pope Francis has finally and officially recognized clerical sexual abuse as a crime as well as a sin, and required that the hierarchy co-operate with penal or civil authorities to adjudicate such predatory clerical behavior.

But the task of eliminating clerical sexual abuse is not over. Pope Francis is now the leader and papal successor who must solve the religious, social, and legal aspects of that dilemma and reform, what is now, a struggling sacred hierarchical organization, but one that still has the potential to be a moral guide in the world.

To be sure, the Church's organization structure needs reform, but its history belies an institutional convulsion to make this happen. A synthesis of successful modern management principles usually includes the development of a pragmatic process to implement consistent unified strategies for the purpose of reaching a specific goal. Current leadership models, which buttress such systems, are often led by managers who are dominant and/or collaborative and task-oriented; with each type of leader focused on the continuous improvement of their organizations.

The Catholic Church, however, functioning as a hierarchical religious institution, historically operates as a unique model, supporting those parts of its administration that work within the context of its salvific mission. As an anomaly and through the lens of time, this managerial model is a unique one, still operating with a single, patrimonial, sacred leader; divinely mandated to bring people to spiritual salvation.

Under the primacy and leadership of one man, the Pope accomplishes this mission with supreme, unquestioned religious and political power, supported with the service of thousands of loyal religious volunteers which include the hierarchy and clergy. The papal leader can, and does, use a pastoral strategy of evangelization to attract followers, often gained through religious engagement and outreach on a geopolitical platform. He presents his spiritual institution as a moral guide for the pursuit of universal values such as peace, human rights, and social justice.

This, in turn, creates the unique global Catholic community of over one billion adherents. It is maintained first, through a sacramental bond. It is one that begins at birth through Baptism and continues with Holy Eucharist, Confirmation, Marriage, and Holy Orders, until Extreme Unction, at death. These religious rites confer and continually reenforce membership in the Church supplemented by teachings and its educational system, missionary work, and social services. All of these bring people to its fold.

To implement the divine mandate and salvific mission of the Church, the leadership model of the Apostles gave rise to the development of processes and procedures that would enable their pastoral commands to become reality. The evolution of the papacy—to its position of prime authority and the subsequent service role of the hierarchy—survived political challenges even from civil rulers who historically claimed "divine right" to be on their side.[41]

Thus, a religious governance prerogative has always maintained a special position within society because of the early establishment of the Church's organization structure that developed prior to that of national states. It has, therefore, allowed the Church to lay claim to religious exemptions and privileges within emerging territories regarding its right to exist and maintain itself. Further, it has been able to champion the right to religious freedom, religious speech, and religious assembly from the Church's inception. As the Church's religious influence and political power grew, so did its civil control of major institutions: churches, schools, orphanages, and hospitals; art, scientific experiments, scholastic philosophy, and governmental involvement.[42]

The spiritual strategies that the Catholic Church has used over its 2,000 years of existence are again a unique means to impose its salvific purpose. It offered religious salvation or a reduction of eternal punishments for sins by granting "indulgences," or time lessened, for financial Church donations. It promised eternal happiness by assuring a heavenly reward for fighting to liberate the Holy Land during the Crusades. It served as a conduit for wealthy families who often purchased high ecclesiastical position and appointments within the ecclesiastical infrastructure of the hierarchy. It served as the patron of the arts and architecture, providing work, establishing towns, and supporting the trades around the building of cathedrals and their environments. The Church raised armies who protected its leaders, properties, and interests. It made significant political alliances.

The most meaningful of these was the Treaty of the Lateran in 1921. It was the treaty by which the Church reached the apogee of its global religious and political power. At that time, the government of Italy and the Catholic Church signed a concordat in which the Church gave up its control over its significant territories in Italy known as the Papal States[43] and established, instead, the Vatican City State. Governed by the Holy See, or Church bureaucracy, it is technically considered a special type of theocracy. In this case, it is one that is ruled by the Pope, the bishop of Rome, who in the holy ordering of authority is the head of the Catholic Church. In return, the government of Italy, under Benito Mussolini, recognized the Vatican as a sovereign and independent state and accepted Catholicism as the official religion of Italy as well. From that point on, the Church had a sovereign geopolitical platform and an opportunity to operate as a worldwide moral presence. It became a political equal with other independent states in the world.

Today, the Vatican has permanent observer status with all the rights of a full member of the United Nations except for a vote in its General Assembly. It has relations with over 170 states and engages with international organizations as well. It is, therefore, able to use both its religious and political positions to impact foreign policy while attempting to serve as a moral guide for the world.

The government of Vatican City has a unique structure that aids and adds to its adaptability to function within civil society. The Pope is the sovereign ruler of the religious, yet civil state. Although legislative authority is vested in the Pontifical Commission for the Vatican State, it consists of an appointed president and cardinals appointed by the Pope for five-year periods. The Vatican's foreign relations are entrusted to the Holy See's bureaucracy known as the Secretariat of State and pastoral governance is largely exercised through the Roman Curia, or the administrative offices of Vatican City. On a more practical level, the governance officials of Vatican City consist of officials who are appointed by the Pope and oversee the central governmental functions that deal with problems concerning the state's territory, including local security, records, transportation, and finances. Judicial functions are delegated to a supreme court, an appellate court, and a trial judge. At the Vatican's request, sentences imposed can be served in Italy.

Thus, the hierarchy of the Catholic Church, from a managerial perspective, operates on several levels: religious, civil, political, and international. An understanding of the political culture, notions of law, and political power makes it possible to understand how the governance structure, led by the Pope and the Holy See, has enabled Church authorities to enforce Catholic traditional, orthodox religious beliefs and its legal system.

This chapter, then, has been able to show that the historical and continued moral influence, political viability, and social relevance of the governance of the Catholic hierarchy has remained significant due to its ability to adapt to new social, legal, and moral challenges. These changes, however, often with negative sociological implications, but with pragmatic interpretations of Catholic social doctrines, still strive to have positive effects. This can be seen in Pope Francis's willingness to shift the past emphasis and priorities on clerical sexual abuse to a new internal approach to contemporary problems,[44] one based on transparency, accountability, and even the reform of the institutional agencies that deal with clerical sexual abuse.

Prior to becoming Pope, Francis guided and edited a type of hierarchical manifesto, known as the *Aparecida Documents* issued by the Latin American Bishops Conference (CELAM) in 2007.[45] At that time, he headed the regional organization as the Archbishop of Buenos Aires and maintained then, as now, two guiding principles that would underlie this religious and social agendas: the support of an option for the poor and marginalized as well as the need to renew notions of the responsibility of the hierarchy and laity to implement these social doctrines.

> A Catholic faith reduced to mere baggage, to a collection of rules and prohibitions, to fragmented devotional practices, to selective and partial adherence to the truths of the faith, to occasional participation in some sacraments, to the repetition of doctrinal principles, to bland or nervous moralizing, that does not convert the life of the baptized would not withstand the trials of time. . . . We must all start again from Christ, recognizing that being Christian is not the result of an ethical choice or a lofty idea, but the encounter with an event, a person, which gives life a new horizon.[46]

As the basis of his pastoral commitment, he reenforced its principles in 2013 after he became Pope, in an encyclical entitled *Evangelium Gaudium.*[47] In it, he outlined his vision for a Church in need of a new approach to attain its salvific goals. He urged clergy and laity alike to recognize the importance of time over space, unity over conflict, reality over ideas, and the whole over the parts.[48] The arguments, though deeply philosophical, were basic: that the Church can work pragmatically and slowly, without being motivated by immediate results. In short, his vision has given credibility to patience, adaptability, as well as a willingness to initiate new processes and engage others "without anxiety, but with clear convictions and tenacity."[49] Most importantly, he has personally acted on these principles, beginning with his own attempt to uncover and reform the internal problems that have allowed clerical sexual abuse to exist and fester during the last two papacies.

In 2014, for example, Pope Francis faced the clerical sexual abuse crisis head on when the United Nations Committee on the Optional Protocols to Protect Minors accused the Catholic Church of being complicit in the sexual abuse of children by adopting policies and policies which essentially led to the continuation of the sexual abuse by clerical perpetrators.[50] As a signatory and a member of the Committee, he denied the accusations, had them investigated, and soon after, established the Pontifical Commission on Clerical Sexual Abuse.

Its purpose, ostensibly, was to draw up systematic strategies for education and communications while also helping to develop solutions to end clerical sexual abuse. Headed by Cardinal O'Malley of Boston, a vocal critic of Catholic responses to the clerical sexual abuse crisis, Pope Francis appointed the Churchman to lead a team composed of medical experts, lay activists, and others. The organization successfully set out principles and processes to accomplish an education goal, however, due to a dispute,[51] the committee was recalled and then reinstated. However, some members questioned the group's continued purpose and value. They resigned from the commission, and left the organization to work in limbo.

Five years later, in 2019, with the clerical abuse crisis still a central problem for the Catholic Church, Pope Francis held a synod, or a global meeting of the Church leadership, to discuss the still festering global crisis. The meetings' organizers emphasized that the synod would share good practices and ways to implement measures for the safety of minors while also discussing the responsibility, transparency, and accountability of the Church. Absent from the meeting, however, were Cardinal Sean O'Malley and representatives from the Pontifical Commission for the Protection of Minors.

While the success of the synod was questionable, it resulted in major directives that set Vatican City State policies for child protection. Most importantly, however, was the apostolic letter in the form of a *moto proprio* issued by Pope Francis entitled *Vos estes lux Mundi (You are the Light of the World).*[52]

In it, he set out the scope of an ecclesial commitment that required new norms for reporting clerical sexual abuse. These included acts of coercion, violence or abuse of a vulnerable person, possession, distribution of pornography, or omissions aimed at interfering with or circumventing civil investigations or canonical, administrative, or criminal investigations, against a cleric or religious in crimes of clerical sexual abuse.[53] There was no longer any question or confusion as to the responsibilities or scope of actions that were to be reported to civil authorities. It was finally clear.

In 2020, Pope Francis continued his work to change various aspects of Church management, particularly as they were related to clerical sexual abuse. At that time, he launched an investigation into the system that supported the ecclesiastical promotion of Theodore Cardinal McCarrick, the highest-ranking cleric in the United States, despite rumors, as well as a later CDF conviction for the sexual abuse of seminarians. Punished by isolation in a monastery, McCarrick reappeared at the Vatican a while later discussing a potential diplomatic assignment for the Pope. This triggered an angry response from a former Vatican diplomat to the United States, Archbishop Vigano,[54] who accused McCarrick of predatory offenses that were reported but not acted on by Church authorities.

The investigation revealed significant flaws in the Church's administration and laid bare the fact that references and votes approving hierarchical promotions by brother bishops and even the Pope often included cover-ups and cronyism among the elite leadership. In a 425-page report,[55] the investigation also showed that some bishops provided incomplete information about McCarrick, and that his relationships with Pope John Paul II likely had an impact on the decision making and appointment of him as a Cardinal. Further, it also showed that Pope Benedict XVI did not initiate a formal canonical inquiry into the McCarrick case or even impose sanctions on him for a variety of questionable reasons.[56]

However, the larger implications of Francis's actions have provided transparency and justified his continued actions to reform the inner works of a flawed managerial system of ecclesiastical promotions. They showed that even with allegations and convictions of sexual abuse, clerics could still be elevated to the highest levels of Church administration, and that the hierarchical organizational structure was in dire need of repair.

ANALYSIS

Even with all these modern managerial changes there are still negative realities that need to be addressed about the hierarchical organization of the Church. Indeed, its functioning during the clerical sexual abuse scandal has been considered by some as the beginning of the end of the Catholic Church. The hierarchy has been accused by civil authorities, the media, and lay activists as leaders who are unwilling and unable to accept responsibility and accountability for the inept way it has managed the crisis.

Some political scientists, particularly Warner,[57] argue that the Church's religious doctrines have had an adverse, yet significant, sociological impact on democracy. She maintains that it has affected the oversight, prosecution, and privileged status of the Church in a serious way, but that it should serve as a warning for laws and procedures when continuing public deference to sacred institutions.

Critics of hierarchical organizations, in general, also claim that as information and directives flow from the top down, that is, from the Pope to Church adherents, and the size of its organization grows, this type of hierarchical governance can give rise to an autocratic infrastructure often distorted by power and corrupted by scandals. Thus, many thinkers consider this type of hierarchy problematic, and maintain that hierarchies can restrict freedom for order, personalize power, and lead to stagnation.[58]

In response, the Catholic leadership has, in its own way over two millennia, honed a unique style of managerial adaptability during its long existence. While democracies can be "polarized and paralyzed,"[59] the modern Church leadership has continually attempted to re-create itself by reforming its special sacred governance to assure the integrity of its religious leadership, management processes, and ecclesiastical legal system.

Activists also claim that the Church hierarchy must listen, take advice, and include the secular concerns of the laity to effect meaningful change. They argue that people in the pews must have a say in agenda setting, policy development, and decision making within the Church that impact their daily lives. To do this, lay organizations such as Voice of the Faithful support the fact that the leadership must change from a top-down autocratic organization structure to a bottom-up democratic, inclusive system of governance, particularly one that recognizes the concerns of women, their lack of any appreciable participation in the governance of the Church, or any significant advisory role in making Church policy.

New voices represent lay activism as well as science, the humanities, medicine, politics, and other social agendas. They want to have the opportunity to bring innovative solutions to policy discussions and decision making and believe that such in-put can provide a viable means to gain acceptance of the values that will emerge from such inclusive governance.

At the same time, Pope Francis is also aware of the need to change the focus of the Church's religious outreach to reflect the demographic changes occurring in its laity. Calling Europe "aged," he has instituted policies to reflect the growth of adherents in new parts of the world. He intends to bolster a global sensitivity to changed social, political, and religious reconciliation, a signal that will continue to upend the Catholic Church's traditional priorities.

Nonetheless, major organizational and sociological challenges remain. Among them are the continued, almost daily, investigations and revelations of clerical sexual abuse even as papal attempts to control the tragedy have been addressed by Pope Francis. Since the beginning of his papacy and attempts to bring the crisis under control, major exposes have dampened hopes that clerical sexual abuse would become a fading problem for the Church.

Instead, the steady and growing supremacy of civil law over canon law has exacerbated due to the focused, aggressive, and successful attempts of society to protect its children. These legal investigations have been supported and impacted by social activism and media attention. Their demands for Church transparency and accountability as well as their insistence on new religious approaches to policies, processes, regulations, and rules can, and most likely will, require a change in official Church priorities.

Ehrlich's theories, then, broadly and in certain circumstances, can also be used to critique the Catholic governance system. They are, for example, still the underpinnings of sociological and legal arguments today that support civil and religious responses to the clerical sexual abuse crisis. The most important of these is the need for the hierarchy to shift its continued attempts *to control of the reputation* of the Church which depends on to accomplish its divine mandate to save souls.

There also exists a constant sociological tension between ideas and realities as Pope Francis philosophized in *Evangelium Gaudium.* His recognition that realities simply are, whereas ideas must be worked out is a profound, pragmatic governance principle. Yet, it needs to be the Church's hierarchical and organizational focus in the future so that continuous dialogue can bring both together. Francis claims that it is dangerous to dwell in the realm of words alone, of images and rhetoric, but while Pope Francis is motivated to move from theology to policy—he is on a hierarchical precipice trying to move from theory to practice with an agenda and processes that still require reform and challenge the Church to continue its efforts to end clerical sexual abuse.

Largely left wanting is still a deeper, objective study of the internal workings of the Vatican. That is, papal calls for hierarchical introspection must be more than a mechanical study of bureaucratic processes. It must be one that involves a broad examination and analysis of papal control of hierarchical governance, the current role of his leaders, and the means to maintain the unique ruling system that is increasingly becoming ideological. Liberal and conservative forces, reflecting the sociological and political climate of the times, are also causing religious splits on issues such as abortion, gay marriage, and assisted suicide. They are leaving the Church at odds with government policies and societies around the world especially in places like Europe and traditional Catholic states causing the Vatican to seek new converts in places such as China, Africa, and India.

The need for a "Vatican III" is an option to renew the moral role of the Church in the world and to provide an external modicum of religious concern during the continuing clerical sexual abuse global crisis. Pope Francis attempted such a meeting in 2019, but met with disaster as its discussions, input, and emphasis on the Church's stances rather than on the needs of victims solved none of the problems it was meant to address.

This author has argued for the need for a total reset of the Church's clerical sexual abuse policy. It should be one based on atonement.[60] Essentially, it must recognize the need for the Church to begin anew, to take responsibility and apologize formally—that is from the pulpit of St. Peter's Basilica—for the clerical sexual abuse crisis that the Church has allowed to not only exist, but to continue to fester openly for more than twenty years. Most importantly, the Church must place victims at the center of its concerns and become a place of healing and protection for children.

With this approach to predatory priestly behavior, that is, with transparency, acceptance of lay input into solving the crisis, and the pursuit of a meaningful introspection by the hierarchy, the Church can begin to achieve its salvific mission even in the tragedy of clerical sexual abuse. Hopefully, it will be able to pursue a sincere reconciliation of the Church leadership and its sacred organizational structure with the religious requirements and social challenges of society around the world, especially as it continues to adjudicate the sins of predatory priestly behavior ecclesiastically, and report the crimes of such clerics to civil authorities.

NOTES

1. Other Biblical texts are also used to legitimize the divine mandate for apostolic leadership in Jesus' Church. For example, in John 21:16, the Biblical text recounts Jesus telling His Apostle Peter to "be the shepherd of my sheep."

2. See Daniel J. Elazar, *The Covenant and Civil Society: The Constitutional Matrix of Modern Democracy* (New York: Routledge, 1997).

3. Stephen Pimentel, "The Master Key: Pope Benedict XVI's Theology of Covenant," *Homiletic and Pastoral Review,* October 2007. pp. 16–20. Accessed on 28 June 2022 @ Library : The Master Key: Pope Benedict XVI's Theology of Covenant | Catholic Culture. This is part of an explanation of the argument of Joseph Cardinal Ratzinger prior to his becoming Pope Benedict XVI in *Many Religions — One Covenant: Israel, the Church, and the World,* trans. Graham Harrison (San Francisco: Ignatius Press, 1999).

4. Mark 14:24.

5. This is a title from Roman antiquity given to a member of its religious class known as the College of Pontiffs. The titles were later given to any high official of the Roman Catholic Church, to a bishop and more particularly to the Bishop of Rome, who was also known as the Pope or "Roman Pontiff."

6. Historically, however, due to geographical distances and a lack of centralized communications, bishops often carried out their duties without major control from the ultimate seat of power, that is, from Rome and by the Pope of the Catholic Church.

7. Cardinals, even to the present, are appointed by the Pope for the purpose of electing a successor on his death. As members of the College of Cardinals, they may also serve as an advisory body to the Pope. They are often chosen to balance the views of their ideologies, geographical needs, specific competencies, and proven loyalty to the Church.

8. The hierarchy also maintained that the Church should not be confused with a political community or bound to any political system. There remained no discussion after that meeting about a juridical appeal in the Church against a possible misuse of papal power, although many theologians argue that a pope can be removed for public heretical or schismatic reasons. Walter M. Abbott, gen. ed., *The Documents of Vatican II* (New York: Herder and Herder, 1966). See: *Lumen Gentium.* Section 41, p. 241.

9. Conference of Latin American Bishops. *Medellin Conference Statement, 1968.* Accessed on 1 July 2022 @Medellín Conference Statement, 1968 (we-are-church .org).

10. Pope John Paul II, "Opening Address at Puebla," 28 January 1979. Accessed on 1 July 2022 @ Library : Pope John Paul II Opening Address at the Puebla Conference | Catholic Culture.

11. Pope John Paul II, *Apostolos Suous,* 21 May 1998. Accessed on 13 June 2022 @ Apostolos Suos (21 May 1998) | John Paul II (vatican.va) Specifically see Section IV, para. 1. This type" of papal directive can reconstitute offices (congregations) processes and powers of the Church bureaucracy known as the Holy See. Accessed on 29 March 2022.

12. Pope John Paul II. *Ad Tuendam Fidem*. 6 March 1998. Accessed on 28 Jun3 2022 @ https://www.vatican.va/content/john-paul-ii/en/motu_proprio/documents/hf_jp-ii_motu-proprio_30061998_ad-tuendam-fidem.html It dealt with the responsibility of those in Church positions of leadership to follow hierarchical teachings. In its preamble, it stated what was expected of Church authorities: to always preserve communion with the Catholic Church, to carry out ones duties toward the Church, both universal and particular, to keep to the deposit of faith, explain in and avoid any teaching contrary to it, and observe all ecclesiastical laws, especially those in the Code of Canon Law.

13. Jo Renee Formicola, *Clerical Sexual Abuse: How the Crisis Changed US Catholic Church-State Relations* (New York: Palgrave Macmillan, 2014). See Chapter 3 for a fuller history of this period and issue.

14. Father Brendan Daly, "Sexual Abuse and Canon Law," *Compass* 43 (Spring 2009): 34.

15. Eugen Ehrlich, *Fundamental Principles of the Sociology of Law* (New Brunswick: Transaction Publishers, 1975).

16. For an early historical, chronological study of the problem of clerical sexual abuse see: Father Thomas Doyle, O. P., F. Ray Mouton, and Father Michael Petersen. "The Problem of Sexual Molestation by Roman Catholic Clergy: Meeting the Problem in a Comprehensiveand Responsible Manner." 8–9 June l985.

17. Some early examples of these accusations were printed in the *Los Angeles Times* from Reuters in "Society Shares the Blame for Scandals," on 26 June 1993, p. B5; William D. Montalbano in "Pontiff Assails U. S. Church, Sex Abuse by Priests," in the *Los Angeles Times*, 15 August 1993, p. A1, Richard Boudreaux and Larry B. Stammer, "US Catholics and Vatican Face a Cultural Chasm in Coping with Sexual Scandal," *Los Angeles Times,* 23 April 2002, p. A1; and Ron Howell "Vatican Focuses on Gay Priests," *Newsday*, 21 March 2002, p. A6.

18. Joshua J. McElwee, "Vatican: John Paul II Took 'immediate' Action on Sexual Abuse," *National Catholic Reporter*, 25 April, Accessed on 6 June 2022, @ Vatican: John Paul II took 'immediate' action on sexual abuse | National Catholic Reporter (ncronline.org).

19. Pope John Paul II and the Cardinals of the United States, *Final Communique of the Extraordinary Meeting Between the Cardinals of the United States at the Sala Bologna Del Palazzo Apostolico Vaticano.* 23–24 April 2002. Accessed on 16 June 2022 @Final Communiqué (vatican.va).

20. Patricia Rice, "Gregory Hails Pope's Response in US Scandal: "He Gets It"," *St. Louis Post-Dispatch,* 18 April 2002, p.B1. Reported statement by Bishop Wilton Gregory.

21. The United States Catholic Conference, *The Charter to Protect Children and Young People,* Accessed @ Charter for the Protection of Children and Young People | USCCB on 13 June 2022. This is the final version that was accepted by the Vatican.

22. The National Review Board of the USCCB. "About the National Review Board." Accessed on 28 June 2022 @National Review Board | USCCB. The USCCB established the National Review Board in June of 2002. The functions of the Board were revised slightly and reconfirmed in June of 2004. Originally, the agency

collected data and made recommendations to provide processes to protect minors. The purpose of the National Review Board, however, has always been to collaborate with the USCCB in preventing the sexual abuse of minors in the United States by persons in the service of the Church, but it also continues to provide information and make recommendations to prevent the sexual abuse of children.

23. These actions were carried out increasingly as civil authorities subpoenaed high Church officials including the Cardinal Archbishop of Boston in 2002 and subsequently others in Los Angeles, Philadelphia, and major dioceses in the United States. Other actions, such as the monitoring of Church agencies that dealt with children occurred in Vermont, and financial settlements for clerical sexual abuse began to require the bankruptcy of many diocese as well.

24. In 2010, Pope Benedict revised Pope John Paul's directive entitled *Sacramentorum sanctitatis tutela,* Accessed on 1 July 2022 @ Sacramentorum sanctitatis tutela - Apostolic Letter in the form of a Motu Proprio (30 April 2001) | John Paul II (vatican.va). It contained norms concerning the sexual abuse of minors by members of the clergy. He added adding specific, uniform guidelines and procedures to be followed by those who would have a responsibility to participate in such proceedings. See these in: Congregation for the Defense of the Faith, *Circular Letter for Dealing with Cases of Sexual Abuses of Minors Perpetrated by Clerics,* 3 May 2011. Accessed on 1 July 2022 @ Circular letter to assist Episcopal Conferences in developing Guidelines for dealing with cases of sexual abuse of minors perpetrated by clerics (vatican.va)

25. Statement made at Good Friday Mass in 2005. The exact quote is: How much filth there is in the Church, even among those who, in the priesthood, should belong entirely to Him. How much pride, how much self- sufficiency. Accessed on 28 June 2022 @ quotefancy.com.

26. Joseph Cardinal Ratzinger and Vittorio Messori. *The Ratzinger Report. (*San Francisco: Ignatius Press, 1985), p. 53.

27. Congregation for Catholic Education. "Concerning the Criteria for the Discernment of Vocations with regard to Persons with Homosexual Tendencies in view of their Admission to the Seminary and to Holy Orders." 31 August 2005. Accessed on 28 June 2022 at Criteria for the Discernment of Vocation for Persons with Homosexual Tendencies (vatican.va).

28. Pope Benedict XVI, "Letter of His Holiness Pope Benedict XVI to the Catholics of Ireland," 21 February 2011. Accessed on 28 June 2022 @ www.ncronline.org /news/text-popes-letter-catholics-ireland.

29. Pope Benedict XVI, *Letter of Pope Emeritus Benedict XVI regarding the Report on Abuse in the Archdiocese of Munich-Freising*, 6 February 2022. Accessed on 1 July 2022 @ Letter of Pope Emeritus Benedict XVI regarding the report on abuse in the Archdiocese of Munich-Freising (vatican.va).

30. Pope Francis. Apostolic Constitution "Pascite Gregem Dei," 23 May 2021. Accessed on 20 June 2021 @ Apostolic Constitution "Pascite gregem Dei" of the Holy Father Francis, Reforming Book VI of the Code of Canon Law (23 May 2021) | Francis (vatican.va).

31. Ibid.

32. Ibid.

33. Pope Francis. Apostolic Constitution, "Praedicate evangelium," 19 March 2022. Accessed on 22 April 2022 @ Apostolic Constitution "Praedicate evangelium" on the Roman Curia and its service to the Church and the World (vatican.va).

34. These judicial tribunals consist of the Apostolic Penitentiary, The Supreme Tribunal of the Apostolic Signatura, and the Tribunal of the Roman Rota. See clarifications of specific duties in Articles 189–204.

35. Preamble. Article 1.

36. Article 12.

37. Article 61.

38. Articles 79 and 147.

39. Article 128.

40. Pontifical Council For Justice and Peace, *Compendium of the Social Doctrine of the Church* (Washington, DC: United States Conference of Catholic Bishops, 2004), Chapter 4.

41. St. Paul. *Letter to the Romans.* Chapter 13. "Let everyone be subject to the higher powers because there is no authority except from God and so whatever authorities exist have been appointed by God. Anyone who disobeys an authority is rebelling against God's ordinance and rebels must expect to receive the condemnation they deserve."

42. This led to the development of a Christian Europe, that is, the "Holy Roman Empire," that endured the until the Reformation of Martin Luther in 1521. Thus, the experience and expertise of the Church in both religious and political matters during all that time gave Catholicism an entrenched hierarchical power model, one already superior to those in the infancy of statehood. The Church could, and did, serve as the moral voice in an emerging nationalistic Europe, using its God-given status and civil approval to spread and implement its own social, religious and political agenda above the civil law and its secular gaze.

43. These territories in the Italian Peninsula were under the sovereign control of the Pope from 756 to 1870 A.D. This came about due to donations by Christian kings such as Charlemagne and Pepin, the fall of the Byzantine Empire, and Papal military force. At one time, the Papal states included major regions of what is now Italy, but in th 1870s as Italy began to pursue unification, the forces of nationalism were eventually able to subdue the military of strength of the Popes. Benito Mussolini in 1921 was able bring about a concordat with Pius IX that brought about the establishment of the civil power of his political party over the entire peninsula of Italy.

44. Pope John Paul II, the first Polish Pope made abortion his central religious concern, pursued outreach to Eastern Europe and has been credited with the fall of Communism in that part of the world. Pope Benedict, a German theologian, scholar, and the most highly appointed individual tasked with the defense of religious orthodoxy in the Church placed his emphasis on reforming the legal structures of the Church to deal with clerical sexual abuse.

45. Conference of Latin American Bishops. *The Aparecida Documents.* Accessed on 2 July 2022 @ Aparecida Document (d2y1pz2y630308.cloudfront.net).

46. Ibid. *Conclusions.*

47. Pope Francis. *Evangelium Gaudium.* 24 November 2013. Accessed on 29 June 2022 @ Evangelii Gaudium : Apostolic Exhortation on the Proclamation of the Gospel in Today's World (24 November 2013) | Francis (vatican.va).

48. Chapter 4, Section 3.

49. Ibid, para. 223.

50. United Nations Committee on the Rights of the Child, "Concluding Observations on the Second Periodic Report of the Holy See, 25 February 2014. Accessed on 29 June @ Committee on the Rights of the Child Concluding Observations on The Second Periodic Report of the Holy See | International Legal Materials | Cambridge Core.

51. This arose over the Pope's original support of Archbishop Barros Madrid in Chile, who was accused of clerical sexual abuse. After an investigation, Francis admitted that he was wrong and that his actions were a source of pain and shame for him.

52. Pope Francis. "You are the Light of the World." 7 May 2019. Accessed on 29 June 2022 @ Apostolic Letter in the form of a "Motu proprio" of the Supreme Pontiff Francis "Vos estis lux mundi" (vatican.va).

53. Section 1.

54. Archbishop Carlo Maria Vigano, The First Testimony, 22 August 2018. Accessed on 14 June 2022 @Archbishop Vigano's Testimony (churchmilitant.com).

55. Secretariat of State of the Holy See of the Vatican City State. Report on the Holy See's Institutional Knowledge and Decision Making *Related to Former Cardinal Theodore Edgar McCarrick (1930 to 2017)* 10 November 2020. Accessed on 14 June 22022 @ resources_rapporto-card-mccarrick_20201110_en.pdf (vatican.va).

56. These were reported in the summary report as a lack of credible allegations of child abuse; "that the Cardinal swore on his 'oath as a bishop' that the allegations were false; the allegations of misconduct with adults related to events in the 1980s; and there was no indication of any recent misconduct."

57. Carolyn Warner, "The Politics of Sex Abuse in Sacred Hierarchies: A comparative Study of the Catholic Church and the Military in the United States," *Religions,* 2019, Accessed on 31 May 2022 @ www.mdpi.com/journal religions.

58. David Brooks, "This is Why Autocracies Fail," *The New York Times*, 3 March 22, p. A22.

59. Ibid.

60. Jo Renee Formicola, *Papal Policies on Clerical Sexual Abuse: God Weeps* (New York, Peter Lang, 2019), pp. 151–157.

REFERENCES

Abbott, Walter M., gen. ed. *The Documents of Vatican II* (New York: Herder and Herder, 1966).

Balboni, Jennifer M. *Clergy Sexual Abuse Litigation* (First Forum Press: Boulder, CO, 2011).

Boudreaux, Richard, and Larry B. Stammer, "US Catholics and Vatican Face a Cultural Chasm in Coping with Sexual Scandal." *Los Angeles Times*, 23 April 2002, p. A1.

Brooks, David. "This is Why Autocracies Fail." *The New York Times*, 3 March 22, p. A22.

Cafardi, Nicholas P. *Before Dallas: The U. S. Bishop's Response to Clerical Sexual Abuse of Children* (Mahwah, NJ: Paulist Press, 2008).

Conference of Latin American Bishops. *Medellin Conference Statement, 1968*. Accessed on 1 July 2022 at Medellín Conference Statement, 1968 (we-are-church.org).

Congregation for the Defense of the Faith. *Circular Letter for Dealing with Cases of Sexual Abuses of Minors Perpetrated by Clerics,* 3 May 2011. Accessed on 1 July 2022 at Circular Letter to Assist Episcopal Conferences in Developing Guidelines for Dealing With Cases of Sexual Abuse of Minors Perpetrated by Clerics (vatican .va).

Daly, Father Brendan. "Sexual Abuse and Canon Law." *Compass*, Vol. 43, (Spring 2009), p. 34.

Dillon, Sam. "Role of Bishops is Now a Focus of Grand Juries." *The New York Times*, 12 July 2002, p. A1.

Doyle, Thomas, O. P., F. Ray Mouton, and Father Michael Petersen. "The Problem of Sexual Molestation by Roman Catholic Clergy: Meeting the Problem in a Comprehensive and Responsible Manner." 1985. Accessed on 4 July 2022 at http://www .bishop-accountability.org.

Doyle, Thomas O. P., and Stephen C. Rubino, Esq. "Catholic Clergy Sexual Abuse Meets the Civil Law." *Fordham Urban Law Journal*, Vol. 31, Issue 2, Article 6, 2003, pp. 1–42. http://bishop-accountability.org/news5/2004_01_01_Doyle _CatholicClergy.pdf.

Doyle, Thomas P., Richard Sipe, and Patrick J. Wall. *Sex, Priests, and Secret Codes: The Catholic Church's 2,000 Year Paper Trail of Sexual Abuse*. Lanham, MD: Taylor Trade, 2006.

Ehrlich, Eugen. *Fundamental Principles of the Sociology of Law*. New Brunswick: Transaction Press, 1975.

Elazar, Daniel J. *The Covenant and Civil Society: The Constitutional Matrix of Modern Democracy* (New York: Routledge, 1997).

Formicola, Jo Renee. "Catholic Clerical Sexual Abuse: Effects on Vatican Sovereignty and Papal Power." *Journal of Church and State*, Vol. 53, No. 4, Autumn 2011, pp. 523–544.

———. "Catholic Moral Demands in American Politics: A New Paradigm." *Journal of Church and State*, Vol. 51, No. 1, Winter 2009, pp. 4–23.

———. *Clerical Sexual Abuse: How the Crisis Changed US Catholic Church-State Relations* (New York: Palgrave Macmillan, 2014).

———. "Clerical Sexual Abuse: The International Church-State Ramifications." *Journal of Church and State,* Vol. 62, No. 1, Winter 2020, pp. 1–4.

———. *John Paul II: Prophetic Politician* (Washington, D. C.: Georgetown University Press, 2000).

———. *Papal Policies on Clerical Sexual Abuse: God Weeps* (New York: Peter Lang, 2019).

———. "Popes and the Policy of Sin." *Journal of Church and State*, Vol. 62, No. 1, Winter 2020, pp. 135–157.

———. "The Further Legal Consequences of Catholic Clerical Sexual Abuse." *Journal of Church and State,* Vol. 49, Summer 2007, pp. 445–466.

———. "The Vatican, the American Bishops and the Church-State Ramifications of Clerical Sexual Abuse." *Journal of Church and State*, Vol. 46, Summer 2004, pp. 479–502.

Gehrke-White, Donna. "Laity Group Scrutinizing Church's Finances." *Miami Herald,* 1 January 2005, p. E1.

Goodstein, Laurie. "Lessons of a Year; Catholic Lay Board Finds Limits to Power Over Bishops in Dealing With Sex Abuse." *The New York Times,* 18 June 2003, pp. A1 and 22.

Holusha, John, and Ian Fisher. "Pope Begins U. S. Visit; Says He is Ashamed of Sex Scandal." *The New York Times,* 16 April 2008. http://www.nytimes.com/2008/04/16/us/nationalspecial2/15cnd-pope.html?pagewanted=all&_r=0.

Horowitz, Jason. "Cardinal Angelo Sodano, 94, Vatican's Ultimate Power Broker, Is Dead." *The New York Times,* 29 May 2022, p. A22.

Howell, Ron. "Vatican Focuses on Gay Priests." *Newsday*, 21 March 2002, p. A6.

John Jay College of Criminal Justice. "The Nature and Scope of Sexual Abuse of Minors by Catholic Priests and Deacons in the U. S. 1950–2002." 25 February 2004a. http://www.usccb.org/nrb/johnjaystudy.

———. *The Nature and Scope of Sexual Abuse of Minors by Catholic Priests and Deacons in the U. S. 1950–2002.* 25 February 2004b. http://www.usccb.org/issues-and-action/child-and-youth-protection/upload/The-Nature-and-Scope-of-Sexual-Abuse-of-Minors-by-Catholic-Priests-and-Deacons-in-the-United-States-1950-2002.pdf.

John Jay College Research Team. *The Causes and Context of Sexual Abuse of Minors by Catholic Priests in the U. S. 1950–2010.* USCCB, May 2011. http://www.bishop-accountability.org.

Kirby, Peter. "The Didache: The Lord's Teaching Through the Twelve Apostles to the Nations." http://www.earlychristianwritings.com/text/didache-roberts.html.

Lyon, Alynna J., Christine A. Gustafson, and Paul Christopher Manuel. *Pope Francis as a Global Actor* (New York: Palgrave-Macmillan, 2018).

McElwee, Joshua. "Vatican: John Paul II Took 'Immediate' Action on Sexual Abuse." *National Catholic Reporter*, 25 April. Accessed on 6 June 2022 at Vatican: John Paul II took 'immediate' action on sexual abuse | National Catholic Reporter (ncronline.org).

Montalbano, William D. "Pontiff Assails U. S. Church, Sex Abuse by Priests." *The Los Angeles Times*, 15 August 1993, p. A1.

Mouton, Ray, and Rev. Thomas P. Doyle, O. P. "The Problem of Sexual Molestation by Roman Catholic Clergy: Meeting the Problem in a Comprehensive and Responsible Manner." Accessed on 5 July 2022 at DoyleManual_NCR_combined.pdf (bishop-accountability.org).

Office of Child and Youth Protection of the USCCB. "Report on the Implementation of the Charter for the Protection of Children and Young People." February 2005. Accessed at http://www.nccbuscc.org/ocyp/diocese0405-039.html.

Pimentel, Stephen. "The Master Key: Pope Benedict XVI's Theology of Covenant." *Homiletic and Pastoral Review*, October 2007, pp. 16–20. Accessed on 28 June 2022 at Library: The Master Key: Pope Benedict XVI's Theology of Covenant | Catholic Culture.

Pontifical Council for Justice and Peace, *Compendium of the Social Doctrine of the Church* (Washington, DC: United States Conference of Catholic Bishops, 2004).

Pope Benedict XVI. "How Much Filth There is in the Church." Statement Made at Good Friday Mass in 2005. Accessed on 28 June 2022 at quotefancy.com.

———. "Letter of His Holiness Pope Benedict XVI to the Catholics of Ireland." 21 February 2011. Accessed on 5 July 2022 at Instruction on the Manner of Proceeding in Causes Involving the Crime of Solicitation (vatican.va).

———. *Letter of Pope Emeritus Benedict XVI Regarding the Report on Abuse in the Archdiocese of Munich-Freising*, 6 February 2022. Accessed on 1 July 2022 at Letter of Pope Emeritus Benedict XVI regarding the report on abuse in the Archdiocese of Munich-Freising (vatican.va).

———. *Sacramentorum sanctitatis tutela,* 30 April 2001. Accessed on 1 July 2022 at Sacramentorum sanctitatis tutela - Apostolic Letter in the form of a Motu Proprio (April 30, 2001) | John Paul II (vatican.va).

Pope Benedict XVI with Peter Seewald. *Benedict XVI: Last Testament in His Own Words* (Bloomsbury: London, 2016).

———. *Light of the World* (San Francisco: Ignatius Press, 2010).

———. *Salt of the Earth* (San Francisco: Ignatius Press, 2007).

Pope Francis. *Evangelium Gaudium,* 24 November 2013. Accessed on 29 June 2022 at Evangelii Gaudium: Apostolic Exhortation on the Proclamation of the Gospel in Today's World (24 November 2013) | Francis (vatican.va).

———. "Pascite gregem Dei." 22 May 2011. Accessed 5 July 2022 at Apostolic Constitution "Pascite gregem Dei" of the Holy Father Francis, Reforming Book VI of the Code of Canon Law (23 May 2021) | Francis (vatican.va).

———. "Praedicate evangelium." 19 March 2022. Accessed on 22 April 2022 at Apostolic Constitution "Praedicate evangelium" on the Roman Curia and Its Service to the Church and the World (vatican.va).

———. *Vos estis lux Mundi*, 7 May 2019. Accessed on 29 June 2022 at Apostolic Letter in the Form of a "Motu proprio" of the Supreme Pontiff Francis "Vos estis lux mundi" (vatican.va).

Pope John Paul II. *Ad Tuenndem Fidem.* 30 June 1998. https://www.vatican.va/content/john-paul-ii/en/motu_proprio/documents/hf_jp-ii_motu-proprio_30061998_ad-tuendam-fidem.html.

———. *Apostolos Suous.* 21 May 1998. Apostolos Suos (May 21, 1998) | John Paul II (vatican.va).

———. *Crimen Sollicitudionis.* Supreme Sacred Congregation of the Holy Office, 16 March 1962. Accessed on 5 July 2022 at Instruction on the Manner of Proceeding in Causes involving the Crime of Solicitation (vatican.va).

———. "Opening Address at Puebla." 28 January 1979. Accessed on 1 July 2022 at Library: Pope John Paul II Opening Address at the Puebla Conference | Catholic Culture.

———. *The Code of Canon Law 1983*. Promulgated 25 January 1983 (Abbreviated as 1983 CIC From Its Latin Title *Codex Iuris Canonici*), also called the Johanno-Pauline Code.

Pope John Paul II and the Cardinals of the United States. *Final Communique of the Extraordinary Meeting Between the Cardinals of the United States at the Sala Bologna Del Palazzo Apostolico Vaticano.* 23–24 April 2002. Accessed on 16 June 2022 at Final Communiqué (vatican.va).

Ratzinger, Joseph Cardinal. *Milestones: Memoirs 1927–1977* (San Francisco: Ignatius Press, 1998).

Ratzinger, Joseph Cardinal, and Vittorio Messori. *The Ratzinger Report* (San Francisco: Ignatius Press, 1986).

Reese, Thomas J. *Inside the Vatican* (Cambridge, MA: Harvard University Press, 1996).

Reuters. "Society Shares the Blame for Scandals." *Los Angeles Times*, 26 June 1993, p. B5.

Rice, Patricia. "Gregory Hails Pope's Response in US Scandal: He Gets It." *St. Louis Post-Dispatch,* 18 April 2002, p. B1. Reported Statement by Bishop Wilton Gregory.

Rourke, Thomas R. *The Roots of Pope Francis's Social and Political Thought* (Lanham, MD: Rowman and Littlefield, 2018).

Secretariat of State of the Holy See of the Vatican City State. "Report on the Holy See's Institutional Knowledge and Decision Making Related to Former Cardinal Theodore Edgar McCarrick (1930 to 2017)." 10 November 2020. resources_rapporto-card-mccarrick_20201110_en.pdf (vatican.va).

Supreme Sacred Congregation of the Holy Office. "Instruction on the Manner of Proceeding in Causes Involving the Crime of Solicitation." 1962. http://www.vatican.va/resources/resources_cimen-sollicitationis-1962_en.html.

The National Review Board for the Protection of Children and Young People. *A Report on the Crisis in the Catholic Church in the United States* (Washington, DC: The United States Conference of Catholic Bishops, 2004).

Tomasi, Silvano Msgr. "Presentation by H. E. Msgr. Silvano Tomasi of the Periodic Report of the Holy See to the Committee on the Convention of the Rights of the Child and the Optional Protocols."16 January 2014. http://www.vatican.va/roman_curia/secretariat_state/2014/documents/rc-seg-st01401 16_tomasi-child-rights_en.html.

United Nations Committee on the Rights of the Child. "Concluding Observations on the Second Periodic Report of the Holy See, 25 February 2014." Accessed on 29 June at Committee on the Rights of the Child Concluding Observations on The Second Periodic Report of the Holy See | International Legal Materials | Cambridge Core.

United States Catholic Conference. *The Charter to Protect Children and Young People,* 13 June 2022.Charter for the Protection of Children and Young People | USCCB. Final Version.

United States Conference of Catholic Bishops. "Report of the National Review Board, 29 July 2003." http://www.bishopaccountability.org/news2003_07_12/2003_07_29_Chicago_ReportOf.html.

———. "The Charter to Protect Children and Young People." 2002. First Version. http://www.bishop-accountability.org/resources/resourcefiles/Churchdocs/Dallas.

———. "The Essential Norms for Diocesan/Eparchical Policies Dealing With Allegation of Sexual Abuse of Minors by Priests of Deacons." 2002. Accessed on 5 July 2022 at The Essential Norms for Diocesan/Eparchial Policies Dealing With Allegations of Sexual Abuse of Minors by Priests or Deacons | USCCB.

———. "The Nature and Scope of Sexual Abuse of Minors by Catholic Priests and Deacons in the U. S. 1950–2002." February 2004. http://www.usccb.org/issues-and-action/child-and-youth-protection/upload/The-Nature-and-Scope-of-Sexual-Abuse-of-Minors-by-Catholic-Priests-and-Deacons-in-the-United-States-1950-2002.pdf.

United States Conference of Catholic Bishops Office of Media Relations. "Effort to Combat Clergy Sexual Abuse Against Minors: A Chronology." http://www.usccb.org/issues-and-action/child-and-youth-protection/upload/The-Nature-and-Scope-of-Sexual-Abuse-of-Minors-by-Catholic-Priests-and-Deacons-in-the-United-States-1950-2002.pdf.

Vigano, Archbishop Carlo Maria. *The First Testimony,* August 22, 2018. Archbishop Vigano's Testimony (churchmilitant.com).

Warner, Carolyn. "The Politics of Sex Abuse in Sacred Hierarchies: A Comparative Study of the Catholic Church and the Military in the United States." *Religions,* 2019. www.mdpi.com/journal religions.

Weakland, Rembert W. O. S. B. *A Pilgrim in a Pilgrim Church* (Grand Rapids, MI: Eerdmans, 2009).

Index

About the Contributors

Ilie Bădescu, doctor in sociology, university professor and researcher, is the director of the Institute of Sociology (Romanian Academy) since 2002. He has been actively dedicated to the revitalization of the research on social problems in rural Romania, establishing and coordinating within the Institute the Laboratory of Rural Studies. He is the author of numerous studies, handbooks, monographies, encyclopedias, and sociology treatises.

Joseph Livni spent thirty-four years (1979–2013) creating and applying mathematical modeling of aircraft physics. The models certified that aircraft systems such as fuel, hydraulic, electrical, flight control, among others, will withstand severe vibrations during flight. Other models served to demonstrate structural integrity during hard landing and during emergency landing on ground and water. For aircraft in service, Joseph generated and utilized models to diagnose and fix failures of systems due to excessive vibration.

After retirement, Joseph turned to use his experience in mathematical modeling to investigate controversial topics in biological and social phenomena; in academic terms he changed direction from aerospace engineering to biophysics and sociophysics. He is the author or co-author of eight articles, one monograph, and one edited collection.

Rachel Christ-Doane is the director of Education at the Salem Witch Museum. She holds a BA in history from Clark University and MA in history and museum studies from Tufts University. She began working at the Salem Witch Museum in 2015 and has been the director of Education since 2017. Within this role she engages in a wide array of research, curates the museum's exhibits, works with students and teachers, and creates educational programming.

Jo Renee Formicola, PhD, is a professor of political science and public affairs at Seton Hall University. A specialist in Church–State relations, she has published and edited nine books as well as written numerous peer-reviewed articles on issues that concern religion and government in the United States. She has appeared on major media outlets to discuss her specific area of expertise, Catholic politics, doing commentary on the visits of Pope Benedict and Pope Francis at the United Nations and the White House. For the last two decades her area of research and publications has focused on clerical sexual abuse. She is currently working on a book on President Joe Biden and continues to teach courses on religion and politics at her university.

Mădălina Măndiţă graduated in 2004 the Faculty of Sociology and Social Work, University of Bucharest, and in 2006 obtained the master's degree in the same institution. Since 2013 she is Phd in sociology, with the thesis *Compared Noology Study Upon Jewish And Romanian Peoples*. Since 2009, she is a member of the research team of the Institute of Sociology, Romanian Academy.

Peter J. Mazzacano, BA (Toronto), MLA (Harvard), MBA (Phoenix), LLM (Osgoode), PhD (Osgoode), is currently an LLM dissertation supervisor at Robert Kennedy College, Zurich, and at Queen Mary University of London. Peter also serves in the Legal Department of Canada's largest privately held commercial landlord and real estate development firm in the Greater Toronto Area and teaches commercial law at Algoma University.

Peter is the founder and editor of *CISG Canada*, which is dedicated to Canadian jurisprudence on the UN International Sale of Goods Convention (CISG). He has taught numerous law courses at various universities and colleges over the years. These include *Legal Aspects of International Business* at Ryerson University, and *Canadian Business Law* at York University, in Toronto. He served as a Visiting Professor and Adjunct Professor at Osgoode Hall Law School, where he taught *Legal Process*, *Civil Procedure*, *Graduate Legal Research and Writing*, and *International Dispute Resolution*. During that time, from 2006 to 2012, Peter also co-coached Osgoode's Vis Moot International Commercial Arbitration Team. Recently, he served as an adjunct faculty member at the University of Guelph and Sheridan College where he taught a number of business law courses and served as a Lecturer in Law at the University of Derby Online.

Peter continues to research and publish in the area of national and international commercial law. He has numerous publications in international law journals on topics related to the CISG and international commercial law generally.

Zeev Safrai is a full professor in the Land of Israel and Archaeology Department of Bar Ilan University, Israel. He specialized in the classical periods (Hellenistic, Roman, and Byzantine periods), mainly from the rabbinic point of view. He published some dozens of books and more than 150 articles on the Jewish community, economy of Roman Judea demographic process, among others. His big project is a sociological and historical commentary for the Mishna (fifty volumes) until now twenty-two volumes were published.

Adela Şerban is researcher in sociology, PhD, specialized in community studies and societal security. She is senior researcher at the Institute of Sociology within Romanian Academy, where coordinates the Research Laboratory on Social Theory, dedicated to the study of community structure and social morphology

www.ingramcontent.com/pod-product-compliance
Ingram Content Group UK Ltd.
Pitfield, Milton Keynes, MK11 3LW, UK
UKHW020838290926
15470UKWH00004B/1428